ORLANDO
& CENTRAL FLORIDA
ACCESS®

Busch Garden

D0465574

Orientation

The sweet, heady scent of grapefruit and orange blossoms still fills the air every balmy winter in Central Florida. But not as much as it used to. From **Tampa** east to **Orlando**, most of the rows of dark green, perfectly tended citrus trees have given way to million-dollar theme parks, glittering high-rise hotels, and trendy shopping districts.

Orientation

Whether you are a poolside chaise-lounge potato, a theme-park denizen, a swimmer, a surfer, or a seafood-lover, Central Florida can accommodate you. From the spires of Cinderella Castle at **Walt Disney World** to the cobblestone streets of old **St. Augustine** or the white, sandy beaches of **St. Petersburg** or **Daytona Beach**, you can find the relaxation and the thrills you seek.

Orlando is the heart of this area, but even after Walt Disney World threw open its gates in October 1971, it was nowheresville in the minds of most visitors. Sure, tourists knew Disney World was in Florida, but where *exactly* was Orlando? Orlando hotels got calls from people asking for a room with a great beach view. No small request since Orlando—Florida's largest inland city—is about 50 miles from the nearest beach.

Foreign tourists were even more confused. Some jetted into Miami International Airport (until 1982 Orlando International didn't have regularly scheduled international service), hopped into a cab, and told the cabbie to take them to Walt Disney World. Imagine their shock when they found out the park was almost 300 miles away.

How times change. Today, South Florida tourism experts call Orlando "The Wall" because it offers so many visitors such a great time, they don't venture downstate. While Central Florida is still famous for its juicy grapefruits and oranges, it's the stupendous theme parks that draw more than 13 million people to town every

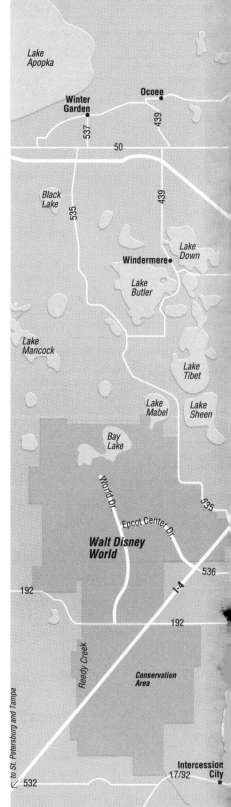

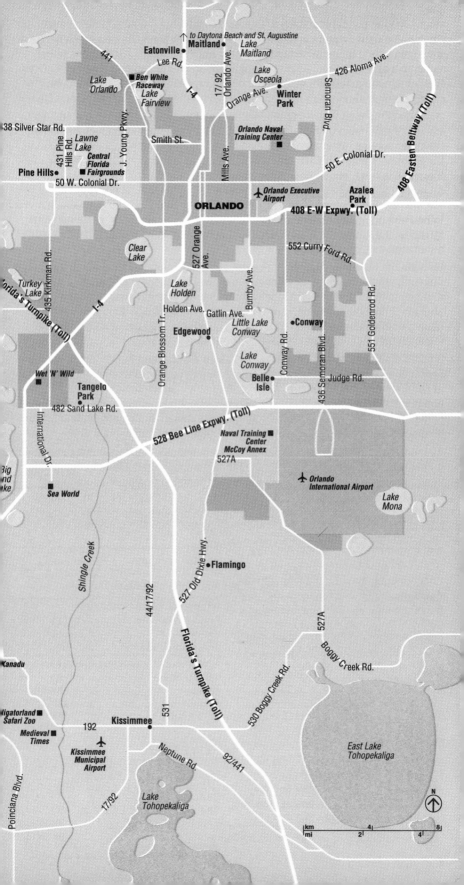

year. If you're the typical tourist, Disney World will be your top destination: It's the No. 1 tourist attraction in the world. At 28,000 acres, its vast size is bound to stun you. You'd be surprised to learn how many die-hard aficionados return again and again; in fact, 70 percent of all visitors to Orlando are repeat visitors. Not a surprising statistic, since some of the gargantuan theme parks in nearby cities can provide even more hours of enjoyment if you've already done Disney.

Orlando is the only place in the world where **Hollywood** is reproduced—some say upstaged—twice. Walk through working sound stages and seek out thrills on the cutting-edge rides at the **Disney-MGM Studios** theme park one day; smell King Kong's banana breath and see how movies are made at **Universal Studios Florida** the next. Scores of smaller attractions compete for the rest of your time, including zoos and dinner theater shows where you can eat while cheering your favorite medieval knight in a joust, tapping your foot to country music in a Wild West show, or gawking at an enormous alligator. (Stick with the mainstream attractions if you want a show suitable for your child—most emphasize family entertainment.)

Outside the theme parks, you'll find every kind of hotel or motel, from glamourous high rises with huge, free-form swimming pools to small, humble mom-and-pops, many in the Kissimmee area south of Orlando. The city has almost 77,000 hotel rooms, more than any other metropolitan area in the country. Still, don't arrive without reservations during national holidays because all the popular inns are likely to be booked.

If you tire of attractions, you can always soak up sun and history in St. Augustine, a great city for walking or bicycling, or put your toes in the surf along any of the beautiful, wide beaches from St. Augustine south to **Melbourne.** And if you haven't gotten your fill of parks, there's **Busch Gardens** with its huge collection of wild animals in Tampa; **Marineland** in St. Augustine; and **Silver Springs**, famous for its glass-bottom boat trips, near **Ocala.**

As for dress, cool is the rule. Orlando is as relaxed as a Jimmy Buffett tune, and it's OK to wear shorts into all but the fanciest restaurants. And, of course, shorts, a loud shirt, and a camera are de rigueur at the theme parks. If you arrive in December or January, the weather can turn chilly, damp, and rainy. Cotton sweaters come in handy, but don't bother toting your umbrella—theme parks pass them out like candy.

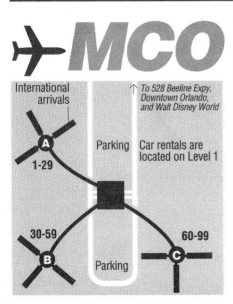

Getting There by Air

Orlando International Airport (MCO)

Airport Information	825.2001
US Customs	648.6847
US Immigration	826.5870

Airlines serving Orlando International Airport:
Gates 1-29:

Aeropostal	800/345.9708
American	800/433.7300
Continental	800/525.0280
Icelandair	800/223.5500
Mexicana	800/531.7921
Midway	800/866.9000
Pan Am	800/221.1111
TWA	800/221.2000

Gates 30-59:

Bahamasair	800/222.4262
Northwest	800/225.2525
United	800/241.6522

USAir 800/428.4322
USAir Express 800/428.4253
Gates 60-99:
British Airways 800/247.9297
ComAir 800/354.9822
Delta 800/221.1212
KLM 800/777.5533
TransBrazil 800/872.3153

Major rental car agencies at the airport:
Avis 851.7600
Budget 850.6749
.... 850.6724
.... 850.6730
Dollar 851.3232
Hertz 859.8400
National 855.4170
Superior 857.2023

Distances in miles from the airport:
Cocoa Beach 47
Daytona Beach 56
Downtown Orlando 18
Kissimmee-St. Cloud 19
Ocala 77
St. Petersburg 113
Tampa 84
Walt Disney World 20

Getting There by Car

Driving to Central Florida is a snap. From North Florida, Interstates 95 and 75 lead to Interstate 4, the route through Orlando and Walt Disney World. Rental cars are so plentiful that, especially in Orlando and the Disney World area, you'll pay some of the lowest rates in the country. Although public transportation in Tampa and Orlando can be awkward and sometimes unreliable, taxis from the airports to hotels and attractions are strictly regulated, efficient, and relatively inexpensive.

FYI

Bicycle Riding

European tourists sometimes rent or bring bicycles to the Orlando area, a city cited by *Bicycling* magazine as one of the 10 worst places to bike in the nation. It's not quite that bad, but cycling isn't much fun unless you're in rural parts of Central Florida. Traffic can be very heavy in Orlando and in the Walt Disney World area. Use caution and never ride at night without a light.

Money

Foreign Currency Exchange

At exchange desks, you must present valid identification (driver's license, passport, etc.). **SunBank, NA** and **Barnett Bank of Florida** buy and sell bank notes in most major foreign currencies at competitive rates. However, there is a service charge assessed for conversion of foreign currency—usually, one percent of the dollar amount. Also, some bank branches may limit the exchange to US $500 per non-customer transaction.

Traveler's Checks

Banks will cash and businesses will accept traveler's checks. In most places, you will need to present valid identification such as a driver's license or passport.

At Walt Disney World

SunBank, NA is Disney's official bank. One is located on Main Street in the Magic Kingdom theme park (828.6101); another at EPCOT Center at 1320 Avenue of the Stars (827.5200); and a SunBank building is at Lake Buena Vista, across from the Disney Village Marketplace (828.6100).

Orientation

How to Read this Guide

ORLANDO & CENTRAL FLORIDA ACCESS® is arranged by neighborhood so you can see at a glance where you are and what is around you. The numbers next to the paragraphs in the following chapters correspond to the numbers on the maps. The paragraphs are color-coded according to the kind of place described:

Restaurants/Nightlife: Red	**Hotels:** Blue
Shops/ 🌳 Outdoors: Green	**Sights/Culture:** Black

Rating the Restaurants and Hotels

The restaurant ratings take into account the service, atmosphere, and uniqueness of the restaurant. An expensive restaurant doesn't necessarily ensure an enjoyable evening; however, a small, relatively unknown spot could have good food, professional service, and a lovely atmosphere. Therefore, on a purely subjective basis, stars are used to judge the overall dining value (see star ratings below). Keep in mind that chefs and owners change, which sometimes drastically affects the quality of a restaurant. The ratings in this book are based on information available at press time.

The price ratings, as categorized below, apply to restaurants and hotels. These figures describe general price-range relationships between other restaurants or hotels; they do not represent specific rates.

★ Good	$ The price is right
★★ Very good	$$ Reasonable
★★★ Excellent	$$$ Expensive
★★★★ Extraordinary	$$$$ A month's pay

Map Key

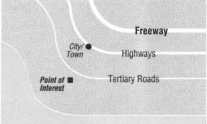

Newspapers/Publications

Tourist publications are free, and many are available along International Drive in south Orlando and in the Kissimmee-St. Cloud area.

Metro Orlando's major newspaper is the morning *Orlando Sentinel,* with a daily circulation of about 280,000 and Sunday circulation topping about 400,000; 407/420.5411.

Other publications: *The Winter Park Observer,* a weekly with columnist Sloan Wilson, author of *The Man in the Gray Flannel Suit;* 407/628.8500. *Orlando*

Orientation

magazine is a slick monthly that offers general local interest features; 407/539.3939. *The Weekly* bills itself as Central Florida's "News and Entertainment Weekly," published by T.S. Publications Inc., a division of Toronto Corp; 407/645.5888. *Florida Trend,* a high-quality statewide publication, is devoted mainly to business issues. *Florida Today,* published in Melbourne, is owned by Gannett Newspapers, with a daily circulation of 80,999; 407/242.3500. In the Tampa Bay area, the *St. Petersburg Times* is the largest daily newspaper. Its daily circulation tops 353,130 and 459,225 on Sundays; 813/893.8111.

In 1991 the *Orlando Sentinel* was surpassed in circulation by the *Tampa Tribune,* with a daily circulation of 289,999 and a Sunday circulation of 385,747; 813/272.7766. In Ocala, the *Star-Banner* is the morning daily, with a 45,543 circulation; 904/867.4010. The *Ledger,* in Lakeland, has a daily circulation of 79,684; 813/687.7000. There's also the *Leesburg Daily Commercial,* with a circulation of 27,674; 904/787.4515.

Street Smarts

Never forget that, while Orlando and other resort towns dedicate themselves to entertaining tourists, crime unfortunately does happen. Always lock your car and hotel room, and don't open the door of your room unless you know who's on the other side. Most tourist places are safe for walking at night, but use common sense, especially if you're alone. Leaving Orlando, one street that has a definitely seedy look is South Orange Blossom Trail, with its row of topless bars. This is not a strip you want to walk down alone, but you'll be fine if you stay in your car.

Phone Book

Area code 407 unless otherwise indicated.

Emergencies

Ambulance/Fire/Police	**911**
AAA Emergency Road Service:	
Orlando area	877.2266
Kissimmee area	396.1556
AAA Local Member Services	894.3333
Poison Control Center	841.5222
Suicide Prevention	628.1227

Important Numbers

US Government, Federal Information Center	422.1800
Visitors Centers:	
Orlando/Orange County	363.5871
Kissimmee/St. Cloud	847.5000
Passport Information	850.6335
Amtrak	843.7611
Better Business Bureau	660.9500
Greyhound-Trailways Lines:	
Fare and Scheduling Information	843.7720
En Español	800/531.5332
Daytona Beach Service	292.3401
Miami Beach Service	292.3403
Tampa Beach Service	292.3404
Emergency Dental Referral	847.7474
Mental Health Services, 24-hour	896.9306
Orange County Medical Society	841.6267
Time and Temperature	646.3131
	834.4545
Weather	851.7510

Major Attractions

Busch Gardens, Tampa	813/998.5171
Fun 'n Wheels	351.5651
Gatorland	855.5496
Kennedy Space Center's Spaceport USA	800/SHUTTLE
	451.2121
Kissimmee	870.2222
Mystery Fun House	351.8500
Nickelodeon Studios	363.8500
Sea World	800/327.2424
	432.1178
Silver Springs	800/342.0297
	904/236.2121
Universal Studios Florida	363.8000
Walt Disney World's Magic Kingdom, EPCOT, Disney-MGM Studios, and Typhoon Lagoon	824.4321
Water Mania	396.2626
Wet 'n Wild	351.1800

Rental Cars (for rentals inside Orlando International Airport, see page 5):

Agency	381.3290
	834.9330
Alamo	800/327.9633
	857.8200
	351.3284
Alamo in the Disney World area	396.0991
American International	851.6910
Dolphin	851.0255
	363.1600
Lindo's	855.0282
	857.8243
	843.1629
Payless	825.4400
Rainbow	363.4696
Thrifty	380.1002
	239.6727

Donald L. Hennessy
Division Vice President, TW Recreational Services, Inc., and General Manager, Kennedy Space Center's Spaceport USA, Cape Canaveral

Enjoying tropical scenery and showboat-style entertainment during a St. John's River dinner cruise on the riverboat *Romance*.

Playing the challenging golf course at **Grandy Cypress Hotel** in Orlando.

Watching the sunrise while walking on the beach at **Cape Canaveral.**

Taking a one-day cruise from **Port Canaveral**...great food, floor show, and game tables...a floating Las Vegas!

Chuck Agostinelli
Director of Public Relations, Canaveral Port Authority, Cape Canaveral

Brunch on Park Avenue in Winter Park, followed by a scenic boat tour of the **Chain of Lakes.**

A stroll around **Lake Eola** in Orlando, followed by a tour of the lake in a paddleboat swan.

An afternoon with a picnic lunch at the **Central Florida Zoo.**

A rainy day at the **Orlando Public Library.**

A Sunday bike ride through downtown Orlando, along its side streets, and around its many lakes.

Robert I. Earl
President, Hard Rock International; President, Planet Hollywood; and President, Rank Leisure USA, Inc., Orlando

Central Florida is perfect for all sports, especially tennis, golf, fishing, and water sports. Many golf and tennis clubs are public. Rafting is available on the Wekiva River.

Stroll down **Park Avenue** in Winter Park for the best shopping in Central Florida. Then, visit the **Charles Hosmer Morse Gallery of American Art** to see the world's largest collection of Louis Comfort Tiffany's stained glass. Top it all off with a canal boat tour and a meal at **Enzo's** in Longwood for wonderful Italian food.

© THE WALT DISNEY COMPANY

Orlando was first called Jernigan, after Aaron Jernigan, a poor settler who came to the lake-dotted region in 1842. No one's quite sure why, but the city's name was changed to Orlando in 1857, probably in memory of a 19th-century soldier, Orlando Reeves, who was killed by Seminole Indians near the banks of the city's Lake Eola.

In the late 1800s Orlando was a rip-roaring frontier cattle town, every bit as colorful as any village in the fabled Wild West. Florida cowboys, immortalized by the artist Frederic Remington, were hardbitten

Orientation

individuals more than capable of accommodating the rugged environment, and they had a special tradition all their own: alligator wrestling in the dirt outside the saloons along Main Street. Cowboys from throughout the region gathered here to test their skills and their courage—usually fortified by locally distilled spirits—against the ferocious alligators, risking hands, fingers, and a foot or two for the roar of the crowds or the favor of a pretty girl. Today Orange Avenue, once Main Street, is a quieter place. Instead of saloons it's lined with banks, law firms, and high-rise office towers.

The St. John's River is the only river in Florida that runs from south to north. It lies wholly within the state and flows northward more than 200 miles, from Lake Helen in south Florida to Jacksonville, where it flows into the Atlantic. Most Floridians know that the St. John's flows north; what many don't know is that it is an ideal river for harvesting eels. One young entrepreneur near Ocala sells much of his catch to Japanese restaurants in New York City.

Orlando may have Walt Disney World, Universal Studios, Sea World, and a domed arena, reports *The Wall Street Journal,* but it doesn't have a major league baseball team, or a supermarket in its downtown area.

Who says you can't work your way to the top? Dick Nunis, chairman of Walt Disney Attractions, got his start in 1955 as a temporary "gofer," or errand-runner, at Disneyland in Anaheim, California. Bill Davis, president of Sea World at Florida, began as a photographer at the San Diego Sea World.

Disneyland, in Anaheim, California, opened in 1955 on 200 former orange-grove acres, and cost about $17 million. When Walt Disney and his brother, Roy, wanted to expand the park, the cost of land had risen to exorbitant levels. Walt felt he'd made a mistake by not buying more land at the start. He was angry about the many hotels and restaurants that sprang up around Disneyland; he said some of the businesses were tacky and tourists were spending money that could have flowed into the Walt Disney Company's coffers if there had only been enough land to build its own hotels and restaurants. Walt didn't want to make that mistake again, which is why his company acquired 27,400 acres in Central Florida, providing plenty of room for the amusement park to grow over the years.

Orlando Area

Orlando began as a tiny settlement carved out of a pine tree wilderness after the Civil War. Seminole Indians bestowed many of the beautiful place names on the region, such as Eola, Osceola, Kissimmee (kis-SIM-ee), and Ocoee (oh-COE-ee). The origin of the name Orlando, though, is obscure. Most people ascribe to the tale of Orlando Reeves (or Rees, depending on which historian you talk to).

In the 1830s, a chain of military forts were scattered across Florida to guard pioneers against hostile attacks by Indians. According to legend, a company of soldiers had engaged a band of Indians near Lake Cherokee, a beautiful, tiny lake that's now at the heart of a residential neighborhood just south of downtown Orlando. The Indians were repelled at first, but they attacked after dark and killed Orlando Reeves, who was believed to be the sentinel on duty that night. But some historians claim Reeves was actually a well-to-do plantation owner; records show a man by that name wrote to the federal government in the 1830s complaining that Indians had stolen several of his black slaves. Reeves may have been standing guard that night for a small group of residents when he was killed. But in any case, a man named Reeves was buried in 1835 just one mile north of Lake Cherokee on Lake Eola, now the center of downtown Orlando. In 1857 Reeves' first name was adopted as the name of the post office in honor of his death; the town then took the name of the post office—Orlando.

Even 15 years after the Civil War, the land surrounding Orlando was open-range cattle country, and on Main St (now Magnolia St), the favorite form of Saturday-afternoon entertainment was alligator wrestling. The area grew when speculators wrote of the wonderful Central Florida land and its climate.

As more people arrived, citrus crops became an increasingly important source of revenue and jobs. By the early 1880s, Orlando was a major marketing and supply center for the citrus industry. From 1910-20 sugarcane, sweet potatoes, and celery joined citrus as significant cash crops.

Long before the name **Walt Disney** would be linked with Orlando, the town became a tourist mecca, albeit a small one, because of its mild climate, pretty lakes, and modest hotel development. In 1924 the completion of the Cheney Highway, now State Route 50, connected Orlando to Florida's east coast and US 1. As automobiles became affordable, people were eager to drive to new and less-developed places, so Orlando started attracting more tourists—particularly when a second major thoroughfare, the Dixie Highway opened through Apopka, Orlando, and Kissimmee in 1925.

It was citrus—not tourism—that remained as Orlando's high-profile industry until the 1960s, when the nation's space program at Cape Canaveral boosted Orlando's growth a bit. The town was still a small one when a mystery buyer began snapping up land in Orange and Osceola counties in 1965.

The buyer, of course, was Walt Disney. On 1 November 1965, the creator of Mickey Mouse promised that his $100-million Walt Disney World would be bigger and better than Disneyland in Anaheim, California. A frenzied building boom started and has slowed little since. In 1990, metropolitan Orlando's population surpassed the one million mark, and largely because of Disney, it attracts 13 million tourists a year.

Area code 407 unless otherwise indicated.

1 Gary's Duck Inn ★$ Long a favorite with old-time Orlandoans, this restaurant doesn't serve duck. Seafood is what it does best, and grouper Oscar, a rendition of the state's best-known fish, is always grilled to perfection. ♦ Seafood ♦ M-Th, Su 11:30AM-10PM; F 11:30AM-11PM; Sa 5-11PM. 3974 S. Orange Blossom Trail (40th-39th Sts) 843.0270

2 The Courtyard at Lake Lucerne $$ Three buildings of varied character make up this collection of three bed-and-breakfast inns. The **Norment Parry Inn** was built in 1895 and is Orlando's oldest house. Each of its six rooms has been decorated by a different artist or designer who had free rein to select colors, fabrics, antiques, and embellishments. The **Wellborn's** Art Deco design is carried througout its 12 rooms. The **I.W. Phillips** building has three rooms, including a honeymoon suite. Nice touches, including fresh flowers, make this a fine choice for travelers weary of sterile, modern hotels. ♦ 211 N. Lucerne Circle East (Orange-Delaney Aves) 648.5188

3 City Hall Fast-growing Orlando has a new, high-profile $33 millon city hall. Designed by **Harwood K. Smith** in 1991, this 267,000-square-foot building is capped with a 120-foot- high copper dome. ♦ 400 S. Orange Ave (Anderson-South Sts)

4 SunBank Center At 35 stories high, this is the tallest building in Orlando and was designed by **Rick Keating** of **Skidmore, Owings and Merrill** in 1988. Four green pyramids top this structure with windows the color of pink champagne, pink granite walls, and teal-green accents. SunBank Center's plaza is dominated by a fountain and plantings, as well as works of art. ♦ 200 S. Orange Ave (Church St)

5 Pebbles ★★$$ The quality of the food and service differentiates this from other yuppie "fern" bars. It looks like just another old storefront from the outside, since it was a five-and-dime store before the inside was transformed into an intimate tropical restaurant. Fresh fish is wonderful here, and there is a long list of imported ales that complement the creative menu. This is the fourth Pebbles restaurant. ♦ American ♦ M-Th 11AM-midnight; F 11AM-1AM; Sa 5PM-1AM; Su 11AM-11PM. 17 W. Church St (Orange-Garland Aves) 839.0892 The others are: Pebbles at the Crossroads,

2551 SR 535, 827.1111; Pebbles in Winter Park, 2516 Aloma Ave, 678.7001; Pebbles in Longwood, 2110 W. SR 434, 774.7111

5 Mulvaney's Irish Pub Lively bar frequented by the locals. It has the feel of a turn-of-the-century Irish pub with its long bar stretching to the back, where live entertainment is often presented. ♦ M-F 11:30AM-2AM; Sa-Su 2PM-2AM. 27 W. Church St (Orange-Garland Aves) 872.3296

5 Behr Shoe Center Owner **Sam Behr** is one of the most well-known characters in Orlando. His abrasive, down-home pitches can be seen on television and he is so popular that people drop in just to say hello. He claims he can fit any human. If you are on Church St after dark, check out the funky neon shoes that walk across the wall above his door. ♦ M-Sa 9:30AM-6PM. 41 W. Church St (Orange-Garland Aves) 423.5746

5 Church Street Market A marketplace and open courtyard with pushcarts, park benches, a clock tower, and turn-of-the-century-style fountains and lamps that connects old downtown buildings with the Church Street Station complex. Built in 1988, the market includes such yuppie favorites as **The Sharper Image, Brookstone, Compagnie Internationale**

Express, and **Häagen Dazs**. Of note is the **Cola Connection,** which has the Coke label on everything imaginable, plus memorabilia and an old-fashioned soda fountain, and at **Southern Candy Corporation** you can watch Southern-style candy being made. The Market is a popular place to dine for the downtown crowd. It has **Pizzeria Uno** (★★$$), **The Olive Garden** (★$) and **Jungle Jim's** (★$), a gourmet burger stop with a diverse menu and rather slow service. ♦ M-Sa 10AM-9PM; Su noon-9PM. 55 W. Church St (Orange-Garland Aves) 872.3500

5 Church Street Station (1974) What used to be a city block of rundown hotels, office buildings, and stores is now a complex of upscale bars, eateries, and shops. The South Florida Railroad train station was built here in 1881 and is now used for administrative offices. Most people refer to the larger street-party scene as "Rosie's," short for **Rosie O'Grady's Good Time Emporium,** a block away and the first bar to open in the complex. What is often overlooked in the revelry is the restoration. **Bob Snow,** the Orlando businessman who founded Church Street, searched all over Europe for antiques used in the complex's bars and restaurant. He also used materials saved from old buildings that were being torn down around the world. ♦ Admission. 129 W. Church St (Orange-Garland Aves) 422.2434

Within Church Street Station:

Rosie O'Grady's Good Time Emporium
This Dixieland bar is in what used to be the Orlando Hotel built in 1904. Look up as you enter and you will see an 800-pound chandelier that once hung in the First National Bank of Boston in 1904. Guests sit on turn-of-the-century benches from the L&N Railroad Depot in Pensacola. The bentwood chairs in the balcony that circles the bar are from the dining room of an English monastery, and when you order a sandwich you talk through an 1870s teller's cage from a Pittsburgh bank. ♦ Shows daily 7:30PM, 9PM, 10:30PM, midnight

Apple Annie's Courtyard This L-shaped room features live bluegrass and folk music in what used to be a meat locker and vacant lot. To enter from Church St you pass through wrought iron gates from an 18th-century English country estate. The bar's mirrors on the east wall were created in the mid-18th century in Vienna, Austria. Some of the booths are old church pews, which fit in quite nicely, considering the bar itself was reconstructed from a communion rail of an 18th-century French-Catholic church. ♦ Shows daily 8:20PM, 2AM

Lili Marlene's Aviator's Pub and Restaurant ★★★$$$ A bit pricey, but where else can you have dinner at **Al Capone's** dining table? It's the one with the green, velvet-covered chairs. The two chairs at the head of the table have steel running through the tall chairback, so someone couldn't sneak up and shoot you from behind. The table sits near a walnut fireplace and wine cabinet carved in 1850 in Gothic-Revival style for a Rothschild townhouse in Paris. The carving above the fireplace depicts the coronation of Louis XVI. The solid brass railing by the bar is 60 feet long and was made in 1903 for the First National Bank of Atlanta. The phone booth between the lavatories is actually an oak confessional from the same old French-Catholic church that provided the pews for the dining booths. This may not be gourmet gobbling, but the veal is good and you can't go wrong with the seafood. The restaurant sits where the Strand Hotel once stood. ♦ American ♦ Daily 11AM-4PM, 5:30PM-midnight. Reservations recommended. 422.2434

Phineas Phogg's Balloon Works This museum is disguised as a disco. When it opened in 1979 it was one of the only places for dancing in downtown. It can still get very crowded, especially with tourists or locals who arrive around midnight after a downtown concert or ball game. The disc jockey's booth is from a London church. If you get here before the crush, you'll be able to see pictures and memorabilia from famous balloonists, including Church Street Station's own **Colonel Joe Kittinger,** best known as the first pilot to cross the Atlantic Ocean in a balloon. At the time it was the world's longest balloon flight. His 1984 trip from Caribou, Maine to Montenette, Italy aboard *Rosie O'Grady's Balloon of Peace.* from 14-18 September lasted 86 hours and covered 3,543 miles. What few people remember is that Kittinger had already set three other world records during his leap from an airplane in August 1960: the first person to exceed the speed of sound without an aircraft or space vehicle (714 mph during his freefall); highest parachute jump from a balloon (102,800 feet); and longest parachute free fall (4 minutes, 32 seconds). ♦ Must be 21. Daily 7PM-2AM

Church Street Station Exchange You can walk out of Apple Annie's into the Exchange, two floors of shopping under Victorian tin ceilings. The Exchange is free if you enter from the street instead of through Rosie's entertainment complex. It has more than 50 shops, including a nifty **Old Town Magic Shop,** with a magician always on hand, and the usual favorites like **Benetton, Victoria's Secret** and **Units. Pewter by Ricker** is a shop selling hand-crafted pewter by artist **Michael Ricker.** ♦ Daily 11AM-11PM. 442.2434

Commander Ragtime's Midway of Fun, Food, and Games Besides pool tables, pinball, and video games, there are large-screen TVs to catch sporting events. Look up

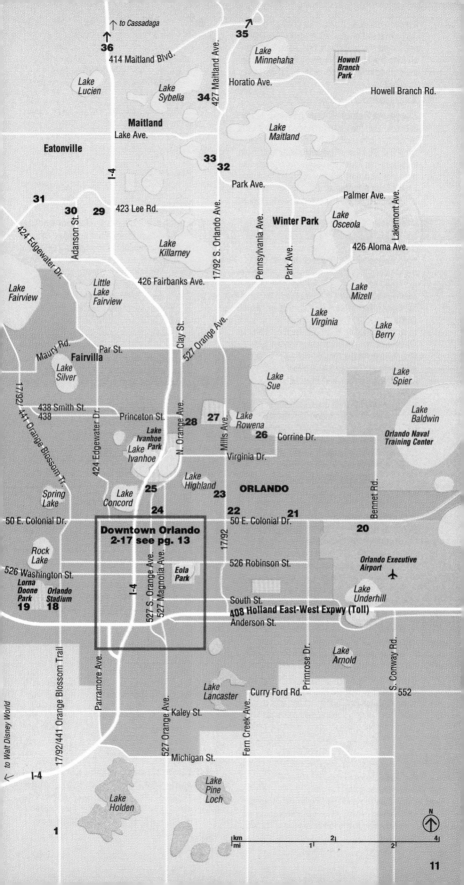

↑ *to Cassadaga*

36
414 Maitland Blvd.

35

Lake Lucien

Lake Minnehaha

Howell Branch Park

Lake Sybelia

34

Horatio Ave.

Howell Branch Rd.

427 Maitland Ave.

Maitland
Lake Ave.

Lake Maitland

Eatonville

I-4

33
32

Park Ave.

Palmer Ave.

Lakemont Ave.

31

30 **29**
423 Lee Rd.

Winter Park

Lake Osceola

424 Edgewater Dr.

Adanson St.

Lake Killarney

17/92 S. Orlando Ave.

Pennsylvania Ave.

Park Ave.

426 Aloma Ave.

426 Fairbanks Ave.

Lake Fairview

Little Lake Fairview

Lake Mizell

Clay St.

527 Orange Ave.

Lake Virginia

Lake Berry

Maury Rd.

Par St.

Fairvilla

Lake Silver

Lake Sue

Lake Spier

17/92/441 Orange Blossom Tr.

438 Smith St.
438

424 Edgewater Dr.

Princeton St.

28 **27**

Mills Ave.

Lake Rowena

26
Corrine Dr.

Lake Baldwin

Orlando Naval Training Center

Lake Ivanhoe Park

N. Orange Ave.

Virginia Dr.

Lake Ivanhoe

Spring Lake

Lake Concord

25

Lake Highland

23

ORLANDO

Bennet Rd.

50 E. Colonial Dr.

24

22

21

50 E. Colonial Dr.

20

Downtown Orlando 2-17 see pg. 13

17/92

526 Robinson St.

Orlando Executive Airport ✈

Rock Lake

526 Washington St.

I-4

527 S. Orange Ave.

527 Magnolia Ave.

Eola Park

Lake Underhill

Lorna Doone Park

Orlando Stadium

South St.

19 **18**

408 **Holland East-West Expwy (Toll)**

Anderson St.

Parramore Ave.

Lake Arnold

Primrose Dr.

S. Conway Rd.

Lake Lancaster

Curry Ford Rd.

552

527 Orange Ave.

Kaley St.

Fern Creek Ave.

← *to Walt Disney World*

I-4

Michigan St.

17/92/441 Orange Blossom Trail

1

Lake Holden

Lake Pine Loch

N
↑

km
mi

1

1

2

2

4

between dangling replicas of WWI planes to find a maze of electric train tracks. Six trains are constantly in motion, crisscrossing and sharing tracks. Don't expect a collision: They are computer-operated. ♦ Daily 11AM-1AM. 422.2434

Across the street:

Cheyenne Saloon & Opera House Many consider this the jewel of the complex. It took more than two years to build this showcase from 250,000 feet of golden oak lumber from a century-old Ohio barn. Anyone who works here will be proud to point out the 11 original **Frederic Remington** sculptures, and the antique guns on the bar room wall; one set was

Orlando Area

once owned by outlaw **Jesse James.** Climb the stairs to the upper level for a great view of the entire saloon. Check out the 1885, solid rosewood Brunswick pool table and the original tapestries from the **Buffalo Bill** and **Annie Oakley's** "Wild West Show." Looking across to the front you'll see an outstanding stained-glass window that once was a memorial to the Grand Army of the Republic in a Philadelphia courthouse. The chandeliers each have a story too: three of them came from beer baron **Joseph Schlitz's** home in St. Louis, and six are from the Philadelphia mint. There is dancing, dining, and often an opportunity to run into big-name country stars. The Cheyenne Saloon is home to the Nashville Network's Church Street Station TV show. ♦ Entertainment daily 8:30PM, 10PM, 11:30PM and 1AM. 422.2434

Orchid Garden Ballroom and Dessert Cafe Music from the 1940s to the present is presented in a Victorian arcade complete with wrought iron, brick floors, and stained-glass windows. The dance floor is a balcony above the bandstand. ♦ Entertainment M-Th 8:30PM, 9:30PM, 10:45PM, midnight; F-Sa 8:30PM, 9:30PM, 10:45PM, midnight, 1:10AM. 422.2434

Cracker's Oyster Bar ★★$$$ The Victorian age is alive in this bar, where you can get a taste of Creole cooking or enjoy ocean goodies such as oysters, gumbos, and clam chowders. ♦ Seafood ♦ Daily 11AM-midnight. 422.2434

Wine Cellar One of the largest wine cellars in Florida is located underneath Cracker's Oyster Bar. There are more than 4,000 bottles, including a $180 bottle of old port. Occasional wine tastings. 422.2434

The Bumby Arcade Once the Bumby Hardware store, it now houses **Bumby Gifts,** a shop filled with Church Street Station souvenirs; **Thomas Sweet Ice Cream** and the **Buffalo Trading Company,** a Western gift shop—check out the size of the stuffed buffalo before you leave. ♦ Daily 11AM-11PM

Metropolitan Orlando and Las Vegas are competing to see which city can build the most hotel rooms. In 1991 Orlando was in the lead with a total of 76,500 hotel rooms.

6 Farmers Market Gaining in popularity, this half-block, open-air market offers good prices on produce, baked goods, gourmet coffee, cheese, dried flowers, and houseplants, including a fine selection of orchids. ♦ Sa 7AM-1PM. Underneath Interstate 4 (Garland-Hughey Aves)

7 Good Times Diner ★$$ Slick vinyl booths, great fifties and sixties tunes on the jukebox, wacky waiters (some dressed as lovable nerds), cold beer, thick shakes, and great burgers and fries. Wine and beer, along with hearty breakfast omelets, make this worth a stop even if you aren't a burger fan. ♦ American ♦ M-Sa 7AM-11PM. 301 W. Church St (Hughey-Bryan Aves) 246.1950

8 Ichiban ★$$ One of the few places in Central Florida where fresh sushi is not only available but worth seeking out. Tangy teriyaki and tempura dishes—the latter even includes a lightly fried banana—round out the menu. No nonsmoking area. ♦ Japanese ♦ M-Th 11:30AM-2:30PM, 5-10PM; F 11:30AM-2:30PM, 5-11PM; Sa 5-11PM. 19 S. Orange Ave (Pine-Central Sts) 423.2688

9 Beijing $ Basic Chinese food. Crisp egg rolls and inexpensive luncheon specials. A good place for an ethnic food fix when you're downtown. ♦ Chinese ♦ M-Th 11AM-10PM; F 11AM-11PM; Sa noon-11PM; Su 1-10PM. 19 N. Orange Ave (Wall St) 423.2522

10 Beacham Theatre Sometimes a weekend disco, the once-proud theater built in 1921 has had many lives as the downtown slowly died with the advent of suburbs and theme parks.The recent resurgence, though, has brought stars here, including **David Byrne** of **Talking Heads** and country-blues crooner **Lyle Lovett.** ♦ Cover ♦ F-Sa 10PM-6AM. 46 N. Orange Ave (Central-Washington Aves) 425.4038

10 Beacham's Blue Note ★$$$ This is one of the few places off Church St that is lively and open late. It's filled with townies who appreciate live blues and jazz. Jam sessions Sunday (blues) and Tuesday (jazz). The food is more than bar fare. If you favor the taste of Cajun, try the crawfish smothered in Creole sauce. ♦ American ♦ M-Sa 11AM-4:30PM, 5PM-1:30AM; Su 5PM-1:30AM. 54 N. Orange Ave (Central-Washington Aves) 843.3078

11 Ha Long ★$ Savory shrimp curry with baked eggplant is a contender for the best lunch in downtown Orlando. For dinner try the grilled beef, pork with vermicelli noodles, or the salted, fried crabs. Lunch buffet. ♦ Vietnamese ♦ M 11AM-2:30PM; Tu-Th 11AM-2:30PM, 6-9:30PM; F 11AM-12:30AM; Sa 10:30AM-12:30AM; Su 10:30AM-9PM. 120 N. Orange Ave (Washington-Jefferson Aves) 648.9685

12 Harley Hotel of Orlando $$$ A recent renovation makes this hotel a good bet if you need to stay downtown. Good lunch buffet in the restaurant, along with a fine view of Lake Eola. ♦ 151 E. Washington St (Rosalind Ave) 841.3220

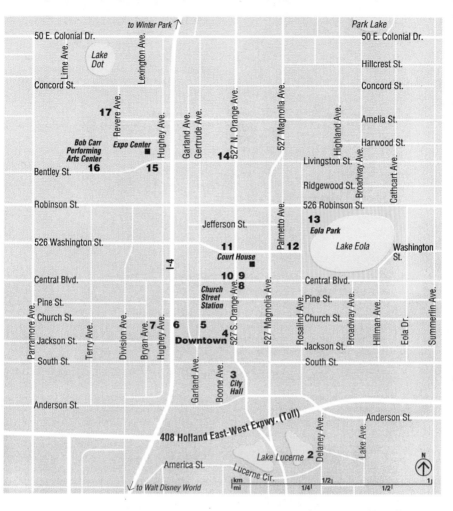

13 Lake Eola Park and Amphitheater Newly refurbished after a donation from the Walt Disney World Co, the Lake Eola bandshell is the home of the annual **Orlando Shakespeare Festival** and occasional free concerts. The Shakespeare Festival, a nonprofit professional repertory theater affiliated with the University of Central Florida, produces two of Shakespeare's plays each spring. ◆ Lake Eola Park (Central-Robinson Sts) Shakespeare Festival information: 605 E. Robinson St, Suite 100. 423.6905

14 DuPont Centre Neo-Victorian spires top this 28-story office building constructed of silvery reflective-glass walls, built in 1987. A stately entrance takes you from an open friendly plaza into elegant lobbies. ◆ 390 N. Orange Ave (Livingston Ave)

15 Omni International Hotel $$$ If you can't find a place to stay near Walt Disney World, this 300-room hotel is the nicest in the area, and is a good bet because it's only a 20- to 25-minute drive from the theme park. It's also across the street from the Orlando Arena and Bob Carr Performing Arts Centre, and right off Interstate 4. ◆ 400 W. Livingston St. 843.6664

16 Bob Carr Performing Arts Centre Home to the **Florida Symphony Orchestra,** the **Orlando Opera Company,** the **Southern Ballet,** touring Broadway shows, and musical groups from rock to classical. This is the big theater in town, despite the less than first-rate acoustics, a small stage and behind-the-scenes working area, and lack of a center aisle. The 32-year-old Orlando Opera Company performs four operas—usually including a lighter operetta—each year. The season usually runs from November to April. (Office: 1900 N. Mills Ave, Suite 4. 896.7664.) ◆ Seats 2,500. 401 W. Livingston St (Hughey-Parramore Aves) Box office 849.2050, event information 849.2001

Orlando, especially in residential neighborhoods near downtown, has many beautiful brick streets. In the teens, the city first used pine straw to build their streets, but it didn't hold up very well, so clay was tried out. Clay worked much better but it was scarce. Finally, brick was chosen, and by 1916, Orlando had about 50 miles of brick streets, many of which were laid out by convicts.

Restaurants/Nightlife: Red   **Hotels:** Blue
Shops/ 🌳 Outdoors: Green   **Sights/Culture:** Black

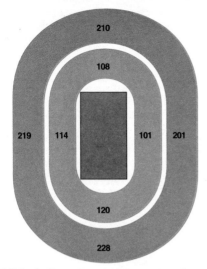

17 Orlando Arena
Taxes levied on tourists who rent hotel rooms or campsites pay for this well-designed, efficient public building that seats 16,000. Popularly known as the "O-rena," it is home to the National Basketball Association's Orlando Magic. The arena, with Art Deco highlights, has aggressively pursued the top names in the entertainment field and is filled almost nightly with a wide range of activities, from hockey, tractor pulls, and the circus to rodeo, wrestling, and music. ◆ 600 W. Amelia St (Hughey-Parramore Aves) Box office 849.2020, event information 849.2001

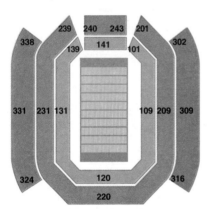

18 Orlando Stadium
The stadium holds 70,000 and plans to expand to 90,000 seats. But it only fills up once a year during the annual **Florida Citrus Bowl,** which is in the prestigious New Year's Day college football lineup. The **Orlando Thunder,** a team in the new World League of American Football, is expected to draw well here; football fans in Orlando have long supported wanna-be football leagues. As the **University of Central Florida** grows, so has its football program. The **Knights** play here in front of a steadily increasing number of fans. The stadium is also home to high school football and a couple of concerts each year. ◆ Church St (Rio Grande-Tampa Aves) 849.2020

19 Tinker Field
Built in 1921 and named for **Joe Tinker** of Tinker-to-Evers-to-Chance fame. Tinker retired to Orlando after his baseball days were over. The stadium seats more than 5,000 and is home to the **Orlando SunRays,** a Class AA minor-league baseball team affiliated with the Minnesota Twins. ◆ 287 S. Tampa Ave (South-Church Sts) 872.7593

20 4th Fighter Group
★$$$ The setting is more memorable than the food, but this restaurant and lounge at the Executive Airport is a cut above the average steak-and-beer stop. The entrance resembles a forti-

fied bunker, and the inside is like a dim old British country pub with its fireplace and exposed beams. The restaurant is dedicated to the 4th Fighter Group, which by the end of WWII was recognized as the elite fighter pilots unit of the American forces. Hanging from the wall are war mementos and pictures of 4th Fighter Group Commander **Colonel Donald Blakeslee,** whose group escorted the first bombers over Berlin on 4 March 1944. The window seats give you a view of airplanes landing and taking off, and far to the west, the green pyramids of the SunBank building are visible. You can eavesdrop on the pilots and the control tower with headphones near the tables away from the window. ◆ American ◆ M-Th 11AM-10PM; F-Sa 11AM-11PM; Su 10:30AM-10PM. 494 Rickenbacker Dr (off E. Colonial Dr, an extension of Bennet Rd, between Lowell-Calvin Aves) 898.4251

21 La Normandie
★★$$$ They serve reliable French fare in three French country dining rooms. Duck with apples is a specialty, and the Grand Marnier souffle is *très magnifique.* One of the owners, **Claude Melchiorri,** was a chef at Maxim's in Paris before becoming executive chef at some of San Francisco's top restaurants. ◆ French ◆ M-F 11:30AM-2PM, 5:30-10PM; Sa 5:30PM-10PM. 2021 E. Colonial Dr (Palm Dr) 896.9976

22 Vinh's
★$ This is a modest restaurant, but it's becoming a big hit with the downtown lunch crowds and adventurous dinner folk. Soups are homemade, delicious, and served in huge bowls. One standout is the seafood soup with its generous serving of translucent rice noodles floating in a clear broth and filled with shrimp, crab claws, and onion. Sliced egg roll, served on noodles, is also a hit. Another can't-miss is the thinly sliced beef that guests cook at the table on an ingenious little stove. ◆ Vietnamese ◆ M-Su 10AM-10PM. 1231 E. Colonial Dr (Shine-Mills Aves) 894.5007

23 The Forbidden City
★★$$ Forget the pricey Chinese food at or near tourist haunts. When chef **Steve Chang** first worked his magic at the Haifeng Restaurant at the Stouffer Orlando Resort hotel near Sea World, Chinese food lovers took note. Now, he's

whipping up good lunches and memorable dinners, including tangy chicken with black bean sauce, orange beef, and an oriental-style barbecue shrimp called *sa chia* shrimp. ♦ Hunan ♦ M-F 11:30AM-2PM, 5-10PM; Sa 5-10PM. 948 N. Mills Ave (Marks-Weber Sts) 894.5005

24 Olympia Place At night, bright, white argon tubes trace the building's crisp, crystalline contours. Pale pink granite walls alternate with glass on the office structure, creating a stairstep effect that attempts to link the building to its less lofty architectural neighbors. Plans are for two more buildings to be built at the site that will make this one—designed by **John Lind** of **Hanson-Lind Meyer** in 1988— look less like a missing puzzle piece. ♦ 800 N. Magnolia Ave (Park Lake-Marks Sts) 422.7773

25 Radisson Plaza Hotel Orlando $$$ Some of the 379 rooms look out over Lake Ivanhoe, while others face a high-rise insurance company. To get rooms with a view, ask for the oddly numbered rooms 03 through 013 on floors 4 through 15. Thanks to a high-rise parking garage, you can avoid getting wet during Orlando's rainy summer months if you forego valet parking. ♦ 60 S. Ivanhoe Blvd (Magnolia-Orange Aves) 425.4455

LEU GARDENS

26 Leu Botanical Gardens Among 56 acres of carefully cultivated gardens, you will find the largest camellia collection in the East. They bloom during the winter months. Small maps are available to help you through a maze of paths. Be sure to see the 50-foot floral clock and the recently renovated rose garden. You can also tour **Harry P. Leu's** house, which was built a century ago. House tours last about 20 minutes and are conducted every half hour. Leu, who grew up in Orlando and was a successful businessman, purchased the land on **Lake Rowena** in 1936. It was once part of a farm owned by **David Mizell**, Winter Park's first settler. ♦ Admission. Daily 9AM-5PM. 1730 N. Forest Ave (Nebraska St) 246.2620

27 Loch Haven Park An Orlando city park that is home to theaters and museums. ♦ Entrance on Princeton St (Mills Ave-Camden Rd)

At Loch Haven Park:

Orlando Museum of Art The focus at this modern, stark structure is on 19th- and 20th-century American art by artists associated

with Florida, including **John Singer Sargent, George Innes,** and **Milton Avery.** It also is noted for its pre-Columbian artifacts. ♦ Admission. Tu-F 9AM-5PM; Sa 10AM-5PM; Su noon-5PM. 2416 N. Mills Ave. 896.4231

Civic Theatre of Central Florida Includes a six-play MainStage Season, a summer musical, a series of plays for children, and a three-play SecondStage Season of adult drama. Civic Theatre consists of **Edyth Bush Theatre** (seats 350), **Ann Giles Densch Theatre for Young People** (seats 400), and **Tupperware Theatre** (seats 140). Edyth Bush is the main stage. ♦ 1001 E. Princeton St. 896.7365

Orlando Science Center A hands-on museum geared toward kids, there is a Foucault pendulum, an astronomical observatory, a natural history collection, science demonstrations, and the **John Young Planetarium.** ♦ Admission. M-Th, Sa 9AM-5PM; F 9AM-9PM; Su noon-5PM. 810 E. Rollins St. 896.7151

Within the Orlando Science Center:

Orange County Historical Museum Exhibits chronicle Orange County's past, and include a country store and pioneer kitchen. ♦ Tu-F 9AM-5PM; Sa-Su noon-5PM

Behind the Orlando Science Center:

Fire Station No. 3 A two-story, redbrick building built in 1926, this is Orlando's oldest standing firehouse and is less than a mile from its original location. On display are Orlando's old fire trucks, including the horse-drawn American LaFrance Metropolitan steam-fire pumper from 1911, and the original leather and

metal buckets from a hundred years ago. It also houses a collection of fire memorabilia such as badges, photos, and helmets. ♦ Nominal admission. Tu-F 9AM-5PM; Sa-Su noon-5PM. 898.8320

Restaurants/Nightlife: Red	Hotels: Blue
Shops/ ☂Outdoors: Green	Sights/Culture: Black

15

28 Theatre Downtown This cozy theater in a former appliance store specializes in American and contemporary plays that have run successfully on and off Broadway. Works by local playwrights are also performed. ♦ Seats 120. 2113 N. Orange Ave. 841.0083

29 The Comedy Zone Affiliated with one of comedy's biggest chains, this zone is for locals, with a sister zone on International Dr. Both clubs are housed in Holiday Inns, and they draw from a regional and national talent pool. ♦ Admission. Shows W-Th, Su 8:30PM; F-Sa 8:30PM, 10:30PM. 626 Lee Rd (Interstate 4-Adanson St) 645.5233

30 Bonkerz Located inside one of the more

popular nightclubs, **J.J. Whispers,** this 250-seat comedy club regularly features the top cablevision comics and professional network stars. ♦ Admission. Shows Tu-Th, Su 9PM; F-Sa 8:30PM, 10:45PM. 5100 Adanson St (Courtland St-Lee Rd) 298.2665

31 Angels's Diner & Bakery ★★$$ This popular hamburger haven is one of the best of the make-believe fifties diners that are sprouting up all over, with booths, little jukeboxes on the tables, and old-time rock 'n' roll. Portions are large. Favorites include Hamburger Max, chili, warm corned beef, and Angel's Famous Reuben. On payday, try the New York sirloin steak. Miniature copies of the menus are free and they contain Angel's Laws, such as law No. four: We hate soggy fries. If yours aren't the way you like them, send them back—the kitchen will get the message. ♦ American ♦ M-Th 7AM-11PM; F-Sa 7-midnight. 1345 Lee Rd (Goddard St) 291.4832

32 Enzian Theatre Central Florida's first art film house, this cozy theater has comfortable chairs, a reasonably large movie screen, and food, wine, and beer service during the movie. ♦ Admission. Seats 250. 1300 S. Orlando Ave (US 17-92), Maitland (Alpine Dr-Orange Pl) 629.1088

32 Jordan's Grove ★★★$$$ Owner and chef **Mark Rodriguez** has made this perhaps the finest example of new American cuisine served in Central Florida. The restaurant features fine Southern fare, including lamb grown in Florida and fish from local fishmongers. The prix fixe dinner menu changes daily, but you'll always find such exotic entrées such as grilled and roasted wild boar with *chipotle* pepper, (a smoked jalapeño pepper) in a red bean marinade. Each night there are six to eight entrées, and you can frequently find wild game, such as mountain hare or fresh seafood, such as grilled Florida wahoo. The setting, a 1912 house

shaded by huge oaks, makes this a romantic and cozy spot perfect for a special occasion. ♦ Continental ♦ Tu-F, Su 11AM-2:30PM; 6-10PM; Sa 6-10PM. 1300 S. Orlando Ave (US 17-92) Maitland (next to Enzian Theatre) 628.0020

33 The Bubble Room ★★★$$$ Innovative cuisine served in kooky rooms lined with mirrors and memorabilia from the thirties through the fifties. You can get anything from a famous Bubble Burger to the Henny Young-One, a boneless breast of young chicken wrapped in bacon and topped with cream sauce. Dinner portions are generous and desserts are mountainous. Try cappuccino chocolate cheesecake or the silk nightie. ♦ American ♦ M-F 11:30AM-2:30PM, 5:30-10PM; Sa 11:30AM-11PM; Su 11:30AM-10PM. 1351 S. Orlando Ave (US 17-92) Maitland (Circle Dr) 628.3331

34 Maitland Art Center This quirky, hand-built museum was created as an artists' retreat in the late 1930s by artist **Andre Smith.** Today, the stucco-and-cast-concrete landmark is on the National Register of Historic Places. The art center features changing exhibitions by local, regional, and national contemporary American artists. The wall carvings in the garden chapel depict the life of Christ. ♦ Free. M, W-F 10AM-4:30PM; Tu 10AM-8M; Sa-Su noon-4:30PM. 231 W. Packwood Ave, Maitland (Maitland Ave-Lake Sybellia Dr) 645.2181

35 Enzo's on the Lake ★$$$ Enzo Perlini has been serving the cuisine of his native Rome for more than a decade in this lively setting, a converted ranch-style house on Fairy Lake. The chef, trained in Venice, prepares delicate pastas and divine desserts. It isn't necessary to spend big bucks if you order a pasta dish like the *bucatini alla Enzo*, long tiny tubes in a light sauce of mushrooms, bacon, and peas, served out of a skillet. If you want to pass on the cakes for dessert, the restaurant holds to European after-dinner tradition by offering cheese and fruits. ♦ Italian ♦ Tu-F noon-2:30PM, 6-11PM; Sa 6-11PM. 1130 S. Highway 17-92, Longwood (Dog Track Rd-SR 434) 834.9872

36 Maison & Jardin ★★$$$ A house and garden reminiscent of a Roman villa provide a serene setting, where the specialties range from fresh poached salmon Niçoise and wild mushrooms over spinach fettuccine to beef Wellington. ♦ French ♦ M-Sa 6-10PM; Su 6-9PM. 430 Wymore Rd, Altamonte Springs (Spring Lake Hills Dr-Spring Valley Rd) Reservations recommended. Jacket and tie required. 862.4410

Bug Off!

There's no denying it—Central Florida is a haven for bugs, from the familiar mosquito to the nearly invisible but singularly annoying "no-see-ums." Modern spraying techniques and truckloads of insecticides, fungicides, and other chemicals have controlled the problem so visitors are rarely bothered by these small beasts. But just in case you do feel something crawling across your arm in the middle of the night, here's a guide to some of these creepy crawlies.

Palmetto bugs

Everywhere else they're called cockroaches, but in Florida they were named by early settlers for the palmetto trees they infested. **Bill Zak,** author of *Florida Critters,* writes that there are more than 3,500 species of cockroaches in the world, and Florida can boast quite a few, including the Florida Woods, the American, the Smoky Brown, the Australian, the German, and the brown-banded cockroach. The bugs love a warm, moist environment, which makes Florida perfect for them. If you're staying in a decent hotel or motel, however, they should never appear; decent pest control will turn their legs up. But don't leave food out to tempt them.

M. BLUM

Chinch bugs Central Florida is home to a type called the Southern chinch bug, which Zak calls "the most injurious and notorious pest of St. Augustine grass in Florida." The bug sucks the plant juices from this popular grass, which causes yellowish to brownish patches in infested lawns. But there's no need to worry about the pesky chinch bug unless you plan to move here and plant a lawn.

Cicadas These critters are known for their nighttime humming concerts (especially during summer months). Some people think the cicada insects are screaming, but their song is actually a mating call: The male species sing to attract females. Frequently misidentified as locusts, these bugs don't wantonly destroy crops (as do locusts), but they will damage vines, shrubs, and trees. If you're in a Central Florida park, you may see the husks of cicada nymphs on tree trunks. This is the harmless skin the insect sheds when it emerges into adulthood.

Chiggers Also known as **redbugs,** these insects won't hop on you while you're inside a park, but they may if you're out in the wild. They are related to ticks and spiders and you can't see them without a magnifying glass; their nasty bites may be your only clue that they've found you. The bites cause intense itching and small reddish welts on the skin. But these creatures don't burrow into your skin, as some people believe. If you start itching, the best course is to shower and apply an over-the-counter remedy, such as an anti-itch lotion, for relief.

Mosquitoes Several Central Florida counties were once lumped together and called "Mosquito County"—and for good reason. There are more than 1,500 species of mosquitoes around the world, and many call Florida home. Florida's tourism industry doesn't like to talk about it, but in 1990 an outbreak of **encephalitis** transmitted by mosquitoes killed 26 people. You have nothing to worry about while visiting the tourist parks, however, because mosquito control at all attractions and in cities is excellent. But if you plan to camp in marsh areas, take along mosquito repellent. Also, bug experts say mosquitoes are often attracted by perfume and after-shave, as well as by dark or blue colors, so dress appropriately.

Termites This is another bug you won't have to worry about unless you decide to become a permanent resident. Termites can turn beautiful wood floors or beloved antiques into sawdust, but they can't do much to ruin a vacation.

No-see-ums It's tough to fight back against creatures you can't see, and the no-see-um is a tiny, almost invisible insect that inflicts a stinging bite. They can be especially pesky along the seashore at dawn or dusk and after dark. Insect repellent helps a great deal, and they will be less attracted to you if you aren't wearing perfume or after-shave.

Bests

Bill Frederick
Mayor, City of Orlando

A swan boat ride on **Lake Eola** at sunset to admire the Orlando skyline.

An early-morning stroll around **Leu Gardens** in Orlando during the winter, when the azaleas and camellias are in bloom.

Dinner at **Vivaldi** and, for dessert, an evening carriage ride around downtown Orlando.

A spring evening concert by the Florida Symphony Orchestra on the lawn at **Loch Haven Park** in Orlando.

The energy of an Orlando Magic basketball game at the **Orlando Arena.**

Harris Rosen
Owner, Tamar Inns Inc.

Shogun Japanese Restaurant—consistently the best food in Orlando.

New Smyrna Beach, south of Daytona Beach.

The **Orange County Convention Center.**

The **Orlando Arena**—the best of its kind anywhere.

Port Canaveral in Brevard County—the best deep-sea fishing around, with extraordinary variety.

Winter Park

This city is synonymous with sophistication, trendiness, and big bucks. Its small-town ambience, tree-lined redbrick roads, and excellent schools make it one of the most desirable places in Central Florida to live. Ever since the well-to-do began retreating from northern winters to cottages and resorts here in the 19th century, Winter Park has been the "proper address" and a haven for the rich and famous.

Winter Park's first white settler, **David Mizell**, arrived in 1858, when the region was mostly wilderness. Most of the native **Seminole Indians** had fled south to the Everglades after losing the Second Seminole War (1835-42). Winter Park's **Lake Osceola** is named after the Indian chief who led the Seminoles in battle against the US military, which was empowered by Congress to resettle them in the Oklahoma Territory.

Significant development didn't occur in Winter Park until 1881, when two friends from Massachusetts, **Loring Chase** and **Oliver Chapman**, bought land for a resort hotel and a residential community. They gave their new town the name it has been known by ever since, and got a boost in 1882 when the South Florida Railroad, financed by a Boston company, linked Sanford to Tampa with a stop in Winter Park.

Winter Park

Today, Winter Park may lack sophistication when measured against New York or San Francisco standards, but this town, with its little parks, nonchain hotels, smart boutiques, and charming lakeside **Rollins College** campus, possesses a graceful character that much of neighboring boomtown Orlando lacks.

When people talk about Winter Park, often they are referring to **Park Avenue**, a favorite among locals and visitors alike for shopping or an evening stroll. Although it has the requisite trendy chain stores—**The Gap, Banana Republic, Polo by Ralph Lauren, Crabtree & Evelyn, Ann Taylor, Talbot's**—its shops and boutiques offer the best alternative to mall shopping in Central Florida.

Parking isn't always easy to find, however. There is free street parking along and off Park Avenue and free parking lots a block west of Park Avenue, on Canton Avenue, Morse Boulevard, and New England Avenue.

Area code 407 unless otherwise indicated.

1 Rollins College At the south end of posh Park Ave is Rollins College, an architectural delight established in 1885. The lakeside liberal arts college is primarily designed in Spanish-Mediterranean style. For those interested in architecture or art, or in need of a quiet moment, an hour strolling the tree-shaded pathways that crisscross the 65-acre campus is a pleasant experience. ♦ 1000 Holt Ave. 646.2000

Within Rollins College:

Knowles Memorial Chapel The most impressive building on the Rollins College campus is the Knowles Memorial Chapel, designed in 1932 by **Dr. Ralph Adams Cram** of Boston, the preeminent Gothic architect of the time. Above the chapel's main door is a carved stone bas-relief depicting a Franciscan friar planting a cross between Seminole Indians on one side and Spanish conquistadors on the other. The linen on the altar is from the 14th century. Take some time to stare at the stained-glass windows, all but two by **Wilbur Herbert Burnham** of Boston, especially if you are planning to compare them with Louis Comfort Tiffany's

Knowles Memorial Chapel

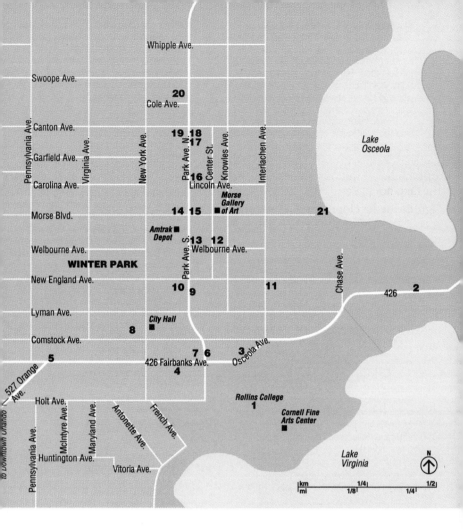

work at the Morse Gallery on Park Ave. Knowles Chapel also plays host to the annual **Winter Park Bach Festival** in the spring.

Annie Russell Theatre A courtyard garden with a tiled fountain connects the theater with Knowles Memorial Chapel. The Spanish-Mediterranean theme is carried through in the theater, home of the **Rollins Players,** students who present a regular season of dramatic and musical productions. ♦ Seats 377

Crummer Hall Designed by **James Gamble Rogers II** in 1966, the hall houses the **Crummer Graduate School of Business**. Hanging in the lobby inside the entrance closest to Fairbanks Ave are two Tiffany medallion window panels depicting scenes from the life of Christ. Originally sections of a Gothic memorial window made in 1929 for the Greeley Presbyterian Church in St. Louis, these panels flanked a dominant panel featuring a figure of Christ. The original window was 15 feet high and 11 feet wide.

Bush Science Center Trimmed on the outside in travertine marble from Italy, the science center displays two Tiffany window

inserts inside. Neither is as spectacular as those in Crummer Hall, and both are smaller sections from the same Greeley Presbyterian Church window. One is lit and tucked away at the end of a hallway to the right as you enter the center's auditorium lobby. The other window panel is unlit and on the back wall of a conference room that is through the doors to your right of the first panel.

Cornell Fine Arts Center Known for its late 19th-century American art and a complete set of tapestries designed by **Alexander Calder.** It also has a fine collection of Baroque and Italian Renaissance paintings, including *Madonna and Child Enthroned* by **Cosimo Rosselli.** The painting was a gift in 1937 from **Samuel H. Kress,** whose collection formed a large part of the National Gallery of Art.

Walk of Fame In the center of campus, on the east side of Carnegie Hall and across the street from the administration building lies the Walk of Fame, created by **Hamilton Holt,** a popular Rollins College president who served from 1925-49. Here you will find hundreds of engraved stones: a rock from the front step of

Woodrow Wilson's home in Princeton, a stone from the garden of the Paris hotel where **Oscar Wilde** died, a rock from the Atlanta home of **Martin Luther King Jr.** are typical of the collection. The idea was inspired from Holt's childhood wanderings with his father, who told his son about the history of the folks around their Woodstock home. The walkways there often were made up of stones taken from ancestral homes and engraved with the names of ancestors. When Holt came to Rollins College, he thought it would be intriguing to start a Walk of Fame with stones from famous people he had met.

Holt was affectionately known as "Prexy" to the students. Besides being very visible on campus by attending social and sports events, he made his mark nationally with his innovative educational ideas, which even included

the design of the campus: He felt the physical environment should be conducive to learning and campus buildings should take advantage of Florida's favorable climate. He, more than anyone else, shaped Rollins College's image. During his tenure, 32 Spanish-Mediterranean-style buildings went up. He also devised the innovative Conference Plan, in which classes were oriented more to discussion than to the traditional lecture approach. He actively recruited around the country for the best professors, and Rollins soon developed a fine national reputation.

Rollins, where 92 percent of the faculty hold a Ph.D. or the highest degree in their field, has approximately 1,400 students and a student-faculty ratio of 12 to 1.

Beal-Maltbie Environmental Studies Building This building was constructed in 1940 to house more than 2,000 shells from **Dr. James Beal,** who began gathering them when he moved from Ohio to Florida in 1888. Beal's lifelong friend, **Dr. Birdsey Maltbie,** built the museum. All the shells have been shipped to a museum in Gainesville.

2 Albin Polasek Galleries Sculptor and painter Albin Polasek (1879-1965) was born in Moravia, Czechoslovakia, and by the time he came to America at age 22, he was an expert woodcarver. After years of studying at the Pennsylvania Academy of Fine Arts in Philadelphia, he became head of the sculpture department at the School of the Art Institute of Chicago where he stayed from 1916-43 and produced much of his acclaimed work. In 1950 he built this home and studio on three acres of land on Lake Osceola. Shortly after it was completed, he suffered a stroke, leaving his left side paralyzed. He continued to sculpt

with his one good hand, and it was during this time he produced *Victory of Moral Law*, a rendering of a horseman slaying a serpent, that represented the American battle against communism following the Soviet demolition of the 1956 Hungarian revolution. In 1961 Polasek married **Emily Kubat,** and with her occasional help, he completed 16 works after he turned 80. In the front gardens, look for a statue of Emily playing a harp with streams of water forming the strings. Another version is in Winter Park's **Central Park.** In front of the gallery is Polasek's favorite piece, *Man Carving His Own Destiny* (1921), a stone statue of a man chiseling himself from a block of marble. Fiberglass replicas of his *14 Stations of the Cross*—the originals were made in bronze for the St. Cecilia Cathedral in Omaha, Nebraska—can be found in a garden courtyard behind the galleries. look for him in the crowd scene of the twelfth station. Inside are a number of his paintings. Pay particular attention to the painting of his bedroom: look at it standing to the left of the painting and then from the right. The bed will appear to have moved from one corner to another. After touring the galleries, walk through his house and peek into his bedroom. In which corner is his bed really located? ♦ Free. W-Sa 10AM-noon, 1-4PM; Su 1-4PM, Oct-June. 633 Osceola Ave (extension of Fairbanks Ave) 647.6294

The Dinky Line

In 1887, the Orlando-Winter Park Railroad was launched and was immediately dubbed the "Dinky Railroad." It ran from the heart of Orlando to Rollins College, just eight miles to the north, and to the little town of Oviedo eight miles east of Orlando. Students at Rollins College who lived in Orlando rode the little railroad the few miles to Rollins. It was described by one student as "a great success, with its narrow-gauge track, yellow-orange cars, and funny little wood-burning engine that used to belch pitch-black pine smoke from its fat little smokestack."

The railroad wasn't bound by a strict timetable, however. Passengers frequently were allowed to get out and pick flowers and fruit, and sometimes the train was delayed when cows were standing on the tracks. It was up to the operator to drive off the cows with a pine club.

But the train was a godsend during a cold spell. If freezing weather was expected, it blew its whistle to warn growers for miles around who then lit piles of old pine stumps and the pitch from pine knots. The smoke and heat was often enough to save fruit and citrus trees from frost damage.

However, wealthy homeowners living around Rollins College complained that the dinky railroad's whistle was a nuisance. So the train made its last run in October 1967.

Rollins College was named for Alonzo Rollins, a wealthy Chicago businessman who contributed $50,000 to the founding of the college. Due, in part, to his gift, the college was built in Winter Park, where Rollins had moved for health reasons.

3 The Fortnightly Inn $$$ Rooms in this beautifully restored, 1922-vintage house are just about perfect. Of the five rooms, the two largest include sitting rooms. Four rooms have double beds; one, a queen-sized bed. Breakfast includes coffee or tea with fresh fruits and pastries. ♦ 377 E. Fairbanks Ave. (Chapman-Interlachen Aves) 645.4440

4 Dexter's ★$$ This trendy *tapas* and wine bar serves light fare to complement its wines. The interior looks like a diner with its black-and-white-tiled floor. Sit at the counter on old-fashioned spinning stools. High tables along the wall and front window are uncomfortable for those who are not sprightly. Dexter's has recently launched a new blues and jazz night at 8PM Monday. It's guaranteed to chase away those beginning-of-the-workweek blues. ♦ American ♦ M-Sa 11AM-2PM, 5-11PM; Su noon-2PM, 5-10PM. 200 W. Fairbanks Ave (New York-Park Aves) 629.1150

5 Le Cordon Bleu ★★★$$$ Long a favorite in Winter Park, this restaurant serves up credible versions of such French classics as chateaubriand and veal *cordon bleu*, as well as lighter fare, including perfectly poached salmon and grouper in a lemon-butter sauce. Even the side dishes are small miracles, including the baked potatoes cut in half-inch rounds and garnished with fresh chives. Noontime is a good time to try out less expensive dishes. Location and complimentary champagne make it a good choice for Sunday brunch. ♦ French ♦ M-F 11:30AM-3PM, 5:30-11PM; Sa 5:30-11PM; Su noon-3PM, 4-8PM. 537 W. Fairbanks Ave (New York-Orange Aves) 647.7575

6 Cafe de France ★★$$$ A small and charming cafe with friendly, unpretentious service. Owner **Dominique Gutierrez** is French; no surprise when you sample the creamy carrot soup or rich French onion soup with chunky onions. For an entrée, the rack of lamb or the fresh salmon are consistently fine. The floating island dessert is a delicious concoction of frozen meringue floating in a sweet sauce of light custard made with vanilla beans. One of the many places on the Avenue recommended for desserts. Nonsmoking section. ♦ French ♦ Tu-F 11:30AM-3PM, 6-10PM; Sa noon-3PM, 6-10PM; Su 6-10PM. 526 Park Ave South (Fairbanks-Comstock Aves) 647.1869

7 Shiki ★$$ The fresh sushi selections here include a variety of fish and octopus. Also, tempura, noodle dishes, and teriyaki for those who don't like raw fish. Try the *gyoza* dumplings—filled with beef and pan-fried—for an appetizer. This restaurant, along with Ichiban in downtown Orlando, ranks at the top for Japanese cuisine in Central Florida. ♦ Japanese ♦ M-Th 5:30-10PM; F-Sa 5:30-11PM; Su 5:30-9:30PM. 525 Park Ave South (Fairbanks-Comstock Aves) 740.8018

Restaurants/Nightlife: Red   **Hotels:** Blue
Shops/ ♥Outdoors: Green   **Sights/Culture:** Black

8 Winter Park Farmers Market A panoply of colors greets visitors to this colorful block-long market, with its fresh flowers, blooming houseplants, and wide variety of vegetables and herbs for sale. This is a wonderful place to buy a delectable homemade dessert of banana bread, fresh bagels, flowers, or a houseplant for the host (prices are more than reasonable) who's putting you up. ♦ Sa dawn-noon. S. New York Ave and W. Lyman Ave

9 Park Books One of Central Florida's few independent bookstores. Owner **Debby Gluckman** and her employees have a frequently changing display of their personal favorites at the front of the uncluttered, brightly lit store. ♦ M-Sa 9AM-9PM; Su noon-6PM. 324 Park Ave South (Lyman-New England Aves) 628.1433

▪Winter Park

10 Albertson-Peterson Gallery Owners **Louise Peterson** and **Judy Albertson** offer an eclectic collection of contemporary art, including works in glass, clay, wood, and metal. Original jewelry and photographs, too. ♦ Tu-F 10AM-5:30PM; Sa 11AM-5:30PM. 329 Park Ave South (Lyman-New England Aves) 628.1258

10 Border Cantina ★$$ Margaritas taste even better after climbing two flights to this casual eatery, where a mounted longhorn steer's head looks down on the herd of diners eating tangy salsa verde with enchiladas and swilling cold Mexican beer. Elevator for those who don't want to climb. Nonsmoking section. ♦ Tex-Mex ♦ M-Th 11:30AM-10:30PM; F-Sa 11:30AM-11PM; Su 11:30AM-9:30PM. 329 Park Ave South (Lyman-New England Aves) 740.7227

PARK PLAZA GARDENS

10 Park Plaza Gardens ★★★$$$ Elegant but not stuffy, this glass-enclosed garden restaurant has an open, airy atmosphere and a creative menu. The grouper *escovitche* is a smart choice. One of the few restaurants in town that prepares a Caesar salad the way it should be done: at the table. ♦ American ♦ Daily 11:30AM-3PM, 6-10PM. 319 Park Ave South (Lyman-New England Aves) Reservations recommended. 645.2475

10 Be Be's Classic clothes and trendy wear, too, for children and infants from such manufacturers as **Florence Eiseman.** Dresses and tuxes for first communion. There is a little play area in the back for fussy children while mom and pop shop. ♦ M-Th, Sa 10AM-5PM; F 10AM-9PM; Su noon-5PM. 311 Park Ave South (Lyman-New England Aves) 628.1680

Park Plaza

10 Park Plaza Hotel $$$ Built in 1921, the Park Plaza feels like a refined, small European hotel. There are only 27 rooms and each one has its own personality, although all have brass beds, ceiling fans, ferns, and flowers. The best rooms are the suites facing the Avenue. While the view overlooking Central Park is idyllic, the trains that pass by might keep you up late. Each room opens onto a balcony of wicker furniture and plants where a complimentary Continental breakfast is served. The

Winter Park

lobby is quietly elegant, reminiscent of a sophisticated British drawing room. Romantics should ask for the honeymoon suite. ♦ 307 Park Ave South (New England Ave) 647.1072, 800/228.7220; fax 647.4081

11 Langford Resort Hotel $$ The rooms are ordinary, but the heated Olympic-sized pool and the nightly dancing make this a good choice for a stay in downtown Winter Park. Just a quick walk to Park Ave. ♦ 300 E. New England Ave (Interlachen Ave) 644.3400; fax 628.1952

12 Vieille Provence This boutique is right out of the French countryside and features French fabrics, antique European dolls, china, and tableware, dried flowers from France and Holland, and other intriguing gift items such as hand-knit sweaters and thyme bath powders. ♦ M-Sa 10AM-5PM. 121 E. Welbourne Ave (Park-Knowles Aves) 628.3858

12 Charles Hosmer Morse Museum of American Art For a closeup of artist **Louis Comfort Tiffany's** works, be sure to visit this small, five-gallery museum. On display are such masterful works as his *Red Peony Lamp*, a breathtaking *Rose Window*, and the dazzling *Four Seasons Window*, made for an international exposition in Paris in 1900, where exposure gave him international recognition as a leader in the Art Nouveau movement. There are also striking examples of ways in which he added an extra dimension to his artwork by folding the glass when it was still soft. Also on display are works of Tiffany's contemporaries. ♦ Nominal admission. Tu-Sa 9:30AM-4PM; Su 1-4PM. 133 E. Welbourne Ave (Park-Knowles Aves) 645.5311, 644.3686

13 Perfumery on Park Hard-to-find perfumes and colognes, including Silence by Jacomo or Animale by Suzanne Delyon, are readily available here, as is a free consultation and a perfume genealogy chart listing the seven families of fragrances. ♦ M-Sa 10AM-5:30PM. 112 Park Ave South (Morse Blvd-Welbourne Ave) 647.4114, 800/552.6279

14 Central Park At the center of Winter Park is Central Park, where the annual springtime **Winter Park Art Festival** reigns as the preeminent outdoor art show in Central Florida, drawing artists from around the country. Each year on the third weekend in March, thousands come to browse and buy everything from acrylic paintings to sculpture and jewelry. ♦ New England-Garfield Aves. For more information on the Winter Park Art Festival, call the Winter Park Chamber of Commerce, 644.8281

15 Tuni's Stylish women's apparel here runs from costly linens and sarongs suitable for the Florida climate to trendy velvet leggings, baby-doll dresses, and brass and bone jewelry from India and East Africa. ♦ M-Sa 10AM-6PM; Su 12:30-5:30PM. 118 Park Ave North (Morse Blvd-Lincoln Ave) 628.1609

16 Timothy's Gallery Unusual jewelry and wearable art make this worth a stop. You'll find hand-loomed silk sweaters from Dia of Boston and one-of-a-kind T-shirts that cost as much as some of the fine dress shirts you will find on the Avenue. Climb the stairs to the loft to find art to hang on your walls rather than from your ears. More than two dozen artists are represented. ♦ M-Sa 10AM-5:30PM. 232 Park Ave North (Lincoln-Canton Aves) 629.0707

16 Caswell-Massey Men's and women's sundries, including badger bristle brushes for shaving and special bath oils designed for all ages from babies to adults, such as a selection from Anton Hubner's Therapeutic Bath Oils from the Black Forest. There are old photos of other Caswell-Massey stores in New York and Rhode Island hanging high on the

wall. ♦ M-Sa 10AM-6PM; Su 12:30-5PM. 234 Park Ave North (Morse-Canton Aves) 647.2455

The MARILINE

17 Three Sheets to the Wind Fine and antique linens are the specialty here, including Egyptian cotton throw pillows, and luxurious 320-thread count Egyptian cotton sheets and pillow shams. Contemporary items, too, including tooled leather tablemats with bold graphics. ♦ M-Sa 10AM-5PM. 316 Park Ave North (Morse-Canton Aves) 644.4448

18 Maison des Crepes ★$$$ Nestled in an intriguing courtyard, the restaurant offers a pleasant place for a casual lunch, a fancy dinner, or for capping off an evening with dessert crepes or a taste of wine in a romantic, secluded setting. The triple lamb chops Bercy is a favorite, or try the crepes St. Jacques, which consists of scallops, shrimp, and sliced fresh mushrooms in Newburg sauce with Gruyere cheese. ♦ French ♦ 348 Park Ave North (Lincoln-Canton Aves, in the Hidden Gardens courtyard) 647.4469

18 Park Avenue Grille $$ A congenial setting for a drink. (If you've started your stroll on the south end of Park Ave, you might be ready for one by now.) A window seat makes up for the unremarkable American fare. ♦ American ♦ M-Th, Su 11:30AM-10:30PM; F-Sa 11:30AM-11:30PM. 358 Park Ave North (Canton Ave) 647.4556

19 Jacobson's Traditional women's clothing, children's and infant's wear, plus a beauty salon. ♦ M-W 10AM-6PM; Th-F 10AM-9PM; Sa 10AM-6PM. 339 Park Ave North (Canton Ave) 645.5005

20 Matis Where Winter Park's well-heeled women go for a manicure, facial, leg-wax, and similar pampering. ♦ M-Sa 10AM-5:30PM 515 Park Ave North (Cole-Swoope Aves) 740.7515

20 Jester Toys Good selection of stuffed animals, baby toys, games, and puzzles. The top names in toydom are found here: **Brio, Steiff, Avanti,** and **Dakin.** A **Cherbuine** doll, which won the 1987 French doll award, has ball bearings in its joints. ♦ M-Sa 10:30AM-6PM. 505 Park Ave North (Canton-Swoope Aves, in the Brandywine Center) 628.5400

20 Brandywine's Deli Restaurant $ Enjoy a beer at an alfresco table, and watch Park Ave's habitues go by. Try the quarter-pound slab of braunschweiger and thinly sliced raw onions served on a poppy-seed Kaiser roll. ♦ Daily 10:30AM-7:30PM. 505 Park Ave North (Canton-Swoope Aves, in the Brandywine Center) 647.0055

21 Scenic Boat Tours For a view of Winter Park from its chain of lakes, take a boat tour from the dock on **Lake Osceola** at the end of Morse Blvd. A revealing and pleasant way to spend an hour, Scenic Boat Tours has been taking passengers on shallow-draft boats around Lakes Osceola, Virginia, and Maitland since 1938. The lakes are connected by old lumbering canals dug during the last century. The tour boat passes Rollins College, formal gardens, and magnificent mansions hidden from the road. Many of these residences began as winter cottages; some were torn down and replaced, while other residents just kept adding on. It also gives you a good view of Albin Polasek's backyard sculptures. ♦ Admission. Daily 10AM-4PM; closed Christmas. 312 Morse Blvd. 644.4056

Winter Park

Bests

Tom Elrod
Senior Vice President, Marketing, Walt Disney Attractions

Spending leisurely Saturday mornings shopping for fresh flowers, fruits, and vegetables at the Winter Park Farmers Market while eating some of the homemade baked goods.

Walking along **New Smyrna Beach** at Ponce Inlet across from the lighthouse among the birds, fishers, and surfers.

Taking a sunset boat cruise around the **Chain of Lakes** in **Winter Park** to admire the many spectacular homes, Rollins College, and Genius Drive's peacocks.

Thaddeus Seymour
Professor, Rollins College

The book sales at the **Winter Park Public Library** in October and April offer a rich variety of choices at reasonable prices. More than 20,000 volumes are offered at each sale—a bibliophile's dream.

The **Maitland Art Center** in Winter Park, with its unique architecture by Andre Smith, was a hub for artistic experimentation in the 1930s. Its exhibitions and resident artists continue to enrich the community today.

You can still get a Blue Plate Special at old-fashioned prices at the **Winter Park Diner** on Fairbanks Ave.

The **Scenic Boat Tour** through the Winter Park lakes and canals provides an unforgettable perspective on the town, enlivened by the boat skipper's entertaining narrative.

Many visitors to Winter Park wonder why there aren't more bed-and-breakfast inns; the city's charm would seem to lend itself perfectly to small, cozy inns. But strict zoning laws preclude many homeowners from going into the B&B business, and many with suitable B&B buildings have found the licensing requirements too daunting to tackle.

International Drive

At first glance, International Drive seems like nothing more than a collection of T-shirt shops and fast-food restaurants. It may look that way at second and third glance too, but if you keep looking you will find a range of hotels to fit all budgets, one of the largest discount malls in the country, restaurants that serve elegant meals in shabby surroundings and shabby meals in elegant surroundings, and enough entertainment to keep a family busy for a week. The area, known as I-Drive or Tourist Town by locals, is also called Florida Center. Included in this section are a number of places a block or two off I-Drive, but the main drag remains the point of reference for visitors. Interstate 4 has International Drive exits at the north end (Exit 30B, Kirkman Rd), in the middle (Exit 29, Sand Lake Rd), and at the south end near Sea World (Exit 28, Beeline Expressway). If you are coming up I-4 from the south, you can get off at the EPCOT exit (Exit 26) and go east on the new extension of I-Drive.

Area code 407 unless otherwise indicated.

1 Parc Corniche Condominium Resort Hotel $$ This all-suite hotel's location on a lightly developed stretch of International

International Drive

makes it a quiet getaway, but you won't be able to walk to any attractions from here unless you're a real trooper. Each suite in this three-story building has a patio or balcony. The building, with its distinctive red-tiled roof, sits on the new **International Golf Club.** ♦ 6300 Parc Corniche Dr (International Dr) 239.8461, 800/446.2721; fax 239.8501

2 Stouffer Orlando Resort $$$ The mega-atrium lobby, said to be the largest in the world, was a pet project of **William Jovanovich,** the former chairman of the publishing company **Harcourt Brace Jovanovich Inc,** which owns a stake in the hotel. The expensive rooms have balconies that look down on the atrium, where there's a little of everything: a fish pond stocked with huge Japanese carp, an aviary, a two-level lounge bar, and glass-enclosed elevators. Amenities include a health club on the second floor, an 18-hole golf course, and seven restaurants. A much-acclaimed Sunday brunch is served in the atrium's **l'Orangerie,** $ which is decked out as a sidewalk cafe. The pastries are particularly delectable. A special touch is the back elevator; guests in bathing attire wanting to avoid the lobby can take it straight to their rooms. ♦ 6677 Sea Harbor Dr (Central Florida Pkwy-International Dr) 351.5555

Within the Stouffer Orlando Resort:

Haifeng $$ A Chinese restaurant where diners can watch the chef prepare their meal. ♦ Chinese ♦ Tu-Su 6-11PM

Atlantis $$$ Art on the walls, crystal shining, and impeccable service. The rack of lamb is delicious. ♦ French ♦ M-Sa 6-11PM

Trade Winds Cafe Coffeehouse by day and steakhouse by night. ♦ Daily 24 hours

3 Sea World of Florida One of Florida's top three theme parks, the biggest stars here are the killer whales. The 135-acre marine life park, imposing as it is, can be done in a day. Take a moment when you get in and look at the map you receive at the ticket booth. In the bottom left corner is a computer-generated plan based on your time of arrival with recommendations of what to do and when. Most visitors circumnavigate the park clockwise, but if you arrive at opening time go straight to **Terrors of the Deep,** which has the longest lines later in the day. From there cross over the lagoon to see **The Legend of Shamu,** and then double-back to circle the park counterclockwise. This way, you will get to **Cap'n Kid's World,** a water playground, just when the kids need a cold splash and can save the water-ski show (the least interesting, perhaps because the stars are human) for last. Snack bars and food kiosks are found throughout the park. As you would expect from a park owned by **Anheuser-Busch,** beer is available. ♦ Admission (parking and kennels are free) Daily 9AM-8PM (longer hours in the summer) 7007 Sea World Dr (International Dr) 351.3600

Within Sea World of Florida:

Terrors of the Deep Formerly known as Sharks!, this exhibit has been converted into one of the world's largest collections for dangerous sea creatures. Eels, lionfish, scorpionfish, blowfish, surgeonfish, and barracudas glide around inside the tanks, looking mean. You may also enter a small theater to watch a short film about sharks. When it is over, the screen rises to reveal an incredibly large shark tank. Unsqueamish visitors may

---

Restaurants/Nightlife: Red   Hotels: Blue
Shops/ 🌳Outdoors: Green   **Sights/Culture:** Black

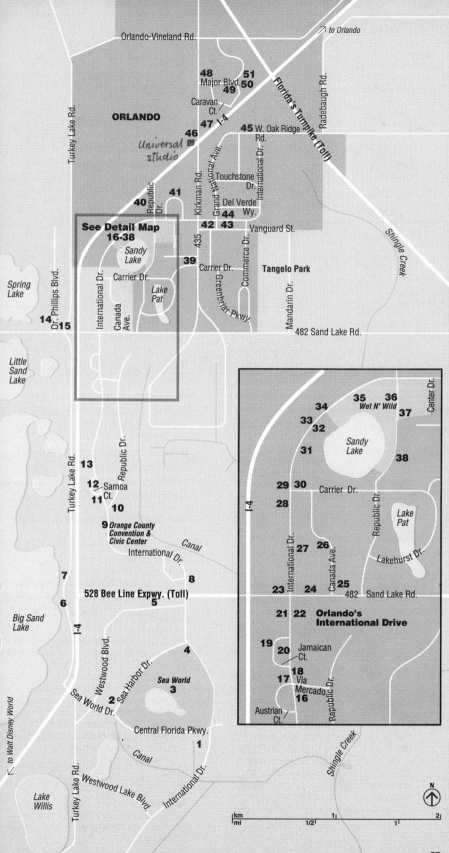

Orlando-Vineland Rd.

to Orlando

ORLANDO

48 Major Blvd. 51
50
49
Caravan Ct.
47 I-4
46 45 W. Oak Ridge Rd.

Universal studio

Touchstone Dr.

41 Del Verde Wy.
40 Republic Dr.
44
42 43 Vanguard St.

See Detail Map 16-38

Sandy Lake

39 Carrier Dr.

Carrier Dr. **Tangelo Park**

Lake Pat

Spring Lake

Shingle Creek

14 Dr. Phillips Blvd.
15

International Dr.
Canada Ave.

Greenbriar Pkwy.
Commerce Dr.
Mandarin Dr.

482 Sand Lake Rd.

Little Sand Lake

35 36
Wet N' Wild
34 37
33
32
31
Sandy Lake
38

Turkey Lake Rd.

13
12 Samoa Ct.
11
10

29 30 Carrier Dr.
28

Republic Dr.

I-4
27 26
23
24 25
482 Sand Lake Rd.

Lake Pat
Lakehurst Dr.

9 Orange County Convention & Civic Center
Canal
International Dr.

7
8
5
528 Bee Line Expwy. (Toll)

6
I-4

21 22 **Orlando's International Drive**

19
20 Jamaican Ct.
18 Via Mercado
17
16
Austrian Ct.

Republic Dr.

Center Dr.

Big Sand Lake

Westwood Blvd.

4

Sea Harbor Dr.

2 **Sea World** 3

Central Florida Pkwy.

1

to Walt Disney World

Sea World Dr.

Turkey Lake Rd.

Canal

Lake Willis

Westwood Lake Blvd.

International Dr.

Shingle Creek

N

km
mi
1/2   1   1   2

Sea World of Florida

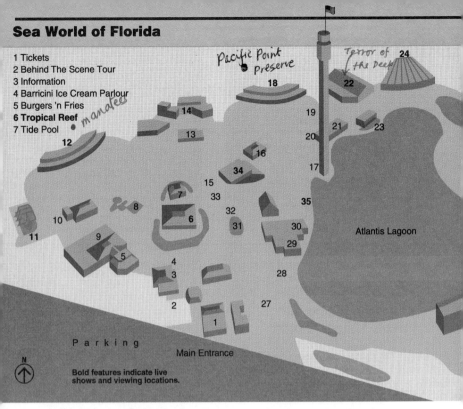

1 Tickets
2 Behind The Scene Tour
3 Information
4 Barricini Ice Cream Parlour
5 Burgers 'n Fries
6 Tropical Reef
7 Tide Pool

manatees

Pacific Point Preserve

Terror of the Deep

Atlantis Lagoon

Parking

Main Entrance

N

**Bold features indicate live
shows and viewing locations.**

step on a moving sidewalk that will slowly slide them 125 feet through a 635,000-gallon shark tank, separated only by a four-inch-thick, clear acrylic tube. As you leave the exhibit, enter a door to the right and spend as much time as you like nose-to-nose with these creatures.

Snack Encounter $ Foot-long hot dogs, beer, and soft drinks. Behind Snack Encounter and the adjoining gift shop, you can pilot your own radio-controlled boats in a tiny lagoon.

Waterfront Sandwich Grille $ Burgers, hot dogs, beer, and soft drinks while overlooking the **Atlantis Lagoon.**

Shamu: New Visions
James Earl Jones narrates a story about the reputation and complex personalities of killer whales. The current Shamu, one of three killer whales born at Sea World of Florida since 1985, frolics with his family in what is billed as the largest marine-mammal habitat in the world—**Shamu Stadium,** holding five million gallons of seawater, some of which will slosh onto the first couple of rows during the show. The stadium seats 5,200 people and includes a large video screen.

Sky Tower For overview of the park or a scenic panorama of the area, take this 400-foot ride into the sky. ♦ Admission.

In the Sky Tower Courtyard:

Chicken 'n Biscuit $ Barbecued and fried chicken, beer, and soft drinks.

Clyde and Seamore 1000 BC A corny yet clever show of performing sea lions, otters, and walruses in the 3,000-seat **Sea Lion and Otter Stadium.**

Penguin Encounter Home to hundreds of these formal looking fellows and other birds native to the Antarctic and Arctic regions. Visitors move through a 120-foot-long people mover where tempered glass separates you from a habitat so natural that 6,000 pounds of manufactured snow falls daily. Besides the viewing area there is the learning hall with videos on the history of polar exploration. In another room is an exhibit where you can get up close and personal with more than 100 buffleheads, puffins, murres, and smews, who, while not related to penguins, are accustomed to the same environment. The white stucco building in which the penguins are housed sits on a five-acre site that includes a 32,000-square-foot science center, a gift shop, a restaurant, and freshwater ponds.

Pizza 'n Pasta $ Antipasto salads, a big Italian-sausage sandwich, and, of course, pizza and spaghetti with beer and soft drinks.

New Friends In the old stadium in which Shamu once reigned, Atlantic bottlenose dolphins share the water with beluga and false killer whales.

Shamu Breeding Pool

25

Mango Joe's Café

Bermuda Triangle

26

Cap'n Kid's World Children scale a 55-foot pirate ship by climbing up rigging nets and battle each other with water cannons. Adults can sit back and watch in the shade. In front of this 2.5-acre play area is the **Seal Feeding Pool** and **Stingray Lagoon,** where you can reach in and touch nasty-looking cownose and southern diamond rays. They are harmless.

Tropical Reef For a good look at more than 1,000 tropical fish, stop here at the largest man-made coral reef display in the country. Surrounding the main exhibit are 17 smaller aquariums. Behind the Tropical Reef is the **Caribbean Tide Pool,** filled with tropical fish and invertebrates such as starfish and crabs. Across the path to the left is the **Sea Lion and Seal Community Pool,** where you can watch the pool or through windows underwater.

The Tropical Reef is surrounded by inexpensive ($) fast-food stops: **Pancho's Tacos, Burgers 'n' Fries** (which has a large eating area and also serves chicken sandwiches and fish), **Barricini Ice Cream Parlor, International Sandwich Shop,** and **Hot Dogs 'n' Spuds.**

Dolphin Feeding Pool Buy some fish and let the dolphins snatch them out of your hand. If you are lucky, you'll be able to reach out and touch them. It's a tough place to leave if it isn't crowded.

Sea World Theatre A cool, dry refuge when afternoons get too hot or rainy. Multimedia shows are presented.

Hawaiian Village Sit on logs and watch the **Hawaiian Rhythms** troupe perform Polynesian dances and songs on the beach at the Atlantis Lagoon. **Al E. Gator's Key West Eatery** (★$) offers traditional fare of the Florida Keys and Caribbean Islands, including exotic drinks. The **Lahaina Trading Post** sells leis, grass skirts, and more fashionable tropical attire.

USO Water Ski Show One of the few shows here starring humans. Familiar but thrilling stunts are loosely held together with a musical plot in the 5,200-seat **Atlantis Water Ski Stadium.**

Aloha! Polynesian Luau ★$$ The Hawaiian Rhythms troupe performs at the nightly luau on the **Luau Terrace,** which includes traditional South Seas dances and dinner. Reservations required, but you don't need to pay regular park admission. ◆ Daily 6:35PM. 363.2195, 351.3600 ext 195, 800/327.2424, 800/227.8048 (FL)

Other nighttime activities at Sea World include a special show with Shamu and a show with sea lions and otters. The evening concludes with **Night Magic,** a fireworks-and-laser extavaganza.

4 **Sheraton World Resort** $$ This large, 800-room hotel on 28 acres next to Sea World, has paved, winding paths through tropically landscaped grounds that lead to three pools and five lighted tennis courts. ◆ 10100 International Dr (Westwood Blvd) 352.1100, 800/327.0363; fax 352.3679

5 **Wynfield Inn** $ A little-known chain that enjoys a fine local reputation. Children 17 and under stay free in their parents' room. Complimentary coffee or tea , and the fruit on the front deck is there for the taking. ◆ 6263 Westwood Blvd (International Dr) 345.8000, 800/346.1551

6 **Sonesta Villa Resort Orlando** $$ Situated on 97 acres alongside a lake, this is one of the most serene all-suite hotels in Central Florida. The spacious 391 suites are single or split level, with fully equipped kitchenettes. A restaurant, cafe, lounge, pool bar and grill, swimming pool, ice cream shop, and grocery delivery service make it a full-service resort. ◆ 10000 Turkey Lake Rd (I-4-Sand Lake Rd) 352.8051

7 **Comfort Suites Orlando** $ A solid alternative to the high-priced hotels in the Disney World area. The free Continental breakfast is a boon to families that want to grab a bite before setting off to the attractions, and the microwaves and refrigerators in this all-suite hotel help cut down on the major cost of eating out for every meal. Other amenities include a restaurant, pool, whirlpool, and cable TV with HBO. ◆ 9350 Turkey Lake Rd (I-4-Sand Lake Rd) 351.5050; fax 363.7953

8 Orlando Heritage Inn $ A good alternative to its larger chain neighbors. The outside verandas and a rotunda lobby with a patterned tin ceiling and hardwood floors convey Southern hospitality, as do the hotel's staff. Rooms have a pleasant, understated decor. ♦ 9861 International Dr (Beeline Expressway-Republic Dr) 352.0008, 800/282.1890 (FL), 800/447.1890

Within the Orlando Heritage Inn:

Plantation Room Dinner Theatre This musical revue makes up with spirit and good humor what it lacks in polish. ♦ Seats 135. Admission. Tu-Sa 7PM

9 Orlando-Orange County Convention/Civic Center Don't ask for a tour; there isn't one. This is a working convention center where trade shows and other events are held. ♦ 9800 International Dr (Hawaiian-Samoa Cts) 345-9800

10 The Peabody Orlando ★★★$$$ Across the street from the Orlando-Orange County Convention/Civic Center, this 27-story luxury hotel caters to both businesspeople and tourists. Its wide range of restaurants makes it unnecessary to venture out onto the International in the evening, but it is best known for another gimmick: Like its sister hotel in Memphis, TN, the famous Peabody ducks march into the marble lobby fountain daily at 11AM and march out at 5PM. The rooms are large and even have small TVs in the bathrooms. There are also four lighted tennis courts, an Olympic-sized pool, a children's pool and outdoor whirlpool, a beauty salon, and the **Peabody Athletic Club** on the fourth floor with 15 Nautilus weight machines open from 6AM to 10PM. The supervised day care center is well run, and there is a complete business center. 891 rooms. ♦ 9801 International Dr (Republic Dr) 352.4000, 800/PEABODY (US), 800/458.4522 (Canada); fax 351.0073

Within the Peabody Orlando:

B-Line Diner ★★$$ This sleek fifties-style diner never closes. The spicy crab cakes and to-kill-for desserts are tempting. For those with more willpower, there is a steamed vegetable plate served with wild rice, lemon, and Asiago cheese. ♦ American ♦ Daily 24 hours. 352.4000 ext 4460

Capriccio ★★$$$ Elegant dining and a wonderful gourmet pizza cooked in a wood-burning stove. Some folks swear by the *pollo alla birra*, which is tender, oak-roasted Petaluma chicken marinated in avocado oil and herbs and basted with Morretti beer. A lavish brunch is served here Sundays. ♦ Italian ♦ Tu-Sa 6-11PM; Su 11AM-3PM, 6-11PM. Reservations recommended. 352.4000 ext 4450

Dux ★★★$$$ The butter is shaped like a little duck here, but there's no duck on the menu. Instead you can enjoy tenderloin of veal lamb, flavored with sage and lemon and topped with California black olives, or fish-and-legume combinations such as sautéed Florida red snapper on a bed of carrots and cucumbers with Chinese black bean sauce. The wine list is impressive, and the service is attentive and knowledgeable. ♦ American ♦ M-Sa 6-10PM. Jacket required. Reservations recommended. 352.4000

Lobby Bar A nice place for a rendezvous, but if you're waiting to see the famous Peabody ducks walk from their home upstairs to the lobby's fountain, you might be caught in the crush. Guests never seem to tire of this show. Afternoon tea is served weekdays from 3-4:30PM.

Mallards Lounge Tucked away from the lobby, you can sit at the black marble-and-brass bar or find a seat on one of the overstuffed sofas. ♦ Daily 11AM-2AM

11 Clarion Plaza $$ Next door to the Orlando-Orange County Convention/Civic Center, this new hotel opened in fall 1991, affording conventioneers a low-cost alternative to the stately Peabody across the street. Each of the large rooms have an in-house safe and most have two double beds, and there are 42 suites. A complete service center for the business traveler includes computer modem hookups. The lobby of this cream-colored, 14-story building overlooks a nicely landscaped area that has a heated pool and Jacuzzi. Express check-in and video check-out. ♦ 9700 International Dr (Hawaiian-Samoa Cts) 352.9700, 800/366.9700; fax 351.9111

Within the Clarion Plaza:

Jack's Place $$ This upscale, 99-seat restaurant is open for dinner only and features Florida seafood, pasta, and steaks. ♦ American ♦ Daily 5-11PM

Cafe Matisse $ A 320-seat restaurant with a buffet and a la carte service. ♦ American ♦ 6:30AM-midnight

Lite Bite $ Primarily a bakery-deli takeout venue, open around the clock.

Hard Rock Cafe Orlando, a veritable museum of rock memorabilia, is the largest Hard Rock Cafe in the world. The original Hard Rock opened in London in 1971, sporting wall hangings such as American road signs and American sports uniforms. That decorating idea didn't fly in New York, where the second Hard Rock opened in 1974, so it was filled with rock memorabilia, and all of the other cafes have since followed suit.

Backstage at the Clarion This 4,000-square-foot lounge with a back-stage theme offers live and recorded Top 40 hits. ♦ Daily 3PM-2AM

MING COURT

12 Ming Court ★★$$$ The serpentine curve of the wall outside, reminiscent of a dragon's back, sets the tone for a delicious meal inside, in a glass-enclosed dining room overlooking a floating garden. The Hunan *kung pao* chicken with cashews, peanuts, and walnuts or the crispy Shanghai noodles topped with shrimp and shiitake mushrooms are good choices. ♦ Chinese ♦ Daily 11AM-2PM, 5PM-midnight. 9188 International Dr (Samoa Ct) Reservations recommended. 351.9988

13 Caruso's Palace ★$$ Some say it's tourist kitsch elevated to a new level; others find this 450-seat restaurant fun and pretty with gold-leaf and faux marble accents offsetting the domed green, peach, rust and blue interior. Corinthian and Doric columns rise up to a ceiling covered with murals of the Italian countryside done in Renaissance style—right down to the chubby cherubs. The walls are covered with tapestry and statues abound. Naturally there is a portrait of **Enrico Caruso,** as well as photographic portraits of other great opera stars. The pasta is fine if not memorable, and you won't leave hungry, since there are four courses: antipasto, salad or soup, entrée, and dessert. Among the favorite dishes are *penne cardinale,* pasta tubes with light lobster sauce, Gulf of Mexico shrimp, and vegetarian lasagna with spinach pasta. ♦ Italian ♦ Daily 5-11PM. 8986 International Dr (Samoa Ct) Reservations recommended. 351.7110

13 King Henry's Feast It's hard not to gawk

at this Tudor-style castle complete with crenellated tower and moat. Once inside, you'll be offered mead, an Old English honey wine. The five-course banquet includes roasted chicken, ribs, soup, salad, vegetables, and pie—along with a show. ♦ Admission. Daily 6:30-9PM (showtimes vary) 8984 International Dr (Samoa-Austrian Cts) 351.5151, 800/347.8181

13 Park Suites Orlando $$ This all-suite hotel is one of the best-planned and-designed properties along Central Florida's tourist strip. Entering the cool atrium lobby with its tile pathways, tropical foliage, and fountains,

you feel as if you're getting away from it all. The suites feature wet bars, microwaves, refrigerators, and two TVs. Breakfast is complimentary. A nice indoor pool with whirlpool and sauna is next to exercise equipment. There is a small restaurant and nonsmoking rooms available. A sister hotel, **Park Suites Orlando North,** is in suburban Altamonte Springs. ♦ 8978 International Dr (Samoa-Austrian Ct) 352.1400, 800/433.7275 (FL), 800/432.7272; fax 363.1120

14 Marketplace This upscale shopping center houses offices, a 24-hour **Gooding's** grocery store, and some of the best restaurants in town. ♦ 7600 Dr. Phillips Blvd (Sand Lake Rd)

Within the Marketplace:

Phoenician Restaurant ★$$ Middle Eastern specialties aren't common in Central Florida, but this restaurant acts as if it has

plenty of competition. The *shwarma* dinner, choice beef marinated in exotic spices, is delicious, as is the accompanying *hummus,* a chickpea puree. The vegetarian couscous, a traditional North African dish, is made up of generous portions of couscous and delicately spiced cooked potatoes and carrots. The Turkish coffee is only for the hardy. ♦ Middle Eastern ♦ Daily 11AM-11PM. 345.1001

Christini's Ristorante Italiano ★★★$$$ Owner **Chris Christini's** culinary expertise and stints at The Fours Seasons in New York and the Copley Plaza Hotel in Boston are evident here. Pasta is homemade, and the fish soup with shrimp, lobster, and clams is unbeatable. The fettuccine Alfredo is a favorite among regulars. Occasionally a strolling musician adds to the restaurant's ambiance. ♦ Italian ♦ M-Sa 6PM-midnight. Reservations recommended. 345.8770

Darbar ★★$$$ Less-pricey Indian fare can be found elsewhere in the I-Drive area, but many locals favor this restaurant because the food is consistently good, the service is helpful, and the atmosphere is inviting despite the chandeliers, omnipresent marble, and red-and-gold walls. The *tandoori* specials are favorites. It's an added treat to watch the chef thwack bread dough against the side of the tandoori oven, and pull it out later, fully risen. ♦ Indian ♦ M-Th 6-10PM; F-Sa 6-10:30PM; Su 6-9:30PM. 345.8128

Donato's Italian Market $ Fully loaded Sicilian pizza and large servings of hearty vegetable calzone, with its warm, doughy covering, are just the sort of dishes you'd expect at this homey restaurant with hardwood floors and noisy congeniality. ♦ Italian ♦ M-Sa 10AM-11PM; Su 11AM-11PM. 352.8772

Restaurants/Nightlife: Red   Hotels: Blue
Shops/ 🌳Outdoors: Green   Sights/Culture: Black

15 **Days Inn Orlando Lakeside** $ Location and price make this 690-room hotel a good choice. It's on the unbusy side of I-4, a block from the Marketplace. Other pluses include three pools and a playground, a romantic boardwalk that leads to a sandy beach, and free meals for children at the on-site restaurant. ♦ 7335 Sand Lake Rd (Dr. Phillips Blvd-Turkey Lake Rd) 351.1900, 800/777-DAYS

16 **Pirate's Cove** Two imaginative 18-hole miniature golf courses reward luck more than skill. Hazards include waterfalls and damp rock grottoes. ♦ Admission. Daily 9AM-midnight. 8601 International Dr (Austrian Ct) 352.7378

17 **Summerfield Suites Hotel** $$ One of the newest all-suite hotels in the I-Drive area. The two-bedroom suites have two bathrooms, two phones, a TV in each bedroom,and a TV with VCR in the living room. One-bedroom suites are also available. All suites have fully

International Drive

equipped kitchens, and breakfasts and the cocktail hour are complimentary. ♦ 8480 International Dr (Austrian Ct) 352.2400

17 **Radisson Inn and Aquatic Center** $$ Besides a convenient, central location on I-Drive, the Radisson offers a heated outdoor pool surrounded by tropical gardens and jogging trails, and a lighted tennis court, but the main attraction is the indoor Olympic-sized pool located in the Aquatic Center and Athletic Club, which has been called one of the fastest in the continent by competitive swimmers; Olympic gold medalists **Matt Biondi** and **Tracy Caukins** set world and national records here. Its deep diving well is fitted for both springboards and a diving platform. If you're lucky, your visit will coincide with a swim or dive meet. The athletic club has a trainer on hand to help familiarize guests with the 23 Nautilus machines, computerized treadmills, and other fitness equipment. The **Waterway Cafe** ★$ serves meals, some low in sodium and fat. The **Sweetwater Lounge's** happy hour is popular with guests. The 300 rooms are large and most have two queen-sized beds and a separate vanity area. ♦ 8444 International Dr (Jamaican Ct) 345.0505

The tradition of the Peabody Hotel's duck march began in the 1930s when Frank Schutt, general manager of The Peabody Memphis, and a friend, Chip Barwick, Sr., returned from a weekend hunting trip in Arkansas. The two men thought it would be humorous to place a couple of their live duck decoys (it was legal for hunters to use live decoys then) in the marble lobby fountain.

At Fun 'n Wheels off International Drive in Orlando, the go-carts get 36 miles per gallon and each one travels about 250,000 miles a year.

18 **Mercado Mediterranean Village** More than 50 specialty shops and restaurants in a Mediterranean-style setting were built in 1986 around an open courtyard where entertainment ranges from mariachi music to clog dancing. In the evening, lights twinkle in the trees. ♦ Daily 10AM-10PM. 8445 International Dr (Austrian Ct) 345.9337

Within the Mercado Mediterranean Village:

Visitor Information Center Here's the place to get all your questions answered, from where to find a vacant hotel room to where to take the kids to eat. There are discount coupons, maps, and a handy book of menus from area restaurants, along with two walls of brochures. The center is operated by the Orlando/ Orange County Convention and Visitors Bureau. ♦ Daily 8AM-8PM

Conch Republic A cute twist on the usual T-shirt shop, this store features tropical clothing suitable for lounging around poolside listening to **Jimmy Buffett** tunes. In fact, there's a Jimmy Buffett clothing line.

Coral Reef Nautical jewelry and shells. It's unschlocky enough to merit a visit.

House of Ireland If there are O'Malleys or O'Connells in your life, you should be able to find something for them here, such as mugs with the appropriate coat of arms.

Jose O'Day's Mexican Restaurant $
Need a Tex-Mex fix? Stop in for guacamole with chips and beer. For dinner, you will find better elsewhere around town. ♦ Tex-Mex ♦ M-Th 5-10PM; F-Sa 5-10:30PM; Su 5-10PM. 363.0613

The Butcher Shop Steakhouse $$ If
you're the kind of person who likes to make dinner even when you're on vacation, here's your chance. Choose a slab of steak from a refrigerated case and cook it at one of the large hickory charcoal pits. If that sounds like too much work, kick back and have a brew while a Butcher Shop chef prepares a steak for you. The building holds about 320 meat-eaters in three dining rooms. ♦ American ♦ M-Th 5-10PM; F-Sa 5-11PM; Su 5-10PM. 363.9727

Mardi Gras This nightclub features a four-course dinner accompanied by a cabaret show with *Carnival* music from Rio and jazz from New Orleans. Dinner includes Venetian vegetable soup, Caesar salad, chicken, broccoli, potatoes, Key lime pie, and unlimited beverages. There is a special children's menu, although kids probably will find any of the dozen or so dinner extravaganzas in the area more entertaining. ♦ Admission. Daily 6, 8:30PM (showtimes vary) Reservations required. 351.5151, 800/347.8181

Bergamo's Italian Restaurant ★$$ Step through the doorway into a New York-style trattoria straight out of Little Italy. The Neopolitan pasta is scrumptious, and they do wonders with chicken. Among the specialties is *zuppa di pesce alla Bergamo*, which is king crab, clams, shrimp, mussels, and whitefish sautéed in white wine and garlic, served with linguine. Imported Italian wines. ♦ Italian ♦ Daily 5-10:30PM. 352.3805

Charlie's Lobster House $$$ This extensive seafood menu includes crab cakes and daily seafood specials, plus steaks and chicken. ♦ Seafood ♦ M-Th 11AM-10PM; F-Sa 11AM-11PM; Su 11AM-10PM. 352.6929

Damon's-The Place for Ribs $$ Let your nose do the walking; the mouth-watering smell of ribs barbecuing will pull you forward as you approach the Mercado from I-Drive. You won't be disappointed. Lunch specials too. ♦ American ♦ Daily 11AM-11PM. 352.5984

The Mercado also includes a food pavilion, where you can get mall-type fast food. One of the best here is **The Greek Place** ($) for gyros, pita bread generously stuffed with lamb and beef, tomatoes, onions, and special sauce.

19 Embassy Suites at Plaza International $$ Among the more inexpensive hotels in the chain, this was the first of the all-suite hotels on I-Drive. **Mississippi Management Inc**, which owns the hotel, has been cited as one of the nation's best-run companies. Suites are equipped with refrigerators, wet bars, microwaves, and two TVs. The hotel has a restaurant, an indoor-outdoor pool (allowing guests to swim in and out of the building), a game room, sauna, steam room, and exercise room. The suites surround an enclosed courtyard where free breakfast and happy hour are offered daily. ♦ 8250 Jamaican Ct (International Dr) 345.8250, 800/826.0778

20 Ran-Getsu ★★$$$ Don't be fooled by this restaurant's location in the midst of Central Florida's big tourist strip; It is authentic and prices are right. Enjoy fresh sushi at the long, curving blond-wood sushi bar or sit at American-style tables overlooking a Japanese garden and reflecting pool. The restaurant excels at teriyaki and sukiyaki, but the menu breaks new ground with *yosenabe*, a Japanese bouillabaisse with fresh Florida seafood. Occasionally, for entertainment, a kimono-clad woman dances sedately to Japanese music. ♦ Japanese ♦ Daily 5-11:30PM. 8400 International Dr (Jamaican Ct) Reservations recommended. 345.0044

Time magazine recently hailed Orlando as "the boomtown of the South."

21 Howard Johnson International Drive $ A recent renovation has helped out this hotel; there's a nice heated swimming pool, a coffeeshop and a restaurant, and Wet 'n' Wild is within walking distance (see page 25). ♦ 8020 International Dr (Jamaican Ct-Sand Lake Rd) 351.1730

22 Orlando Marriott International Drive $$ This pink and teal hotel has recently undergone a major renovation. Its 16 two-story stucco buildings sit on 48 acres along with a lagoon. A new health club was added and, with an eye toward the business traveler, all meeting rooms were upgraded and concierge suites were created. There are three heated outdoor swimming pools and four lighted tennis courts. The **Marmalade Tree Restaurant** ($$) is a cozy new poolside bistro. ♦ 8001 International Dr (Sand Lake Rd) 351.2420

23 Quality Inn International $ Orlando hotelier and owner **Harris Rosen** boasts that

he has the cheapest rates in town, and it's true that his prices are hard to beat. However, you may have difficulty getting in if you haven't booked ahead, since the hotel is a frequent choice for domestic and international tour groups. The hotel's biggest drawback may be the traffic on I-Drive during high season, which can make getting in and out of the parking lot an adventure. If this place is full, Rosen has two other inexpensive choices on I-Drive: **Quality Inn Plaza** and **International Inn.** ♦ 7600 International Dr (Sand Lake Rd) 351.1600

24 Fun 'n Wheels This family amusement park draws about a million people a year and is so popular it added a second park in Kissimmee. The go-kart track is always buzzing; in fact, the 43 go-karts here wear out 200 tires each year. There's also a waterslide, miniature golf, bumper boats and cars, video and arcade games, and now **Tank Tag**, where two-person teams battle other tanks and battlefield obstacles. ♦ Nominal fee for each amusement. M-F 4-11PM; Sa-Su and daily in the summer 10AM-midnight. 6739 Sand Lake Rd (International Dr-Canada Ave) 351.5651

They're getting along better now, but there once was considerable bad blood betweeen Universal Studios Florida and the Walt Disney Co., which owns Disney World. When Disney's Michael Eisner declared in 1985 that his company would build a studio tour, Universal's top executives reacted with fury, claiming they had shown Eisner their own plans to build a studio tour in Orlando when Eisner was head of Paramount Pictures Corp. Eisner has always heatedly denied the allegation. Universal threatened to cancel its plans to build a studio tour in Orlando, saying it would leave the city to become a Disney "company town." Today there's no more name calling, and both Disney's and Universal's studio tours are raking in big bucks.

25 Residence Inn by Marriott $ If you have a large family or just need some room to spread out, this all-suite hotel is a dependable choice. Pool, fully equipped kitchens, and free buffet breakfasts daily. ◆ 7610 Canada Ave (Sand Lake Rd) 345.0117, 800/426.6260 (FL), 800/227.3978

26 Dowdy Pavilion Looking for a little rainy-day recreation? Under one big roof here are 32 bowling lanes and ice-skating rink. Snacks and places to eat them are available at both the lanes and the rink. ◆ Admission, rental fee. Bowling: M-F 9AM-11PM; Sa 9AM-2AM; Su 9AM-11PM. Skating: Tu-F 7:30-10PM; Sa-Su 1-4PM; 7:30-10PM. 7500 Canada Ave (Sand Lake-Carrier Rds) 352.2695 (bowling), 363.7465 (skating)

27 New Punjab Restaurant ★$$ The service can be a tad surly, but the food is special. The Murgh curried chicken or lamb with curry sauce is served with fragrant rice; the teardrop-shaped flat cakes baked in the

International Drive

tandoori, or clay oven, are heavenly. ◆ Indian ◆ M, Su 5-11PM; Tu-F 11:30AM-11PM. 7451 International Dr (Sand Lake Rd-Carrier Rd). 352.7887

28 China Coast $ If you've got a craving for Cantonese, Mandarin, or Szechuan food, you won't go wrong at this inexpensive restaurant. The menu isn't imaginative, but you'll find all your old favorites; dinner entrees come with hot Chinese bread, tea, steamed rice, and a choice of soup or salad. Lunch and early-bird specials. ◆ Chinese ◆ Daily 11AM-10:30PM. 7500 International Dr (Sand Lake Rd-Visitors Cir) 351.9776

DANSK

29 Dansk Factory Outlet Typically pricey Dansk dinnerware is available here at discounts of 10 to 60 percent. You will find limited editions, alongside overstocks, seconds, and discontinued patterns. Good place for wedding gifts. ◆ Daily 9AM-7PM. 7000 International Dr (Sand Lake Rd-Visitors Cir) 351.2425

30 The Enclave Suites at Orlando $$ Overlooking a private lake, this all-suite hotel is far enough off I-Drive for you to enjoy a touch of serenity, but close enough to walk to Wet 'n Wild or for a bite to eat. Ask for a room with a lake view. The little outdoor cafe is a pleasant place to unwind. There are VCRs in every room, and suites are spacious, ranging from 660 to 1,200 square feet. The kitchens are fully equipped, and there is an outdoor and an indoor pool, plus sauna, tennis courts, and an exercise room. ◆ 6165 Carrier Dr (International Dr) 351.1155; fax 351.2001

31 Shell World Lusting after a nightlight, a lamp, or a lucite toilet seat decorated with shells? Inexpensive mother-of-pearl or coral shell jewelry? This is the place for shells of every imaginable kind and shape. ◆ Daily 8:30AM-midnight (Carrier Rd-Republic Dr) 6464 International Dr 351.0900

32 Congo River Golf & Exploration Co. Two 18-hole miniature golf courses with a jungle motif. ◆ Admission. Daily 10AM-10PM. 6312 International Dr (Carrier Rd-Republic Dr) 352.0042

33 Holiday Inn International Drive $$ There are many newer hotels along the tourist strip, but this one is well managed and always spick-and-span. Huge, free-form heated pool, whirlpool, and pool bar. ◆ 6515 International Dr (Sand Lake Rd-Visitors Cir) 351.3500

Within the Holiday Inn International Drive:

Comedy Zone Stand-up comics try their luck with the crowds. ◆ Admission. Tu-Th 8:30 PM; F-Sa 8:30-10:30PM. Reservations recommended. 351.3500

34 Las Palmas Inn $ Palm trees surround a heated pool in the back, away from the commotion of I-Drive. The hotel is across the street from Wet 'n Wild and is within walking distance of just about anything you need in the way of dining or shopping. ◆ 6233 International Dr (Sand Lake Rd-Visitors Cir) 351.3900, 800/833.8389

Wet 'n Wild

35 Wet 'n Wild This ever-expanding water-thrill park has spawned a host of imitators, but many think the 25-acre granddaddy remains the best of the bunch. Wet 'n Wild, which now includes four parks across the country, was founded by **George Millay,** a former president of Sea World of Florida. Teens who find Disney's Typhoon Lagoon or River Country too tame will be satisfied here; the adventurous love **Der Stuka,** a steep six-story slide into a pool of water, or **Black Hole,** a wild journey in near-total darkness through a tube with special lighting and sound effects. A favorite is **Blue Niagara,** two CK intertwined tubes six stories high and 300 feet long. Although the slides seem daunting from the street, the park has a new children's water playground that contains miniature versions of some of the big rides as well as a pool for toddlers. The park also sports a surf lagoon, and the relaxing **Lazy River,** where you can float gently in an inner tube and work on your tan. Don't expect more than a hot

---

Restaurants/Nightlife: Red   **Hotels:** Blue
Shops/ 🌴Outdoors: Green   **Sights/Culture:** Black

dog and snack foods from the kiosks. ♦ Admission. Daily mid Feb-Dec 10AM-6PM; extended hours summer and holidays. 6200 International Dr (Republic Dr) 351.3200; fax 363.1147

Sleuth

36 Sleuths A novel entry in the dinner-show circuit there's a mystery afoot, and you're the detective. You start the evening in an English drawing room complete with period furnishings and secret panels; hot and cold hors d'oeuvres are served as you mingle with other guests and the characters. The mystery unfolds in the next 40 minutes, while you eat a four-course dinner. Honey-glazed cornish hen is the main entrée. Unlimited drinks are served. ♦ Admission. Daily 6, 9PM (showtimes may vary) 7508 Republic Dr (Republic Square Shopping Center, Carrier Rd-International Dr) 363.1985

37 Siam Orchid ★$$ Authentic Thai food served by waitresses in native dress. Specialties include deep-fried fish in a sauce of chili, garlic and peppers or the roast duck with honey. The building sits back off the road in a serene setting. If you are new to Thai food, try the Sunday brunch. ♦ Thai ♦ M-Sa 4-11PM; Su 11AM-2:30PM, 4-11PM. 7575 Republic Dr (Carrier Rd-International Dr) 351.0821

38 The Floridian of Orlando $ A great location—right off I-Drive but away from the Drive's heavy traffic and within walking distance of Wet 'n Wild. The 300 rooms are simply but nicely furnished, and the food in the restaurant is basic but good. Also a pool, game room, and small gift shop. ♦ 7299 Republic Dr (Carrier Rd-International Dr) 351.5009, 800/237-0730 (FL), 800/445-7299

39 Gateway Inn $ This reasonably priced hotel is perennially popular with British tourists. Wet 'n Wild is an easy walk, and the hotel has a free shuttle to Disney and other area attractions. It has two pools, a children's playground, and family restaurant. ♦ 7050 Kirkman Rd (Carrier Rd) 351.2000; 800/432.1179 (FL), 800/327-3808; fax 363.1835

40 Citrus Circus You might be able to find the same items for less elsewhere, but one-stop shopping here offers T-shirts, shells, and Central Florida citrus for the folks back home. They'll ship it for you. ♦ M-Sa 8AM-11PM; Su 9AM-1PM. 6813 Visitors Cir (International Dr) 351.1694

41 Malibu Grand Prix and Castle With its batting cages for hardball and softball, and its formula-style race cars, Malibu draws an older crowd than does Mystery Fun House up the street. Arcade games, rides, and miniature golf. ♦ Fee for each activity. Daily 10AM-midnight. 5863 American Way (International Dr) 351.7093

42 Original Pancake House ★$ Huge omelets, good coffee, and French toast with a hint of almond. Not the cheapest place for breakfast, but one of the best. ♦ American ♦ Daily 6AM-9PM 5728. International Dr (Kirkman Rd) 351.9342

42 Jonathan's Restaurant $$$ The dining room features an 18-foot waterfall that cascades through tropical

foliage into a Japanese *koi* lagoon. The food is worthy of the setting. You can make a dinner out of the seafood salad; the Dungeness crab claw is a nice touch. Filet mignon, marinated in blue cheese is a good choice. Along with fresh crabs and lobsters try the grouper or snapper cooked in parchment paper with fresh vegetables and seasonings. ♦ American ♦ M-Th 11AM-10:30PM; F-Sa 11AM-11PM. 5600

International Drive

International Dr (Kirkman Rd) 351.7001

43 Passage to India ★★$$ Owner **Uday Kadam,** a native of Bombay, left an 11-year career with Marriott Corp to open this warmly hospitable ethnic restaurant. Experiment by ordering a selection of appetizers that are served with a variety of chutneys. ♦ Indian ♦ Daily 11:30AM-2:30PM; 6-11PM. 5532 International Dr (Grand National Ave-Municipal Dr) 351.3456

44 Great Western Boot Company There is usually a good selection of men's western cowboy boots by **Justin** and **Dan Post,** and a small selection of handmade boots by lesser-known makers, such as **Stewart** of Arizona. The women's selection isn't very broad, but all boots are discounted. ♦ M-Sa 9:30AM-9PM; Su 11AM-7PM. 5597 International Dr (Grand National Ave-Municipal Dr) 345.8103

45 Belz Factory Outlet Mall If you're a careful shopper and know your merchandise, you won't have trouble finding the good buys. Brand-name stores include **Gitano, Bass, Anne Klein II, Capezio,** and **Levi's,** plus **Ruff Hewn** and **Old Mill Ladies' Sportswear.** Belz claims this is one of the largest non-anchored factory outlet complexes in the country and the second-largest tourist attraction in Central Florida, with its nine million visitors annually. The complex is made up of two large unconnected malls and three smaller annexes. Annex II has a new carousel for kids to ride for a nominal fee. ♦ M-Sa 10AM-9PM; Su 10AM-6PM. 5401 W. Oak Ridge Rd (International Dr) 352-9611

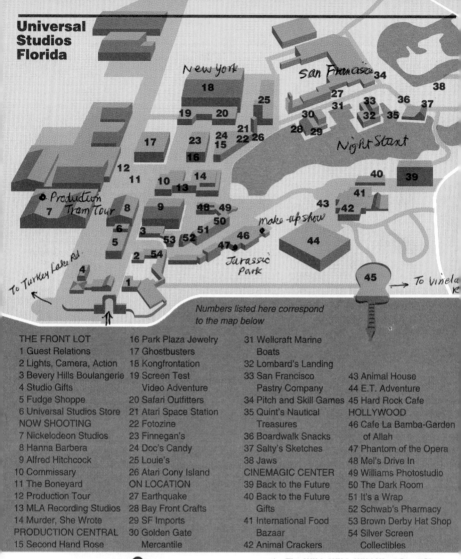

Universal Studios Florida

New York
San Francisco
Night Stunt
Production Tram Tour
make-up show
Jurassic Park
To Turkey Lake Rd
To Vineland Rd

Numbers listed here correspond to the map below

46 Universal Studios Florida The largest active motion picture and television production studios outside of Hollywood, this 444-acre theme park boasts more than 50 attractions and 40 individual street sets. You could walk around a corner and find a television show or movie being filmed, and you could even be asked to be an extra. The park opened in June 1990. Recent attractions include **The American Tail Show,** a musical production based on the animated movie starring **Fievel Mousekewitz;** an AT&T exhibit about the history of moviemaking; and the **The Wild, Wild, Wild West Stunt Show,** an action production featuring stunt actors in a 2,000-seat amphitheater. The park is divided into six areas: **The Front Lot, Hollywood, Now Shooting, Production Central, On Location,** and **Cinemagic Center.**
♦ Admission. Daily 9AM-6PM (longer hours summer and holidays) 1000 Universal Studios Plaza (off Kirkman Rd between I-4 and Major Blvd) 363.8000

Within Universal Studios Florida:

The Front Lot No need to spend a lot of time here. To your right as you pass through the Universal Studios arch is **Guest Relations,** the lost and found for children and personal property. Help is available for the hearing impaired and for non-English speaking guests; a Disabled Guests Guidebook also is available. Check out the chalkboard listing the day's production schedule. You can also sign up here to be in a live TV studio audience. Behind Guest Relations is a bank and pay lockers. On the path leading into the rest of the park is **Lights**

Camera Action, a camera shop where you can rent a camera and buy film, and **Beverly Hills Boulangerie,** the first of many food stops, this one serving light snacks. To the left is **Studio Gifts,** and more pay lockers. As you pass through the Front Lot, **The Fudge Shoppe** and **Universal Studios Store** will be on your left.

Now Shooting If you have children, stop here first. Let the kids run to **Nickelodeon Studios** and see what is available for them. At times, they will have an opportunity to audition for a show, test games, or be part of a live studio audience.

In this area:

Nickelodeon Studios This 90,000-square-foot facility includes two 16,500-square-foot sound stages each seating 250 people. It flanks a 3-story main building, which houses the production control rooms, administrative center and rehearsal stage. Everything is behind glass walls, so you can see what's going on. Of particular interest is the "gak" kitchen, where that famous, gooey, green slime is cooked.

The Funtastic World of Hanna-Barbera
The lines are long and slow, and the Hanna-Barbera shorts repeated above you on conveniently placed monitors get old fast. Once inside, you'll experience the best of the Central Florida simulator-type productions. The show starts with **Bill Hanna** and **Joe Barbera** talking about animation, and before you know it, you're a part of it. After a breathtaking movie, you will have an opportunity to get your hands on some toys—making sound effects, creating voices, and playing the Flintstones' piano with your feet. There is also a **Hanna-Barbera Store** that you pass through on your way out.

Alfred Hitchcock: The Art of Making Movies This three-part attraction begins with clips of Alfred Hitchcock movies, including a 3-D version of *Dial M for Murder,* on a giant screen in the **Tribute Theater;** it's a bit disconcerting because the clips are so brief. The second stop is the **Psycho Sound Stage,** where **Tony Perkins** reveals on screen how the shower scene was filmed using 78 camera angles. If you are with children under 13, you might want to skip these first two features, which can be pretty intense, and go straight to the interactive area, where audience members are chosen to star in some of Hitchcock's thrillers on recreated sets. You leave via **The Bates Motel Gift Shop.**

Universal Studios Commissary ★$$ A wide variety is offered on the menu, including interesting wines. Seafood off the grill is tasty; there also is chicken, salads, steaks and rack of lamb. If you're wanting something different for dessert try the frangipane strawberry flan. Good food aside, you may luck out and see a star. ♦ California ♦ Daily 11AM-closing. Reservations recommended. 363.8769

Across from the Commissary is **The Boneyard,** a corner lot filled with such famous props as Ben Hur's chariot and the original mechanical great white shark from *Jaws.* Beyond is a courtyard where you can wait in line for a **Production Tour.** Here you'll get quick glimpses into large warehouses where the detail work of moviemaking takes place, such as casting, editing, costuming, lighting, and special effects. A popular part of the tour is walking through a live set. Behind the Commissary is **MCA Recording Studios,** where you can cut your own record or music video.

***Murder, She Wrote* Post Production Theater** An interactive attraction in which you'll learn about the **Foley Sound Effects Stage,** editing, and how all the pieces fit together to make a film. Members of the audience are chosen to complete the editing, scoring, and special effects—while a clock ticks toward deadline.

Production Central The big attraction here is **Kongfrontation,** but the street sets are amazing, including **Little Italy** and **Sting Alley,** where **Paul Newman** got his signal in *The Sting.*

In this area:

Second Hand Rose A thrift shop with old clothing, and **Park Plaza Jewelry,** with china and crystal, are en route as you leave Now Shooting, enter Production Central, and head over to Ghostbusters.

Ghostbusters An entertaining special effects show where performers interact with ghosts at the **Temple of Gozer,** the site of the movie's climax. The Ghostbusters battle the Terror Dogs, Gozer, and the Stay-Puff Marshmallow Man. More than 2,300 separate computer cues and 11 tons of liquid nitrogen are used in each performance. **Ghostbusters Paranormal Merchandise** is housed in a re-creation of the movie's fire station.

Kongfrontation In the back streets of the New York set, you come to Penn Central and the Roosevelt Island Tramway Station. Once aboard the tram, you'll hear that King Kong has escaped and is menacing New York. You'll first spot him hanging from the Queensboro Bridge; next thing you know he's grabbed your vehicle and raised it up

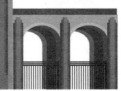

so close to his face that you can smell his banana breath when he hurls you down; one cable remains attached to save you, but not before you experience 1.75 g's of force as you fall 12 feet per second. The tram then takes you to Roosevelt Island, where your reaction to the King's fling plays on a screen above you. Flanking Kongfrontation, on your left, is **Screen Test Video Adventure,** offering you the chance to be a star in your own 8- to 10-minute video. On your right, **Safari Outfitters Ltd,** for safari clothes and a photo opportunity with King Kong; **Atari Space Station** has arcade games; and at **Fotozine,** you can get your face on the cover of any of several magazines. Across the street is **Finnegan's,** serving Irish pub grub, and **Doc's Candy.**

The Lagoon The Lagoon is used almost daily for shooting, rehearsing, or just trying out new stunts. Since it's in the middle of the park, it's easy to keep your eye on it as you pass from one area to the next. One of the best places to

International Drive

watch the action is in the park across the lagoon from the San Francisco set.

Two new features have opened in this area: **The Blues Brothers Show,** a musical production on a small stage on the streets of New York set; and **The Ghostbusters/Slimer/Beetlejuice Show,** an action production centered around the library steps in the New York set.

On your way out of Production Central and into On Location, you will pass **Louie's Italian Restaurant** on your left and **Atari Coney Island,** with midway-type games of skill.

On Location Two blockbuster rides, **Earthquake** and **Jaws,** are in this area; the sets include a Louisiana bayou and San Francisco Fisherman's Wharf.

In this area:

Earthquake, The Big One Charlton Heston, star of the movie *Earthquake,* is the on-screen host at this attraction in which you see how miniaturization, high-speed photography, matte painting, blue screen, and stunts combine to create dazzling disasters. Everyone is herded into a re-creation of an Oakland subway station. Your subway car goes under San Francisco Bay, and as it pulls up to the Embarcadero station it begins to shake. Soon chaos reigns, with lights blinking and chunks of street falling from above. It's a good thing that slab of roadway doesn't hit your car—it weighs 45,000 pounds. There is an on-

coming subway train and a runaway propane tanker truck heading your way and suddenly a deluge of 60,000 gallons of water rushes down the subway stairs directly at your car. What is even more amazing is how quickly everything on the set goes back into position before your eyes. This mock earthquake measures 8.3 on the Richter scale.

Across the street: **Bayfront Crafts,** studio artisans creating movie props alongside crystal cutters and glassblowers; **San Francisco Imports,** kimonos, jade, and other oriental imports; **Golden Gate Mercantile,** earthquake souvenirs; **Chez Alcatraz,** seafood and sourdough rolls; **Wellcraft Marine Boats,** a display of the newest in powerboats.

Lombard's Landing ★★$$ The largest of the restaurants in the park, in a San Francisco Fisherman's Wharf setting. It sticks out into the lagoon and has a second floor accessible by elevator. ♦ Seafood ♦ Daily 11AM-4PM, 4:30PM-closing. Reservations recommended. 351.9955

San Francisco Pastry Company Adjacent to Lombard's Landing, it provides specialty coffees and pastries.

On the way to Jaws, you will pass through the **Amityville** section, which includes **Pitch & Skill Games,** 16 midway-type games; **Quint's Nautical Treasures,** Jaws memorabilia along with ship models and offbeat jewelry; **Boardwalk Snacks,** lemonade, ice cream, yogurt and hot dogs of all kinds; **Salty's Sketches,** a portraiture artist.

Jaws There have been snags in this attraction. Check with the studio to learn if it's functioning.

Cinemagic Center Two blockbusters are here: *Back to the Future* and *E.T. Adventure.* The Hard Rock Cafe is behind the Psycho House and Doc Brown's Science Center sets.

In this area:

Back to the Future After climbing into your DeLorean-style car, you zoom through time with the help of a seven-story-high Omnimax surround screen, flight simulators and special effects. **Christopher Lloyd,** the star of *Back to the Future,* sends you on a mission to recover a stolen DeLorean. Your bumpy journey takes you through various time periods as the car pitches on hydraulic lifts some 12 feet above the ground.

Across from *Back to the Future* is **Back to the Future Gifts** and **International Food Bazaar,** where you are surrounded with monitors playing famous movies and TV shows. Listen carefully: the stars' voices are dubbed to match the language represented by the cuisine.

Animal Actors Stage Benji, Lassie,and **Mr. Ed** join about 50 animals as their trainers put them through their paces.

In the attraction "Earthquake, The Big One," a simulated disaster ride at Universal Studios Florida, 60,000 gallons of water are recycled every six minutes.

Restaurants/Nightlife: Red   **Hotels:** Blue
Shops/ ♠Outdoors: Green   **Sights/Culture:** Black

On the way from Animal Actors Stage to E.T. Adventure, there is **Animal Crackers,** where you can get yogurt, chicken fingers and, hot dogs; and **Animal House,** filled with plushy, stuffed animal stars.

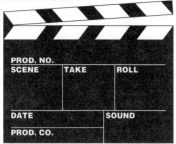

E.T. Adventure Steven Spielberg held up the opening of this attraction until he was satisfied with it. He also had **John Williams,** who won the Academy Award for the movie's score, compose original music for the ride. Spielberg then put together a new story—an E.T. sequel for those of us who were disappointed a movie follow-up never materialized. The ride begins with Spielberg setting the scene: E.T.'s planet is dying, and unless you can get E.T. back to his planet, it will turn into a wasteland. After walking through a perilous redwood forest, you hop aboard dirt bikes with E.T. in the basket on the front. The bikes climb into the sky. Beneath you is a large city, made up of 250 cars, 1000 street lights and 3340 miniature city buildings. As you soar higher, there are 4,400 illuminated stars. You pedal past the moon through purple perfumed fog. Soon you are on E.T.'s planet, and he begins the work of saving it. If the ride is working properly, E.T. will thank you ... personally. In front of the building is **E.T.'s Toy Closet & Photo Spot,** where you can buy intergalactic phones and, E.T. jewelry, and have your photo taken with E.T.

Hard Rock Cafe ★★$$ Rock memorabilia and murals depicting rock stars cover the wall as music blasts so loud it's difficult to hear your tablemates. You can enter this two-story guitar-shaped building that seats nearly 400 from the back of Cinemagic Center or from the Universal parking lot for those going to the club who don't want to do the park. It's burgers-and-fries type fare with mouth-watering desserts. You might want to stand in line to buy T-shirts or sweatshirts (10AM-1AM) while you wait to be seated. It stays quite busy, even during the off-hours. ♦ American ♦ Daily 11AM-2AM. 5401 S. Kirkman Rd (Universal Studios Florida) 363.ROLL

The Animal Actors Stage at Universal Studios Florida is the largest assembly of motion picture and TV animal actors in the world. Most of the dogs and cats are from the Humane Society.

Each year "The Phantom of the Opera Horror Make-Up Show" at Universal Studios Florida uses approximately 365 straight-edge razors, 14,600 pistol blanks, 912 quarts of stage blood, and 547 gallons of Universal's special blood-and-guts mixture.

Hollywood The smallest of the areas and it lacks a blockbuster attraction. The street sets include Hollywood Boulevard, and Schwab's Pharmacy.

In this area:

On the way into Hollywood from Cinemagic Center, you'll pass **Cafe La Bamba** (indoors) and **Garden of Allah** (outdoors). Both serve tacos, Mexican beer, and margaritas.

The Phantom of the Opera Horror Make-Up Show Although there is a warning that this attraction might be too intense for children under 13, all the stunts are explained and there are more laughs than gross-outs. You'll see how **Michael Keaton** was changed in *Beetlejuice,* how **David Naughton** was transformed in *An American Werewolf in London,* and how **Linda Blair** became a head-turner in *The Exorcist.* Next door is **Hollywood Make-Up and Movie Masks,** where you can buy fake body parts and greasepaint, or have monster

International Drive

makeup put on while you wait.
Mel's Drive-In Diner dinners from the movie *American Graffiti,* **Williams of Hollywood Photo Studio,** you choose the wardrobe, they take the picture; **The Dark Room,** a one-hour film developer; **It's A Wrap,** hip, Hollywood boutique; **Schwab's Pharmacy,** a re-creation of the ice cream parlor in which Lana Turner was discovered; **Brown Derby Hat Shop,** chapeaus for sale in this reproduction of the landmark restaurant.

Silver Screen Collectibles A large building filled with costumes worn by stars, movie posters, scripts, and old letters.

47 Howard Johnson Florida Center $$ Across the street from the entrance to Universal Studios. Pretty much like all other Ho-Jo's, with extra-large rooms, cable TV with HBO, and the kids stay free. ♦ 5905 Kirkman Rd (I-4-Major Blvd) 351.3333

48 Twin Towers Hotel and Convention Center $$ The Twin Towers completed a $29 million renovation in time to welcome its new neighbor across the street, Universal Studios Florida. Here is one hotel that keeps the lights on at night for you—it is now outlined in neon. Besides sprucing the place up, it added a business center with computer hookups, and 24-hour room service. Among the amenities are two restaurants, a 24-hour deli, tennis courts, a health club, and a small pool with a poolside bar. ♦ 5780 Major Blvd (Kirkman Rd) 351.1000, 800/327.2110

If you visit "The Art of Making Movies" attraction at Universal Studios Florida, you'll find out how the famous and frightening shower scene was filmed in Alfred Hitchcock's movie, *Psycho.* By the way, Tony Perkins was never in that scene; he was in New York rehearsing for a play.

49 Mystery Fun House A 15-room house with a rolling barrel, a mirror maze, a topsy-turvy room, and a coward's bypass if you are too old and bored or too young and scared. You enter the chambers through a secret door in the fireplace. The Fun House complex also has miniature golf, arcade games, and a little racetrack, but the star attraction is **Starbase Omega,** a laser tag game. ♦ Admission. Daily 10AM-11PM (box office closes at 10PM) 5767 Major Blvd (Caravan Ct) 351.3355

50 Days Inn-East of Universal Studios $ A good, basic motel with in-room safes, color TVs, and separate pools for adults and children. **Denny's** restaurant next door is open 24 hours. ♦ 5827 Caravan Ct (Major Blvd) 351.3800

51 Delta Orlando Resort $$ This sprawling, 800-room hotel on 25 acres of tropical landscaping has undergone a $6 million face-lift, and it's now a reasonable choice for families. One plus is that it lies within a block

International Drive

of Universal Studios Florida. Amenities include **Mango's,** a Key West-styled restaurant; **Center Court Cafe; Hollywood Nites,** a dance club; tennis courts; and three heated outdoor pools. **Wally's Kids Club** will look after your kids if you need a break. ♦ 5715 Major Blvd (Caravan Ct.-Vineland Rd) 351.3340; fax 351.5117

Up, Up, and Away

To be transported into the air in something other than a jet is a wonderful way to see Central Florida, and riding in a **hot-air balloon** is a most serene experience. Many balloon crews take off just after dawn from fields southwest of Orlando near major attractions. While prevailing winds govern the flight, there's a fair chance you'll get a bird's-eye view of the sprawling Disney property. At the very least, you'll fly over lovely, mist-shrouded forests and lakes. As the haze burns off, you might glimpse replanted citrus groves. Be sure to take binoculars or a camera to take pictures of the farm animals or the occasional deer startled by the noisy heater that keeps the balloon afloat.

If you opt for ballooning, get to bed early. You'll be picked up at your hotel about an hour before dawn. Considerate pilots often soften the early morning blow with coffee and a sweet roll, and then ask you to help with the flight preparations. Helping to roll out the balloon will make you appreciate the eccentricity of a balloon flight. Once the basket and balloon are hitched together, the wind direction determined, and fuel lines and supplies checked, it's inflation time. In about 10 minutes, what looks like an enormous bolt of fabric is transformed into a bulbous, colorful, and whimsical craft.

The flight always seems to end too soon. But it's

The grapefruit was introduced in Florida by Count Odet Philippe, a Frenchman who became the first white settler on the Pinellas peninsula.

usually celebrated with champagne and flight certificates—and the drive back to the starting point. Good sports offer to help repack the equipment, so budget four to six hours for the entire adventure.

Fewer time constraints apply to the traveler who chooses a **helicopter** ride. There's a chopper base in the middle of the dozens of hotels that line International Drive. Another stands at the Hyatt Orlando at the intersection of Interstate 4 and US 192.

Zipping about at 120mph in a roaring machine is a sure-fire way to get the adrenaline flowing. The most popular helicopter flights last about 15 minutes and carry four passengers. Pilots fly around—not over—the major attractions, including the Disney complex and Shamu Stadium at Sea World, then head for the Butler chain of lakes in southwest Orange County.

Newlyweds often book choppers instead of the more conventional limousines—one way to avoid a honeymoon traffic jam. High-powered business execs, looking to impress, don't flinch at the $60 or $70 cost of staging such a power retreat. Most of the air space within Orlando's under-construction beltway—a loop around the city—is restricted, so you'll need to plan any flight that varies from normally approved patterns well in advance.

No such restrictions appear to apply to the **blimps** you see wandering the skies over Orlando. The most recognizable are Airport International's Shamu send-ups. Painted to resemble the killer whale that serves as Sea World's mascot, the airships (as their owners prefer to call them) amble around town at their own pace and seemingly with no particular destination in mind.

For hot-air balloon trips, contact:

Balloons by Terry	422.3529
Central Florida Balloon Co.	895.1686
High Expectations Balloon Tours Inc.	846.1110, 847.3421
Orange Blossom Balloons	239. 7677
Rise & Float Balloon Tours	352.8191
Rosie O'Grady's Flying Circus	422.2434
Wind Drifters	295.4153

For helicopter tours and charter flights, contact:

Falcon Helicopter Services Inc.	352.1753
Helicopters Inc. of Orlando	354.5203

For blimp rides, contact:

Airship International	870.7426 (reservations)
	351.0011 (office)
Virgin Lightships Inc.	841.8787 (reservations)
	363.7777 (office)

Orlando's Bargain Hotels

These may not be the cheapest hotels in town, but the following accommodations will provide a lot of bang for your buck.

Crossway Inn This newly redecorated motel has ground-level rooms with kitchenettes that face an interior courtyard with a pool, charcoal grills, a shuffleboard court, and a sand volleyball court. Mini-suites are in a tower. Located across the street from the ocean. 3901 N. Atlantic Ave (Marion-Brevard Lns) Cocoa Beach. 407/783.2221, 800/247.2221 (FL only), 800/327.2224 (US)

Disney's Caribbean Beach Resort Disney's first venture into moderately priced (under $100) hotel rooms. Large rooms, lush landscaping, swimming pools, and a sandy beach outside your door. 10100 Buena Vista Dr (World-EPCOT Center Drs) 407/934.3400

El Caribe Resort & Conference Center Reasonable prices for the older rooms; plenty of amenities in the new tower with suites that can comfortably accommodate a crowd. 2125 S. Atlantic Ave (Browning-Bonner Aves) Daytona Beach. 904/252.1550

Embassy Suites USF/Busch Gardens A good value for a family planning to visit Busch Gardens. Free breakfasts, heated pool, and a free shuttle to Busch Gardens. Prices go up on the weekend. 1310 N. 30th St (E. Fowler-E. Busch Blvds) Tampa. 813/971.7690

The Floridian of Orlando Good location in the middle of the International Drive area. A well-kept motel with a pool, game room, and restaurant. 7299 Republic Dr (Carrier Rd-International Dr) 407/351.5009, 800/237.0730 (FL only), 800/445.7299 (US)

Holiday Inn Maingate West No. 2 Clean, convenient, and just far enough off the main drag to be quiet. 7601 Black Lake Rd (near the US 192 entrance to Disney World) 407/396.1100

Kenwood Inn Rooms with private baths and a swimming pool. Complimentary breakfasts include breads and cakes. 38 Marine St (Bridge St-Bravo Ln) St. Augustine. 904/824.2116

Las Palmas Inn Located in the middle of the International Drive area and across the street from Wet 'n Wild, this motel has a heated pool. 6233 International Dr (Sand Lake Rd-Visitors Cir) 407/351.3900, 800/833.8389

Orlando Heritage Inn A motel with Southern charm that still manages to keep the price down. There is a dinner theater inside, and a wrap-around veranda outside. 9861 International Dr (Beeline Expy-Republic Dr) 407/352.0888, 800/282.1890 (FL only), 800/447.1890

Quality Inn International Great prices, but call ahead for reservations. 7600 International Dr (Sand Lake Rd) 407/351.1600

Quality Suites An affordable, all-suites hotel built in 1989 with designated non-smoking rooms and a heated pool. Adjacent to Old Town, and an entertainment, dining, and shopping complex. 5870 W. US 192 (Holiday Trail) 407/396.8040

Wynfield Inn Children 17 and under stay free if they sleep in their parents' room. Free coffee, tea, and fruit are available at the front desk. 6323 Westwood Blvd (International Dr) 407/345.8000, 800/346.1551

Orlando's Bargain Restaurants

Here's where you can get the most for your dining dollar.

Ted Peters' Famous Smoked Fish The best smoked fish in Florida is at this sidewalk cafe. 1350 S. Pasadena Ave (Gulfport Blvd-14th Ave South) St. Petersburg. 813/381.7931

Crabby Bill's India Rocks Beach. Generous portions of seafood at rock-bottom prices. 401 Gulf Blvd (4th-5th Aves) Tampa Bay. 813/595.4825

Doe-Al Southern Cooking Heaping plates of Southern food, including chitterlings, collards, and black-eyed peas. 85 Corey Circle (St Petersburg

International Drive

Beach Causeway-Blind Pass Dr) St Petersburg Beach. 813/360.7976

Paul's Seafood Seafood prepared in the traditional Greek manner. 630 Athens St (Doddecanese-Grand Blvds) Tarpon Springs. 813/938.5093

Paradise Pier Hard to find and not well known, but the locals crowd this seafood stop. 196 128th Ave East (Gulf Blvd) Madeira Beach (Tampa Bay area) 813/393.1824

Aunt Catfish's For Sunday brunch try their flapjacks, for breakfast try their cheese grits, and any other time try their catfish. The restaurant sits on the Halifax River. 4009 Halifax Dr (Dunlawton Blvd) Port Orange (Volusia County) 904/767.4768

Old Spanish Sugar Mill & Griddle House You can cook your own flapjacks at an old stone water-wheel house here. Deleon Springs State Recreation Area (Volusia County) 904/985.5644

Tex-Mex Cantina Generous portions of the best Tex-Mex food around. 8994 Palm Parkway (SR 535-Lake Ave) Lake Buena Vista (Disney World area) 407/239.8223

Border Cantina A close second to **Tex-Mex Cantina** for Tex-Mex fare, and an affordable food break on trendy Park Ave. 329 Park Ave South (Lyman-New England Aves) Winter Park. 407/740.7227

Tio Pepe's The spot for affordable authentic Spanish meals. 2930 Gulf-to-Bay (US 19-Bayview Ave) Clearwater. 813/799.3082

Capt. Appleby's Inn The salad bar and sticky buns make it impossible to leave this family restaurant hungry. US 441 (west of Donnelly St) Mount Dora. 904/383.6662

The Forbidden City Chinese food at a good price. 948 N. Mills Ave (Marks-Weber Sts) Orlando. 407/894.5005

Restaurants/Nightlife: Red   Hotels: Blue
Shops/ Outdoors: Green   Sights/Culture: Black

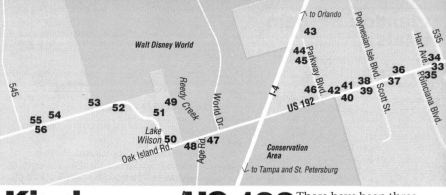

Kissimmee/US 192

There have been three distinct periods in the history of Kissimmee and US 192. In the first, **Chief Osceola**, a Seminole warrior, and his followers arrived in the Lake Tohopekaliga area in the late 1830s. By 1837, the chief had led his people farther south, near Lake Okeechobee, where he was reportedly captured by US General Joseph M. Hernandez while standing under a flag of truce. The chief was sent to Fort Moultrie in Charleston, South Carolina, where he died of malaria in 1838.

In 1881, **Hamilton Disston**, a Philadelphia businessman, purchased four million acres from Florida's bankrupt Internal Improvement Fund for 25 cents an acre. Part of the land became Allendale, a trading post named after pioneer Major J.H. Allen. It was later called **Kissimmee**, a Calusa Indian word meaning "heaven's place." Kissimmee became a minor transportation hub thanks to Lake Toho and a rail line running east to the St. Johns River.

Ninety years later, Walt Disney World opened, and the town started looking northeast toward US 192. The highway, which connects Kissimmee with Walt Disney World, soon sprouted attractions and low-cost lodging to entertain and house thousands of tourists.

Now the strip looks pretty tacky with its string of "bed-and-blacktops"—hotels surrounded by parking lots and the occasional pool. But you can find double rooms for under $40, and even less in the fall. Don't be bashful about asking to see a room before you hand over your plastic. If you don't like it, you're sure to find something better, since there are almost 19,000 rooms to choose from, most along US 192.

Today Kissimmee and neighboring **St. Cloud** are the two largest cities in Osceola County, with a combined population of 98,000. Of the 13 million visitors who come to Central Florida every year, approximately five million stay in this area. Annual events include the **Silver Spurs Rodeo** in February and July, the **Kissimmee Bluegrass Festival** in March, the **Osceola Art Festival** on Lake Toho in November, and the **Christmas Boat Parade** and **Warbird Air Show**, both in December.

Area code 407 unless otherwise indicated.

1 Quality Inn Kissimmee East $ Thanks to a refurbishment in 1991, the facade is new, and the 279 guest rooms have new carpeting, furniture, drapes, and bedspreads. It's a short distance but a long drive from here to Walt Disney World because of the traffic; however, there is a free shuttle. Other amenities include a lounge, two pools, and a restaurant. ♦ 661 E. US 192 (Florida's Turnpike, Exit 244) 846.2221, 800/KIS.EAST, 800/322.0062 (FL)

2 Save Inn $ A well-maintained, econo-priced hotel, but there's probably one just as inexpensive closer to Walt Disney World. It has a small pool and a game room. Pets are allowed. ♦ 2225 E. US 192 (Florida's Turnpike-Simpson Rd) 846.0777

3 Pasta Garden $ Breakfast is served here, along with pasta dishes, salads, and sandwiches. ♦ Italian ♦ Daily 7AM-midnight. 2215 E. US 192 (Florida's Turnpike-Simpson Rd) 870.1773

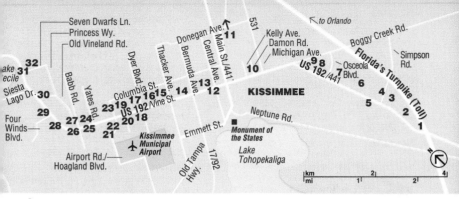

4 Holiday Inn Kissimmee $$ This motel offers the usual Holiday Inn package—lounge, pool, and restaurant—plus **Buster's**, a popular nightspot with live entertainment. There are rooms for the physically disabled. ♦ 2145 E. US 192 (Simpson Rd-Osceola Blvd) 846.4646, 800/465.4329

5 Action Kartways There are four different tracks and bumper boats at this park. You must be 13 or older to race on two of the tracks, one with slick corners, and the other a quarter-mile grand-prix setup for twin-engine Indy cars. The other tracks are tame: Kids must be at least seven years old or able to reach the pedals to go alone on the big family oval, and there is a smaller track for younger children. A new bumper boat ride was added last year. An air-conditioned game room has arcade games and refreshments. ♦ Admission is free, and you pay a nominal fee for each ride. Daily 10AM-11PM 2120 E. US 192 (Simpson Rd-Osceola Blvd) 846.8585

6 Days Inn of Kissimmee $$ This small, moderately priced motel with 122 rooms has a pool, a laundry room, some efficiencies, and rooms for the physically disabled. A **Tasty World** restaurant is on the premises. ♦ 22095 E. US 192 (Simpson Rd-Osceola Blvd) 846.7136, 800/325.2525

7 Park Inn International $$ The 112 rooms here sleep up to four people, and each has a dining area and a fully equipped kitchen. Some rooms connect to make two-room suites. The pool isn't large, but there's a Jacuzzi. The motel is near **Osceola Stadium**, where the Houston Astros hold spring training. ♦ 2039 E. US 192 (Simpson Rd-Osceola Blvd) 846.7814, 800/437.PARK

8 Kissimmee-St. Cloud Convention and Visitors Bureau Stop here for brochures, discounts, and help in finding accommodations. The bureau is the first in the southeastern US to have a toll-free central reservation system (800/333.KISS), which operates from 7AM-2AM EST daily. This is one of four information centers along US 192; the others are east of the turnpike toward St. Cloud, at

Fort Liberty, and west of Walt Disney World's main entrance. ♦ Daily 8AM-6PM. 1925 E. US 192 (Osceola Blvd) 847.5000; fax 847.0878

8 Osceola County Stadium The spring training home of the **Houston Astros.** When the major league team moves out in mid-April, the complex is taken over by the **Osceola Astros,** Houston's Class A Florida State League team. It is also home to the **Senior Little League World Series** (14-15

year olds) in August. ♦ 100 Osceola Blvd (E. US 192-Boggy Creek Rd) 933.5400

9 Silver Spurs Arena This arena hosts two professional rodeos each year. The first, usually held during the last weekend of February, concludes the week-long **Kissimmee Valley Livestock Show** and **Osceola County Fair** at the adjoining **Agricultural Center.** The **Silver Spurs Rodeo** generally takes place on the last weekend in July. In this land of make-believe, it's the real thing. Members of the **Professional Rodeo Cowboys Association** participate in bareback and saddle riding, calf roping, and steer wrestling, and winners walk off with big money. The arena is also used for the annual **Kissimmee Bluegrass Festival** in the spring. ♦1875 E. US 192 (Osceola Blvd-Shakerag Rd) Ticket office opens two months before each rodeo, 847.5118; at other times call the Kissimmee-St. Cloud Convention and Visitors Bureau 847.5000; fax 847.0878

10 Flamingo Motel $ This two-story, pink stucco motel is clean, well appointed, and has some efficiencies. A new pool was added in 1991. ♦ 801 E. US 192 (Damon Rd-Kelley Ave) 846.1935

Tupperware

11 Tupperware International Headquarters The lushly landscaped complex houses a museum of containers (what else?), a theater, and a banquet/exhibit hall. Tours take about 25 minutes and are conducted every 15 to 30 minutes. The museum features food containers used throughout the ages, such as an earthenware *krater*, a bowl—from about

300 BC—typically used to mix wine and water. There are no freebies at the end of the tour, but you can order products and have them shipped to your home if you live in the continental United States. ♦ M-F 9AM-4PM except holidays. US 441 (Barn St-Hunters Creek Blvd) Tours: 847.3111 or in Orlando 826.5050; Convention Center: 847.1800 or in Orlando 826.4475; Theater box office: 847.1802 or in Orlando 826.4450.

11 Gatorland This is Florida B.D. (Before Disney), and the price is right! You enter what is

billed as the world's largest alligator farm through 20-foot-high gaping gator jaws, a landmark in Central Florida since 1962. The jaws lead to a boardwalk bridge spanning a seven-acre lake filled with alligators of all sizes. You can buy fish to feed the gators; children like to flip them onto the backs of the scaly reptiles, who often ignore the offerings

Kissimmee/US 192

because they're so well-fed. Or maybe they prefer chicken: Besides the famous gator jaws at the entrance, the zoo is best known for its **Gator Jumparoo**, where chicken halves are suspended from a cable to entice alligators to jump out of the water and snatch them. The Jumparoo is held about four times a day. Check the hours for show time.

Board the **Gatorland Zoo Express** (which runs continuously) at the train station for a tour of the park's 35 acres. On the other side of the lake are covered walkways that lead past monkeys, pygmy goats, Barbados sheep, deer, bears, zebras, wild birds, and even a tapir. Children love to sit on Albert, a 300-pound tortoise from the Galapagos Islands.

At the far end of the park is a 2,000-foot-long walkway through a cypress swamp that gives you an idea of what the area must have been like before civilization arrived. Gators of all ages can be observed at the zoo, since this is an active alligator farm and research center that works closely with the **University of Florida.** Bug-eyed baby gators, less than a foot long, are kept in a nursery; gators from 1-3 feet long stay in *grow-out* houses, while gators 3-6 feet long are moved to *grow-out* pools. Gatorland also hosts the annual **Great Gator Cookoff,** in which chefs from around Central Florida compete to produce the most

Frank King, creator of the comic strip "Gasoline Alley," lived in Kissimmee for 25 years, and many of his cartoon scenes are spin-offs of buildings and figures around the town. For example, the courthouse in the comic strip is the Osceola Courthouse, which was built in 1889, and is Florida's oldest courthouse still in use.

delectable and imaginatively prepared gator. In 1991 Gatorland began development of 22 additional acres, an 800-seat, open-air gator wrestling stadium, and a four-acre alligator breeding marsh with a boardwalk and three-level observation area. Alligator hide accessories (belts, ladies handbags, boots) are available at the gift shop, and the snack bar offers fried alligator tail. ♦ Admission. Daily 8AM-6PM, later in the summer. 14501 S. Orange Blossom Trail (Barn St-Hunters Creek Blvd) 855.5496, 800/777.9044

12 Lambert Inn $ If you are looking for a clean bed, cable TV, and a cool pool, this two-story, 44-room motel will fill the bill. ♦ 410 W. US 192 (Central-Bermuda Ave) 846.2015

13 Walgreen When you have an upset stomach, it's nice to know this huge drugstore never closes. ♦ 1003 W. US 192 in the Green Acres Shopping Center (Bermuda Ave) 847.4222; prescription service 847.5252

14 Lucy Bluz Cafe One of the few lively nightspots in the area. You can chow down on chicken wings and chase them with beer, all brought to your table by waitresses who zip across the hardwood floors on roller skates. ♦ M-Th 11AM-12:30AM; F-Sa 11AM-1AM; Su noon-midnight. 1707 W. US 192 (Bermuda-Palm Aves) 870.9111

15 Larson's Lodge Kissimmee $$ Local owners keep loyal fans coming back to this sprawling, 200-room motel, complete with a big swimming pool, game room, Jacuzzi, and tennis court. Children under 18 stay free with their parents. Pets are allowed, and there are rooms for the physically disabled. ♦ 2009 W. US 192 (Thacker Ave) 846.2713, 800/624.5905

Within Larson's Lodge Kissimmee:

Black Angus Restaurant $$ The specialty here is steaks and seafood, but it's also a good place to start your day with an all-you-can-eat breakfast buffet, served from 8AM to noon, before beginning your assault on nearby theme parks. There is also a children's menu. American. M-Su, 7AM-11:30PM; 846.7117

16 Travelodge Kissimmee Flags $$ A real steal for the price. Clean, efficiently run, and well located, it has all the amenities of larger, higher-priced motels, including a lounge, pool, restaurant, baby-sitting service, car rental, and rooms for the physically disabled. There's a **Denny's** restaurant next door. ♦ 22407 W. US 192 (Thacker Ave-Orange Blvd) 933.2400, 800/FLAG.PAK, 800/432.4554 (FL)

Restaurants/Nightlife: Red	**Hotels:** Blue
Shops/ 🌳Outdoors: Green	**Sights/Culture:** Black

16 **Lone Star Bar and Grill** $$ This may be a steak joint, but try the chicken fajitas and quesadillas. It's cool inside, and the grub is good. ♦ Tex-Mex ♦ M-W, Su 11AM-2AM; Th-Sa 11AM-3AM. 3109 W. US 192 (Orange-Dyer Blvds) 870.8118

17 **Tony Roma's** $$ If you're looking for a big slab of baby back ribs, this is the place to go. ♦ M-Th 11AM-11:30PM; F-Sa 11AM-12:30AM; Su noon-11:30PM. 3415 W. US 192 (Dyer-Armstrong Blvds) 870.9299

18 **Fox and Hounds Pub** $ Ready for a black-and-tan? If you're a fan of British beer, you'll know that's Guinness Stout topped with a pale ale, such as Bass. This combination is just the ticket for mellowing out after a hard day waiting in line at theme parks. Traditional pub grub, such as a ploughman's plate (cheese, bread, pickle, and salad) or steak-and-kidney pie. Look for the red British phone booth out front. ♦ British ♦ M 5PM-2AM; Tu-Sa 11:30AM-2AM; Su 5PM-2AM. 3514 W. US 192 (Dyer-Armstrong Blvds) 847.9927

19 **Fun 'n Wheels** This spot has everything its sister park on International Drive has except for a Ferris wheel and miniature golf course. There are go-karts, bumper boats, a waterslide, video and arcade games, and the popular **Tank Tag,** where two-person tanks battle it out among themselves and against other battlefield obstacles. One person drives, while a teammate handles the gun in the revolving turret. Among the dangers are racquetballs fired from cannons on the sidelines. If targets on the tank are hit, the tank automatically shuts down for 10 seconds. ♦ Nominal fee for each ride. M-F 4-11PM; Sa-Su and daily in the summer 10AM-midnight. 3711 W. US 192 in the Osceola Square Mall (Armstrong Blvd) 870.2222. Also located on 6739 Sand Lake Rd, Orlando, 351.5651

20 **Comfort Suites** $$ One of the nicer places on this tourist strip. It's relatively new (1988) and has 120 suites on five floors. In-room safes, a nicely landscaped pool deck with a Jacuzzi, a free Continental breakfast, a lounge, a game room, and rooms for the physically disabled. Children under 12 stay free. ♦ 4018 W. US 192 (Armstrong-Hoagland Blvds) 870.2000, 800/228.5151; fax 870.2010

20 **A-1 Motel** $ Nothing fancy here, but there's a decent swimming pool and 45 clean rooms, some with kitchenettes. ♦ 4030 W. US 192 (Hoagland Blvd) 847.9270, 800/662.1920, 800/231.9196 (FL)

21 **Flying Tigers Warbird Air Museum** This WWII aircraft restoration facility is home to a terrific, down-to-earth museum filled with decals, models, and other WWII memorabilia, most for sale. The museum also offers a tour of the huge hangar and field where planes are being restored. The whole setup is a refreshing change after the nearby high-tech attractions: There are no neon signs, no fancy buttons to push, and the refreshment stand consists of a soft-drink machine and a box filled with candy. On a recent visit, coffee was brewing on a card table in the corner; it's like dropping in on a neighbor who is tinkering in his backyard. A small, hand-painted sign directs you from the unpaved parking lot to the entrance through a gate. Once inside, it is best to go straight to the barracks-like building and sign up for the tour, though there is no charge to just wander around. Mechanics always seem willing to answer questions. Among the planes you will see are a brightly colored 1931 *DeHavilland Tiger Moth* and a 1941 *Ryan PT22 Traine,* both of which are frequently in the air. Restored aircraft include a *Flying Fortress Boeing B-17 Heavy Bomber 909,* which completed 140 missions; and a *North American B-25J Mitchell,* a medium bomber used on the **Doolittle Raid** on Tokyo in 1942. Planes are in the air regularly on test flights or for the

fun of it, but there is no set schedule. **Bombertown, USA,** as the museum is sometimes called, sponsors the annual **Warbird Air Show** on the last weekend of the year. Finding the museum is a bit tricky; Hoagland Blvd is also known as Airport Rd south of US 192. ♦ Fee for a guided tour. Daily 9AM-5PM. 231 Hoagland Blvd (US 192) 933.1942

22 **Days Inn** $ Another good-value motel with a pool. There are efficiencies and rooms for the physically disabled. ♦ 24104 W. US 192 (Hoagland Blvd) 846.4714, 800/874.5557, 800/423.1460 (FL)

23 **Tropicana Motel** $ This is an economical choice if you're going to be out all day and just want a place with a clean bed and a pool. Free coffee is always available, and there are rooms equipped for the physically disabled. ♦ 24131 W. US 192 (Hoagland Blvd) 847.4707

24 **192 Flea Market** In four bright-blue buildings under big oak trees, more than 400 vendors sell everything from Nintendo games to athletic gear and Florida souvenirs. There is also a food court inside. ♦ 2Daily 8AM-dusk. 4301 W. US 192 (Yates Rd) 396.4555

24 **EconoLodge Main Gate East** $$ This 173-room motel sits back from the tourist strip, which means peace and quiet. Ask for a room in the rear by the large, heated pool—tranquillity, at last. There is also a children's pool, video game room, shuffleboard court, horseshoe-pitching area, and rooms for the physically disabled. Another smart touch: a do-it-yourself laundry. ♦ 24311 W. US 192 (Yates-Old Vineland Rds) 396.7100, 800/365.6935

25 Pirate's Island Adventure Golf One of the area's many theme miniature golf courses, this course offers two wildly landscaped,18-hole forays among waterfalls, caves, and streams. ♦ Admission. Daily 9AM-11PM. 4330 W. US 192 (Yates-Old Vineland Rds) 396.4660

26 Medieval Times Considering everything else you see on US 192, a replica of an 11th-century European castle doesn't seem out of place. The castle features jousting knights and other tournament games while visitors feast on a four-course meal consisting of an appetizer, vegetable soup, roasted chicken or spare ribs with an herb-basted potato, drinks, and pastry for dessert. There is also a cash bar. And you get to eat just like they did in the olden days—with your fingers! Naturally, everyone is in costume, including the serfs and wenches serving you. As you cross a drawbridge to enter the castle, you, too, must don a colorful cardboard crown. The Hall of Arms displays shields, a deed signed and sealed by Pope Pius V, a 12th-century psalm book, a 350-year-old carved oak podium, and

suits of armor. ♦ Castle is free between 9AM-4PM; admission to the shows M-F, Su 8PM; Sa 6, 8:30PM (times vary) 4510 US 192 (Old Vineland Rd) 239.0214, 800/327.4024, 800/432.0768 (FL)

26 Medieval Life Adjoining Medieval Times, this $2 million expansion completed in 1989 is a re-creation of a village from the Middle Ages, complete with artisan demonstrations and a torture chamber. The village consists of a series of exhibitions by various village craftspeople, such as carpenters, architects, basketweavers, glassblowers, potters, coppersmiths, enamalists, and blacksmiths. Highlights include the falconer show, which involves hawks, falcons, and a European eagle owl, and a close-up look at a dungeon and its instruments of torture (including an interrogation chair covered with iron spikes), which is very popular with children. There's also a medieval kitchen, wine cellar, and a gift shop. ♦ Admission. Daily 9AM-9PM. Same phone as Medieval Times

27 River Adventure Golf This miniature golf course, next to the distinctive Viking Motel, has all the bridges, ponds, streams, and waterfalls that the others do. What makes it more challenging are the breaks in the greens. ♦ Admission. Daily 9AM-midnight. 4535 W. US 192 (Old Vineland Rd) 396.4666

27 Viking Motel $ Campy. You can't miss the tower with turrets. There's a little Viking playhouse for kids, miniature golf, a pool, and an area for outdoor grilling. The 48 rooms face right out onto the parking lot. Some efficiencies and rooms for the physically disabled. ♦ 4539 W. US 192 (Old Vineland Rd) 396.8860

27 Hawaiian Village Inn $$ This motel has 114 tropically decorated rooms, some with kitchenettes, some for the physically disabled. Amenities include two long double beds in each room, a restaurant, a swimming pool, and a playground. ♦ 4559 W. US 192 (Old Vineland Rd) 396.1212

28 Gator Motel $ A two-story motel next door to **Alligatorland Safari Zoo.** Basic and clean with a pool out front. Each of the 38 rooms is equipped with two double beds and cable TV. ♦ 4576 W. US 192 (Old Vineland Rd-Four Winds Blvd) 396.0127

28 Alligatorland Safari Zoo A big alligator statue sits in the parking lot, but you shouldn't confuse this attraction with **Gatorland Zoo.** Walk through the gift shop to buy admission tickets. The petting zoo is to your right as you enter, but save it for the end unless you want to smell like a farm throughout your visit. There are more than 1,000 animals in the zoo, which began in 1977 as a refuge for abused, injured, and unwanted animals. Among the more exotic are Vietnamese pot-bellied pigs, striped hyenas, and endangered species such as the black jaguar and the Siberian tiger. Of course, there are plenty of gators. ♦ Admission. Daily 8:30AM-dusk. 4580 US 192 (Old Vineland Rd-Four Winds Blvd) 396.1012

29 Casa Rosa Inn $ This small, pink, Mediterranean-style motel has been popular with families for years. Accommodations include suites, efficiencies, and rooms with adjoining doors. Free coffee, nonsmoking rooms, a small pool, and rooms for the physically disabled. ♦ 4600 W. US 192 (Four Winds Blvd-Siesta Lago Dr) 396.2020

29 Gemini Motel $ Look for the arches and the redbrick trim when searching for this budget stop, which also offers free donuts and coffee. Efficiencies and rooms for the physically disabled, plus a pool and a restaurant next door. ♦ 4624 W. US 192 (Four Winds Blvd-Siesta Lago Dr) 396.2151

29 Citrus House Gifts Arrange for delicious fresh fruit to be shipped to your home. ♦ 4724 W. US 192 (Old Vineland Rd) 396.4391

Orlando International Airport is the nation's 18th busiest airport, and the 28th busiest in the world.

30 Shell Factory Outlet Like its sister store on International Dr, this shop has shells, shells, shells: loose shells, shells that form jewelry, and shells encased in lucite paperweights and clear toilet seats. ◆ Daily 11:30AM-11PM. 4690 W. US 192 (Old Vineland Rd-Siesta Lago Dr) 396.9000. Also at: 4727 W. US 192; 7550 W. US 192 at Shell World Plaza; 6464 International Dr, Orlando

31 Xanadu With all there is to do in Central Florida, you have to be pretty bored to come here. This 15-room, polyurethane, domed creation is billed as the home of the future, but the presentation is what you would expect from a high school science project. The tour starts in the **Energy Room,** where you're given a preview on a television monitor by a man decked out in something that's a cross between the Jetsons and Salvation Army thrift. The self-guided tour of the house winds through the learning center, a nook with some home computers; the master bedroom with its solar sauna; and a children's room tucked away in a stuffy corner. To make matters worse, the place suffers from such mundane 20th-century problems as cobwebs, dust, and mildew. On a recent visit, a young man at a desk by the door was selling timeshares for a nearby property. ◆ Admission. Daily 10AM-9PM 4800 US 192 (Seven Dwarfs Ln-SR 535) 396.1992

31 Murphy's Lobster House $$ Popular for Maine lobster, but the filet mignon isn't bad either, and you can't go wrong with any of the fresh Florida seafood, especially the broiled swordfish. If you want to save some bucks, Murphy's offers an all-you-can-eat buffet daily. **Kokamo Kafe and Dance Palace** is part of the scene here and provides dancing and live entertainment most nights. There's no cover charge if you eat dinner here. ◆ Seafood ◆ Daily 4:30-11PM; buffet daily 4:30-10PM; cafe daily 9:30PM-2AM; happy hour daily 4:30-9PM. 4736 W. US 192 (Seven Dwarfs Ln-SR 535) Restaurant 396.0401 or 239.7171 in Orlando; nightclub 396.SHOW

32 Congo River Golf and Exploration Company With all the new miniature golf courses chock-ful of the requisite mountains, waterfalls, and caves, new gimmicks are hard to come by. Congo River Golf has an Exploration Game, in which clues on the scorecard lead you to six treasures on the courses. Collect them all, and you win a prize. Also soft drinks and a video arcade. ◆ Admission. Daily 10AM-10PM. 4777 W. US 192 (Seven Dwarfs Ln-SR 535) 396.6900. Also at: 6312 International Dr, Orlando 352.0042

32 Sol Orlando Village Resort ★$$ A cut above the competition. Owned by Spain's biggest hotelier, this pretty, tile-roofed hotel has 150 spacious one-, two-, and three-bedroom villas, each with a family-sized living and dining area, a fully equipped kitchen, and two color TVs with cable. Also a convenience store and air-conditioned

squash and racquetball courts. A good value for the money! ◆ 4787 W. US 192 (SR 535) 397.0555, 800/336.3542; fax: 397.0553

33 Golden Link Motel $ This two-story, brickfront motel, fronted by a small pool, is on **Lake Cecile** and has a fishing pier and a pool. Its rooms are neat and clean, with two double beds and satellite TV. You can rent a Jet Ski or water-ski on the lake. ◆ 4914 W. US 192 (SR 535) 396.0555, 800/336.6621

33 Travelodge Golden Triangle $$ This futuristic-looking, pink-and-turquoise motel has some nice touches: a VCR and video library in every room, TV with free HBO, and balconies (ask for the ones overlooking Lake Cecile). The pool in back is beside Lake Cecile, where there's a private beach, and Jet Ski and paddleboat rentals. Non-smoking rooms and rooms for the physically disabled. ◆ 4944 W. US 192 (Hart Ave) 396.4455, 800/432.1022

34 Park Plantation Inn $$ A well-run, three-story motel, with two double beds and cable TV (including the Disney Channel) in each of the 108 rooms. It offers a family-style buffet,

which is convenient if you are rushing to hit the nearby attractions. ◆ 5055 W. US 192 (S.R. 535-Hart Ave) 396.2212, 800/446.5669

35 Howard Johnson Fountain Park Plaza Hotel $$ Another well-managed hotel, with 413 oversized rooms, transportation to Disney parks, lighted tennis courts, a heated pool with saunas and a hot tub, a restaurant, a lounge, and lakeside picnic grounds. There is a nine-hole putting green, shuffleboard courts, and a playground. ◆ 5150 US 192 (Poinciana Blvd) 396.1111, 800/327.9179

36 Rodeway Inn Eastgate $$ This four-story hotel is a good bargain, offering many of the amenities found in more expensive motels nearby. The lounge often offers live entertainment, and there is a restaurant, a game room, and a large pool. ◆ 5245 W. US 192 (Poinciana-Polynesian Isle Blvds) 396.7700

36 Jungle Falls Go-Karts and Amusements Squeezed in between two motels, Jungle Falls provides go-kart racing for all ages, including a quarter-mile jungle raceway. There are also bumper boats and bumper cars, an arcade, 36 holes of jungle miniature golf, and batting cages. ◆ Nominal fee for each ride. M-Th, Su 10AM-11PM; F-Sa 10AM-midnight. 5285 W. US 192 (Poinciana Blvd-I-4) 396.1996

37 Fort Liberty Wild West Dinner Show and Trading Post The main draw at this recreation of an 1876 stockade is the dinner show, but there are also shops, a museum, a Miccosukee Indian village, and alligator wrestling. The entertainment complex has doubled in size to 22 acres since it opened in 1987. ◆ 5260 W. US 192 (Poinciana-Polynesian Isle Blvds) 351.5151, 800/347.8181

Within Fort Liberty Wild West Dinner Show and Trading Post:

Dinner Show Tables for 12 on two tiers surround center stage in this 600-seat arena, where **Professor Gladstone's Traveling Medicine Show** entertains with gun fighting, singing, roping, and good humor for adults and youngsters alike. The four-course meal consists of hearty western fare: chicken, corn on the cob, and pork and beans. Unlimited beer, soft drinks, and wine. ♦ Admission. Reservations requested. Daily 6 and 9PM

Liberty Village and Trading Post Twenty stores, most based on Old West themes, surround a courtyard with the dinner theater at one end. There's no admission for entering the village, which is decked out with suitable props— teepees, totem poles, and horses. Occasionally, cowboys and Indians demonstrate craft skills here. ♦ Daily 10AM-10PM

Brave Warrior Wax Museum It only takes 15 minutes to walk through this small mu-

seum at the stockade, guided by a timed narrative. The museum opens with the Lewis and Clark expedition to the Missouri River, illustrates through costumed wax figures six Native American nations, and finishes with photos of **General George Custer** and his wife, **Libby.** ♦ Admission; ticket holders for dinner show receive a 50 percent discount. Daily 10:30AM-8:30PM

Alligator Wrestling Bo Jim, a full-blooded Miccosukee, wrestles an alligator five times daily, something he has been doing for about 15 years. The Miccosukee Indian village is 35 miles west of Miami in the Everglades. ♦ Daily 11:30AM, 1, 2:30, 4 and 5:45PM.

38 Best Western Eastgate $$ This 403-room motel, fronted by a small pond, is set back from the road and features a whirlpool spa, game room, tennis courts, playground, and gift shop. It's about two miles from the entrance to Walt Disney World's Magic Kingdom. ♦ 5565 W. US 192 (Polynesian Isle Blvd-Holiday Tr) 396.0707, 800/223.5361

39 Old Town The Big Eli Ferris wheel next to **Wolfman Jack's Rock 'N' Roll Palace** is the landmark for Old Town and its four-block, 70-store dining, entertainment and shopping complex. When you stroll along the redbrick pedestrian mall with distinctive turn-of-the-century Florida architecture, you will want to swing open some of those old, creaky doors. Inside you'll find Disney souvenirs,

glassworks with glass-blowing demonstrations, a magic shop, music boxes and cuckoo clocks, saltwater taffy, a candle store with candle-making demonstrations, gifts and jewelry from Czechoslovakia, a train museum, an **Elvis Presley** museum, and an old-time general store, where you can still get a nickel Coke. (You can keep the small bottle or get your quarter deposit returned.) The road winds to an 80-year-old carousel with 44 hand-painted animals, which came from the Harvey Lakes Amusement Park near the Poconos Mountains in Pennsylvania. Between Big Eli and the carousel is a fountain and a tall, standing clock; live entertainment can often be found here. If you have trouble walking on bricks or are in a wheelchair, don't let that keep you away: There are sidewalks. ♦ Daily 10AM-10PM. 5770 W. US 192 (Frontage Rd) 396.4888, 800/843.4202, 800/331.5093

Within Old Town:

Wolfman Jack's Rock 'N' Roll Palace This is the top 1950s nightclub in the area, with nightly live performances and some of  Wolfman Jack's rock memorabilia. It was started by **Glenn Stetson,** leader of **The Diamonds,** and was previously known as Little Darlin's Rock 'N' Roll Palace. The name of the nightclub came from "Little Darlin," one of The Diamond's big hits. The club opened in 1986, and since then a steady stream of Stetson's singing sidekicks have performed. The house band, **the Rockin Robin Band,** backs up the headliner acts, such as the **Platters** and **Little Anthony,** and keeps things lively when the big names aren't playing. The building itself will knock your bobby socks off: The facade is a 23-foot-high jukebox, with 12-foot-high doors and colored lights and bubbles. Walk down to the black-and-white-tiled dance floor and tables, or head upstairs, where there are more tables. Even if you don't end up sitting upstairs, at least check out the memorial windows there on the east side—**Frankie Lyman, Clyde McPhatter, Rick Nelson, Elvis Presley, The Big Bopper,** and **Ritchie Valens;** on the west side—**Buddy Holly, Johnny Horton, Alan Freed, Bill Haley, Sam Cooke,** and **Bobby Darin.** The restaurant serves fifties fare, which isn't as memorable as the waitreses in poodle skirts, sweaters, and saddle shoes. If you don't happen to be wearing your poodle skirt, you can buy one in the gift shop along with records, tapes, T-shirts, letter sweaters, and satin jackets. ♦ Cover. Daily noon-2AM. 396.6499

Orlando was first called Jernigan, after Aaron Jernigan, a poor settler who came to the lake-dotted region in 1842. No one's quite sure why, but the city's name was changed to Orlando in 1857, probably in memory of a 19th-century soldier, Orlando Reeves.

Restaurants/Nightlife: Red   Hotels: Blue
Shops/ 🌳Outdoors: Green   **Sights/Culture:** Black

Key Largo Steak & Seafood ★$$ On the other side of the Ferris wheel is this laid-back restaurant, one of the few places to dine at Old Town. A stuffed marlin is mounted on the wall and the wooden fanback chairs are painted in pastels. The calamari and grouper are good.
♦ American ♦ Daily 7:30-11PM. 396.6244

Elvis Presley Museum This small museum crammed with Elvis memorabilia is a must-see if you are an Elvis fan. Highlights include some of his cars, like a 1969 Mercedes Benz 600 limousine and a 1966 Rolls Royce Silver Cloud III. There are plenty of photos, gold records, instruments, costumes, and furniture. An interesting document tucked away at the back of the museum is Elvis' birth record from the doctor who delivered him and his twin brother, Jessie, who died at birth. "Evis", as the doctor mistakenly wrote, was born 35 minutes later. ♦ Admission. Daily 10AM-10PM. 396.8594

40 Days Lodge Maingate East $$ Two all-suite buildings across the street from each other off Holiday Trail next to Old Town, with three pools and a restaurant. Pets are allowed. ♦ 5820 W. US 192 (Holiday Trail) 396.7900, 800/327.9126, 800/432.9103 (FL)

40 Days Inn Maingate East $ If you don't need a suite, save a couple of bucks and stay next door at the 404-room Days Inn. Each room has two double beds. Amenities include a lounge, a pool, and a restaurant, along with a gift shop and game room. Pets are allowed. ♦ 5840 W. US 192 (Holiday Trail) 396.7969, 800/327.9126, 800/432.9103 (FL)

40 Quality Suites $$ This relatively new hotel stands out from the rest because it looks like a freshly painted European village. It has a beautifully landscaped pool area with a children's pool and whirlpool, and **Kokomos,** a poolside bar that serves drinks and snacks. Amenities include coffeemaker, game room and microwave. 225 suites, some nonsmoking. ♦ 5870 W. US 192 (Holiday Trail) 396.8040, 800/228.5151

41 Water Mania It doesn't have as many thrill rides as Wet 'n Wild on International Drive, and it isn't as lushly landscaped as Typhoon Lagoon at Walt Disney World, but Water Mania has its own faithful following and is a very pleasant way to cool off if you want more than a motel pool. The **Wave Pool** is always popular, as is the **Banana Peel,** a two-person raft ride down a water-filled chute. On the **Screamer**, you plummet down what feels like a near-vertical slide, and on the **Double Berzerker** slide you bump over an undulating surface. The **Rain Forest,** a children's water playground, was developed in 1990. Behind the waterslides is a wooded picnic area and a sandy beach. You are allowed to bring your own food, but not alcoholic beverages or glass containers. Dry off while playing miniature golf or testing your skills in a maze. Concerts are often held on a stage in front of the Wave Pool, and you can enjoy the music

while floating on rafts during the show.
♦ Admission. Daily 10AM-5PM, Mar-Apr, Sep-Nov; daily 9AM-9PM, June-Aug. 6073 W. US 192 (Polynesian Isle Blvd-Park Equus Rd) 396.2626, 800/527.3092 (outside FL)

41 Larson's Lodge Main Gate ★$$ Family-owned and -operated, this well-run motel has a loyal following, so you may need reservations during peak seasons. Tall people will appreciate the extra-long double beds. There is a bright and airy dining room, heated pool, Jacuzzi, and game room. Children under 18 stay free in rooms with their parents. A sister hotel is at 2009 W. US 192.
♦ 6075 W. US 192 (Polynesian Isle Blvd-Park Equus Rd) 396.6100, 800/327.9074

Arabian Nights

41 Arabian Nights The chariot race is still the hit at this show, despite more than 60 beautiful and well-trained performing horses. The performance of the **Royal Lipizzans,** which dance and prance, is incredible. The 25

acts are thinly held together by the story of a princess searching for her true love with the help of a genie. A four-course dinner with unlimited drinks is served in the 1,200-seat arena. Choose between prime rib or a vegetarian dish. A low-cholesterol meal is available if you order it when you make your reservations. ♦ Admission. Daily 6:30 and 9PM (showtimes vary). 6225 W. US 192 (Park Equus Rd) Reservations recommended. 396.7400, 239.9221 in Orlando, 800/553.6116

42 Time-Out If you are looking for a place where the kids can burn off energy, this amusement center is an option, and convenient if you are staying around Parkway Blvd. There are plenty of things to hit, throw, and roll, and the building is clean and large. ♦ Nominal fee for each game. M-Sa 10AM-11PM; Su noon-10PM. 2901 Parkway Blvd in the Parkway Pavilion (W. US 192) 396.8808

43 Hampton Inn $$ If you're searching for a bargain, but trying to avoid the ubiquitous "bed-and-blacktop," this is a good find. The 164-room motel boasts a fine location on tranquil Parkway Blvd, far from busy, crowded US 192. Rooms are fine; there's a pool and courts for shuffleboard, tennis, and basketball. ♦ 3104 Parkway Blvd N. (US 192) 396.8484, 800/243.8440

44 Homewood Suites $$$ Designed for businesspeople or for families enjoying a longer-than-average vacation, the 156 suites at this handsome new hotel feature king-sized beds, fully equipped kitchens, and plenty of workspace, including computer jacks. Some suites have wood-burning fireplaces. There is also an up-to-date business center with personal computers, typewriters, calculators, copiers, and a fax machine. Breakfasts and weekday social hours are free, and the 24-hour **Suite Shop** is stocked with snacks, videos, and microwave meals. There is a fitness center with a Jacuzzi, and a pool, children's pool, basketball court, and play area. ♦ 3100 Parkway Blvd (W. US 192) 396.2229, 800/255.4543; fax: 396.4833

45 Ramada Resort Maingate at the Parkway $$ If you want a full-service hotel near the Magic Kingdom's main gate without paying the Hyatt Orlando's prices, this is a fine choice. The six-building, 716-room hotel, removed from the heavy traffic on US 192, has spacious, nicely landscaped grounds. There are two pools (including one that has a waterfall and slide), a sauna, a new lounge, a restaurant, and an expanded deli. Tennis, jogging trails, and rooms for the physically disabled. ♦ 2900 Parkway Blvd N. (US 192) 396.7000, 800/634.4774, 800/225.3939 (FL); fax 396.6792

46 Hyatt Orlando $$$ Kissimmee folks will remind you that this hotel is *not* in Orlando.

Kissimmee/US 192

Still, it's very convenient to Walt Disney World, especially to the Magic Kingdom. It has all the requisite Hyatt touches, including well-appointed rooms in four major clusters, each cluster with its own heated pool, whirlpool, kids' pool, and playground. There are jogging trails and three lighted tennis courts. The food in the restaurant is generally much better than average, though pricey. A huge breakfast buffet is served each morning. 924 rooms. ♦ 6375 W. US 192 (Parkway Blvd) 396.1234, 800/544.7178

Within the Hyatt Orlando:

Fio Fio $$$ This is Hyatt's top-of-the-line restaurant at the hotel, and it serves up well-prepared Italian staples, including fettucine Alfredo and chicken parmigiana. But for the money, you could do better elsewhere. ♦ Italian ♦ Daily 6-10PM

Spectacular Helicopter Tours This helicopter service on the Hyatt grounds offers four tours. All require booking by at least two adults. Children receive a discount if they're under 11 and accompanied by two adults. Separate trips take you over EPCOT Center, the Lake Buena Vista Shopping Village at Walt Disney World, or all of the Disney attractions. The grand tour combines the above three trips with aerial views of Sea World, Universal Studios Florida, Wet 'N Wild, and the exclusive Bay Hill residential community. A sister tour begins at the **Falcon Helicopters Heliport** at 8990 International Dr. ♦ Fee. Daily 9AM-dusk. Reservations recommended. 396.7222

Paradise Plantation Miniature golf, a game room, gifts, and snacks available for munching at a small outdoor patio at the entrance to the **Hyatt Orlando.**

47 Holiday Inn $$$ A sprawling, 529-room, two-story motel across busy US 192 from the entrance to Walt Disney World. There are three pools, three restaurants, whirlpool spa, lighted tennis courts, a small playground, and a game room. ♦ 7300 W. US 192 (Disney World entrance-Age Rd) 396.7300, 800/HOLIDAY

48 Hilton Inn Gateway $$ Six one-bedroom suites were added in a recent renovation, along with new furniture, telephone equipment to accommodate personal computers, and new television sets with remote control, HBO, and, of course, the Disney Channel. All rooms have either king- or queen-sized beds. There is the **Palms Restaurant** and a lounge serving deli goodies. Game room, miniature golf, outdoor fitness center, two pools, and rooms for the physically disabled. ♦ 7470 US 192 (Age-Oak Island Rds) 396.4400, 800/327.9170, 800/325.4400 (FL); fax 396.4320

49 Ramada Resort Maingate $$$ The location is great if you want to take a break from Disney World crowds. Two pools, a kiddie pool, tennis courts. Nonsmoking rooms and rooms for the physically disabled, a restaurant, a lounge, and a game room. ♦ 2950 Reedy Creek Blvd (US 192) 396.4466, 800/327.9127, 800/432.9195 (FL)

50 Econolodge Maingate Hawaiian Resort $$ The entrance to this hotel looks like the wooden prow of a Hawaiian boat, and a recent renovation was done with care. Each room has two double beds, individual temperature controls, and cable TV with in-room video movies and room safes. The dining room, while attractive, has mediocre food. The hotel also has a big pool, and is one of the larger, non-Disney hotels that is very close to Disney World's Magic Kingdom. ♦ 7514 W. US 192 (High Point Blvd) 396.2000, 800/638.7829, 800/432.9101 (FL)

51 Wilson World Hotel Maingate $$ From the road this is just another motel, but once inside, you'll be surprised. A four-story atrium has an indoor heated swimming pool with a waterfall and a large cafeteria. There is a game room, gift shop, indoor whirlpool spa, and a large outdoor pool with a sandy beach. The lounge generally has free live entertainment. ♦ 7491 W. US 192 (High Point Blvd-Oak Island Rd) 396.6000, 800/66.WORLD.

When Walt Disney World got under way in the late 1960s, it was billed as the greatest construction project ever undertaken by a private-sector employer. The Walt Disney Co. spent $400 million and created 50,000 jobs when it turned 27,400 acres of mostly marsh lowlands into the nation's No. 1 tourist attraction. Soon after the park opened in October 1971, fewer tourists visited Florida's famous beaches, and Miami was deposed as Florida's tourism capital.

One third of all Florida tourists in 1990 had household incomes of more than $60,000. Walt Disney World was the top destination for all tourists entering the state.

51 Radisson Inn Maingate $$ Another consistent chain offering reasonable prices. Set back from the hubbub of US 192, rooms include cable TV, free in-room movies, and baths with shower massage. Laundry facilities are available, as well as a heated outdoor pool, tennis courts, whirlpool, and game room. Also a restaurant, take-out deli, **T.J's Lounge** and a pool bar. ♦ 7501 W. US 192 (High Point Blvd-Oak Island Rd) 396.1400, 800/777.7800

51 Comfort Inn Maingate $$ A step above the regular pool-bed-and-TV motel. Restaurant, pets OK, and rooms for the physically disabled. ♦ 7571 W. US 192 (High Point Blvd-Oak Island Rd) 396.7500, 800/ 223.1628, 800/432.0887 (FL)

52 Howard Johnson Maingate West $$ This well-managed hotel has rooms that are a bit larger than the usual, with a color TV, double vanities, and a patio or balcony. Two swimming pools, shuffleboard courts, a putting green, a restaurant, a game room and a gift shop. ♦ 7600 W. US 192 (Sherbeth St) 396.2500, 800/654.2000, 800/4324335 (FL)

53 Holiday Inn Maingate West No. 2 $$ Put this at the top of your list of moderately priced hotels near the Magic Kingdom's main gate. It's new, well maintained, and well run, with a pretty pink exterior, and is set on a small road far from the crowds along US 192. Small but attractive pool. ♦ 7601 Black Lake Rd. 396.1100

54 Sheraton-Lakeside Inn $$$ This hotel offers some special frills. The grounds are lushly landscaped, and there's a small lake with paddleboats, plus four lighted tennis courts, two large, heated pools, and children's pools, too. The coin laundries are a boon for families. Following a $5-million renovation, the hotel now has a lounge, a lakeview restaurant, a buffet restaurant, and a deli. 653 rooms with double beds (king-sized beds available) and small refrigerators. ♦ 7769 W. US 192 (Sherbeth St-SR 545) 396.2222, 800/334.8484

54 Travelodge Maingate West $ This economy hotel, sitting on a private lake, has an attractive pool and patio area, a laundry room, and a game room. ♦ 7785 W. US 192 (Sherbeth St-SR 545) 396.1828, 800/ 322.3056, 800/423.4336 (FL)

55 Orange Lake Country Club $$$ From the man who brought you Holiday Inn and Wilson World, **Kemmons Wilson** has built a timeshare complex with 27 challenging holes of golf designed by renowned golf architect **Joe Lee**, 16 lighted tennis courts, racquetball courts, and watersports of all kinds on an 80-acre lake with a 300-foot sandy beach. Orange Lake has taken in guests who find themselves without a room for one reason or another, but it isn't cheap. The two-bedroom, fully equipped townhomes line the fairways. The clubhouse has hotel-type rooms, a restaurant, lounge, a coffee shop, pool bar, pizza parlor, video game room, miniature golf, and 155-seat movie theater. ♦ 8505 W. US 192 (Sherbeth St-SR 545) 396.6800, 800/877.6522

55 Yogi Bear's Jellystone Park Camp Resort Campsites on Orange Lake, with full water and electric hookups. Miniature golf, a pool, and many planned activities throughout the day and evening. ♦ 8555 W. US 192 (Sherbeth St-SR 545) 396.1311

At the Park:

J.T.'s Prime Time $ A restaurant and bar housed in a large log cabin with a screened-in porch. Prime rib and barbecue are the usual fare. The general store next door is equipped with supplies and liquor. ♦ Daily 11AM-midnight

56 Best Western Maingate $$ One of many budget hotels on the quiet side of I-4, but it has a free shuttle to Walt Disney World, and kids under 13 stay and eat free. Each room has two double beds and cable TV with free HBO. ♦ 8600 W. US 192 (Sherbeth St-SR 545) 396.0100, 800/327.9151

How to Weather through a Hurricane

Orlando has never suffered from a truly devastating hurricane, but the fearsome storms have swept up out of the Gulf of Mexico, the Caribbean, and the Atlantic to batter cites on both Florida coasts. Tampa residents and Miami folks may whip out the hurricane tracking maps the minute they hear about a storm, but Central Floridians tend to shrug their shoulders. They're fond of telling newcomers that hurricanes aren't so bad and that you can outrun them a lot easier than you can a tornado. But don't be quite that blasé. If you're staying in a beachside hotel or condo, you'll want to head inland. If you expect to have to evacuate, make sure your car has a full tank of gas, refill any prescriptions, and get some cash. Remember that automatic teller machines may not be in operation if there's no electricity. Florida has well-planned evacuation routes, and you can learn what those are from the local news media. Hurricane season lasts from June to November, with September historically the month with the most hurricane activity.

In the 1880s thirsty, on-the-go cowpunchers could mosey their mounts over to a horseback-high service window outside a wood-frame building in downtown Kissimmee (The world's first "drive-in"), and order up their favorite frothy beverage.

Walt Disney World is built primarily on swampland. Although much of it was drained, deluges during the rainy season could have been a serious problem if it weren't for Disney's elaborate water-control system that uses 47 miles of canals, 22 miles of levees, 24 water-control structures, and control gates that automatically float open when water reaches a peak level and close when high waters subside.

Walt Disney World

For years, Cape Canaveral was the best-known area in Central Florida. Yet even NASA couldn't compete with the world's most famous mouse. When Walt Disney World opened in 1971 more than 10 million visitors flocked to the park that year. These days it attracts about 13 million people annually, making it *the most popular tourist spot in the world*. And why not? This city-sized world of fantasy (nearly 43 square miles) offers spectacular rides and attractions, eye-boggling hotels, revealing glimpses into the future, and a working movie studio that takes you behind the scenes and sometimes puts you in front of the cameras.

All this came about because of the vision of one man, **Walt Disney.** When Disney created Disneyland in California, he made one mistake: He didn't buy enough land for the amusement park, which limited his ability to expand it and permitted non-Disney enterprises to rake in the profits through hotels and souvenir shops. So in 1965, the man who created Mickey Mouse began snapping up acreage of swampy pine shrub about 20 miles south of Orlando.

By the time Disney had finished buying property, he had amassed an amazing 27,400 acres. Today, even with three huge theme parks—Magic Kingdom, EPCOT

Disney World (Nos. 1-14, 33-38, 64-66, 87-93)

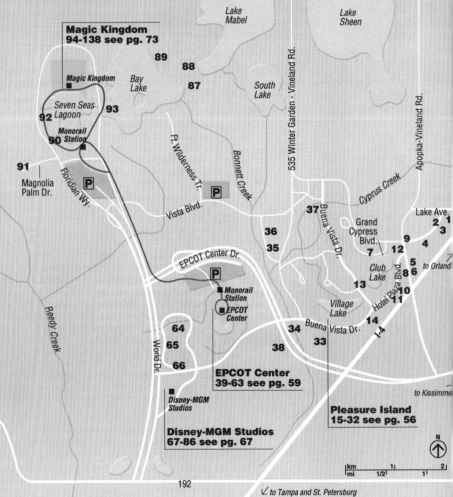

Center, and Disney-MGM Studios — only about one-fifth of those acres is developed, leaving plenty of room for more. And **more** is coming.

In the next decade, plans will be implemented to build another 5,000 hotel rooms, including luxury and moderately priced inns, as well as a fourth theme park that will incorporate animals or music as its theme. New Disney hotels on the drawing board will have plenty of pizzazz, too. The Hollywood Horror Hotel, for example, will be "haunted" with Disney-style ghosts. And the Disney-MGM Studios will double in size, gaining 16 new attractions, while the Magic Kingdom will add seven major attractions, including Splash Mountain. Billed as "the ultimate thrill ride," Splash Mountain will be the tallest (five stories), fastest (at speeds close to 40mph), and longest (80 feet) flume ride in the world. At EPCOT Center, three new attractions will be in place before the year 2000: a Soviet pavilion, a Swiss pavilion with a Matterhorn thrill ride, and a Journeys in Space pavilion.

Walt Disney, who died in 1966, wanted his theme park to remain in a state of perpetual growth–and apparently that's a wish his successors plan to make come true.

© THE WALT DISNEY COMPANY

Walt Disney World

Area code 407 unless otherwise indicated.

1 Embassy Suites Resort Orlando $$$ Opened in July 1991, this hotel, painted a wild combination of pink, tangerine, and aqua, has 280 two-room suites that, while smallish, bristle with amenities, including a TV in the bedroom and a TV with VCR in the living room. Kitchens have a coffeemaker and microwave. A free breakfast, including eggs made to order, is served in a sunny atrium, where the Tropix Grille, a dinner restaurant, is also located. The hotel also includes a pool with a small indoor section, a children's pool, a tidy health club with up-to-date equipment, a sauna, a whirlpool, and a poolside bar and grill. Six suites for the physically disabled. ♦ 8100 Lake Ave (Palm Pkwy) 239.1144; fax 239.1718

2 Howard Johnson Park Square Inn & Suites $$ This 222-room hotel offers good values for families. It includes 86 two-room suites, and has a large interior courtyard with two pools, a whirlpool spa, playground, and shuffleboard courts. Suites have two double beds, a pullout queen sofa bed, two color TVs, and a kitchenette area with microwave. There is a small restaurant at the hotel. ♦ 8501 Palm Pkwy (SR 535-Lake Ave) 239.6900, 800/635.8684; fax 239.1287

3 Comfort Inn Lake Buena Vista $$ Owned by Orlando hotelier **Harris Rosen,** who offers some of the lowest rates in town, the rooms at this sprawling hotel face the street or the Interstate. Still, a real bargain. ♦ 8442 Palm Pkwy (SR 535-Lake Ave) 239.7300; fax 239.7740

4 Radisson Vista Centre $$$ A pretty, 200-room hotel that's not on Disney's property but offers free transportation to Walt Disney World attractions. The hotel has a beautiful outdoor pool with a rock grotto that includes a waterslide and waterfall, a kids' play area, a poolside snack shop, and a whirlpool. All rooms have balconies and small refrigerators. ♦ 8686 Palm Pkwy (SR 535-Lake Ave) 239.8400, 800/333.3333; fax 239.8025

Restaurants/Nightlife: Red   **Hotels:** Blue
Shops/ ♥Outdoors: Green   **Sights/Culture:** Black

Ever wonder how much that person in the Mickey Mouse suit is paid to get pulled, punched, and hugged by the mobs at Walt Disney World? Starting pay is $7 an hour, and Mickey's work week is usually 32 to 40 hours long.

4 Compri Hotel $$$ Not on Disney property, but so close you'll hardly notice the difference. Free shuttle bus service is provided to the Disney attractions, and the hotel throws in a full, cooked-to-order breakfast and late-night snacks as well. Rooms are spacious, and there's a pool, sun deck, health club, sauna, and whirlpool. There's also a playroom for kids with games, toys, and a TV tuned to (what else?) the Disney Channel. ♦ 8688 Palm Pkwy (SR 535-Lake Ave) 239.8500, 800/228.2846; fax 239.8591

5 Tex-Mex Cantina ★★$$ This restaurant does a fine job with Tex-Mex specialties, including wonderfully gooey cheese enchiladas in green sauce, and beans *a la charra*—that is, beans that aren't refried, but served in their own delicious juices. Ask your waiter if the tamales are fresh. You'll blow your diet, but you'll leave happy. ♦ Tex-Mex ♦ Daily 11:30AM-1AM. 8994 Palm Pkwy (SR 535-Lake Ave) 239.8223

6 The Crossroads at Lake Buena Vista This shopping center, on land owned by Disney, boasts a miniature golf course, fast-food joints, including McDonald's, and even a nice bookstore among its 29 stores and restaurants. ♦ SR 535 (opposite Hotel Plaza Blvd)

Walt Disney World

At the Crossroads at Lake Buena Vista:

Pebbles ★★$$
An upscale eatery with a creative menu and a large variety of imported beer to drink while polishing off a plate of snails in morel sauce or a goat cheese-and-tomato *concasse*. Don't be afraid to bring the kids; there are burgers, too. It overlooks a small lake. ♦ American ♦ Daily 11AM-midnight. 827.1111

Pirate's Cove Adventure Golf
An imaginative, 18-hole miniature golf course where golfers climb mountains, walk under waterfalls, and play through caves.

♦ Admission. Daily 9AM-midnight. 827.1242

White's Bookstore All your favorite best-sellers for great vacation and poolside reading. A nice magazine selection, too. ♦ 12542 SR 535. 827.1268

Gooding's This large grocery store never closes. ♦ 827.1200

Jungle Jim's $
This is a gourmet burger stop with a diverse menu and a funky decor that includes walls lined with movie posters and jungle paraphernalia. It has a children's menu. ♦ American ♦ Daily 11AM-2:30AM. 827.1257

7 Grand Cypress Resort A 1,500-acre luxury playground nestled right up against Disney property, the resort has become a local landmark that attracts an international clientele. The complex includes the **Hyatt Regency-Grand Cypress** hotel, the **Villas at Grand Cypress,** and a 45-hole Jack Nicklaus-designed golf course, selected as one of the 25 best resort golf courses in the US by *Golf Digest*. In addition, there is a lavish equestrian center. Restored trolleys ferry guests to different parts of the resort. ♦ Deluxe ♦ 60 Grand Cypress Blvd (SR 535) 239.4700, 800/835.7377; fax 876.5880

Within Grand Cypress Resort

Hyatt Regency-Grand Cypress Hotel $$$$

It's not the rooms, which are fine, that make the hotel special, but the extra touches—from the half-acre free-form pool to the Chinese statuary and gorgeous rugs in the lobby. There's also a health club with sauna, steam room, and massage area, and a 1,000-foot sandy beach complete with paddleboats, canoes, and small sailboats to frolic about with on their 21-acre lake. ♦ 239.1234, 800/233.1234; fax 239.3800.

Within the Hyatt Regency-Grand Cypress Hotel:

LA C♦QUINA

La Coquina ★★$$$ Famous in these parts for its lavish Sunday brunch. The seafood is of very high quality, and the fruit is always fresh. The pastel-hued decor sets a smart tone for this multilevel restaurant. Try the tender lobster in champagne sauce. ♦ American ♦ Tu-Sa 6-11PM; Su 10:30AM-3:30PM. 239.1234

Hemingway's $$$ A dining room with Key West-style ambience and perfectly cooked seafood. ♦ Seafood ♦ M-Th 11:30AM-2:30PM, 6-11PM; F-Sa 11:30AM-2:30PM, 5:30-11PM. 239-1234

Cascade $$ A place for the family to sit down and enjoy meals throughout the day. ♦ Italian ♦ Daily 7AM-4PM, 6-11PM. 239-123

White Horse Saloon $$$ You'll feel as if you have been transported back into an elegant Old West restaurant when you dine here. The steaks are juicy and a thoroughly professional band of singing cowboys entertains nightly except Sunday. ♦ American ♦ Daily 6-11PM. 239-1234

The Villas at Grand Cypress $$$ Built along the **Jack Nicklaus**-designed golf course, these rooms are among the most elegant in Central Florida. Choose from one-, two-, three- or four-bedroom villas, some with fireplaces and whirlpools. All have full kitchens, dining and living rooms, as well as private patios or verandas. You're never too far away from the Villas' many swimming pools and whirlpools, and you can't beat the twice-daily housekeeping service, as well as room service. ♦ 1 N. Jacaranda Place (SR 535) 239.4700, 800/835.7377; fax 239.7219

Grand Cypress Equestrian Center This luxurious stable has a professional staff and offers private lessons as well as trail riding with guides. ◆ 239.1234

The Lake Buena Vista Hotels

There are seven hotels on Walt Disney World property at Lake Buena Vista, an incorporated city: the Guest Quarters Suite Resort, the Travelodge, the Hotel Royal Plaza, the Howard Johnson Resort Hotel, the Hilton at Walt Disney World Village, the Grosvenor Resort Hotel, and the Buena Vista Palace. You may be steered to one of these hotels if you call Disney's reservation number and its hotels are full or too pricey for your budget. The Lake Buena Vista hotels sell discounted tickets to Disney World attractions and each is linked by Disney's efficient shuttle buses to its parks. Additional perks for visitors who stay here are priority for EPCOT reservations and preferred starting times for golf courses. None of the Lake Buena Vista hotels is on Disney's monorail line, and room prices are generally higher here than for comparable hotels not located on Disney property.

8 Guest Quarters Suite Hotel at Walt Disney World Village $$$ A pretty hotel with spacious suites. Each has a living room with a sofa bed and dining area, plus a separate bedroom with two double beds and a vanity dressing area. Suites are packed with amenities, too, including three remote-controlled TVs (one in the bathroom), a wet bar, and a small refrigerator. Free breakfast. ◆ 2305 Hotel Plaza Blvd (Buena Vista Dr-SR 535) 934.1000, 800/424.2900; fax 934.1011

9 Travelodge Hotel at Walt Disney World $$$ One of the smaller hotels at Disney Village, the 325 rooms are spacious and were recently renovated. Club Calypso, a nightclub on the 18th floor, has a splendid view. The hotel offers a game room, playground, and pool. ◆ 2000 Hotel Plaza Blvd (Buena Vista Dr-SR 535) 828.2424, 800/432.1022 (FL), 800/255.3050; fax 828.8933

10 Hotel Royal Plaza $$$ A solid choice for families, each room has a private balcony, and the grounds include four lighted tennis courts, a swimming pool, sauna, and whirlpool. If you're feeling flush, the hotel also has Burt Reynolds and Barbara Mandrell celebrity suites, with furniture lent by the stars. ◆ 1905 Hotel Plaza Blvd (Buena Vista Dr-SR 535) 828.2828, 800/248.7890; fax 827.6338

10 Howard Johnson Hotel at Disney Village $$$ This is a popular hotel for families because kids under 18 stay free, and there is a 24-hour restaurant on the property. Most of the rooms have private balconies. Rooms in the 14-story tower circle an unspectacular atrium with a circular bar on the ground floor. There are two heated pools. ◆ 1805 Hotel Plaza Blvd (Buena Vista Dr-SR 535) 828.8888; 800/654.2000 (FL only), 800/223.9930; fax 827.4623

Hilton at Walt Disney World Village
$$$$ With its pink marble lobby, this 813-room hotel is the most elegant at Disney's hotel village. It has two pools—one with a poolside bar—a health club, and lighted tennis courts. ◆ 1751 Hotel Plaza Blvd (Buena Vista Dr-SR 535) 827.4000, 800/782.4414; fax 827.6380

Within the Hilton at Walt Disney World Village:

American Vineyards ★★$$$ The restaurant specializes in American cuisine, has a good selection of wine, and is one of the best gourmet restaurants in the Disney area. Specials such as venison and rabbit in a curry sauce are available, though the restaurant is best known for its prime rib. You can also select your favorite cut of steak or fish to be grilled, broiled, blackened, sautéed, or roasted with any of 10 sauces, including one made of green peppercorn and another from brandy. ◆ American ◆ Daily 6-10:30PM. Reservations recommended. 827.4000

Benihana ★$$$ A well-known chain, you'll find light but satisfying Japanese food cooked by graceful, dexterous chefs right at your table. ◆ Japanese ◆ Daily 5-10:30PM. 827.4000

Walt Disney World

12 Grosvenor Resort at Walt Disney World Village $$$ A recent renovation has added grace to this still-affordable hotel on Disney property. The hotel has two heated swimming pools, a hot tub, and lighted tennis and racquetball courts, as well as an electronic game room for video kids. ◆ 1850 Hotel Plaza Blvd (Buena Vista Dr-SR 535) 828.4444, 800/624.4109; fax 827.6314

13 Buena Vista Palace $$$$ Without being affiliated with a well-known chain, this 841-room hotel has attracted a loyal clientele because of its well-trained staff and multiple amenities, including three swimming pools, lighted tennis courts, spa, sauna, and health club. A summer program for kids is popular. A separate wing houses 200 roomy suites that were added in 1991. The hotel has standout restaurants, too. ◆ 1900 Buena Vista Dr (Hotel Plaza Blvd-Vista Ave) 827.2727, 800/432.2920 (FL only), 800/327.2990; fax 827.6034

Within the Buena Vista Palace:

Arthur's 27 ★★★$$$$ This sleek, elegant restaurant provides a panoramic view from the 27th floor of the hotel and serves a seven-course prix fix feast. Dover sole has been one of the star entrées, but venison and sautéed breast of duck with honey-ginger sauce are highly recommended. Caviar or sautéed foie gras in champagne sauce often starts the meal, and a cool sorbet separates two courses. ◆ American ◆ M-Th, Su 7-10:30PM; F-Sa 6-10:30PM. Reservations recommended. 827.3450

Outback Restaurant ★★$$$ A touch of Australia in Central Florida, the specialty here is choice, tender steaks grilled over pits in the middle of the restaurant. A glass elevator takes you from the third-floor lobby to the restaurant on the first floor. Choose from 99 brands of beer. ♦ Australian ♦ Daily 6-11PM. 827.3430

14 Casting Center You say you've visited Disney World as a tourist and now you want to work here? Disney will take your application at the Casting Center, whose bold gold letters have been an eye-catching sight from Interstate 4 since **Robert Stern** built the structure in 1988. If you decide to file an application here, you'll first walk into a small rotunda, then up a broad ramp, where the whimsical murals on either side depict great moments in Disney's history. Once at the receptionist's desk, you can fill out your application form. Disney has always referred to every one of its workers, from street sweepers to on-stage performers, as members of its "cast," because everyone is part of the ongoing show. ♦ M, Tu, F 8AM-5PM; W 10AM-5PM; Th 7:30AM-5PM. 824.4254

Disney Village Marketplace

This is a beautifully landscaped, upscale shopping area of more than 25 stores and restaurants. If you need a break from the parks, you could spend a few pleasant hours roaming through the shops or boating on the Buena Vista Lagoon in little motorboats, pontoons, or paddleboats. It is also a pleasant place to stroll before or after a dinner at one of the restaurants. The Marketplace is connected to Pleasure Island, a nightclub and restaurant complex, which is free to visitors until 7PM. ♦ Daily 10AM-10PM. 828.3058

15 Chef Mickey's Village Restaurant ★$$$ Chef Mickey Mouse wanders through each evening to make sure everything is OK with the families who are eating here. Seasonings seem to be kept at a minimum to appeal to kids' palates. You might want to ask for more spices, especially with the pasta. ♦ American ♦ Daily 9-11AM, 11:30AM-2PM, 5:30-10PM. Dinner reservations recommended. 828.3723

16 Cap'n Jack's Oyster Bar ★★$$ Walk through **Windjammer Dock Shop** to this bar of hardwood floors, exposed beams, large windows overlooking the Buena Vista Lagoon, and famous frozen margaritas. This is a wonderful place for a meal; it doesn't get very crowded, and it offers a pleasant view. The salads are loaded with smoked fish, marinated scallops and shrimp, and the conch chowder is spicy. Finish off with a big piece of Key lime pie. ♦ Seafood ♦ Daily 11:30AM-10PM.

17 Mickey's Character Shop If you've been to the parks, but still need gifts to take home, this is your one-stop shop for Disney merchandise. It is enormous, and it has Mickey, Minnie, and even the Muppets emblazoned on virtually everything—from games to clothes.

18 Personal Message A fancy stationery shop that sells costly fountain pens, leather portfolios, and electronic gifts, including neon wall clocks and Mickey Mouse telephones.

19 Empress Lilly This triple-deck stern wheeler riverboat, which is moored at Pleasure Island, has been a Disney landmark since 1977. It has three restaurants and the lively **Baton Rouge Lounge** on board. There is no cover charge to enter Pleasure Island if you are dining here. One way to check the ship out is to schedule a breakfast there. Disney characters are always on hand to entertain the kids ♦ Two seatings: 8:30 and 10AM. Reservations required. 828.3900 or W-DISNEY.

Aboard Empress Lilly:

Empress Room ★★$$$$ The Empress Lilly's finest restaurant specializes in traditional favorites with a French flair. Waiters hover around you in this rather small but spectacular room furnished with a glittering chandelier and mahogany wood paneling. Recent standouts have been the roasted rack of baby lamb, sizzling in its natural juices and topped with fresh thyme, and the roasted breast of duck topped with a perfectly balanced mandarin and honey vinegar sauce, and served with Peking kumquats. No smoking allowed. There is a 20 percent gratuity added to your bill. A harpist performs in the lovely **Empress Lounge.** ♦ American ♦ Daily 6-9:30PM. Jackets required for men. Reservations are required and may be made up to 30 days in advance. 828.3900

Fisherman's Deck ★★$$$ For perfectly prepared seafood, try the fresh speckled trout with sautéed cashews and topped with sprigs of cilantro; for a more down-home meal, sample the fresh catfish marinated in Creole mustards and dusted in fresh corn flour. No smoking allowed. ♦ Seafood ♦ Daily noon-2PM, 5:30-10PM. Reservations recommended; call between 7:30AM-10PM up to seven days in advance. 828.3900

Steerman's Quarters ★★$$$ A simple, no-frills menu with tender steaks, including filet mignon and a 10-ounce Kansas City strip steak. Most are served with fresh veggies or a baked potato. For non-meat eaters, there is whole roasted chicken or fresh seafood. No smoking allowed. ♦ American ♦ Daily 5:30-10PM. Reservations recommended; call between 7:30AM-10PM up to seven days in advance. 828.3900

Restaurants/Nightlife: Red   Hotels: Blue
Shops/ ♦Outdoors: Green   Sights/Culture: Black

The world's tallest, fastest, and longest flume ride will open at Walt Disney World's Magic Kingdom in late 1992. Called Splash Mountain, riders will plummet down a height of five stories at speeds of 80 mph.

Pleasure Island

When **Michael Eisner**, chairman of the Walt Disney Company, asked for something that would entertain tourists at night, Disney's design and real estate arm, Walt Disney Imagineering, came up with Pleasure Island, a collection of retail shops, nightclubs, and restaurants located next to Disney's Village Marketplace. The complex struggled, however, until Disney came up with a clever gimmick: every night is New Year's Eve on Pleasure Island. By day, tourists explore the island and dine in its restaurants, but after dusk, the fun begins. Stick around until midnight, when cannons boom from the rooftops, showering everyone with confetti. An admission fee is required after dusk unless you are dining at the Fireworks Factory or the Portobello Yacht Club.

Area code 407 unless otherwise indicated.

20 Portobello Yacht Club ★★$$$ There is wonderful, if pricey, food at this restaurant run by the **Levy Brothers** of Chicago. Even if you're not a pizza fan, try a small one as an appetizer; with their very thin crusts and perfect spices, they redefine the word pizza. The Pizza Verdure, with sun-dried tomatoes, eggplant, mushrooms, zucchini, and provolone cheese makes a fine starter, as does the velvety baked garlic on house bread. For an entrée, forget your diet and try *salsiccia e polenta*, home-made Italian sausage served over creamy polenta, with caramelized onions. ◆ Italian ◆ Daily 11:30AM–midnight. 934.8888

21 Fireworks Factory ★★$$ This restaurant's specialty is barbecue and it is some of the best in Central Florida. Meals start with heaping portions of perfectly prepared cornbread. Entrées are large, and offer a combination of baby back ribs, chicken, and beef. Wash all this down with one of more than 40 varieties of beer. Or, just belly up to the bar for an ale without the food. ◆ American ◆ Daily 11:30AM–3AM. 934.8989

22 XZFR Rock & Roll Beach Club This nightclub specializes in rock 'n' roll from the fifties to the present, played by usually decent live bands. A rather bizarre show stars cats and trainer **Dominique Lefort**. Yes, apparently those stubborn creatures can be trained, as Lefort has them jumping from stool to stool and even sitting up on their haunches like dogs. ◆ Daily 7AM–2AM. 934.7781

23 Changing Attitudes Here you'll find trendy, youthful fashions with much of the clothing offered either black, white, or a combination thereof. ◆ Daily 10AM–1AM.

24 Mannequins Dance Palace This is primarily a disco for the young, lycra-clad set, with a post-Industrial look that was the rage in New York some years ago. Still, it's a fine place for people-watching. There's Top 40 music and a revolving dance floor. If you no longer dance the lambada or don't look so great in skin-tight duds, stop in anyhow: Disney will thrill you with some great special effects. ◆ Daily 8PM–2AM. 934.7781

25 The Front Page Here's your chance to be *Time* magazine's man or woman of the year or a cover girl for *Cosmopolitan*. Splash your face across any of more than 60 magazines. ◆ Daily 10AM–1AM

26 Superstar Studios Ever longed to strap on a guitar and swivel your hips like Elvis? For a fee, you can star in your own rock video and take it home to show friends. ◆ Daily noon–midnight

27 Cage This is Disney's version of a club that plays "alternative" music in an "underground" environment. The rock 'n' roll isn't the usual Top 40 pop, but lovers of the avant garde won't get much cutting-edge stuff here. It's a good place for wilder dancing, though. ◆ Daily 9PM–2AM. 934.7781

28 Avigator's This is a trendy shop with some pricey but tempting goods. It's Disney's version of Banana Republic. ◆ Daily 10AM–1AM. 934.7781

29 Adventurers Club A nightclub styled as a Victorian-era private club for eccentric world travelers, this club has some clever touches. Old photographs and talking African masks hang on the walls. Guests are supposed to interact with waiters and waitresses who also are actors playing the parts of maids, butlers, and other Victorian-period characters. ◆ Daily 7PM–2AM. 934.7781

30 Neon Armadillo Music Saloon Disney has

been trying hard to bring strong country-and-western talent to this nightclub. But, unlike a real country dance hall, the Neon Armadillo has been hampered by its small dance floor, which is often too packed for real rug-cutting. ◆ Daily 7PM–2AM. 934.7781

31 The Comedy Warehouse Disney World takes itself much too seriously at times, and this place is the perfect antidote. Stand-up comedians perform a 45-minute skit lampooning corporate Disney. ◆ Daily 7PM–2AM. 934.7781

32 AMC Pleasure Island 10 Theatres After a long, hard day at the theme parks, you may be ready to take in a movie before hitting the nightclubs at Pleasure Island. As you might expect, the 10 screens here are heavy on Disney fare, including movies put out by Disney's adult label, Touchstone Pictures. ◆ 827.1300

Restaurants/Nightlife: Red   **Hotels:** Blue
Shops/ 🌳 Outdoors: Green   **Sights/Culture:** Black

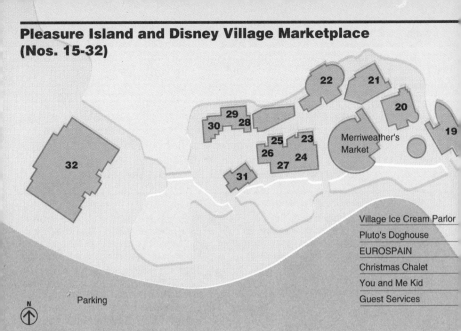

Village Ice Cream Parlor

Pluto's Doghouse

EUROSPAIN

Christmas Chalet

You and Me Kid

Guest Services

Parking

33 Team Disney Building Although the Walt Disney Co. is based in Burbank, CA, it obviously has sizable operations in Florida. About 1,000 employees moved into this 401,000-square-foot office building constructed by **Arata Isozaki & Associates** in 1991. Many have joked that the rose-and-green cone that rises from the center of the building makes it look like a nuclear power plant. Actually, the hollow cone houses an ingenious, eight-story-high sundial, complete with viewing platform. The main entrance is shaded by a canopy shaped like the famous Mouse's ears. It could only have come from the mind of Tokyo architect **Arata Isozaki,** who proves that the Walt Disney Co.'s desire to be a patron of great architects is

Pleasure Island

working out nicely. Inside, each of the office building wings are hung with panels designed by artist **Sol LeWitt.** To arrange tours, call Walt Disney Guest Information Services. 824.4321

34 Typhoon Lagoon This 56-acre water park is so thoroughly landscaped that you feel, at times, as if you're on a tropical island. But its eight waterslides and wave pool, while thrilling, aren't enough to keep most teenagers happy; Wet 'n Wild, a competing attraction on International Drive, is their favorite. But for mom, dad, and smaller kids, this has something for everyone, including, unfortunately, long lines. Two restaurants, **Leaning Palms** ($) and **Typhoon Tilly's Galley & Grog** ($), serve salads, burgers, fries, and other snacks. Leaning Palms has a more extensive menu. Changing rooms and coin lockers are available. ♦ Daily 9:30AM-4:30PM. 560.4142

The main attractions at Typhoon Lagoon:

Typhoon Lagoon The wave pool that gives the park its name is a monster wave machine—the world's largest—that creates surfing-sized waves up to six feet high. A caution: if you have small children, watch them carefully. These waves will definitely be over their heads.

Humunga Kowabgunga Actually two waterslides that drop you down a man-made mountain, through a cave, and out again at speeds of 25 mph.

The Storm Slides These three slides—Rudder Buster, Stern Burner, and Jib Jammer—take you zooming through a rain forest, bat caves, and flotsam and jetsam before plunking you down into one of several lagoons.

Rafting Falls You can take one of three falls here aboard oversized inner tubes. Mayday Falls takes you down a 460-foot slide through whitewater, Keelhaul Falls whips you through a triple vortex (a twisting slide), and Gangplank Falls lets families ride together on four-passenger rafts. This is a don't-miss ride.

Shark Reef In a hurry? Skip this. Yes, the lure of swimming in a 362,000-gallon saltwater pool among real fish, including small, nonbiting sharks, and alongside a wrecked ship, even if it is a fake, is mighty tempting, but hordes of other swimmers make it much less fun. First, you must wait in line to get your snorkel gear, then wait in line again to be instructed in how to use it (even if you already know how), all for a five-minute swim at best. You must swim in one direction only, then you're outta there to make room for more people. Somehow, the thrill is gone.

35 Port Orleans Resort $$ Disney has done a good job at making what it calls its "affordable" hotels pretty, welcoming, and efficient. Although this hotel is very big, its wings are cleverly arranged around a beautifully landscaped square. The hotel's courtyard has a

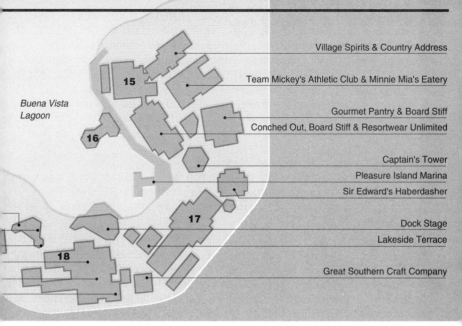

Village Spirits & Country Address

Team Mickey's Athletic Club & Minnie Mia's Eatery

Gourmet Pantry & Board Stiff

Conched Out, Board Stiff & Resortwear Unlimited

Captain's Tower

Pleasure Island Marina

Sir Edward's Haberdasher

Dock Stage

Lakeside Terrace

Great Southern Craft Company

Buena Vista Lagoon

New Orleans look: Wrought-iron balconies look down on courtyards lined with azaleas and magnolias. ♦ 1661 Old South Rd (Vista Blvd-Bonnet Creek Rd) 934.5000

Within the Port Orleans Resort:

Sassagoula Floatworks and Food Factory ★$$ This informal dining area, decorated with real Mardi Gras floats, does a credible job at serving a spicy chicken jambalaya. Food is served in a trendy new "food court," which offers plenty of selections, including New Orleans-style donuts called *beignets*. There's good ice cream, and baked goods are made on the premises. ♦ Hours vary at the food court's counters, but something is always open from 6AM-midnight.

Bonfamille's Cafe ★★$$$ This smallish, 156-seat cafe is a nice addition serving excellent cuts of steak and spicy Creole crawfish entrees. A fountain adds a bit of splash to the shaded courtyard restaurant. ♦ American ♦ Daily 7AM-11:30AM, 5-10PM. 934.5412

Scat Cat's Club $$ This jazz lounge serves up light hors d'oeuvres and specialty drinks. It doesn't quite have that funky feel of a New Orleans bar, but you'll appreciate the beautiful photographic prints of jazz stars on the walls. ♦ Daily 11AM-10PM

36 Dixie Landing Resort $$ A meandering river connects Port Orleans with Dixie Landing Resort. The newest of Disney's moderately priced hotels, this vast, sprawling complex with an Old South ambience consists of two types of lodging: a stately plantation home, and a backwoods bayou dwelling topped with tin roofs. Rooms are well outfitted, most with two double beds and a few with kings. The complex has a themed play area, a swimming pool, and two restaurants. There are plans for another restaurant to be built with a working waterwheel and cotton press. In addition, the

complex, like Port Orleans, is accessible to two new golf courses designed by well-known golf course architects **Tom Fazio** and **Pete Dye.** ♦ 800/647.7900

37 Disney's Village Resort $$$ Choose from an airy townhouse with open interior spaces, a multilevel villa with lofts and skylights, a spacious circular tree house nestled in the woods, or a one-bedroom suite that is large enough for a small family. All villas have fully equipped kitchens and living areas, while the one-bedroom suites offer a refrigerator, wet bar, and coffeemaker. Daily housekeeping service is provided. The resort backs up on Lake Buena Vista golf course. ♦ 1901 Buena Vista Dr (Com-

Pleasure Island

munity Dr-Vista Ave) 827.1100

38 Disney's Caribbean Beach Resort $$ Disney's first venture into moderately priced (for Disney) hotel rooms, this sprawling complex was an instant success. Each of the five lodges at the resort is painted a different pastel color, and all borrow heavily from Caribbean architecture; windows look shuttered (but aren't really) and peak roofs are reminiscent of tin-roofed structures so prevalent in mild Caribbean climes. Each of the "island villages" has its own sandy beach, pool, and laundry facilities. There are seven swimming pools, and a marina with rental boats on the 42-acre Barefoot Bay, a man-made lake. You can bike or jog on a 1.4-mile trail. ♦ 10100 Buena Vista Dr (World-EPCOT Center Drs) 934.3400

At Disney's Caribbean Beach Resort:

Old Port Royale $$ This food court has six counter-service snack bars serving everything from burgers to snacks. ♦ Daily 6AM-midnight

EPCOT Center

Walt Disney World's EPCOT Center, which opened in October 1982, is like a grand world's fair: Favorite attractions include **World Showcase**, several pavilions representing 11 different countries, and **Future World**, the center of hundreds of displays based on the world's most advanced technology. The best advice for enjoying EPCOT (which stands for Experimental Prototype Community of Tomorrow) is to *arrive early*, especially on holidays or during holiday periods, such as the week between Christmas Day and New Year's Day, as well as Easter week, and during the summer months. All Disney parks are very crowded at these times, but if you run counter to the usual dining patterns by eating lunch early or in the mid-afternoon, or coming to the park late after an early dinner, you can minimize the time you spend waiting in line. You can also avoid the biggest crowds by starting your visit at the back of the park, either at the American Adventure, Italy, or Japan pavilions, and then work your way forward.

Plan on having at least one meal in World Showcase, where the food of the different nations is prepared by native chefs; several of these restaurants are among the best in Central Florida. To make reservations, go to WorldKey information service kiosks as soon as you enter the park. WorldKey terminals are located at Earth Station, on the left side of Future World and beside the water taxi next to Morocco. If you are staying on Disney property, call 828.4000 for advance reservations. You can't make same-day reservations by phone; you must book at least one day in advance.

Area code 407 unless otherwise indicated.

39 EPCOT Center Entrance Plaza At the Guest Relations window on the right side of the entrance plaza, Florida residents may wish to buy an annual pass to Disney attractions.

EPCOT Center

Here, too, is the lost and found. To the west of the Entrance Plaza is the pet care kennel, where you can stash Fido for a nominal fee until you've seen all of EPCOT Center. Remember, it's much too hot in Florida to keep your pooch in the car, and it is also against the law. West of the ticket booths is an automatic teller machine that accepts major bank network cards, as well as a window for renting strollers and wheelchairs.

40 Spaceship Earth This is EPCOT Center's signature pavilion, the one that looks like a giant golf ball or a dimpled geodesic dome. But unlike a dome, this 180-foot-high geosphere is completely round. Little cars take you through the history of human communications, from early cave drawings to communications by satellite. What's fun about the trip is that you're moving up a steep incline in near-total darkness; only the communications show is illuminated. Don't wait in a long line, though, at this pavilion. If it's very crowded, come back at a mealtime, when lines are likely to be much shorter.

In Spaceship Earth:

Earth Station At the base of Spaceship is EPCOT Center's information central. Check here for hours of parades; live performances; and IllumiNations, a spectacular laser, sound, and fireworks show presented each night over World Showcase Lagoon.

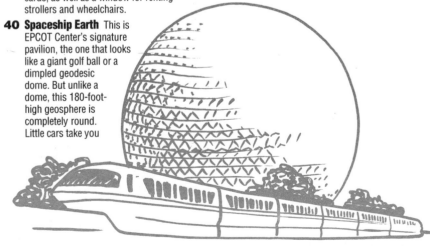

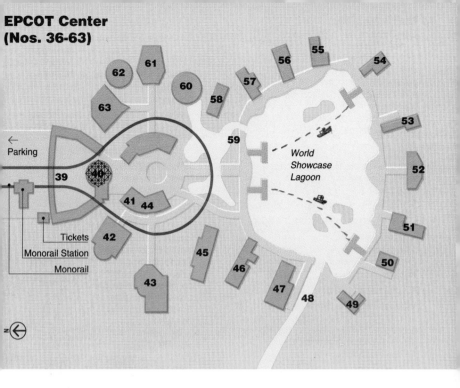

41 Camera Center Here you can buy Kodak film, get your snapshots processed in two hours, or rent a camera or RCA Video Camcorder. (You'll have to leave a deposit for the video recorder.) Employees here will help you with camera problems and can suggest the best photo locations.

42 The Living Seas This is probably the best pavilion at EPCOT. Reputed to have cost more than $90 million, it is the world's largest man-made saltwater aquarium. It holds 5.7 million gallons of seawater, and has a coral reef sheltering more than 80 species of tropical fish, including sharks, and mammals, such as dolphins. Start your trip here aboard "hydrolator" (actually an elevator) which takes you to the bottom of the sea (to be honest, the hydrolator shakes you around without descending even an inch; the view through the glass rotates to simulate motion). You're dumped out at "Sea Base Alpha," a large area where you'll want to linger. Here you can talk to divers entering or leaving the aquarium via a gigantic acrylic tube that fills up with seawater when the diver is ready. There are also special displays of sea life, including one that houses evil-looking moray eels.

Within the Living Seas pavilion:

Coral Reef Restaurant ★★$$ Dine on seafood as you watch it swim by. One wall of the restaurant is made up of specially engineered acrylic panels of the Living Seas giant aquarium. For those who like to watch but not eat animals of the sea, the restaurant also serves some pasta dishes. ◆ Seafood ◆ Daily 11:30AM-3PM, 4:30-8:45PM. Reservations recommended

43 The Land The main show here is "Listen to the Land," an overly earnest, already outdated "cruise" through time that purports to show the way food has been produced. You get a

glimpse of a tropical rain forest, the African desert, the American Plains, and an old-fashioned farm. The only thing that consistently grabs people's imagination is the quick look at a greenhouse where futuristic agricultural methods are employed. Unfortunately, the "cruise ship" is moving almost too fast for you to see much. If you're a real agriculture freak, though, you can schedule a tour of the greenhouse led by an agricultural expert. The tour takes 45 minutes and requires reservations.

Within the Land pavilion:

The Land Grille Room $$ This revolving restaurant serves steak, chops, chicken, and seafood that's overshadowed by the more exotic restaurants at EPCOT Center. A better bet, if your kids need immediate feeding, is **Farmer's Market,** a food court with a little of everything, including pasta and sandwiches. Both restaurants serve breakfast, lunch, and dinner. ◆ Daily 9-10:30AM, 11:15AM-3PM, 4:30-8:30PM

Grapefruit is Florida's second most important crop after oranges. But unlike the Florida orange business, which has been battered at times by Brazil's huge orange juice industry, the grapefruit has virtually no competition.

44 Communicore West Here at Expo Robotics you can have your portrait drawn by a robot, or watch five robots put on a show with spinning tops. As you stand in an assigned spot, a TV camera scans your face, transmitting information about it back to a computer. High-speed image processing is fed to the robot and your portrait is complete in less than three minutes. At the opposite end of the room, other robots delicately balance spinning tops on the edge of a sword, atop a wooden stick, on a rope, etc.

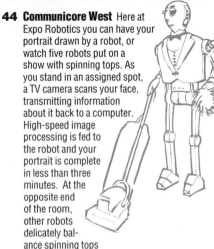

At Communicore West:

Sunrise Terrace Restaurant ★$$ Mostly serving fast food, this restaurant has finally added a decent salad and pasta dishes. It serves only lunch and dinner. ♦ American ♦ Daily 11AM-5PM

45 Journey Into Imagination After **Michael Eisner** and **Frank Wells** were appointed to head Walt Disney Co. in 1984, they paid big bucks to rework this pavilion, with stunning results. The most talked-about change was the replacement of the too-sweet 3-D movie with another 3-D flick directed by **Francis Ford Coppola** and starring rock star **Michael Jackson** as "Captain EO," who fights the forces of evil. The lasers and special effects make the movie worth waiting for. Elsewhere in the pavilion there are appealing shows, including one starring **Dreamfinder** and his devilish companion, **Figment,** who charmingly illustrate how our imagination works.

46 Canada The 360-degree Circlevision film about Canada in this pavilion doesn't seem to dazzle most visitors, although it's well worth seeing. There are the usual shots of Canadian mounties on horseback, but the film also depicts the magical ways in which this nation celebrates winter. The images of snowy, icy Canadian cities are enchantingly beautiful.

Within the Canada pavilion:

Le Cellier $$ The buffet-cafeteria here serves lunch and dinner only, and features Canadian fare, including pork pie and rib roast. Canadian beer is served, too. ♦ Canadian ♦ Daily 11AM-8:30PM

Northwest Mercantile A shop with Canadian crafts, including Indian and Eskimo clothing, moccasins, and luxurious sheepskin rugs that look perfect for dozing on near an open hearth. ♦ Daily 9AM-9PM

47 United Kingdom When EPCOT first opened, this pavilion was often bypassed because it didn't have a glitzy travelogue film on Great Britain. But that was before people discovered the **Rose and Crown Pub.** Now the cozy pub is always packed. American tourists delight in the British accents of the convivial employees— many of them British students working in a special Disney employment program—as they serve up Bass, Guinness, and Harp ales and stouts from behind the bar. Brews are also served outside on a terrace overlooking World Showcase Lagoon. It is an excellent place to watch IllumiNations.

Also at the United Kingdom pavilion:

Rose & Crown Dining Room $$ Americans who have crossed the Atlantic often come back grousing about the British food, but it's hard to understand why if you eat here. The meat pies and delicious teas make a fine meal. ♦ British ♦ Daily 11AM-closing. Reservations recommended

Pringle of Scotland It's hard to get excited about sweaters most of the time in Florida, but these are the real thing. The shop also sells rich tartan kilts and ties. ♦ 9AM-9PM

48 International Gateway Here, between the pavilions of the United Kingdom and France, you can catch trams and boats for Disney resort hotels—including the Walt Disney World Swan and Dolphin hotels and the Port Orleans Resort—and to the Disney-MGM Studios Theme Park.

The Living Seas at Walt Disney World's EPCOT Center is the world's largest aquarium, with a 27-foot-deep tank that holds almost six million gallons of seawater. It was built in 1986 at a cost of $90 million. Disney's animal-care experts collected many of the fish (including sharks) and marine mammals during numerous trips to the Florida Keys. When the time came to dedicate the pavilion, Frank Wells, president of the Walt Disney Co., donned a wetsuit and scuba gear to cut the ribbon under 20 feet of water.

49 France Although the 360-degree Circlevision film at the China pavilion wins consistent raves, the more conventional show here, *Impressions de France,* is the favorite of many EPCOT aficionados. You'll be ready to book your trip to France afterward. Enhanced by a ravishingly beautiful soundtrack with snippets of **Debussy** and **Saint-Saëns,** the film takes you on a quick tour of present-day France, through a lively marketplace, past stately châteaux, and into the countryside.

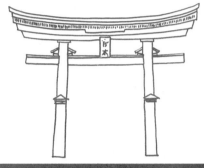

And, unlike the Circlevision movies, you get to watch sitting down, in comfortable, theater-style seats. This is a don't-miss film.

At the France pavilion:

Chefs de France ★★$$$ This restaurant serves up traditional French cuisine, but some dishes have lighter sauces than you might find in Paris. Start with baked oysters in champagne sauce. For a main dish try the roast duck with prunes and wine sauce or filet of grouper baked in puff pastry. ◆ French ◆ Daily 11AM-9PM. Reservations required

Boulangerie Patisserie ★★★$ Delectable pastries and croissants are served here. ◆ French ◆ Daily 9AM-9PM

Plume et Palette Stop here for delicate Limoges porcelain items and mementos; next door **La Maison du Vin** sells wine and wine accessories, including many vintages that are hard to find in Central Florida. **Tout Pour Le Gourmet** has, as the name suggests, everything for the gourmet cook, including exotic foodstuffs. ◆ Daily 9AM-9PM

50 Morocco The winding entrance into this pavilion gives you the feel of a Middle Eastern bazaar. Along the way, **Casablanca Carpets** sells handmade rugs and wall hangings, and **Tangier Traders** sells leather goods and Moroccan clothing. But the real reason to go to the Morocco pavilion is **Restaurant Marrakesh.**

Restaurant Marrakesh ★★★$$$ You say you don't know what Moroccan food is? Come

on, take a chance. Start with the fragrant bread dusted with poppy seeds, and move on to a Middle Eastern favorite, couscous. For an entrée try the roast lamb or a sampler platter offered at lunch and consisting of broiled chicken brochette, chicken bastila (chopped chicken with almonds and cinnamon wrapped in phillo dough), beef brewat (similar to a meat-filled egg roll), and couscous. For dinner there's a similar sampler. ◆ Moroccan ◆ Daily 11:30AM-9PM. Reservations recommended

51 Japan The show here is basically at the restaurant, where food is prepared at your table. However, **Bijutsu-kan Gallery** has a permanent exhibit that features both traditional and modern Japanese art.

At the Japan pavilion:

Mitsukoshi Restaurant The restaurant is divided into two parts. For tempura, try **Tempura Kiku,** a cozy corner spot near the front; if you want stir-fry, wait to be seated in one of the **Teppanyaki Dining Rooms.**

Tempura Kiku ★$$ The quality of the batter-fried meats, seafood, and vegetables varies here. Real Japanese-food lovers are likely to be disappointed. But the Kirin beer is always cold. ◆ Japanese ◆ Daily 11AM-9PM

Teppanyaki Dining Rooms ★★$$$ You'll be escorted with your party to one of many small dining rooms here, where your chef introduces himself and you choose an entrée of steak or seafood that he or she chops and stir-fries, with much panache, on the grill at your table. The restaurant also serves Kirin beer and sake. ◆ Japanese ◆ Daily 11AM-9PM. Reservations recommended

Matsu No Ma Lounge ★$$ This is a great place to take a respite from the Florida heat. The bar serves exotic mixed drinks, sushi, and other small appetizers. ◆ Japanese ◆ Daily 11AM-9PM

Mitsukoshi Department Store It's fun to look around here, but it seems that Mitsukoshi, the giant Tokyo department store, has stocked this EPCOT store with the lowest common denominator of goods. There are some pretty Japanese dolls, though, as well as beautiful fine porcelain and unusual stationery items.

52 The American Adventure If you consider yourself a real patriot, you won't mind waiting to see the show in this pavilion, which is billed as the "dramatic and inspirational story of America and its people" told through a mix of motion pictures and Disney's famous audio-animatronic figures. But others should be warned that the show here has been criticized for its sanitized, Disneyized version of American history that leaves out the sorrows of Vietnam and other tragedies.

At the American Adventure pavilion:

Liberty Inn $ Appropriately, hamburgers, hot dogs, and apple pie are available at this restaurant. ♦ American ♦ Daily 11AM-9PM

American Garden Theatre Across from the American Adventure pavilion and overlooking World Showcase Lagoon, this open-air stage features entertainment, some of it from around the world. Check with pavilion employees for a schedule of entertainment.

53 Italy There's no film on Italy and its wonders here, but the pavilion does house EPCOT's favorite eatery, **L'Originale Alfredo di Roma Ristorante.**

At the Italy pavilion:

L'Originale Alfredo di Roma Ristorante ★★★$$$ This restaurant serves up a creamy, delicious version of—what

else?—fettuccine Alfredo. Try an Italian wine to make your meal even that much more like the real thing. In the evening, waiters belt out arias from favorite operas as they serve you. ♦ Italian ♦ Daily noon-9PM. Reservations recommended

Delizie Italiane Perugina chocolate, cookies, and candies can all be found here. **La Bottega Italiane** features pretty leather and straw purses, belts, and ties. **Il Bel Cristallo** specializes in inlaid music boxes and alabaster figures.

54 Germany This is another pavilion without a travelogue film, but the **Biergarten Restaurant,** serving hearty German fare, is worth a visit.

At the Germany pavilion:

Biergarten Restaurant $$ An oompah band plays from a bandstand while you dine at communal tables in a large indoor beer garden. Beck's beer and H. Schmitt Sohne wines are served to make the meal merrier. Sauerbraten (roast beef marinated in vinegar, water, wine, and spices) or grilled bratwurst with potato salad makes for a filling meal. ♦ German ♦ Daily noon-9PM

Sommerfest $ Here you can buy soft pretzels, bratwurst, desserts, and beer.

Glas und Porzellan This is the place for the Hummel figurine lover. Goebel giftware is also sold here. ♦ Daily 9AM-9PM

Die Weihnachts Ecke This cute shop features nutcrackers and German Christmas items. ♦ Daily 9AM-9PM

Der Teddybar Traditional German toys including dolls and that perennial favorite, the teddy bear, can be found here. ♦ Daily 9AM-9PM

55 China *Wonders of China*, a 360-degree Circlevision film, has been a longstanding favorite since EPCOT threw open its gates in late 1982. The enchanting movie manages, in less than 20 minutes, to give you a glimpse of the vastness and diversity of that huge nation. You stand and watch the film all around you, with its breathtaking scenery, from the mysterious stone forest of the Yunnan Province to the Great Wall, where you feel you are actually on the wall with people in front of and behind you.

At the China pavilion:

Nine Dragons Restaurant $$ The restaurant offers tastes from many different provinces. The fare here isn't bad, but it's often bland and uninspired. ♦ Chinese ♦ Daily 11AM-9PM

Lotus Blossom Cafe ★$ The sweet-and-sour chicken is fine, and the egg rolls are always good for a quick snack. ♦ Chinese ♦ Daily 10:30AM-9PM

Walt Disney wanted the EPCOT Center to be a city where people could live, work, and play. The late visionary wanted EPCOT to include schools, churches, recreational areas, residential housing, people movers (like monorails), and an "airport of the future." When Disney died, executives thought his plans were too sketchy and abandoned the idea. Although EPCOT Center doesn't have the residential environment Walt Disney envisioned, a new Disney project may. Called "Celebration," the development planned for Disney's land in Osceola County calls for residential housing, a huge shopping mall, hiking and bicycling trails, a center for the performing arts, and maybe a "think tank" on a campus-like setting where business, civic, and art groups can brainstorm. Celebration is expected to take 25 years to complete.

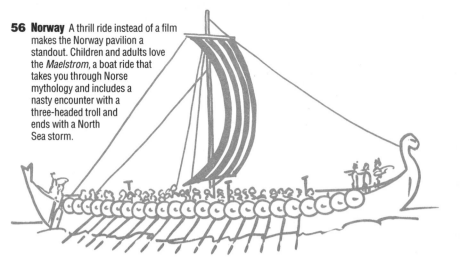

56 Norway A thrill ride instead of a film makes the Norway pavilion a standout. Children and adults love the *Maelstrom*, a boat ride that takes you through Norse mythology and includes a nasty encounter with a three-headed troll and ends with a North Sea storm.

At the Norway pavilion:

Restaurant Akershus ★★$$$ Norwegian food isn't something that Americans easily identify with, and that's too bad. This restaurant offers much more diversity than most, serving up a varied buffet that features authentically prepared cold dishes, such as delicate herring or salmon, as well as hot and hearty meatballs, and roast chicken. And don't forget the wonderful bread. There's Ringnes beer, too. ◆ Norwegian ◆ Daily 11:30AM-8:30PM. Reservations recommended

Kringla Bakeri og Kafe ★★$ For a nice change from hot dogs, try a Norwegian pastry. Scandinavians practically wrote the book on open-faced sandwiches, and these are splendid. ◆ Norwegian ◆ Daily 9AM-9PM

The Puffin's Roost Porcelain, glass, pewter, and wood knickknacks are sold here. ◆ Daily 9AM-9PM

57 Mexico The ride here, El Rio del Tiempo, takes visitors on boats down that so-called river of time, providing a wholly inadequate glimpse of Mexican history. Unless you are with a small child, skip it and enjoy a meal at the excellent restaurant instead.

Within the Mexico pavilion:

San Angel Inn Restaurant ★★★$$$ A sister restaurant to the renowned San Angel Inn in Mexico City, this is one of the standout restaurants at EPCOT Center. The ambience is unmatched: The restaurant is lit to a purple shade at dusk, while the still-active volcano Popocatepetl looms. It's Disney Imagineering at its best. As for food, try the tender chicken enchiladas, or if you're daring, anything with *mole* (chocolate) sauce. You can get Dos Equis and Sol beers, or a mean margarita. But remember, this isn't Tex-Mex food, so you won't get chips with hot sauce the minute you sit down. ◆ Mexican ◆ Daily 11AM-9PM. Reservations recommended

Plaza de Los Amigos Here's the place to buy that sombrero you need to protect yourself from the Florida sun. ◆ Daily 9AM-9PM

Artesanias Mexicanas Here you'll find ceramics for sale and edifying glass-blowing demonstrations. ◆ Daily 9AM-9PM

Cantina de San Angel ★$ Mexican fast food and a patio on the World Showcase Lagoon are the attractions here. This is also a good place to view IllumiNations. ◆ Mexican ◆ Daily 10:30AM-9PM

58 Odyssey Restaurant $ Routine fare is served here, with hamburgers, hot dogs, and chicken sandwiches. There are some decent salads for calorie-watchers. ◆ American ◆ Daily 11AM-9PM

59 Lost Children Office You can get help in finding your lost child here, or by calling 560.7928. Next door is a **First Aid** station.

60 World of Motion This often humorous show is a ride through the evolution of transportation, and includes 22 tableaux filled with Disney's patented audio-animatronic figures.

Another worthwhile stop within the World of Motion pavilion is **Transcenter.** Here you can get a hands-on look at futuristic automobiles, as well as more familiar models.

Restaurants/Nightlife: Red   **Hotels:** Blue
Shops/ ☂ Outdoors: Green   **Sights/Culture:** Black

61 Horizons This show is an enjoyable mish-mash. Portions of the "ride through the lifestyles of the 21st century" become tiresome, such as the look at the visions of futurists of the past, including **Jules Verne,** who was never so bland. Then it's off to explore four Disneyized visions of the future, including a desert farm run by robots and a "space city" where people mine asteroids. The show ends in a clever way, though, as visitors choose one of several possible endings.

62 Wonders of Life The big attraction here is Body Wars, a thrill ride that pairs a genuine flight simulator—basically a fancy platform whose pneumatically controlled motion mimics that of an airplane—with a film. Once strapped into your seat, you're taken on a fast-moving trip through the human body. Veering and swooping, the simulator is real enough to give some people motion-sickness, but most everyone loves it. A similar ride called Star Tours is at the Disney-MGM Studios Theme Park.

Inside the Wonders of Life pavilion:

Cranium Command This is a clever show in which the audience gets a look at what happens inside the head of a 12-year-old boy as he negotiates his way through a typical day. Audio-animatronic figures representing parts of the body argue in lively fashion with Cranium Commando, his brain.

The Making of Me It's hard to believe, but this endearing film about pregnancy and birth was criticized by some Disney-loving diehards, who initially felt it was out of character for

EPCOT Center

Disney when the pavilion opened a few years ago. But Walt Disney Co. chairman **Michael Eisner** backed it from the beginning. The film manages to deal with the mysteries of human reproduction in a charming way.

Coach's Corner Here you swing a golf club, baseball bat, or tennis racquet, and you'll get a videotaped comment from a sports pro. An instant replay also compares your swing, captured on videotape, with that of a professional.

Met Lifestyle Revue Embarrass yourself in front of your friends by punching your health habits into the computer. You'll get a printout telling you what you can do to live a more healthful lifestyle.

AnaComical Players A troupe of actors presents skits on various health-related topics.

Pure & Simple ★★$ A good place for a healthful, low-fat snack, the restaurant serves salads, sandwiches, and good waffles with fruit toppings. There are fruit drinks instead of the usually ubiquitous sodas. ♦ American ♦ Daily 9AM-9PN '

Walt Disney World stopped announcing its attendance figures in 1984, but *Amusement Business* magazine, a trade journal, estimates the turnstiles at the giant resort click about 28 to 30 million times a year (a figure that includes multiple-day ticket holders who enter the park more than once).

63 Universe of Energy This don't-miss pavilion opens with an entertaining multiscreen slide show, then moves on to a short film about the mysteries of the forces of energy within the earth. The whiz-bang stuff begins as you ride on "sunshine," or solar-powered, cars through a primeval jungle where dinosaurs roam. The show ends with an erupting volcano.

64 Disney's Yacht & Beach Club Resorts $$$$ Designed by **Robert Stern** in 1990 to look like two distinctly different New England turn-of-the-century inns set down in Florida, these sister hotels have a combined 1,214 rooms. The Yacht Club is a five-story, oyster-gray clapboard seaside summer cottage, and the Beach Club is a blue-and-white seaside hotel. Rooms have private balconies and one king-sized bed or two queens. There are 200 rooms on the concierge level. Rooms are available for the physically disabled and non-smokers. **Stormalong Bay,** a 2.5-acre water park behind the resort, features waterslides from the deck of a shipwrecked vessel and one of Disney's niftiest touches: a freshwater pool stocked with live fish and another pool with a sandy bottom. They're a gas for swimmers. From both hotels you can walk to EPCOT Center or take a water taxi to the Disney-MGM Studios Theme Park. The hotels also share a beauty salon, laundry facilities, a daycare center, and a game arcade. Another attraction is the nightly clambake on the hotels' sandy beach. ♦ 1700 and 1800 EPCOT Resort Blvd (Buena Vista Dr) 934.7639

At the Disney's Yacht & Beach Club Resorts:

Yachtsman's Steakhouse ★★$$$ This restaurant displays prime cuts of beef in a glass-enclosed, beef-aging room where you can watch the chefs cook your steak and vegetables over hardwood-fired grills. For breakfast, try the "crow's nest," a batter-dipped, french-fried bagel rolled in cinnamon sugar and topped with a cranberry-apple compote. ♦ American ♦ Daily 6-10PM

Yacht Club Galley $$ Economically priced meals are served here all day. Breakfast is buffet-style or à la carte, and lunch and dinner include hearty soups, salads, and tasty sandwiches served on fresh-baked bread. Entrées include tender fried clams or prime rib. ♦ American ♦ Daily 7-11AM, 11:30AM-4PM, 5-10PM

Ariel's at the Beach Club ★★$$$ This New England-style restaurant overlooks the hotel's Stormalong Bay; inside it has an eye-catching, 2,000-gallon aquarium stocked with brightly hued tropical fish and wild, colorful fish mobiles hanging overhead. Fresh fish, as you might guess, is the specialty. Try the catch of the day, which is cooked over a flame and served on fine porcelain dishes. Other goodies include the New England silver dollar crabcakes and the sweet lobster pasta with lemon-garlic butter. ♦ Seafood ♦ Daily 6-10PM

Beaches & Cream ★$ An original Wurlitzer jukebox pumps out hits from the forties, fifties, and sixties as you dine on a juicy "Fenway Park burger" or dig into an ice cream concoction. ♦ American ♦ Daily 7-10:30AM, 11AM-midnight

65 Walt Disney World Dolphin $$$$ Some critics are put off by the looks of this hotel and its sister, the Walt Disney World Swan, but others think both hotels' fanciful touches are perfect, given their location next to the world's most popular theme parks. When Walt Disney Co. chairman Michael Eisner commissioned Princeton architect **Michael Graves** (with New York architect **Alan Lapidus**) to design the hotels, Eisner told them he didn't want the hotels to be boring. They aren't. Those who prefer something a little more austere are taken aback by chandeliers that look like monkeys and hallway benches that sprout giant palm trees. Perhaps these critics can't take a joke. This hotel's namesake dolphins—actually two mythical, funny-looking fish—rise 55 feet above the hotel's roof, and the 27-story triangular tower is dramatic when viewed from below. A pattern of waves and banana leaves decorate the exterior walls. Inside, the walls are hung with beautifully framed but inexpensive prints by **Matisse, Chagall,** and California artist **Ken Done.** The 1,509-room Dolphin is the largest hotel in Florida. Rooms aren't cheap, but the location is excellent: Hotel guests can walk or take a tram or water taxi from the hotel to EPCOT Center or to the Disney-MGM Studios Theme Park. The hotel has three pools, including a beautifully landscaped rock grotto, a health club with up-to-the-minute equipment, a beauty salon, eight lighted tennis courts, and desks for National Rent A Car and Delta Air Lines. ♦ 1500 EPCOT Resort Blvd (Buena Vista Dr) 934.4000, 800/227.1500; fax 934.4099

Tourism is Florida's biggest business; the state lured about 40.9 million tourists in 1990, up from 38.7 million in 1989. Who are these folks? The typical tourist is from New York and has a household income of about $44,000 a year, stays 7.8 nights in a hotel or motel, and rents a car. His or her (and it's more likely to be a woman) number one destination is the Orlando-Walt Disney World area.

Within the Walt Disney World Dolphin Hotel:

Sum Chows ★★$$$ This stylish but casual restaurant serves a variety of regional Chinese foods. ♦ Chinese ♦ Daily 6-11PM. Reservations recommended

Ristorante Carnevale $$ Italian specialties, especially from northern Italy, highlight the menu. In the manner of a Venetian festival, strolling musicians, jugglers, and opera singers entertain while you dine. ♦ Italian ♦ Tu-Sa 6-11PM. Reservations recommended; character brunch with Chip and Dale, Donald Duck, and Goofy. Su 9AM-1PM. 934.4000

66 Walt Disney World Swan Hotel $$$$ Designed by **Michael Graves** in 1989, the 758-room Swan is half the size of its sister hotel. Two 47-foot-high, 56,000-pound swans grace the crown of the hotel, which is painted in a colorful pattern of aquamarine-and-coral waves. The 12-story building has two seven-story wings, and it overlooks **Crescent Lake,** which has a beach, playground, and wading area. West of the hotel is a free-form grotto pool with waterslides, three Jacuzzi tubs, and a patio bar. Next to the grotto is a tennis center with eight hard courts, four of them lighted. Guests can walk, take a tram, or ride a water taxi to EPCOT Center or to the Disney-MGM Studios Theme Park. ♦ 1200 EPCOT Resort Blvd (Buena Vista Dr) 934:3000, 800/228.3000; fax 934.1399

Within the Walt Disney World Swan Hotel:

Palio ★★$$$ Fine Italian specialties, from anti-pasti and salads to pizzas made in a wood-fired

brick oven and pasta dishes topped with veal, shrimp, or calamari. As you enter the restaurant, located in the east lobby wing, you can watch chefs work in the open kitchen. Hand-painted porcelain plates line the walls, and flags representing different counties of Italy hang from the ceiling. The Tuscan scene on the enormous mural hanging in the restaurant was painted by **Ani Rosskam.** The restaurant also has an extensive Italian wine list. ♦ Italian ♦ Daily 5-11PM. Reservations recommended. 934.3000

Kimonos ★★$$ This posh lounge, with touches of rich teakwood and authentic kimonos on display, has a sushi bar serving tuna, octopus, yellowtail, salmon, and squid. There are selection for non-sushi fanciers, too, including hot hors d'oeuvres and teriyaki. ♦ Japanese ♦ Daily 4PM-1AM. 934.3000

Garden Grove Cafe $$ Enter this restaurant by walking past an open window where bakers are creating tempting pastries. The cafe, which looks like a large greenhouse, is also a good place to dine on fresh fish. Hot and cold buffets are available. ♦ American ♦ Daily 6:30AM-11PM. 934.3000

Restaurants/Nightlife: Red Hotels: Blue
Shops/ ♟Outdoors: Green Sights/Culture: Black

Disney-MGM Studios

Looming over Disney's 110-acre version of Hollywood is a 13-story water tower topped with—what else—Mickey Mouse ears. Besides the "Earffel Tower," as it's been dubbed, this park features television and movie studios and a plethora of entertaining attractions, not to mention a large selection of restaurants.

Disney-MGM Studios is arranged in four segments: **Hollywood Boulevard, Studio Courtyard, Backstage Studio Tour,** and **Backlot Annex.** If you want to dine in one of the four full-service restaurants, go immediately to the **50's Prime Time Cafe, Studio Pizzeria, Sci-Fi Dine-In The-ater Restaurant,** or **The Hollywood Brown Derby** and make reservations. Reserved seating can also be arranged at **Guest Relations** or at **Restaurant Reservations,** and the booths are set up to the right of The Hollywood Brown Derby. If you are staying on Disney property, you can make reservations up to two days in advance. From Disney-owned hotels, call 828.4000; from Disney-property hotels, call 824.8800. Most of the restaurants offer low-cholesterol, low-fat selections.

Area code 407 unless otherwise indicated.

Hollywood Boulevard

After passing through the Entrance Plaza, which is designed to look like the lobby area of the grand old movie studios of the thirties and forties, you will enter a small plaza dominated by a statue of Mickey Mouse on top of a circular kiosk. It's called **Crossroads of the World,** and this is where you can get information and souvenirs. Check for times of live performances, parades, and the spectacular evening fireworks display. If you get to the park just after the gates open, walk straight down Hollywood Boulevard, through the Studio Gate Arch, and begin with the animation and Backlot tours. Save the souvenirs for the end of your visit. And as you walk down the boulevard keep your eyes open for any one of a number of street actors, such as the autograph hound or the flim-flam man.

In this area:

Oscar's Super Service, an old-time gas station with a 1947 Buick parked in front, is where you will find lockers, strollers, wheelchairs, and automotive memorabilia such as vanity license plates, key chains, mugs, and models. To your left is the hospitality building (first aid, lost and found, guest relations, baby services). Up the street is **Movieland Memorabilia** (souvenirs) and **Sid Cahuenga's One-of-a-Kind,** which is worth wandering through to see authentic old costumes, old movie posters, and promotional photos. All items are for sale.

Heading up the boulevard, on your right is **The Darkroom,** where you can rent cameras or purchase film; **Cover Story,** where you can dress up and have your picture put on the cover of a magazine; **Celebrity 5 & 10,** where movie memorabilia is housed in what looks like an old five-and-dime store; **Sweet Success,** purveyors of fancy candy, including postcards made of chocolate; and **Legends of Hollywood,** where you can dress up and star in your own home video, plus buy a bunch of movie merchandise. On the left going up the boulevard is **Mickey's of Hollywood,** this park's one-stop Disney merchandise mart.

If you cross the street and continue up the boulevard, there is a small island of three stores on your left: **Keystone Clothiers,** where you can buy just about any article of clothing with Mickey or Minnie on it; **Lakeside News** offers comic books, old magazines, and souvenirs; and **Sights & Sounds** provides an opportunity to record your own video.

Hollywood Boulevard eventually spills into a pleasantly landscaped plaza where you'll see **Theatre of the Stars,** an open-air stage where Disney characters perform song-and-dance shows with a movie theme. A posted schedule announces when the Star of the Week will be on hand to perform or just talk with the guests. Next to the theater is **Starring Roles,** a bakery attached to **The Hollywood Brown Derby.**

Restaurants/Nightlife: Red
Shops/ 🌴Outdoors: Green
Hotels: Blue
Sights/Culture: Black

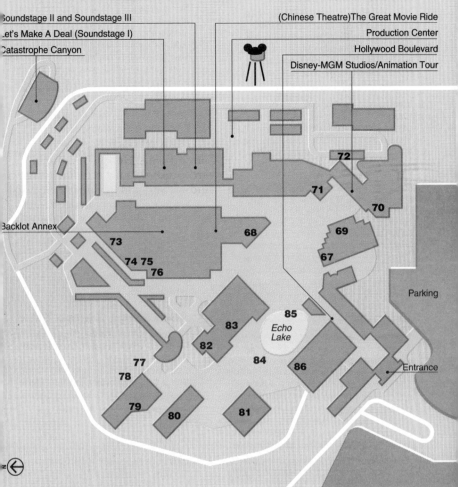

Soundstage II and Soundstage III

Let's Make A Deal (Soundstage I)

Catastrophe Canyon

(Chinese Theatre)The Great Movie Ride

Production Center

Hollywood Boulevard

Disney-MGM Studios/Animation Tour

Backlot Annex

Echo Lake

Parking

Entrance

67 The Hollywood Brown Derby ★★$$$
From the pictures of the stars on the walls to the little derby-shaped brass lamps, this restaurant is modeled faithfully after the famous Brown Derby in Hollywood. The Cobb salad of Brown Derby fame is served here, and although the restaurant is usually filled with adults, a children's menu is available. ♦ American ♦ Daily 11AM-3:30PM, 4:30-7PM. Reservations recommended

68 Chinese Theatre At the end of Hollywood Boulevard is this remarkable reproduction of Grauman's (now Mann Corp's) Chinese Theater. After watching some big-screen action, visitors board a tram for **The Great Movie Ride.** It travels past about 60 audio-animatronic figures right out of the movies. Old-time movie buffs will enjoy this immensely, as will youngsters, who may not have seen some of the flicks, but who will get a kick out of the interaction between live and audio-animatronic figures. Highlights include a Gene Kelly figure dancing in the rain, John Wayne fighting bank robbers, and scenes from *Casablanca* and *The Wizard of Oz.*

Studio Courtyard

To avoid long lines, go to the **Disney-MGM Studios Animation Tour** first thing in the morning, immediately after making dining reservations. Remember, the artists are real; they have a life and they don't usually stick around after working hours.

In the Studio Courtyard area:

69 **Soundstage Restaurant** ★$$ The entrance is a movie set of the Plaza Hotel in New York City, as seen in the movie, *Big Business*. Walk through the set to the back, where there are three serving areas. One serves pasta and pizza (don't overlook the cold pasta salad), another makes sandwiches (chicken salad, meatball, and the big meat and cheese combination), the third offers soup and salad. Each has a children's menu, with such delicacies as peanut butter-jelly-marshmallow cream sandwiches and chocolate chip pie. Tables are scattered everywhere through the set, which includes phony elevators, a glittering chandelier, and a formal staircase that leads to an upstairs bar and restrooms. ◆ Daily, pizza and pasta 10AM-7PM, sandwiches 11AM-6PM, soup and salad 11AM-5PM

Within the Soundstage Restaurant:

The Catwalk Bar $$ This is the niftiest place to wash down a plate of shrimp with a cold, wet one or just to relax with cheese, fruit, and wine. To get to the bar above the food serving area, walk up the formal staircase of the movie set to the right of the entrance, or up a backstage staircase to the left of the entrance. The bar gives the feeling of being up on a catwalk—those narrow walkways used by technicians to move around above stages. This one, however,

is wide enough for tables, chairs, a bar, and plenty of props. ◆ Daily 11AM-6:30 PM

70 **Disney-MGM Studios Animation Tour** This could have been a disaster, where parents, who grew up with Disney animated cartoons, drag their bored children through a building of people working behind glass windows. But it is saved by the unlikely duo of **Robin Williams** and **Walter Cronkite,** who are

introduced in a film at a movie theater where Williams becomes an animated figure. After this short feature, you proceed into the working area, and with Williams and Cronkite appearing on monitors, you have the opportunity to stop at each animation department and to view the artists as they work. You will see how story line and characters are developed right on through to the final step of editing, where the scenes are finally put together. Along the way you'll see artists create characters, develop backgrounds, and add color. When you leave this two-level room, you enter the **Disney Classics Theater** to watch highlights of Disney's best animated movies. The **Animation Gallery** is a gift shop attached to the Animation Building.

71 **"Here Come the Muppets"** Rolf entertains you from overhead monitors as you wait to enter; unfortunately there are only two monitors, and it is difficult to hear. Once inside, Kermit is the host of a song-and-dance show, which includes favorite jokes and songs from the Muppet menagerie. **The Muppet Store** is next door to **The Disney Studio Store** for souvenirs.

Backstage Studio Tour

This tour can take a couple of hours, depending on how long you care to spend in the backlot area. It begins with a tram ride through the production center, and follows with an hour-long walking tour through the sound stages and the special effects studios.

In the Backstage Studio Tour are:

72 **Tram Tour** If you are traveling with children, let them get on the tram first so they can sit on the left side; there will be a surprise in store for them along the way. If you hit this attraction early, the lines won't be too long. Even so, as you wait, you are entertained by overhead monitors in which **Carol Burnett** and **Tom Selleck** host a quick history of the Disney Studios. Once aboard, the tram rolls past an area where trees and shrubbery are grown and sculpted for use on sets, and then past costuming and crafts shops. The tram then emerges onto what looks like a residential street. Actually, these are shells used for outdoor scenes. The house where **The Golden Girls** live is here, and you will also see **Herbie the Love Bug.** After winding around some more props, you will come to **Catastrophe Canyon,** where you don't just get to see special effects, but will actually experience some. First there is a rainstorm, then an explosion in which you will feel the heat of the flames, followed by a flash flood; those sitting on the left get sprayed with water, those on the right don't. When it is over, the tram goes behind Catastrophe Canyon to show you the water cannons and sophisticated machinery that creates the realistic disaster. The tram then shuttles you to the New York street scene.

After getting off the tram, follow the large, purple paw prints of **Roger Rabbit.** It will lead you into **The Loony Bin** and **Fototoons.** Better than the souvenirs on sale here, this is a place where weird sounds emerge from a variety of boxes as you open them. There are large cutouts of Toontown favorites and plenty of fun photo opportunities.

If you feel like taking a detour before continuing on the tour, walk down the two blocks of New York City toward the removable Empire State Building and Chrysler Building props. The path on the right leads behind these buildings, back into the park, and right to the entrance of **Star Tours** (see Backlot Annex). If the line isn't long, go to Star Tours, a ride you will probably want to do twice, anyway. Then return and go to **Jim Henson's Muppet Vision 3D.**

73 Walking Tour Stroll back down the New York street scene to a sign marked **Inside the Magic;** this is the beginning of the **Special Effects and Production Tour.** Lines get long for this portion of the backstage studio tour, but **Goldie Hawn** and **Rick Moranis** keep you entertained on overhead monitors. Two volunteers among the visitors are given raincoats as they help demonstrate how a storm at sea and a sea battle are filmed at the **Water Effects Tank.** The next building is the **Special Effects Workshop and Shooting Stage**—better known as the prop room. A gigantic bee is suspended from the ceiling, and two children picked from among the guests show how filming against a blue screen works. One child is placed on the bee's back and another on its wing. A scene from *Honey, I Shrunk the Kids,* is re-created and then the action is played back with different backgrounds and bits of the real movie spliced in. Generally, something is going on in one of the three **soundstages** you walk through next. When the first soundstage is empty, it is sometimes used as the **"Let's Make a Deal"** attraction, where guests can play, and the show is taped to be sold as a souvenir. Guests interested in participating in the game-show taping should call 560.8225. For showtimes for the not-for-TV Let's Make a Deal, check at Soundstage 1 or at the Production and Information window at the main entrance. Then it's on to a funny film by **Bette Midler** about a lucky lottery ticket. The film incorporates just about everything that you have learned on this tour—from stunts to blue screens. The next stop is a building housing props from the Midler film you have just seen. The **Post Production Editing and Audio** area is where the finishing touches are put on a movie. The final stop is **The Walt Disney Theater,** where you get previews of soon-to-be-released movies.

Backlot Annex

The Monster Sound Show, SuperStar Television, Star Tours, and Indiana Jones Epic Stunt Spectacular are the big attractions.

74 Studio Catering Company $$ If you haven't made lunch reservations, this is a good place to refuel. There are sandwiches, salads, plus a plate of cheese and fresh fruit on the menu. Beer, wine, and soft drinks are available.
♦ American ♦ Daily 9AM-6PM

75 *Honey I Shrunk The Kids* Movie Set Adventure In this 11,000-square-foot playground, kids play among 30-foot blades of grass, a 20-foot paper clip, and cereal loops that are nine feet in diameter. Tree stumps are slides, a giant mushroom is actually three levels of interconnecting tunnels, and there is a multilevel spider web that gives kids a pretty good overview once they manage to climb to the top. Youngsters are constantly amazed when they climb the fern sprouts, which emit sounds as they get stepped on.

The Costume Shop Besides masks and makeup, here is where you will find the largest selection of villains at the park. They can be found as toys and even on T-shirts.

76 Sci-Fi Dine-In Theater Restaurant ★★★$$$ The 250-seat restaurant is set up as a 1950s drive-in movie theater. You enter through a ticket lobby and eat in re-creations of old cars. Fiber-optic stars are in the Hollywood Hills night sky. Once you are seated, you are served popcorn, which, by the way, is very good throughout all of Disney World. The club sandwiches and salads are popular, but the Reuben; the sub of grilled, shaved beef; or the

vegetable lasagna are the best bets. While you munch, you can watch old monster and science-fiction films. The sound is delivered through drive-in speakers mounted next to each car. ♦ American ♦ Daily 9 AM-6PM. Reservations recommended.

77 Jim Henson's Muppet Vision 3D The newest Muppet attraction is Jim Henson's Muppet Vision 3D in a 584-seat theater, decorated with red velvet drapes and gilded columns. Muppets will entertain visitors on TV monitors before the theater doors open. Live characters and audio-animatronics interact seamlessly with the movie. **Statler** and **Waldorf** are in mezzanine seats to your right, and behind you, high on the wall, is the **Swedish Chef,** who is the projectionist. A mischievous new character, **Waldo C. Graphic,** is introduced, and he talks to you—face to face. The kids will love the fireworks, and everyone will be astonished when they are actually squirted by a boutonniere. This is the best 3-D movie you will see at any of the parks.

Restaurants/Nightlife: Red   Hotels: Blue
Shops/ 🌳 Outdoors: Green   **Sights/Culture: Black**

Stage One Company Store A large souvenir store, featuring a substantial supply of Toontown trinkets.

78 Studio Pizzeria ★$$$ At the New York street scene set is a back street with the park's newest restaurant, a pizza palace that bakes its pies in brick ovens. Here you can also create your own meal by choosing among fettuccine, rigatoni, or tricolored linguine, and then selecting a topping such as tomato-basil-garlic or white clam sauce. One of the more inexpensive yet tasty entrées on the menu is *pollo al caraibi,* a chicken with Jamaican jerky spice, mushrooms, relish, and papaya. ♦ Italian ♦ Daily 11:30AM–9PM. Reservations recommended.

79 Star Tours A flight simulator ride that really rocks and rolls you. Try to sit near the middle, and remember you can take you eyes off the screen and focus them elsewhere if the motion is getting to you. The story line involves a rookie pilot who is flying off to the Moon of Endor when trouble occurs. Not allowed on board this ride are those with back problems, heart conditions, or women who are pregnant. Children under three are not allowed; children under seven must be accompanied by an adult. **Endor Vendors** is a Star Tours-related gift shop next to Star Tours.

80 Backlot Express ★$$ This is a cafeteria disguised as a workshop. The left side is filled with props and looks like a room in which stunt artists would gather; the right side is set up like a paint shop, complete with paint-splattered decor. There are salad bars in both sections, and another in a glass-enclosed, air conditioned paint shop on the patio. Besides hot dogs and burgers, there is chocolate chip cheesecake. ♦ American ♦ Daily 10:30AM–6PM

Disney-MGM Studios

81 Indiana Jones Epic Stunt Spectacular The lines may look daunting, but the outdoor covered theater holds 2,000. A number of extras are chosen from the audience. The stunts are for real, but the extras are never in any danger. Not so for the stunt people, who fall from buildings and escape from an overturned truck. Three scenes are played out from *Raiders of the Lost Ark.* The stunts are explained amid much action.

82 The Monster Sound Show Visitors are picked from the audience of this 270-seat theater to create the sounds for a haunted-house movie. **David Letterman** is the host on the outdoor monitors. Inside, visitors view a short, funny film with **Chevy Chase** and **Martin Short,** complete with squeaking doors and claps of thunder. Following an explanation of how the sounds were created, the movie is played again, and the volunteer sound-effect artists try to create the correct sounds at the correct times. The results are funny, and so is the surprise ending to the movie. Exit through **SoundWorks,** a hands-on sound effects exhibit.

83 SuperStar Television If there's a bit of the ham in you, or if you've ever wanted to play a part in "I Love Lucy," "Gilligan's Island," "Cheers," or a number of other TV shows, this may be your chance. As you wait to be admitted, volunteers are chosen for parts in 11 segments. (Try to get near the front of the crowd and don't be afraid to raise your voice.) Inside the 1,000-seat theater, the chosen are led backstage for costuming and makeup; other guests take their seats. Amateurs act out their roles on stage, but they appear to be acting opposite the stars of various TV shows on the eight projection screens hanging in the theater. One volunteer plays Ethel Mertz in a classic "I Love Lucy" comic routine, and another hits a home run and is interviewed by **Howard Cosell;** a bar scene from "Cheers" with four volunteers always provides loud laughs.

Golden Age Souvenirs Mainly gifts reflecting old-time television and radio.

84 Dinosaur Gertie's Ice Cream of Extinction $$ Ice cream, yogurt, or a frozen banana for those long waits in line. ♦ Daily 10AM–7PM.

85 Mim and Bill's Dockside Diner $$ This old tub doesn't leave its dock on Echo Lake, but serves salads, sandwiches, and snacks. ♦ Daily 9AM–7PM

86 50's Prime Time Cafe ★★★$$$ Guests sit at kitchen tables or counters straight out of the 1950s and are served meals on Fiesta Ware or TV dinner trays by a family dressed up in fifties garb. TV sets showing clips of old sitcoms in black and white are strategically placed so you will be able to see from wherever you sit. Unfortunately, you end up watching the same clips over and over. You can have a beer with your burger here, and most of the food is straight out of Mom's kitchen: meat loaf, chicken, soup, and salad. While you wait to be served, relax in the **Tune in Lounge.** This place looks like the elephant burial ground for patio furniture. TVs are placed around the room. Beer, wine, and soft drinks are served. ♦ American ♦ Daily 11AM–7PM. Reservations recommended

87 Disney's Fort Wilderness Campground Resort $$$ This 750-acre resort is the best bargain on Walt Disney World property, so book early. There are 785 campsites for hooking up your Winnebago, as well as 407 trailer homes for rent. The trailer homes sleep six and come equipped with a double bed and a bunk bed, a vanity area, a pull-down double bed in the living room, and a fully equipped kitchen and bath. There's also a color TV, telephone, picnic table, and grill. Best of all, a housekeeper stops in daily.

At Disney's Fort Wilderness Campground Resort:

Fort Wilderness Campsites $$ You can hook up your own camper to electrical outlets at these campsites that come with grills and picnic tables. Each campsite section has restrooms, showers, ice machine, laundry, and telephones. No more than 10 people per campsite are allowed, though. This is one of the most heavily wooded and prettiest parts of Walt Disney World's 43 square miles. There are two swimming pools, two lighted tennis courts, biking and jogging paths, and a marina with boats for rent. You can rent horses and ride the trails, or play volleyball, tetherball, or basketball.

88 **Disney's River Country** Conceived as an updated version of Tom Sawyer's swimming hole, River Country doesn't have the plethora of thrill rides present at its sister park, Typhoon Lagoon, but the slides here are plenty of fun. Swing on a rope into Bay Cove or tube through whitewater rapids. A sandy beach has scores of lawn chairs if you just want to soak up some sun. There's a swimming pool with a rock grotto and slide, as well as towels and lockers for rent. ♦ Admission. Daily 10AM-7PM

89 **Discovery Island** Don't let your children miss this chance to see unusual, free-roaming animals and rare waterfowl. Take a short boat ride across Bay Lake from Disney's Contemporary Resort hotel to this 11.5-acre island nature preserve. Once on the island, which is an accredited zoological park, you can wander at your leisure and see more than 100 types of birds. The animal collection also houses Galapagos tortoises, alligators, and some small primates.

90 **Disney's Polynesian Resort** $$$ The first hotel to be built at Walt Disney World, the Polynesian looks a bit dated, but has a loyal following. Not everyone finds the lushly landscaped lobby too hokey—called the Great Ceremonial House, it has three-story coconut palms and a waterfall cascading over lava rock. The hotel has an efficient staff, and rooms are comfortable and well-equipped, most featuring a balcony or patio, two queen beds, and one day bed. The hotel has two swimming pools, and there's a white, sandy beach with a marina. Accessible by monorail. ♦ 800/647.7900

At Disney's Polynesian Resort:

Polynesian Revue Hula dancing, fire jugglers, and a South Seas buffet are part of this outdoor luau, which has won a loyal following of local folks. ♦ Admission. Daily 6:45 and 9:30PM. Reservations required. 934.7639

91 **The Disney Inn** $$$ If you love to play golf and you're touring Disney for the kids' sake, this is a good choice. With just 287 rooms and off the beaten track, the inn is quiet, comfortable, and efficient, and it's located between two PGA Tour championship golf courses: the Magnolia and the Palm. Each of the inn's rooms has two queen-sized beds and a day bed, as well as a patio or balcony with a view of a golf course or one of the two swimming pools. One pool is in the shape of Mickey Mouse. Rooms for nonsmokers. The inn also has a buffet-style restaurant and a snack bar. ♦ 824.2200, 800/647.7900

92 **Disney's Grand Floridian Beach Resort** $$$$ Conceived as Disney's top-of-the-line hotel when it was built in 1988, the Grand Flo-

ridian doesn't disappoint. Patterned after the landmark turn-of-the-century Hotel Del Coronado in San Diego, the Grand Floridian isn't opulent in a European way, but has sweeping verandas and crystal chandeliers. Many rooms have balconies, and the "dormer rooms" feel as if you're staying in a cozy attic in your rich aunt's mansion. Disney's monorail conveniently stops on the hotel's second level. Located on a marina with rental boats, there's a sandy beach along Seven Seas Lagoon, which lies just south of the Magic Kingdom theme park. The 8,000-square-foot swimming pool is a beauty. St. John's Health Club is staffed with knowledgeable personnel, and lawn croquet adds a special touch. Rooms are available for nonsmokers and the physically disabled. There are also suites and concierge rooms with restricted access and free Continental breakfasts. ♦ Deluxe. ♦ 10100 Buena Vista Dr (Floridian Way) 824.3000

At Disney's Grand Floridian Beach Resort:

Victoria & Albert's ★★★$$$$ Standards at this small, sumptuous restaurant probably are the most exacting at Walt Disney World. You'll be seated in an elegant, dome-topped room and served by two waiters, Victoria and Albert. This is a little silly, since neither Queen Victoria nor her prince consort ever served anyone a meal, but that doesn't mean you won't enjoy your prix fix dinner. The menu changes daily. The sautéed breast of duck, succulent and not the least bit fatty, is served with exotic wild rice. For dessert, try one of the restaurant's signature souffles. ♦ American ♦ Daily 6-9:30PM. Jacket and tie required. Reservations required. 824.2383

Narcoosee's ★★$$$ This octagon-shaped restaurant, with its big windows and exposed

beams, has a marvelous view of Seven Seas Lagoon. It serves seafood steamed, sautéed, smoked, or broiled. ♦ Seafood ♦ Daily 11:30AM-10PM

93 **Disney's Contemporary Resort** $$$ A recent renovation has made this 15-story, perennially popular hotel into something out of the Jetsons. But don't hesitate to book a room in this efficiently run resort; you can't beat the convenience or the pure pizazz of the monorail zipping right through its center. The hotel also boasts two swimming pools, a health club, a hair salon, and laundry facilities. It sits on a lagoon with a beach and a marina with rental boats.

At Disney's Contemporary Resort:

Top of the World ★$$ During the daytime, breakfast buffets are the draw; in the evening a musical revue, Broadway at the Top, is the main attraction. Don't miss the Lucite grand piano. ♦ American ♦ Daily 6, 9:15PM. Jackets required, ties optional. Reservations required. Four to 30 days in advance: 934.7639; three days or less in advance: 824.3611. Sunday brunch served 9AM-2PM. 824.3611

Magic Kingdom

This 98-acre park is divided into **Main Street USA** and five lands: **Adventureland**; **Frontierland**, which includes **Liberty Square**; **Fantasyland**; **Mickey's Starland**; and **Tomorrowland**. Each area has at least one major attraction that will have long, long lines. As always, the best strategy is to arrive at least a half hour before the park opens. Besides avoiding the worst of the traffic, you will have time to go from the parking lot to the Transportation and Ticket Center (TTC) and stroll down Main Street USA, where by 8:30 AM there will be a couple of places open for breakfast. Before you arrive, pick out the one can't-miss ride and get there first before it opens at 9AM. Then start in Adventureland and walk clockwise around the park. That way, if you don't get to Tomorrowland, you haven't missed much. If **Space Mountain** (in Tomorrowland) isn't your first ride, save it for dinnertime or later when the lines are shorter, but avoid it right after a *big* dinner (lest you get sick). If you have young children who will get a thrill meeting Mickey Mouse, take the Walt Disney World Railroad to Mickey's Starland to see the characters, then make your way around the park counterclockwise. No matter which way you tour the park, however, your first stop should be City Hall at the entrance to Main Street to check the times of parades, live performances, and the fireworks display.

Trams circle the parking lots regularly, shuttling guests to the TTC. From there, you have a choice of taking the monorail or a ferry across the **Seven Seas Lagoon**. It's more fun to take the monorail because it goes right through the **Contemporary Resort** about halfway up the 15-story, A-frame hotel. Monorail drivers have, on occasion, invited a guest to sit up front with them, which is something children will talk about long after Dumbo the Flying Elephant is forgotten. The ride takes about five minutes by monorail, or a minute or two longer by ferry, which is a nice way to leave the park and lets you avoid the long lines at the monorail station.

Area code 407 unless otherwise indicated.

Main Street USA

There are no major attractions in this portion of the park; this is where you get information, reservations, and souvenirs. If you are here

Restaurants/Nightlife: Red   Hotels: Blue
Shops/ 🌳Outdoors: Green   Sights/Culture: Black

when the hours are extended (during the summer and on holidays), you might consider doing your shopping in the afternoon when the lines at the attractions are the longest. Purchase your Mickey Mouse ears and other gifts and store them in the lockers under the Main Street Station. Some visitors shop in the afternoon and then go back to their hotels for naps or a swim, and return to the park at dinnertime when the crowds start thinning out. If you do this, don't forget to get your hand stamped so you will be able to return to the park. Also, hang on to your parking ticket so you won't have to pay again. Main Street USA empties onto an island hub directly in front of **Cinderella Castle.** Going clockwise around this hub, the first path to the left goes to Adventureland, the next one goes to Liberty Square and Frontierland, the path through Cinderella Castle takes you to Fantasyland, the one next to that goes to Fantasyland and Mickey's Starland, and the final path goes to Tomorrowland. If you want to bypass one "land" to get to another, it is quicker to cut through the hub. For instance, if you are in Adventureland and think the time is right to do Space Mountain in Tomorrowland, don't walk through all the lands, instead cut through the hub.

94 Walt Disney World Railroad There are four trains in the Magic Kingdom roundhouse, all built in the early 1900s and all of which now run on diesel fuel. The trains used

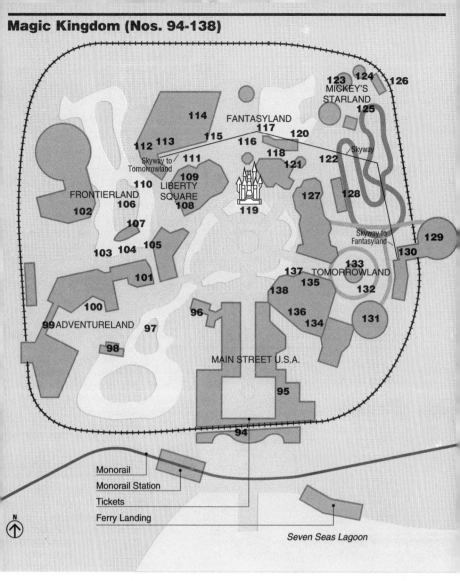

to circle the park clockwise in about 15 minutes with stops at Frontierland and Mickey's Starland. But construction of **Splash Mountain,** a log flume ride with a five-story plunge scheduled to open in Adventureland by 1993, has caused the WDW Railroad to change its name and route. **Goofy's Back-Track Express** now travels in reverse from Main Street Station to Duckburg Station in Mickey's Starland. Once Splash Mountain is on line, the WDW Railroad will chug through the attraction.

At City Hall Square:

City Hall and **SunBank** are on the left as you enter the town square and before you head up Main Street. You can also catch free transportation up Main Street in front of City Hall. Choose from horse-pulled trolleys, a firetruck, old cars, and a double-decker bus. You might want to skip **The Walt Disney Story** if you are with kids. It is the life story of Walt Disney,

and there is some rare film footage here of Walt, plus some memorabilia. **Disneyana Collectibles** is a souvenir shop. There is a booth outside to get reservations for **The Diamond Horseshoe Jamboree,** a live floor show in Frontierland. If the jamboree is something you want to attend, get your reservations first thing in the morning as you enter the park. Seating is limited and by reservation only, and there are only five shows during the day.

95 Tony's Town Square Restaurant ★$$$
One of four full-service restaurants in the Magic Kingdom. If you have ever seen *Lady and the Tramp,* you will feel right at home in this Victorian-style restaurant inspired by the movie. This is a popular spot to stop for breakfast if you arrive before 9AM. You can order waffles in the shape of Mickey Mouse and, although this is mainly a pasta place, they also make good burgers. ◆ Italian ◆ Daily 8:30AM-11AM, 11:45AM-6PM.

Also in City Hall Square:

The Chapeau Hats of all kinds, including Goofy hats and Mickey Mouse ears, can be monogrammed here; **Kodak Camera Center,** film, tips, two-hour processing, and rentals; **Main Street Confectionery.**

On the east side of Main Street:

Main Street Cinema Silent films, including *Steamboat Willie,* the first movie in which Mickey Mouse appeared. An air-conditioned respite on a hot, summer afternoon, but there are no seats. A couple of films run continuously here.

Uptown Jewelers, Main Street Market House Gifts, snacks, and tobacco products are found here. Other stores include **Disney & Co.** (souvenirs), **The Shadow Box** (silhouettes created and framed while you wait), and **Crystal Arts** (glass cutting, blowing, and engraving).

The Plaza Restaurant $$$ A good location to view fireworks in the evening, but the meals aren't as memorable as the desserts.
♦ American ♦ Daily 11AM-7PM

Main Street Bake Shop and **Plaza Ice Cream Parlor** flank the restaurant.

On the west side of Main Street:

Emporium This is a large Disney merchandise store. **Harmony Barber Shop** (besides a shave and a haircut, there are shaving cream bowls and brushes, and moustache cups), **Disney Clothiers, House of Magic,** and **Main Street Book Store** lead to the **Penny Arcade,** featuring games dating back to the turn of the century.

Refreshment Corner A shady place to grab a snack if you are heading over to Adventureland or allowing your children a few minutes in the arcade.

Magic Kingdom

First Aid Center This as well as a **Magic Kingdom Baby Center** are on the way to Adventureland, right before you get to The Crystal Palace.

96 The Crystal Palace $$ The Victorian-style building at the end of Main Street is a large cafeteria often overlooked by tourists for breakfasts because of the location and cuteness of Tony's Town Square Restaurant. Even if you don't make this your morning cereal stop, you might want to come back later in the day for prime rib. Ask for a seat in the front of the restaurant: It has a good view.
♦ American ♦ Daily 8:30AM-7PM

Adventureland

Jungle Cruise and **Pirates of the Caribbean** are the big attractions. Jungle Cruise has the longest lines. This is one you might want to come back to in the evening if the line sign indicates a 45-minute or longer wait.

97 Swiss Family Robinson Climb up, around, and through an elaborate tree house. Children will like the climb, but many adults find this incredible prop pretty boring.

98 Jungle Cruise Children love this boat ride through tropical jungles where they will encounter many audio-animatronic animals of the wild. The captain's corny jokes will be fresh for the kids, who strain to see what awaits around each corner on this 10-minute ride.

99 Pirates of the Caribbean This is one of those rides where you see something new each time you take it. Keep your eyes open to catch all the Disney detail of these drunken, brawling pirates.

100 Tropical Serenade Unless you are bringing along very young, impressionable children, you can pass on this one. This was Disney's first adventure into audio-animatronics. It's boring, it's old, and it's slow.

101 Adventureland Veranda $$ With its colorful, winding vines, lazy fans, and patio dining near the water separating Main Street USA and Adventureland, the restaurant looks as if it were transplanted from the South Seas. Burgers, dogs, and chicken are served here with an oriental flavor. ♦ American-Chinese ♦ Daily 11AM-6PM

Attached to Adventureland Veranda are two snack stop spots—**Aloha Isle** and **Egg Roll Wagon.**

Frontierland

Big Thunder Mountain Railroad is the favorite attraction here, judging from the length of lines at midafternoon, but even better is **The Haunted Mansion** at Liberty Square.

102 Big Thunder Mountain Railroad This is a  roller coaster ride for those who thought they didn't like roller coasters—sort of a roller coaster with training wheels. There are plenty of dips, twirls, and surprises to make it exciting, but the scenery and action make you keep your eyes open so you won't miss any of the dandy details. There are floods, tumbleweeds, and waterfalls, and one trip isn't enough to appreciate all the goodies. Come back in the evening, when you will get a different view of the scenery, and you won't have to wait an hour for a three-minute ride. There are health and other boarding restrictions.

103 Pecos Bill Cafe $$ A place for chili or chicken, and the burgers aren't bad.
♦ American ♦ Daily 10AM-6PM

103 Mile Long Bar $$ Be careful if you want to walk from one end to the other of this seemingly mile-long bar, and keep your eyes on the animal heads on the wall. You'll know you have had enough when one head turns to another and winks. No, your eyes aren't betraying you, it's just more of Disney's audio-animatronics. ♦ Tex-Mex ♦ Daily 11AM-5PM

104 Country Bear Jamboree A song-and-dance show performed by a pack of audio-animatronic bears stars Henry, but it is Big Al who steals the show. Another showstopper is Teddi Beara, who is lowered from the ceiling on a swing while belting out "Singing in the Rain."

105 The Diamond Horseshoe Jamboree Here you get songs, dances, and corny jokes from real, live humans. Those of you who are making the Magic Kingdom a short day better skip this one; young children probably will be bored. Since seating is by reservation only, there is no waiting in line, but you do sit for about 45 minutes in a big dance hall. Sandwiches and drinks are served while you wait for the 30-minute performance. ♦ Reservations required. You get them out front of Disneyana Collectibles on Main Street USA on a first-come, first-serve basis. Daily 10:45AM, 12:15, 1:45, 3:30, 4:45PM

106 Tom Sawyer Island When you find your energy level isn't keeping up with the kids in your party, mosey back here. Take a raft to the island and then, keeping Rivers of America to your right, follow the path to **Aunt Polly's Landing.** While you sit sipping lemonade, let the kids explore the island with its cave, bridges, dirt paths, and fort. **Fort Sam Clemens** has guns to fire on the upper level, and you can exit through a secret passageway.

On Tom Sawyer Island:

Aunt Polly's Landing $$ A two-story wooden structure with a covered patio protruding out into the water. It is one of the least-known eateries at the park, but you can get a sandwich, cookies, or a piece of pie with iced tea, lemonade, or a soft drink. Signs warn you that the island closes at dusk. ♦ American ♦ Daily 11AM-4PM

107 Liberty Square Riverboat This triple-decker ship is a real steamboat, although it glides through Rivers of America via rail. It doesn't hold much amusement for children because the ride is slow and the only action comes from fake figures on shore.

108 The Hall of Presidents Strictly for the history buff, this attraction opens with a patriotic movie about the importance of our Constitution, and then introduces each of our country's 41 presidents. On both sides of a little passageway to Adventureland is a cluster of shops: **Heritage House, The Courtyard, Silversmith, Olde World Antiques, Umbrella Cart,** and **Silhouette Cart.** At **Sleepy Hollow** and **Liberty Square Wagon** you can grab a snack.

109 Liberty Tree Tavern $$$ Built to look like a 200-year-old tavern with hardwood floors, fireplace, and Colonial-style furniture. You can easily make a meal of New England clam chowder and one of the salads. ♦ American ♦ Reservations, taken at the door, are recommended. Daily 11:30AM-6PM

110 Mike Fink Keel Boats If you ever saw Disney's original *Davy Crockett,* you will recall the memorable episode where Crockett and Mike Fink have a keelboat race. This isn't nearly as memorable. It goes down the Rivers of America, so you won't want to do both this and the riverboat, and you may not want to do either.

111 Columbia Harbour House $$ Furnished with a nautical theme, this small fast-food favorite serves fresh shrimp. ♦ Seafood ♦ Daily 11AM-6PM

112 The Haunted Mansion It's not scary, but it is a showcase of all of Disney's special effects. The walkway up to the mansion with its funny tombstones sets the tone. The suit of armor that moves is predictable, but try to figure out how the floor you are standing on in the portrait gallery starts sinking.

Fantasyland

The attraction with the longest line is **20,000 Leagues Under the Sea. It's a Small World** is the one the kids will want to ride over and over, and **Peter Pan's Flight** may be the best.

113 Skyway Taking a gondola ride in the sky is a pleasant way to get from Fantasyland to Tomorrowland, but not if there is a long line. If you want to ride Skyway, take it from Tomorrowland, where the lines are always shorter.

114 It's a Small World The first time through it's fun to watch all the early Disney audio-

animatronic dolls perform and sing the catchy tune. The second time through it's fun to watch the bright-eyed delight on small childrens' faces as the boat passes through several rooms and past hundreds of dolls, which all look the same except for costumes. Warning: If you go more than once, the song will haunt you the rest of the day.

In the back of Fantasyland there is **Pinocchio Village Haus,** a fast-food restaurant that is very large, **Fantasyland Pretzel Wagon, Fantasy Faire,** where there are live performances at different times of the day, and **Tournament Tent,** another snack place.

115 Peter Pan's Flight Once you fly over London at night in your pirate ship, you'll fall in love with this ride. The attraction travels through the highlights of the magical story of Peter Pan.

116 Cinderella's Golden Carrousel This carousel is the real thing. Built in 1917, much of it has been refurbished.

117 Dumbo, the Flying Elephant Climb aboard Dumbo and go around and around, controlling how high and low he'll fly.
Troubador Tavern, The Mad Hatter (another place to get monogrammed Mickey Mouse ears), and **Kodak Kiosk** are next to **Magic Journeys,** a 3-D movie that used to be at the Imagination pavilion at EPCOT. On the other side of Magic Journeys is **Tinkerbell's Toy Shop,** next to a little-used path that leads to Liberty Square.

118 Snow White's Adventures A fun ride through a dark and scary forest to meet the Seven Dwarfs. The wicked witch pops up often; Disney officials warn parents that small children might be frightened.

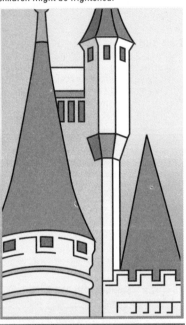

Magic Kingdom

119 Cinderella's Castle Most visitors to the Magic Kingdom recognize the castle as a landmark, but don't realize that it is a functioning building, which houses one of the nicer restaurants in the park. This mostly fiberglass castle was patterned after King Ludwig's castle at Neuschwanstein in southern Germany.

Within Cinderella's Castle:

King Stefan's Banquet Hall The furnishings and the dress of the persons staffing the hall are all designed to be true to the 13th century. The great hall serves roast beef sandwiches for lunch; the chicken is a good bet for dinner. ♦ American ♦ Reservations required; make them at the restaurant as soon as you get to the park. Daily 11:30AM-6:15PM

Across the moat entrance at the **Castle Forecourt Stage** there is often live entertainment.

Restaurants/Nightlife: Red	Hotels: Blue
Shops/ 🌲Outdoors: Green	**Sights/Culture:** Black

120 20,000 Leagues Under the Sea The props and the special effects are kind of hokey, but the ride enjoys great popularity. As you stand in line or go past the ride, you can see the subs going under, adding to the wonderment of the ride.

121 Mr. Toad's Wild Ride Similar to the Snow White attraction, the intensity here comes from the sudden turns and near disasters, such as a close call with an oncoming train, and slamming through a barn door.
The shops and snack spots around these two rides are **Mickey's Christmas Carol** (Christmas accessories), **The AristoCats** (gifts), **Royal Candy Shoppe, Gurgi's Munchies & Crunchies, The Round Table,**and **Nemo's Niche.**

122 Mad Tea Party Climb into the Mad Hatter's tea cups for a ride.

Mickey's Starland

There are no major rides in this land, but it does give children an opportunity for one-on-one photos with Mickey Mouse without having to battle an army of kids. You enter a room where Mickey waits with a helper; snap a photo of your child with the mouse, or ask the helper to take a snapshot of all of you with Mickey.

123 Meet Mickey Mouse Here is your opportunity to go backstage and have your picture taken with Mickey, one-on-one. You can even ask a friend of Mickey's, who is always back there with him, to take the picture for you, so you and your child can be in it together.

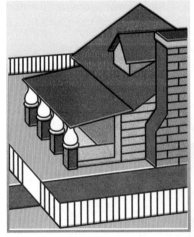

124 Mickey's House Follow the signs from the Duckburg Station to Mickey's House. It's the one with Pluto's doghouse out front. Inside, there are pictures on the walls of Mickey with the original Mouseketeers, Walt Disney, and even former First Lady Nancy Reagan. As you leave by the back door, you head over to Mickey's **Magical TV World.** It starts with film clips from *Ducktales, Gummi Bears,* and *Chip 'n Dale Rescue Rangers,* setting you up to see stars from these three television programs in a live stage show. When the show concludes, follow the crowd into the **Mickey Mouse Club Funland** tent, where you can see yourself on TV. A pathway leads you out of Mickey's yard, but not before passing **Mickey's Walk of Fame.** The stars on the walkway have Disney characters in them, and when you step on a star you hear the character's voice.

125 Grandma Duck's Farm Let the kids loose here, while you sit back and relax. The area contains a petting zoo, a maze, and props to climb in and explore.

126 Walt Disney World Railroad Duckburg Station is one of three stops on the line.

Tomorrowland

Space Mountain is the big attraction here, and about the only reason to be in Tomorrowland until 1996, when the land will be turned into an "intergalactic spaceport for arriving aliens."

127 Tomorrowland Terrace $$ This is the place to eat if you are looking for a wide variety of food, a place to sit down, and no long lines. It is the biggest of the cafeterias in the Magic Kingdom, and it serves large salads, along with soups and sandwiches. ♦ American ♦ 10AM-7PM

128 Grand Prix Raceway Little gas-powered go-karts put-put along on tracks. This isn't a very exciting ride, and the cars don't go faster than seven miles per hour.

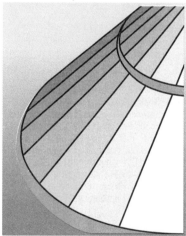

129 Space Mountain This roller coaster ride in the dark is the one that everybody will ask you about when you return home from a trip to Disney World. The lines are long, and as you wait for a place in a six-seat rocket, you'll hear the screams and the sounds of the coaster screeching on the rails. The apprehension isn't lessened with the well-posted warning signs and restrictions. Try to keep your eyes open during the two-and-a-half-minute ride, so you can fully enjoy the shooting stars. And don't tell your friends back home that this roller coaster never reaches 30 miles per hour. If you chicken out once you are in line, there is a moving

walkway that will lead you out past the **RYCA 1 Dream of a New World,** an exhibit exploring electronic media of the future.

130 Skyway A gondola sweeps you into the air and transports you to Fantasyland.

131 Carousel of Progress In a revolving theater, an audio-animatronic family demonstrates how electricity has improved our lives.

132 WEDway PeopleMover These little nonpolluting, electric vehicles take you on a tour of Tomorrowland, including a brief inside look at Space Mountain.

133 StarJets This is a high-flying ride along the lines of Dumbo, perfect for children who feel they are too old for the Fantasyland attraction.

134 Tomorrowland Theatre Live song-and-dance presentations are held on this stage at different times during the day.

135 Dreamflight This enjoyable ride lasts just under five minutes, but in that time you learn a bit of aviation history. You will see early efforts of people attempting to fly, and then the barnstormers and stunt flyers take you up to the beginning of the modern age of commercial flight. The ride travels through an engine, recreates a take-off, and concludes with some beautiful scenes from the air.

136 American Journeys This is a wonderful Circlevision film of the US. You stand in this theater and the sounds and sights surround you. Among the most impressive are Mount St. Helens and a space shuttle launch from Cape Canaveral.

137 Mission to Mars Until the rash of space simulator rides (Star Tours at Disney-MGM, Body Wars at EPCOT), this ride was considered pretty good. Now it seems rather tame: you sit in your capsule, your seat jiggles, and the sound surrounds you while

you blast-off on a mission to Mars piloted by an audio-animatronic captain. Actual NASA film of Mars is used.

138 The Plaza Pavilion $$ This establishment, behind the Plaza Restaurant on Main Street USA, is a step above fast food. They have deep-dish pizza and sandwiches. The pasta salad is good, as are the Italian hoagies. There are tables indoors and out. ♦ Italian ♦ Daily 10AM-7PM

Walt Disney World's Electrical Light Parade was famous from 1977 to October 1991. But just like a long-running Broadway hit, it eventually ran its course and was replaced by another nightly parade, SpectroMagic. The new, high-tech parade uses fiber-optic technology to light its floats, and computers control the lights, motors, special effects, and street speakers. It took almost 300 people laboring over 37 floats for nine months to create the parade. And just where did the Electrical Light Parade go? It was sent to Euro Disneyland, about 18 miles east of Paris.

Brevard County/Kennedy Space Center

In 1825 **Douglas Dummitt** settled on Merritt Island, in eastern Brevard County, and began planting citrus trees. Dummitt has been given credit for establishing Indian River citrus, a brand that became world famous and led to the development of the citrus industry for which the entire state of Florida has become renowned. Dummitt's father had been a wealthy planter in Barbados, but the Dummitt family fled the Caribbean after an uprising in the early 1800s. In 1807 young Dummitt smelled a delightfully sweet fragrance as he sailed up the coast of Florida to his father's new sugarcane plantation near St. Augustine. Dummitt later discovered that he'd smelled orange blossoms, and vowed to return one day to establish his own grove. By 1828 Dummitt was shipping his first fruit in large Indian canoes made from cypress logs. The fruit was then poled up the Indian River by black slaves.

Today, Brevard County is still home to Indian River citrus, but it was the space race that put this region on the map. Titusville, Cocoa, and other cities are home to thousands of workers at Kennedy Space Center. And Spaceport USA at Kennedy Space Center is one of Florida's most popular tourist attractions.

1 Sebastian Inlet State Recreation Area A favorite with surfers, this 576-acre park that stretches between the Atlantic Ocean and the Indian River has a separate beach for surfers and swimmers, a visitor center, a fishing pier, a protected lagoon for snorkelers, a boat ramp, campgrounds, and a concession stand. The **McLarty State Museum and Visitor Center**, two miles south of the Sebastian Inlet Bridge on SR A1A, features treasures from a 1715 shipwreck and other historic exhibits. ♦ SR A1A. 984.4852

Melbourne

The heart of Melbourne was once Front Street, near the Indian River. There, in the 1880s, one could find dry-goods stores, grocery stores, and a fish house with a brothel upstairs. Melbourne's city center remained on Front Street until 1919, when all the small businesses burned to the ground in a tragic fire.

Brevard County/JFK Space Center

2 Nannie Lee's Strawberry Mansion & Mister BeauJean's Restaurant ★★$$ Beneath the spreading branches of towering live oaks, wide brick walkways lead into this charmingly restored house, with flowered wallpaper and rich woodwork. Chef and co-owner **Peter Wynkoop** serves up quiches, soups, and specials of the day. Any restaurant that can prepare oysters Rockefeller just right is worth a visit, and the mansion does just that. The seafood sampler—all fresh—is broiled to perfection. **Mister BeauJean's,** a cafe and grill on the property, is a great option for more casual dining on burgers or snack foods. ♦ American ♦ Nannie Lee's daily 5-10PM; Mister BeauJean's daily 7-10PM. 1218 E. New Haven Ave (Harbor City Blvd-Front St) Reservations recommended. 724.8627

3 Melbourne Square Mall If you are in the south end of the county and feel the need for a mall fix, this one is anchored by Belk Lindsey, Burdines, Dillards, JC Penney, Jordan Marsh, and includes 132 specialty stores. ♦ M-Sa 10AM-9PM; Su noon-5:30PM. 1700 W. New Haven Ave (Evans Rd-Piney Branch Way) 727.2000

4 Melbourne Greyhound Park Minors aren't allowed near the wagering windows, but this new greyhound track encourages families to come to the races anyway. Air-conditioned clubhouse dining, with TV monitors on your table for a close-up view of the racing. ♦ M, W, F 7:45PM; Tu, Th, Sa 1 and 7:45PM. 1100 N. Wickham Rd (Sarno Rd) 259.9800

5 Brevard Art Center and Museum There are six galleries, a museum shop, an auditorium, and an educational wing in this large, modern facility. The galleries' exhibits generally feature Florida themes by Florida artists. Among the most popular works are valuable **Ansel Adams** photographs. ♦ Tu-F 10AM-5PM; Sa 10AM-4PM; Su noon-4PM. 1463 N. Highland Ave (Creel-St. Clair Sts) 242.0737

SPACE COAST SCIENCE CENTER

5 Space Coast Science Center More than 30 hands-on activities are featured here, and that doesn't include the computers where you can experiment with games and graphics. This is a great rainy-afternoon activity for restless children. ♦ Tu-F 10AM-5PM; Sa 10AM-4PM. 1510 Highland Ave (Law-Creel Sts) 259.5572

6 Maxwell C. King Center for the Performing Arts Small-scale touring versions of Broadway shows, such as M. Butterfly and Ziegfield, are presented, as well as dance productions, chamber ensembles, and community theater. Located on the **Brevard Community College** campus. ♦ Seats 2,000. 3865 N. Wickham Rd (Post Rd-Parkway Dr) 242.2219

Indialantic

Ernest Kouwen-Hoven, one of the many land developers and promoters who've stalked Florida since the turn of the century, founded Indialantic in 1918 as a resort community. He started construction on a bridge across the Indian River in 1919, and the narrow, wooden structure was completed in 1921. It was replaced by a concrete and steel bridge in 1947.

7 Quality Suites Hotel $$ These two eight-story buildings are a good value for a beachfront hotel. Each of the 208 two-room suites have ocean views, two TVs, two telephones, a VCR, a cassette deck, and a private balcony. But the hotel's most unusual feature has to be the heated outdoor pool with an underwater sound system. A breakfast buffet is free. Rooms for the physically disabled and nonsmokers are available. ♦ 1665 N. SR A1A (Pine Tree Dr) 723.4222, 800/876.4222; fax 768.2438

8 Holiday Inn Melbourne Oceanfront $$ The reliability of a chain hotel, ocean views, and fine beach access—the sand is just steps away down a wooden staircase—combine to make this recently renovated hotel a good choice. An activities director on site plans adventures for children and groups, and there are four tennis courts, a Jacuzzi, a big sun deck, and indoor and outdoor pools. A 4,000-square-foot penthouse suite is available to those who feel like splurging. ♦ 2605 N. SR A1A (Coral Wy E.-Ponce de Leon Rd) 777.4100, 800/HOLIDAY; fax 773.6132

Brevard County/JFK Space Center

9 Melbourne Beach Hilton $$$ All 118 rooms and 10 suites have dramatic ocean views at this glitzy Hilton. The breezy outdoor pool bar is a great place to relax during the day. At night, **Encore's,** a high-energy nightclub, becomes a local hangout. Gift shop and three lounges. ♦ 3003 N. SR A1A (Eau Gallie Blvd-Coral Wy E.) 777.5000, 800/HILTONS; fax 777.3713

9 Radisson Suite Hotel Oceanfront $$$ This is the priciest hotel on the beach, but its 168 generously proportioned suites, all with ocean views and full kitchens, are worth it. The hotel has 551 feet of secluded beach, along with an outdoor pool, two spas, and an exercise room. It includes a reasonably priced restaurant, **Nick's Coco de Mer** (daily 7AM-10PM); **La Bistro Lounge** (daily 11AM-10PM); and a pool bar. Rooms for the physically disabled and nonsmokers are available. ♦ 3101 N. SR A1A (Eau Gallie Blvd-Coral Wy E.) 773.9260, 800/777.7800; fax 777.3190

Cocoa Beach

Cocoa Beach became a municipality in 1925, just a month after developer Gus Edwards sold it to a New York syndicate for $1.3 million. The city's population at that time isn't known, but few people must have lived in the new municipality because by 1939 there were only nine houses on today's jam-packed S. Atlantic Avenue, and there were no telephones.

It took the nation's space program to bring Cocoa Beach to its current size. When the space program took off in the late 1950s, dozens of large missile contractors began moving into the Cape Canaveral and Cocoa Beach areas, and houses, apartments, and hotels couldn't be built fast enough to accommodate everyone who needed a place to stay. Newspaper accounts of the day say that people coming into the area to look for jobs often had to sleep in their cars, and a few even slept in the huge water pipes waiting to be installed along SR 520. The pipes were there as part of the construction of Cocoa Beach's first public water system in 1958.

10 Coconuts on the Beach $$ Nobody really comes here for the food as much as for the beach, the beer, and the bodies. The restaurant and bar are air-conditioned, but it is more fun to sup and sip on the large patio overlooking the beach, where greased guys play volleyball and bikini contests are often held. Sunday brunch buffet, surf contests, live music most nights. ♦ American ♦ M-Sa 11AM-2AM; Su 10AM-2AM. 2 Minuteman Causeway (SR A1A) 784.1422

11 Bernard's Surf ★★$$$ You might think they're joking when they hand you the menu—it's almost three feet across and just as long—but the food is no laughing matter. Few places in this area do seafood in as many ways or as imaginatively. The restaurant opened in 1948 with **Bernard Fischer** serving fish from his fleet of boats. His nephew **Rusty Fischer** now supplements the family fleet's catch with such delicacies as lobsters from Maine and oysters from the Chesapeake River. **Rusty's Raw Bar** is a popular new addition, decorated with sports pictures and pennants, that serves seafood and burgers. The main entrance to Rusty's Raw Bar is on the west side of the restaurant. ♦ Seafood ♦ M-Sa 11AM-1AM; Su noon-1AM. 2 S. Atlantic Ave (Minuteman Causeway) Dinner reservations recommended. 783.2401

12 The Prince of Wales Dining and Piano Bar ★$$$ This dimly lit restaurant is a cool retreat from the relentless beach sun. Heavy-duty menu items include beef Wellington and prime rib, but lighter fare, such as Dover sole, poached salmon, and a local catch of the day, gets the vote for best prepared. ♦ British ♦ Daily 11:30AM-2PM, 5:30-10:30PM. 2 N. Atlantic Ave (Minuteman Causeway) 783.9512

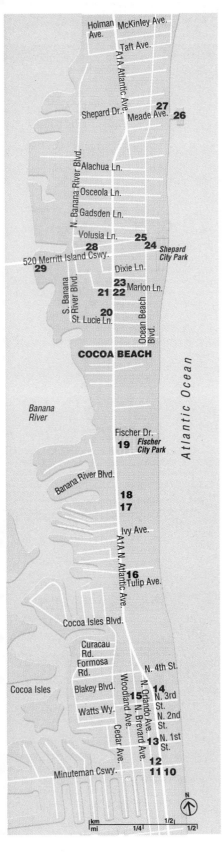

12 Heidelberg $$ Some of the lunch sandwiches have ridiculously cute names, such as *Yes Sir, Cheese My Baby*, but the imported Swiss and Muenster cheeses are good. A variety of savory German wursts served with rye or Bavarian black bread also make a tasty lunch. The dinner menu is German through and through: roast duckling served with potato dumplings, or the house specialty: melt-in-your-mouth sauerbraten (marinated lean beef served with a potato dumpling and tangy red cabbage). ♦ German ♦ M-Sa 10AM-10PM. 7 N. Orlando Ave (Minuteman Causeway) Reservations recommended. 783.6806

13 Mango Tree ★★$$$ Owners **Betty Price** and her son **Bob** cook up something special in this charming restaurant, whose wooden-frame exterior behind a brightly painted picket fence seems almost out of place among the ordinary buildings lining N. Atlantic Ave. Inside, a waterfall splashes gently into a lily pond and palms crowd the ceiling. Straight-backed wooden chairs at tables with starched white tablecloths make a comfortable but elegant setting for the restaurant's wonderful creations, such as juicy roast Long Island duckling in orange sauce with macadamia nuts or flaky Florida grouper grilled with olive oil, garlic, and fresh herbs. The restaurant's vegetables are always fresh and perfectly prepared, so the pasta primavera with steamed vegetables is a fine choice. ♦ American ♦ Tu-Sa 6-10PM; Su 6-

8:30PM. Hours vary seasonally. 118 N. Atlantic Ave (N. Second-N. First Sts) Reservations recommended. 799.0513, 783.5533

14 Desperados $ Drink your tequila or *cervezas* atop Desperados' outdoor deck or at the beachside cantina, which is open only for breakfast and lunch and is located behind the restaurant. Find some other place to dine, though, if you hanker for Tex-Mex. While the enchiladas are passable, Desperados was woefully shy of *carne* in some meat dishes, and its quesadillas are more worthy of a fast-food restaurant than one that bills itself as having "fine Mexican food." ♦ Tex-Mex ♦ 301 N. Atlantic Ave (N. Third St) 784.3363

Restaurants/Nightlife: Red	**Hotels:** Blue
Shops/ 🎋Outdoors: Green	**Sights/Culture:** Black

81

15 Alma's Italian Restaurant ★$$ Instead of knocking down walls to make large dining rooms, this old house was pretty much left intact. Alma's has an excellent wine cellar, cozy dining areas, good pasta dishes, and seafood entries that are well prepared. Children's menu

and early-bird dinners, too. ♦ Italian ♦ M-Th 5-10:30PM; F-Sa 5-11PM. 306 N. Orlando Ave (N. Third St) 783.1981

16 Holiday Inn Cocoa Beach $$$ Located right on the Atlantic, this hotel is about a 20-minute drive from Kennedy Space Center and Spaceport USA. The hotel has an Olympic-size pool, 625 feet of sandy beach, a wading pool for kids, a Jacuzzi, two lighted tennis courts, shuffleboard courts, and a game room. A plus for parents: a recreational program for children run by a qualified recreational pro. **Willard's** restaurant does a brisk local business with its lunch buffet (M-Sa 11:30AM-2PM) and its seafood buffet (F-Sa 5:30-10PM). **Plum's Lounge** has live entertainment daily from 9PM-1AM. ♦ 1300 N. Atlantic Ave (Holiday Ln) 783.2271, 800/HOLIDAY; fax 784.8878

17 Cocoa Beach Hilton and Towers $$$ Sleek and modern, this hotel has all you need. There are 11 suites among its 300 rooms, along with a hot and cold whirlpool, an out-door pool, **Sea Shells** oceanfront restaurant, **Coco's Lounge,** and a pool bar. From the hotel's expansive pool deck, a wooden bridge crosses dune vegetation to the sandy beach. One floor has a concierge to pamper guests, another is only for nonsmokers, and some rooms are specially equipped for the handi-

Brevard County/JFK Space Center

capped. ♦ 1550 N. Atlantic Ave (Banana River Blvd-Ivy Ave) 799.0003, 800/526.2609; fax 799.0344

18 Satellite Motel $ Recommended only if you have to stay in the motel that was the temporary home of the first seven astronauts. There are better rooms near the beach, but the Satellite is inexpensive, has a pool, and is right on the coast. In other words, it has some of the right stuff. ♦ 1600 N. Atlantic Ave (Banana River Blvd-Ivy Ave) 783.2252

19 Howard Johnson Plaza Hotel Cocoa Beach $$ This is a hotel that tries hard, and offers something for everyone: a beachfront location; surfboard, sailboard, and Jet Ski rentals for adventurous types; and a pool deck and gazebo bar for those who like to relax. There are two big swimming pools, one with a swim-up bar. Choose between a 62-

room cabana lodge, with tiny kitchens, or 148 rooms in an oceanfront tower, where the rooms have balconies overlooking the Atlantic. There are efficiencies and some suites, as well as rooms for nonsmokers and the physically handicapped. If you want to be pampered, there is a concierge floor. **Carlyle's Beachside Bistro** is a casual restaurant with an ocean view and live entertainment. ♦ 2080 N. Atlantic Ave (Fischer Dr-Banana River Blvd) 783.9222, 800/654.2000; fax 799.3234

At the Howard Johnson Plaza Hotel Cocoa Beach:

Herbie K's ★$ This 24-hour, fifties-style diner is part of a three-unit chain, but don't hold that against the place. Sassy waitresses sit down at your booth to take your order, and if they like the rock 'n' roll tune you pick from the jukebox selector at your table, they'll start bopping. Happily, the food isn't an after-thought. Good breakfasts, with non-greasy-spoon selections such as blueberry pancakes, and for lunch and dinner, good burgers, are served. Through a black back door is **Bumper**'s, which has dancing on weekend nights. The diner sits in the parking lot in front of the hotel. ♦ American ♦ M-Th, Su 6AM-midnight; F-Sa 24 hours. 783.6740

20 Motel 6 $ The econo-chain is OK if you're searching for a bargain near the beaches. It has a pool and shuffleboard courts, plus rooms for the physically disabled and nonsmokers. ♦ 3701 N. Atlantic Ave (St. Lucie Ln) 783.3103

21 Sunrise Motel Bed and Breakfast $$ This isn't a classic B&B, but the two-story inn's pretty pink exterior, meticulously maintained rooms, and small pool ringed with Queen palms make it a fine, reasonably priced getaway. It's across a busy highway from the beach, but there's easy access. ♦ 3185 N. Atlantic Ave (Marion-Brevard Lns) 783.0500

CROSSWAY INN

22 Crossway Inn $$ Newly redecorated, this inn has a homey feel. Ground-level rooms with kitchenettes face an interior courtyard with a pool, charcoal grills, a shuffleboard court, and a sand volleyball court. Minisuites are located in a tower, where ocean views are partially blocked by a condo. But you can still appreciate the sea breezes from your balcony. The suites have two TVs, two queen-sized beds, and a sofa bed. The inn also offers lighted tennis courts. ♦ 3901 N. Atlantic Ave (Marion-Brevard Lns) 783.2221, 800/327.2224, 800/247.2221 (FL only)

23 Ron Jon Surf Shop This vast retail establishment is a testament to the great staying power of T-shirts and the appeal of casual beachwear and bikinis. Even if you don't plan to hit the sand, this landmark store is a must-see. Bronzed youths wearing tiny headsets attached to walkie-talkies will direct you to your parking place. A glass elevator zips from a grotto near the back of the store up to the mezzanine level. The pseudo-Art Deco shopping palace has just gone through a $2.2 million expansion and face-lift. What was built in 1963 as a brick and glass, one-story shop is now a two-story structure painted purple, pink, and blue with turrets, glass blocks, and miles of cathode lighting that is controlled by a computer capable of giving the building 16 different looks. Inside there is mostly clothing, but Ron Jon's also sells every type of flip-flop known to humankind, as well as some fancy sporting goods, including roller blades, surfboards, and bicycle gear. You can buy or rent any kind of water-related equipment here—from boogie boards to beach bikes. ♦ Daily 24 hours. 4151 N. Atlantic Ave (Marion Ln) 799.8888

24 The Inn at Cocoa Beach Bed and Breakfast $$$ This is perhaps the nicest inn on the beach. All 50 rooms have ocean views. Ground-floor rooms have patios, upper floors have balconies, and the honeymoon suite boasts a Jacuzzi. The hotel is small enough to give you plenty of personal attention, as well as a free Continental breakfast in a room with French Country furniture, oriental rugs, and tile floors. Wine and cheese are served in the lobby as the sun sets. One complaint: The inn feels more like a hotel than a cozy B&B. ♦ 4300 Ocean Beach Blvd (SR 520) 799.3460, 800/343.5307; fax 784.8632

25 Bimini's Raw Bar $ This hangout caters to a boisterous young crowd and serves oysters and clams on the half-shell and juicy Florida rock shrimp. ♦ Seafood ♦ Daily 10AM-11PM. 4301 Ocean Beach Blvd (SR 520) 784.2788

26 The Cocoa Beach Pier This dining, entertainment, and shopping complex stretches 840 feet out into the Atlantic. First opened in 1962, the pier has expanded bit by bit and now is home to three restaurants, a fine, open-air bar with an ocean view, a T-shirt shop, and a place where you can buy bait. The pier is a hangout for all ages, and is a good spot to quaff a brew and watch bathing brutes and beauties below you on the beach. ♦ Parking fee. 401 Meade Ave (Ocean Beach Blvd) 783.7549

On the Cocoa Beach Pier:

Oh Shucks $ An outdoor "raw bar" (the name Floridians give any place that sells oysters on the half-shell) located at the beginning of the pier to your left on a casual deck above the beach. Munchies such as burgers and hot dogs are also served. ♦ M-Th, Su 11AM-midnight; F-Sa 11AM-2AM. 783.4050

Oceanotions The tropical gift shop is up the boardwalk and past the showers. You'll find all you need for the beach—sunglasses, hats, caps, and, of course, the ever-popular Panama Jack T-shirts that seem to have become requisite Florida beachwear. ♦ M-Th 8:30AM-11PM; F-Su 8:30AM-11:30PM.

Boardwalk This outdoor bar usually has live music. Set over the ocean and a good spot to watch beach volleyball.

The Pier House Restaurant ★★$$$ Behind the outdoor tables of the Boardwalk is the entrance to this fine dining establishment with floor-to-ceiling windows overlooking the ocean. The seafood selections are solid but predictable. The restaurant gets a little adventurous with Shrimp à la Pier House, a tasty concoction of broiled shrimp served with crispy apples and snow peas in a rich cognac cream sauce. The fresh catch of the day is a better choice if you don't want seafood in a heavy sauce. ♦ American ♦ M-Sa 5-10PM; Su 10AM-2PM, 5-10PM. Reservations recommended. 783.7549

Spinnaker's ★$$ Past the public restrooms is this casual restaurant with laminated wood booths, a beamed ceiling, and windows that frame the Atlantic on three sides. Shorts—but not swimsuits—are OK in Spinnaker's, which serves good, basic burgers and lighter fare, including tuna and chicken salads. Look for the daily specials, especially Monday's rock shrimp. These hard-shelled shrimp are native to Florida and delectable when fresh. ♦ American ♦ Daily 8AM-12:30AM. 783.7549

Brevard County/JFK Space Center

Bait & Tackle Rent fishing equipment here, near the end of the pier. ♦ Daily 6:30AM-5PM for rental equipment; 6:30AM-1AM if you use your own equipment.

27 Oceanside Inn $$ Many hotels tout their ocean views, but this inn really has them. All 74 rooms face the Atlantic, and each has a balcony and two double beds. A low wall keeps the pool area private from the beach. Rooms for the physically disabled available, too. ♦ 1 Hendry Ave (Ocean Beach Blvd) 784.3126

27 Ocean Suite Hotel $$ A good bet if you want to be near the surfing action at Cocoa Beach Pier, but ocean views from some

Alan Shepard was the first American launched into space; he made a 15-minute suborbital flight in May 1961.

suites in this five-story building are somewhat obscured by the Oceanside Inn. All two-room suites have a wet bar, refrigerator, and two TVs. There's a heated pool, **Pierre's** restaurant, and a lounge. Among the 50 suites are some designated for nonsmokers and the physically disabled. ♦ 5500 Ocean Beach Blvd (Hendry-Meade Aves) 784.4343, 800/367.1223; fax 783.6514

28 Sunseed Co-op You don't have to be a member of the food co-op to shop in this natural foods store, which has the ambience of a well-organized natural foods store in a college setting. In addition to all types of yogurt, organic produce, exotic teas, and other goodies, there are Birkenstock sandals, yoga videos, and one of the best T-shirt collections in Central Florida—everything from tie-dyed attire to shirts bearing **Gary Larson's** *Far Side* cartoons. ♦ Daily 10AM-6PM. 275 SR 520 (SR A1A) 784.0930

28 Old Fish House Restaurant $$ A convenient place to stop for fried or steamed oysters, shrimp, and crab as you leave Cocoa Beach. Thankfully, it doesn't attract the large crowds that pack the Cocoa Beach Pier restaurants. ♦ Seafood ♦ M-F 11AM-10PM; Sa noon-10PM; Su 1-9:30PM. 273 SR 520 (SR A1A) 784.6468

29 Gatsby's World Gatsby's is a dining and entertainment complex that includes four buildings and a boat on both sides of SR 520, the Merritt Island Causeway, which is sometimes called the Cocoa Beach Causeway. ♦ 500 SR 520 (east shore of the Banana River) 783.2389

At Gatsby's World:

Little River Queen This ship, fashioned after a Southern riverboat paddle wheeler with an open upper deck, makes a daily two-hour cruise up the Banana River in the afternoons. Regular dinner cruises are scheduled Sundays through Thursdays, with a big buffet on Thursday nights. Dixieland jazz dinner cruises are Fridays and Saturdays and always include prime rib, broiled grouper, or chilled shrimp platters. ♦ Admission. Sight-seeing cruises daily 2PM; dinner cruises M-Th, Su 6:30-9PM; Dixieland cruise F-Sa 7-10PM. Reservations required. 783.2380

Gatsby's Dockside ★$$ Dining on the riverside deck makes this a fun place for a drink or a light dinner. Sunday champagne brunch and live entertainment on weekends. ♦ American ♦ M-Th 11:30AM-midnight; F-Sa 11:30AM-1AM; Su 10AM-1PM. 783.2380

Gatsby's Food & Spirits ★$$ Best known for its prime rib and Roaring Twenties atmosphere, specialties here are the Sheik, a filet covered with bernaise sauce, and Garbo, a sautéed veal cutlet with asparagus and crab meat served with hollandaise sauce. Or try the popular Legs Diamond—Alaskan king crab. ♦ American ♦ M-Th 4:30-10PM; F-Sa 4:30-11PM. 783.2380

Jay Gatsby's Sports Emporium This popular sports bar is across the street from the rest of the action at Gatsby's World. With three satellites, two big screens, 11 monitors, free pizza, and munchies at halftime, Monday Night Football is big here. ♦ Daily 11AM-2AM. 784.4514

Gatsby's Fitzgerald Seafood Restaurant $$ Next to the Sports Emporium, this restaurant is known for its fresh seafood. Try the lobster dinner or the filet mignon wrapped in bacon. ♦ Seafood ♦ Daily 5PM-1AM. 784.8322

Cocoa Village

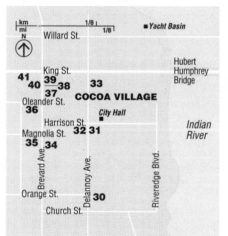

Pioneer families arrived in **Cocoa** around 1860, and the first commercial building was a general store built by **B.C.** and **C.A. Willard** around 1881. Cocoa was once known as **Indian River City,** but US postal authorities said the name was too long. Their decision was announced at the Willard brothers' store, where **Mrs. James,** a poor black woman who was well known for her charitable deeds, suggested the name Cocoa after she spotted a box of Baker's Cocoa on a store shelf.

30 Cocoa Village The heart of Cocoa is contained in this four-square-block area of cobblestone streets, shade trees, patios, parks, and restored turn-of-the-century buildings. Here you'll find restaurants, craft shops, a historical house to tour, and a theater. ♦ Bordered by Church St, Brevard Ave, Willard St, and Riveredge

Within Cocoa Village:

Restaurants/Nightlife: Red	**Hotels:** Blue
Shops/ 🌳Outdoors: Green	**Sights/Culture:** Black

30 Porcher House An example of 20th-century Classic Revival architecture, this house is made primarily of local coquina rock. It was built in 1916 by **Edward Postell Porcher** and his wife, **Byrnina Peck Porcher.** Byrnina, who was the first postmistress of Merritt Island, loved to play bridge so much that she had playing card symbols worked into the coquina rock around the front entrance. During the recent renovation, this feature was incorporated into the new stonework at the rear entrance.

Edward is credited with being the first citrus grower to grade his fruit, as well as the first to inspect and wash it after taking it out of the fields. He established the Deerfield Citrus Groves on Merritt Island in 1883, and it soon grew to be the largest in the county. He was also cofounder of the Florida Citrus Commission and the city of Cocoa.

The **Brevard Museum of History and Natural Science,** along with the **Brevard Arts Council,** has set up a **Victorian Library** on the first floor. ♦ Admission. Tu-F 10AM-1PM. 434 Delannoy Ave (Harrison-Church Sts) 639.3500

31 Taylor Park Shuffleboard courts stand today on the site of land homesteaded in 1886 by **Albert A. Taylor.** The home burned down in 1940. The Taylors were one of many families that took advantage of the Homestead Act of 1862, which gave Southern land away for free to those who agreed to settle on it. Visit the Brevard Museum of History and Natural Science (see page 86) to look at furniture from the Taylor estate (removed before the fire). ♦ Delannoy Ave (Harrison St.)

32 Flashbacks! A pack rat's dream come true, this small store is filled with old magazine art, catalogs, and maps, some more than one hundred years old. Old ads for Lockheed, Motorola, and automobiles are very popular. ♦ Tu-Th 10AM-6PM. 103 Harrison St (Brevard-Delannoy Aves) 633.7366

33 The S.F. Travis Company Colonel **Fred S. Travis Jr.** bought this 1885 building around 1900, and the Travis family still runs this one-block-square hardware store. Step in to see the tin ceiling and the track ladders (just like those used in libraries). Before Commodore Plaza, Riveredge Blvd, and Lee Werner Park were added behind it on landfill, ships used to pull up to the Travis docks to unload supplies. The **Mutual Moving Picture House,** where traveling vaudevillians performed, was also back there, and that building is now part of the Travis Co. ♦ M-F 7AM-5:30PM; Sa 7AM-4PM. 300 Delannoy Ave (King St) 636.1441

34 Forget Me Not This eclectic combination of women's clothes and accessories includes antique and estate jewelry. ♦ M-Sa 10AM-5PM. 404 Brevard Ave (Harrison-Orange Sts) 632.4700

35 Village Country Store & Antiques China and glassware are now sold in what was once the residence of **Mrs. James,** who came up with the idea of naming the city after Baker's Cocoa, a chocolate product sold in the area. ♦ M-Sa 10AM-5PM. 401 Brevard Ave (Magnolia St) 639.4980

36 Bath Cottage This little shop features Crabtree & Evelyn and Caswell-Massey products. It also makes up gift baskets and sells wallpaper and window furnishings. ♦ M-Sa 10AM-6PM; Su 1-5PM. 301 Brevard Ave (Oleander St) 690.2284

37 Cocoa Village Playhouse Built in 1924 as the Aladdin Theatre, a leading vaudeville theater of its time, this stately redbrick building was restored in 1988 and now features regularly scheduled performances. A children's theater shares the facilities. The theater is also used for a rock 'n' roll festival, the Miss Cocoa High pageant, and ballet productions. ♦ 300 Brevard Ave (King-Harrison Sts) 636.5050

38 Cafe Margaux ★$$ Tucked away in the corner of a little courtyard next to the Cocoa Village Playhouse, this cafe is a good place for an afternoon break from shopping or an evening meal if you are going to the theater. Their homemade pastas make for inexpensive but tasty fare. Try the fettuccine Alfredo or the pasta primavera. The chicken Kiev has a great garlic flavor, or if you want something that isn't fried, try the pork dish garnished with

Brevard County/JFK Space Center

sliced apples. ♦ French/Italian ♦ Daily 11AM-9PM. 220 Brevard Ave (King-Harrison Sts) 639.8343

39 J.P.'s Gallery of Gifts An interesting collection of antiques, dolls, and jewelry is sold in a Victorian-style shop opening onto a small, pleasant courtyard. ♦ Tu-Th noon-6PM; F-Sa noon-8PM. 212 Brevard Ave (King-Harrison Sts) 631.1019

40 The Black Tulip ★★$$$ Not to worry; dining on fresh dolphin doesn't mean you're eating Flipper, the former TV star, but a wonderful light fish, also known as mahimahi. The restaurant serves it three ways: with an imaginative banana and lemon butter sauce, a crab stuffing, or baked in parchment

paper with scallops and herbs. The espresso is strong, as it should be ♦ American ♦ M-Sa 11AM-2:30PM, 5-10PM. 207 Brevard Ave (King-Oleander Sts) 631.1133

41 The Village Plate Collector Fine china, miniature figurines, and delicate bells make this shop a good stop for gifts. ♦ M-Sa 10AM-5PM. 217 King St (Brevard Ct-Brevard Ave) 636.6914

42 Byrd Plaza This shopping center is the largest mall in the Cocoa-Rockledge area. Belk Lindsey dominates the recently renovated 40-store center. ♦ M-Sa 10AM-9PM; Su noon-5:30PM. US 1 and Dixon

43 Brevard Museum of History and Natural Science Worth a quick visit, this museum has a vast color chart showing the fish that inhabit the Brevard reef and a display of artifacts—including furniture, clothing, and children's toys—from the family of **Albert A. Taylor**, one of the region's first pioneer families. Children will be fascinated by the live bee colony in the small activity center, although the museum's nature walks—22 acres through three of Florida's ecological systems: a swamp, a sand pine hill, and a Florida hammock—are disappointing. ♦ Admission Tu-Sa 10AM-4PM; Su 1-4PM. 2201 Michigan Blvd (Mercer Dr-Clearlake Rd) 632.1830

Cape Canaveral

When the US government decided in the late 1940s that it needed a long-range missile testing site, it settled on Cape Canaveral, a relatively unpopulated peninsula that juts into the Atlantic. The region was mostly rural, and all of Brevard County had a population of only 16,142 people in 1940. Most made their living raising cattle or crops, or by fishing.

By 1958 the National Aeronautics and Space Administration (NASA) began operations at Cape Canaveral, where it launched scientific, meteorological, and communications satellites. But things changed on 25 August 1961, when President John Kennedy accelerated the space exploration program. Today, Cape Canaveral remains home to Kennedy Space Center.

44 Cape Sierra ★$$$ A semicircular dining room next to the lounge provides a view of a dance floor and stage, featuring piano concertos, to dance bands, and comedy on Mondays. There is also a dining room tucked away from the action. Entrées vary from seafood Alfredo, a combination of gulf shrimp, lobster tail, and scallops served with fettuccine, to pork loin stuffed with cheese, garlic, ham, pimentos, and spinach. The restaurant offers luncheon buffets Tuesdays through Fridays, as well as Cajun grouper sandwiches. ♦ American ♦ M-Th 11AM-midnight; F-Sa 11AM-2AM. 8625 Astronaut Blvd (SR A1A at Cleveland Ave) 799.9996

45 Port Canaveral Port Canaveral, already the third-largest cruise port in the US, is currently undergoing a multimillion-dollar expansion to add more cruise and cargo berths. The military shares the port with cruise ships, private boats, and small commercial operations.

The flags pictured around the map below, provide a means of communication for the various crafts. Some say Love is the international language, but for sailors the language is "wigwag," a slang term for the International Code of Symbols, examples of which border the map below. These semaphores can be decoded in several ways: each corresponds phonetically to the military alphabet (Alpha, Bravo, Charlie, etc.) and can be used to spell out directions. At the same time, each flag symbolizes a condition or warning. For example, **B** means "transporting ammunition," while **P** signifies "man overboard." These ensigns, when used in configurations of two or more, can also signify a more complex situation. **MTG**, for instance, means medical staff and equipment is on its way.

Often docked on the north end of the port is a ship that tracks underwater test missiles launched from submarines. Three cruise lines operate out of the port:

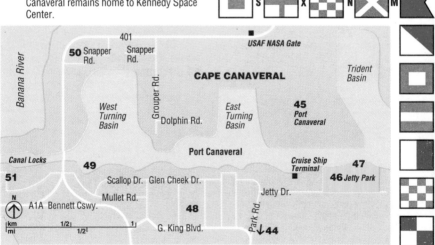

Carnival Cruise Lines *Carnivale* and *Mardi Gras* leave on Thursdays and Sundays for three- and four-night cruises to Nassau in the Bahamas. The four-night cruise includes a stop at Freeport. ◆ 800/327.9501

Europa Cruise Line The *Europa Star* offers six-hour "cruises to nowhere" on the Atlantic for dancing, dining, and gambling. ◆ M-W 10AM-4PM; Th 7PM-midnight; F-Sa 10AM-4PM, 7PM-1AM; Su 1-7PM. 799.0400, 800/688-PLAY

Premier Cruise Lines The *Starship Oceanic* and *Starship Atlantic* leave every Monday and Friday for three- and four-night cruises to Nassau and Salt Cay in the Bahamas. The *Starship Majestic* takes three- and four-night cruises to the Abaco Islands in the northern Bahamas, including Green Turtle Cay, Man-O-War Cay, Treasure Cay, and Great Guana Cay. ◆ 783.5061, 800/432.2545, 800/327.7113 (FL)

46 Jetty Park On the eastern tip of the cape, this 35-acre park offers swimming, fishing, surfing, and camping with grills, bathrooms, and shower facilities. A boardwalk and dunes are hidden from the road. It is a popular stop to watch the cruise ships or view a shuttle launch. ◆ 799.0519

47 Cruise Terminals 2, 3, and 4 These terminals are 9,000-square-foot geodesic domes that are filled with tropical landscaping. Passengers walk through them to get to the docks. ◆ Jetty Park

48 Central Park This 10-acre park has three double-wide boat-launching ramps, boat-wash stations, fish-cleaning tables, pavilions, picnic tables, restrooms, and a parking lot that accommodates vehicles hauling trailers. Its big playing field is home to the **Space Coast Rugby Association** (and their grames are free). At other times the park is full of people playing softball, flying kites, or working on their golf game.

49 Port's End Park This new four-acre park is perfect for the fishing enthusiast. You can fish from a seawall or launch your own boat from a double-wide launching ramp. There are covered picnic tables and bathrooms and an observation tower to view port activities. You also get a clear view of NASA's launch pads five miles away.

50 Cruise Terminal 5 This 42,000-square-foot triangular building, designed by **Post Buckley, Schuh & Jernigan** in 1991, holds 2,500 passengers and can accommodate the largest cruise ships. ◆ Snapper Rd

51 Locks Park The newest of the four port parks, this one is at the far west end where the locks connect the Banana River to the Intercoastal Waterway leading through the port facilities and out into the ocean. This park has covered picnic tables, pavilions, and restrooms, and it is hard to find. There is talk about making a road from SR 528 directly to the park, but until then you must go through the main entrance to the port and keep bearing left until you have gone past Port's

End Park, and under SR 401. The road will dead-end at the park. ◆ Port's End Park

Merritt Island

Merritt Island is 40 miles long and only seven miles across at its widest point near the north end. Samuel Field and his family came to the island in 1868 and created a community called Indianola. The Fields donated land for the first community building, the first school, and the first church, and Samuel became its first minister. He also opened the first store and post office.

52 Merritt Island Dragon A 100-foot dragon created by **Lewis Vandercar** in 1971 is made up of more than 20 tons of concrete and steel and is perched at the southern tip of Merritt Island, where the Banana and Indian rivers converge. Legend has it that hundreds of years ago a dragon rose out of the river to chase away enemies attacking the Native Americans who lived on the island. In 1982 four hatchling dragons were added. ◆ S. tip of Merritt Island

53 Holiday Inn of Merritt Island $$ A typical two-story Holiday Inn, but this one has gone through a recent renovation and is set off the highway a bit. It has tennis courts and a pool, rooms for the physically disabled, and nonsmoking rooms. **C.W. Dandy's Restaurant & Lounge** (daily 7AM-2PM, 5:30-10PM) is on the premises. There are luncheon specials, and the baby back ribs and boneless chicken breast are popular at dinner. The lounge has a lingerie show every Wednesday, and it's home to **Coconuts Comedy Club.** ◆ 260 SR 520 (Formosa Ave) 452.7711, 800/HOLIDAY

54 Merritt Square Mall If you're in a hurry and need a place to go for one-stop shopping, you'll probably find what you need here. There are about a hundred stores, including **Maas Brothers/Jordan Marsh, JC Penney, Dillard's,** and **Sears.** ◆ M-Sa

Brevard County/JFK Space Center

10AM-9PM; Su noon-5:30PM. 777 SR 520 (Plumosa St-Sykes Creek Pkwy) 452.3270

54 Jungle Jim's $$ A step above the average gourmet burger bistro, this spot is heavy on the chrome and greenery and has also become a popular after-work watering hole, thanks to its free hors d'oeuvres. Two tropical birds greet you as you enter; old movie posters, jungle paraphernalia, and tables designed as animals keep you entertained. This isn't native Florida food, but it's a good place for a family and has a children's menu. If you are in the mood for an expensive but popular drink, try their Jungle Jim, which is a mix of tropical juices, jungle cola extracts, and four secret shots of liquor. ◆ American ◆ M-Th, Su 11AM-midnight; F-Sa 11AM-2AM. 777 SR 520 (behind Merritt Square Mall) 459.2332

Kennedy Space Center, Spaceport USA

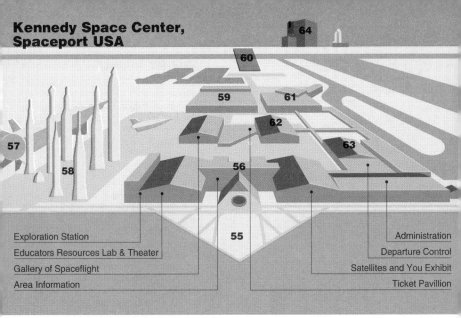

- Exploration Station — 56
- Educators Resources Lab & Theater
- Gallery of Spaceflight
- Area Information
- 55
- Administration
- Departure Control
- Satellites and You Exhibit
- Ticket Pavillion

KENNEDY SPACE CENTER Spaceport USA

55 Kennedy Space Center, Spaceport USA

Combining a visit to this extensive hands-on space museum with a trip to the beach may end up being one of your favorite—and least expensive—days in Central Florida. Except for two IMAX films and two 2-hour bus tours, everything else at this center is free. Get here early and go straight through the entrance at **Spaceport Central.** Directly ahead will be the **Ticket Pavilion.** Purchase your tour and

Brevard County/JFK Space Center

movie tickets to reserve your seats on the bus tours and in the theater (tour and theater times are listed at the Ticket Pavilion). For the most current shuttle launch information, call 900/321.5438 (75 cents per call). The center lies within a 140,000-acre wildlife sanctuary managed for NASA by the US Department of the Interior. If you head north on SR 3 when you leave, you will pass the space shuttle landing site on your left. Once past the security gate, you can turn left on SR 402 and go to the **Merritt Island Wildlife Refuge,** or turn right and head for popular **Playalinda Beach.** ◆ Free. Daily 9AM-7:30PM; closed Christmas. SR 405 (NASA Pkwy between SR 407-Kennedy Pkwy) 452.2121

Restaurants/Nightlife: Red   **Hotels:** Blue
Shops/ 🌳**Outdoors:** Green   **Sights/Culture:** Black

Within Kennedy Space Center, Spaceport USA:

56 Spaceport Central

Here you will find telephones, restrooms, drinking fountains, mailboxes, snacks, and information. As you walk in the first set of doors, touch-screen computers to your left will answer almost any question you might have about Spaceport. If you prefer to talk to humans, they are behind a counter further down. In the main section of the building is **Satellites and You,** a 45-minute, simulated space station walk-through exhibit featuring animatronics and audiovisual effects that demonstrate how satellite technology has affected our lives. On the left as you enter Spaceport Central is a small kiosk with tourist information on Brevard County. Past the kiosk is **Exploration Station, Educators Resources Laboratory,** and **Spaceport Theater.** Exploration Station is a hands-on exhibit open at various times during the day; the times are posted at the entrance. Spaceport Theater shows a number of short films.

57 Rocket Garden

Outside the Spaceport Theater side of Spaceport Central is the Rocket Garden, where NASA displays many of its rockets. Sometimes there is a replica of a space shuttle here that's open for a walk-through tour. In the back of the garden is an Apollo access arm and a lunar excursion module.

58 Gallery of Spaceflight

Between the Rocket Garden and the Ticket Pavilion is the Gallery of Spaceflight, where a moon rock draws the most attention. Models of spacecraft,

Apollo

The Space Shuttle Orbiter

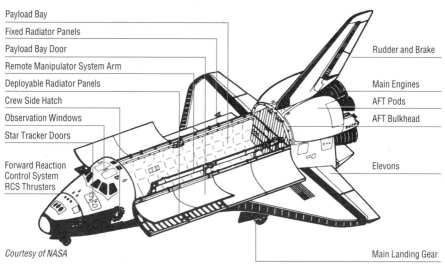

Payload Bay
Fixed Radiator Panels
Payload Bay Door
Remote Manipulator System Arm
Deployable Radiator Panels
Crew Side Hatch
Observation Windows
Star Tracker Doors
Forward Reaction Control System RCS Thrusters

Rudder and Brake
Main Engines
AFT Pods
AFT Bulkhead
Elevons
Main Landing Gear

Courtesy of NASA

including Soviet satellites, space clothes, and lots of photographs are also on display. The Apollo spacecraft that docked with the Russian Soyuz spacecraft in 1975 is here, along with full-size models of a Lunar Rover and a Viking Mars Lander, which landed on Mars in 1976.

59 Galaxy Center Along with the Galaxy and IMAX theaters, Galaxy Center houses more than 250 paintings and sculptures commissioned by the NASA Art Program. A replica of the Hubble Space Telescope hangs from the ceiling. The Galaxy Theater shows a free, 22-minute film, *The Boy from Mars,* throughout the day, starting at 10:50AM, with the last showing at 4:20PM. The IMAX Theater features a variety of films including *Blue Planet,* a beautiful, 42-minute movie about the future of planet Earth. ◆ Admission. *Blue Planet,* daily 9:55AM and 6:15PM.

60 Astronauts Memorial A magnificent, 42-foot-high and 50-foot-wide polished granite monument is carved with the names of the 14 American astronauts who lost their lives in the line of duty. The memorial is a rotating space mirror that tracks the sun throughout the day. Reflectors direct the sunlight back through the names, making it appear as if the astronauts' names are floating in the sky. The $6 million memorial, funded largely by the sale of Challenger license plates in Florida, is located on six acres of land at the back of Spaceport, overlooking a pristine lagoon.

61 Orbit Cafeteria $ Step up to a rotating serving wheel and grab what you want to eat at this air-conditioned cafeteria. ◆ American ◆ Daily 9AM-5PM

62 Gift Gantry Souvenirs ranging from clothes with NASA insignias to space food and postcards are sold here. ◆ Daily 9AM-7:15PM. 452.1634

63 Lunch Pad $ One small step above cafeteria food, where you can get ribs, chicken, and fish. ◆ Daily 11:30AM-7PM.

64 Bus Tours A walkway between the Orbit Cafeteria and the Lunch Pad takes you to the bus boarding area. The **Red Tour** is the more exciting of the tours because you get to see the sights that are so familiar from TV coverage of the space shuttle program, such as the shuttle launch pads and the large Vehicle Assembly Building. Other highlights are a simulated launch countdown, a Saturn rocket, and the six-million-pound Crawler Transporters that move space shuttles to the launch pads. The **Blue Tour** takes you to the Cape Canaveral Air Force Station and the Air Force Space Museum, where there are more than 70 missiles and space launch vehicles on display. The museum is on the site where Explorer 1,

Brevard County/JFK Space Center

America's first satellite, was launched. Both tours may be altered due to actual launch schedules. ◆ Fee. Daily 9:45AM-5PM.

Viewing Space Shuttle Launches

Eager to watch a shuttle launch up close? Here are a few suggestions for a good view:

Get a hotel room overlooking the ocean. Rooms fill up, especially in northern Brevard County, around the launch dates, so book early.

Launch dates are merely target dates; there are many factors that might cause a delay. When it gets close to a launch date, call 900/321.5438 for updated information. The call costs 75 cents.

If you are in Central Florida, you can drive close to the space center for a better view but beware: There are massive traffic jams on launch dates along the highways around the space center, and the usual 45-minute drive between Orlando and Titusville may take more than three hours.

The most popular place to watch a launch is along US 1 between SR 528 and SR 406. Get there early, bring refreshments, and pull off the road where you can find an unobstructed view to the east. One of the best spots is Jetty Park (see page 89) in Port Canaveral. There are refreshments, picnic areas, camping, swimming, fishing, and it is a great place to wait out the traffic. A little less dramatic but also pleasant is Sebastian Inlet State Recreation Area (see page 78).

If you are staying in an Orlando hotel, you can watch the space shuttle launch on TV. After you see the blast-off on TV, run outside and keep your eyes focused to the east. On a clear day, you will be able to see the glint of the rocket.

65 United States Astronaut Hall of Fame

This white building at Kennedy Space Center's Gate 3 is a high-tech warehouse filled with NASA memorabilia and videotapes. The Hall of Fame is basically a tribute to the

original Mercury Seven, America's first astronauts. Among the items on display are **Virgil "Gus" Grissom's** Congressional Space Medal of Honor and a checklist that was strapped to the arm of **Alan Shepard** when he made his moon walk. A timeline can be seen in a tunnel-like display exhibiting a replica of Sputnik, the world's first satellite, which was launched by the Soviet Union in 1957. Also look for a copy of **President John Kennedy's** pledge to put a man in space by the end of the 1960s. A gift shop offers all the usual T-shirts, mugs, and postcards, as well as dinners just like the ones the astronauts used to eat—freeze-dried chicken, rice, peas, peaches, and ice cream in a plastic envelope. ♦ Admission. Daily 9AM-5PM (extended hours in the summer, closed Christmas) SR 405 (US 1-SR 3) 269.6100

65 United States Space Camp

The camp shares the grounds with the Hall of Fame and offers five-day programs for children in grades four to seven from March through October. The camp isn't cheap, but where else can kids wear flight suits, eat freeze-dried food, experience one-sixth gravity, and perform simulated shuttle missions? Also, a single-day camp, lasting about four hours, is available year-round to both youth and adult groups. ♦ Admission. Pre-registration is required. SR 405 (US 1-SR 3) 800/63-SPACE

66 Canaveral National Seashore/Merritt Island National Wildlife Refuge

The national seashore and wildlife refuge are within easy reach of Orlando and Kennedy Space Center's Spaceport USA. With minimal planning, you can enjoy this unspoiled seashore, a welcome alternative to the expensive, manufactured attractions in the Orlando area. The wildlife refuge is home to 310 species of birds, 25 species of mammals, 117 species of fishes, and 23 species of migratory waterfowl. For backcountry hiking permits and details on the trails and beaches, stop by the Information Center ♦ Daily 8AM-4:30PM. One-fourth mile south of Turtle Mound on SR A1A. 904/428.3384

At the Canaveral National Seashore:

Beaches Locals use the anglicized pronunciation of **Playalinda Beach** (Spanish for "pretty beach"), Central Florida's version of a hedonistic, unsullied beach. There is some nude bathing here, but the main attraction is the sand, sun, and ocean. One warning: Playalinda is closed at times because of launches from Cape Canaveral. Call before you visit (867.2805 or 267.1110). Take SR 406 east from Titusville to SR 402 until you get to the beach. Lesser-known and less accessible **Apollo Beach** is at the north end of the National Seashore in Volusia County. You can take SR 3 north from Spaceport USA; then, at the city of **New Smyrna Beach**, head south on SR A1A to the beach. Both Apollo and Playalinda beaches have parking areas. Take water or refreshments, because there is nothing to drink once you get there. You can hike north from Playalinda or south from Apollo Beach to the less populated **Klondike Beach**, which is accessible only by foot. Consult tide charts before walking in, however, since there may be little beach to walk on at high tide.

Drives No American wildlife area would be complete without accommodating the automobile, and the National Seashore has two drives that offer good views of the wildlife. The 30 to 45-minute **Black Point Wildlife Drive** meanders through pine flatwoods and marsh and is a great place to see waterfowl and wading birds, especially in the winter. The 20-minute **Max Hoeck Creek Wildlife Drive** (closed occasionally because of space center operations) follows a railroad bed through a marsh and uplands just west of Playalinda Beach. If you're lucky, you'll get a glimpse of alligators and waterfowl, as well as marsh and wading birds.

 Hiking Trails The paths are clearly marked and afford some of the most rewarding glimpses of flora and fauna. And they are short enough not to tire even small kids. **Oak Hammock Trail** is a 30-minute hiking loop that wanders through a hardwood hammock—a dense coastal forest. It lies off SR 402 about halfway between Titusville and Playalinda Beach. A shorter, 15-minute hike at **Turtle Mound,** north of Apollo Beach, is well marked and takes you to the top of an Indian shell mound (a 50-foot mound so prominent it shows up on 16th-century Spanish maps) for a view of the Atlantic Ocean and Mosquito Lagoon.

Ranger Walks Another great way to introduce yourself or your kids to Florida's wildlife is to ask about ranger-sponsored hikes at the **National Seashore.** Rangers give guided tours of hammocks that last from one to two hours. They also lead nature walks along the beach and teach you about seashells, marine life, sand dunes, and beach vegetation. Rangers will even give you points on how to fish in the surf; you'll learn about proper equipment, bait, what fish you are trying to catch, and how to cast your fishing line. Fishing equipment is provided for practice, or you can bring your own gear.

So Long, Dusky

As Central Florida has boomed, it's taken its toll on the environment. One of the most famous casualties is the dusky seaside sparrow. The aging, half-blind, sole survivor of the species died on 16 June 1987 at Disney's Discovery Island, an island nature preserve. Central Florida bird-lovers mourned. The 20-year battle to save the little bird—shy in its youth and bold at maturity—was over.

The cry of the bold dusky seaside sparrow used to be heard in the marshes of Brevard County, within a 10-mile radius of Titusville. Thousands of the duskies thrived until land development, dikes, and controlled floods required for mosquito control, along with pesticides, highways, and fires, destroyed their habitat. During its tenure at Disney's Discovery Island, the dusky was treated like a prince. The public didn't have access to him; he could only be observed by scientists or others for the very best of reasons. The dusky's handlers treated him tenderly, dipping their feet in disinfectant before entering his sandy-bottomed cage planted with marsh grass to simulate, as much as possible, his habitat.

Even though the dusky is now extinct, there's a chance your kids or grandchildren will one day see a clone of this bird. Some of the dusky's tissue sits in a laboratory at Clark-Atlanta University, where it has been frozen in anticipation of some future technology that may allow a pure strain of the bird to be resurrected through genetic cloning.

 Primitive Camping If you really want to rough it, the Canaveral National Seashore has a number of backcountry camping sites that are located among the many islands in the northern part of **Mosquito Lagoon.** They can be reached only by boat or canoe, and those near Klondike Beach are closed from 15 May to 30 September to protect the sea turtle during its nesting period. A backcountry hiking permit is required to stay overnight at campsites, but the permit is free. For permit information, call 904/428.3384.

Titusville

The county seat of Brevard County, Titusville was named for Colonel Henry T. Titus. He was a soldier of fortune before the Civil War, and then a relatively rich man after it, because he acquired a contract to sell supplies to the Confederate Army. After the war, Titus became a saloon-keeper and hotelier in a little city on Florida's east coast called Sand Point. Feeling no lack of ego, he became postmaster and had the name of the post-office station changed from Sand Point to Titusville.

67 Holiday Inn Kennedy Space Center $$ Take your choice of a room that faces either a pool or the Indian River. All come with two double-sized beds. The hotel has a do-it-yourself laundry room and rents fishing equipment. ◆ 4951 S. Washington Ave (Cheney Hwy) 267.4739, 800/HOLIDAY

68 Best Western Space Shuttle Inn $$ A good value. This 125-room motel has recently been renovated and has a pool, sauna, and rooms with king-sized beds. There are even waterbeds for sixties diehards. The motel has easy access to I-95 near Kennedy Space Center. ◆ 3455 Cheney Hwy (I-95-SR 405) 269.9100, 800/523.7654; fax 383.4674

69 Ramada Inn Kennedy Space Center $$
Low rates make this motel a hit with shuttle fans. It has tennis courts, an exercise room, a game room, a sauna, and a restaurant. There are also rooms for the physically disabled and nonsmokers. ◆ 3500 Cheney Hwy (I-95-SR 405) 269.5510, 800/228.3838

70 Rodeway Inn Kennedy Space Center $$
Convenient access to I-95 and SR 50 make this motel a good location for shuttle watching. You can watch the launch from your room, and among the amenities are a pool, rooms for the physically disabled, nonsmoking rooms, rooms that allow pets, a restaurant, and a lounge. ◆ 3655 Cheney Hwy (I-95) 269.7110

71 Quality Inn Kennedy Space Center $$
This motel has a convenient location off the interstate, a large pool, some suites, nonsmoking rooms, and rooms for the physically disabled. ◆ 3755 Cheney Hwy (I-95) 269.4480; fax 383.0646

Turtles See the Light

"Save the baby loggerheads!" has become a rallying cry for nature lovers in Brevard County. And businesses and the governments of Central Florida's Brevard and Volusia counties, especially in the coastal regions of Daytona Beach and Melbourne, are becoming sensitive to the problem of lighting along the beaches during turtle-nesting season.

Biologists say artificial lights confuse and disorient baby sea turtles, which hatch in beachside nests, and are instinctively drawn to the moonlight shimmering off the Atlantic Ocean. But sometimes that glow isn't the moon's reflection, but the lights shining from condos, beachfront restaurants, or street lights. When the hatchlings crawl toward those lights, they become easy prey for birds, or are squashed by cars in parking lots or streets. The tiny hatchlings that survive the first night usually die from intense heat from the sun the next day.

Both Volusia and Brevard counties have enacted lighting ordinances, vowing to crack down on lights that endanger the sea turtles. From May through October, residents and businesses in Brevard County coastal areas must turn off or shade bright ocean-front lights. Violators can be fined up to $250 a day.

The rest is up to nature. Thousands of sea turtles swim toward Brevard County to nest in its sandy beaches during spring and summer. The female turtles are mostly loggerhead, a threatened species, but there also are smaller green turtles and an

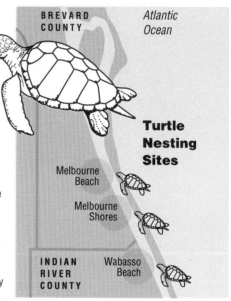

occasional leatherback. In 1990 researchers counted 20,000 nests along a 28-mile stretch of Brevard beaches. An encouraging sign: it was a 40 percent increase in the number of nests compared to 1989.

Hatchlings incubate from 45 to 75 days and crawl out in the evening when the sand is damp and cool. You can get a fascinating glimpse of nesting turtles, but don't get too close to the female until she actually starts laying eggs. Nesting turtles are easily frightened, but once the female, some weighing as much as 350 pounds, digs her nest and the process of egg-laying begins, spectators can approach without disturbing her. The turtle will lay as many as 120 eggs about the size of Ping-Pong balls. A female loggerhead may dig five nests in one season.

For more information about proper turtle-watching protocol, take a guided turtle walk, usually scheduled from 9PM to midnight. Reservations are mandatory; and it is best to make them at least two weeks in advance. The following offer guided tours:

Brevard Turtle Preservation Society (donations) 676.1701
Sebastian Inlet State Recreation Area (free) 589.2147
Merritt Island National Wildlife Refuge (free) 867.0667

Brevard County/JFK Space Center

	Tips for Turtle Watching
1.	Wear dark-colored clothes.
2.	Bring insect repellent to ward off mosquitoes.
3.	Use your flashlight only to help you get to the beach, then turn it off.
4.	Use high-speed film in your camera instead of a flash.
5.	Do not disturb the turtles. Let them crawl about without having to go around you.
6.	Do not kick up sand around a nest or a nesting turtle.
7.	Do not disturb or get too close to a turtle making a nest.
8.	Clean up after yourself—leave *nothing* on the beach.
9.	Remember it is a federal offense to touch or even disturb a sea turtle.

72 Miracle City Mall Belk-Lindsey and JC Penney are a part of this 46-store mall. ♦ M-Sa 10AM-9PM; Su noon-5:30PM. 2500 S. Washington Ave (Jackson-Harrison Sts) 269.7521

73 Emma Parrish Theatre An amateur community theater group presents two musicals and four dramas a year in this 1920s restored movie theater in downtown Titusville. ♦ 301 Julia St (Hopkins Ave) 268.3711; box office 268.1125

74 North Brevard Historical Museum This small storefront museum has a surprisingly large amount of articles detailing what life was like in the Titusville area around the turn of the century. Displays include farming equipment, pictures, and furniture. ♦ Free. Tu, Th, Sa 10AM-2PM. 301 S. Washington Ave (Main St) 269.3658

75 Dixie Crossroads ★$$ This spot is much larger inside than it appears from the outside, and it's always crowded with locals. The menu features seafood caught in the Atlantic, and the customers keep coming back for the all-you-can-eat rock shrimp (small, hard-shelled shrimp that taste a lot like lobster) specials. The broiled or fried calico scallops with corn fritters are also good. ♦ Seafood ♦ Daily 11AM-10PM. 1475 Garden St (Dixie Ave) 268.5000

Space Exploration Timeline

24 July 1950—The first missile launched from Cape Canaveral is a modified German V-2.

31 January 1958—*Explorer 1,* the first US satellite, discovers Van Allen Radiation Belt.

17 March 1958—*Vanguard 1,* the second US satellite, determines that the Earth is slightly pear-shaped.

7 August 1959—*Explorer 6* sends back a crude cloud-cover image, the first Earth photo from space.

1961—NASA begins acquiring land next to the Cape Canaveral Air Force Station on Merritt Island for its primary launch facility.

5 May 1961—**Alan Shepard's** suborbital flight aboard *Freedom 7,* the first manned Mercury flight in the US, lasts 15 minutes.

21 July 1961—**Virgil Grissom's** flight aboard *Liberty Bell 7,* the second manned Mercury flight, lasts 16 minutes.

20 February 1962—**John Glenn** becomes the first US astronaut to orbit the Earth, making three complete revolutions aboard *Friendship 7.*

27 August 1962—*Mariner 2* is launched and flies by Venus on 14 December 1962.

23 March 1965—Grissom and **John Young** are the first to change orbital altitude. They are aboard the premier launch of the Gemini program.

3 June 1965—**Edward White** becomes the first US astronaut to walk in space, spending 21 minutes outside a *Gemini 4* capsule.

30 May 1966—*Surveyor 1* makes the first soft lunar landing in the Ocean of Storms, and sends back 11,237 pictures.

27 January 1967—*Apollo 1* explodes, killing astronauts Grissom, White, and **Roger Chaffee.**

11 October 1968—*Apollo 7* is the first successful manned flight of the Apollo spaceship; aboard are **Walter Schirra, Donn Eisele,** and **Walter Cunningham.**

21 December 1968—*Apollo 8* goes to the moon, marking the first time humans leave the gravity of the Earth for another planetary body.

16 July 1969—*Apollo 11* is launched. Its mission is to land men on the moon and return them safely to Earth—a national goal set in May 1961 by **President John Kennedy.** The lunar landing takes place on 20 July. **Neil Armstrong** takes the first step on the moon at 10:56PM EDT of the same day.

28 November 1971—*Mariner 9* is launched into orbit around Mars, sending back 6,876 pictures of the planet's surface.

2 March 1972—*Pioneer 10* is launched. It is the first Jupiter probe, sending back close-up pictures of a Jovian moon.

5 April 1973—*Pioneer 11* is launched. It is the first spacecraft to fly by Saturn and send back pictures.

3 November 1973—*Mariner 10* is launched and sends back the first TV pictures of Mercury.

17 July 1975—*The Apollo,* a US spacecraft, and the *Soyuz,* a USSR satellite, launched 6,500 miles and seven and a half hours apart, dock with each other over Europe. Aboard *Apollo* are **Donald Slayton, Thomas Stafford,** and **Vance Brand.** Aboard *Soyuz* are **Alexei Leonov,** who was the first person to walk in space on 18 March 1965, and **Valeriy Kubasov.**

20 August and 9 September 1975—*Viking 1* and *Viking 2* are sent to Mars in search of microscopic life in the planet's soil samples. Research finds no positive indications of life.

12 April 1981—*Columbia,* the first space shuttle, is launched.

4 April 1983—The *Challenger* is used for the first time in the sixth space shuttle mission.

18 June 1983—**Sally Ride** becomes the first woman in space. Her flight aboard *Challenger* is the seventh space shuttle mission.

30 August 1983—**Guion Bluford** becomes the first black person to fly in space. His flight aboard the

Brevard County/JFK Space Center

Challenger is the eighth space shuttle mission.

7 February 1984—The first untethered space walk is accomplished by **Bruce McCandless.** Two hours later **Robert Stewart** does the same.

6 April 1984—The SMM (Solar Maximum Mission) satellite, launched 14 February 1980 to study the sun, is the first satellite to be retrieved and repaired in space by a shuttle crew.

11 October 1984—**Kathryn Sullivan** becomes the first woman to walk in space.

31 August 1985—**James van Hoften** and **William Fisher** spend seven hours and eight minutes outside *Discovery 6* fixing a damaged satellite.

28 January 1986—An explosion 73 seconds after lift-off kills the crew of *Challenger 10,* including **Christa McAuliffe,** a member of the Teacher in Space program.

24 April 1990—*Discovery 10* is launched to deploy the Hubble Space Telescope.

Volusia County/ Daytona Beach

Sand, sun, and speed is the famous mix that draws visitors to Volusia County and its biggest city, Daytona Beach. The Atlantic beaches here are among Central Florida's most dramatic; they're broad and sweeping—so wide that some sections are open to auto traffic. At any time of day or night you can walk on the beach at Daytona, billed in these parts as "The World's Most Famous Beach," and you can drive on it beginning an hour before sunrise and ending an hour after sundown. Park your car in the sand if you want—it's a Volusia County tradition.

Every spring, successive waves of racing fans flock to Daytona Beach for **Speed Weeks**. First come the auto-racing fans, who jam-pack Daytona International Speedway. The grassy infield area is notorious for its wild beer parties, but teetotalers love the races as well. Speed Weeks climaxes in mid-February with the **Daytona 500**, the world's biggest and most lucrative stock-car race.

No sooner do the auto diehards leave than thousands of leather-clad motorcyclists roar into town from all over the country for **Cycle Week**—seven days in March of motorcycle races held at the Speedway. The bikers represent a varied bunch that includes some pin-striped types, but even so, most come to Daytona Beach to down brews at the bikers' unofficial headquarters: the Main Street bars.

Before the bikers leave, the third wave has already arrived: college students on spring break, ready to party heartily in the beachfront hotels. If you stop for a visit, you'll likely witness around-the-clock wet T-shirt and "hot buns" contests, as well as countless beer bashes. Companies that make everything from suntan oil to condoms and baseball caps set up shop along the beach and at the Ocean Center, a convention hall, where plenty of samples and freebies are distributed.

Not everyone enjoys the wild party atmosphere, and if heavy traffic really gets to you, don't venture into the Daytona Beach area during race weeks or spring break, which traditionally runs from March until mid-April. A more bucolic setting can be found year-round in West Volusia, which is sparsely populated except for the coastal areas and the small towns that dot its western borders. Western Volusia County is famous for its crystalline springs and swamp oaks dripping with moss. Don't miss **Blue Spring State Park**, two miles west of Orange City in Volusia County, which is home to the Florida manatee (or sea cow) during the cool winter months.

Area Code 904 unless otherwise indicated.

Orange City

1 Blue Spring State Park Once a riverboat stop on the St. Johns River, this 518-acre state park is now best known as a manatee refuge. These gentle sea cows, which are about 12 feet long and weigh almost a ton, are drawn to the spring in winter because of its constant 72-degree water temperature. There is a wheelchair-accessible trail that follows Blue Spring Run from the river to the spring. Swimming is allowed in a roped-off area that the manatees slip in and out of as they cruise the run. The mammals are an endangered species, and rangers are on hand to make sure they are not harassed. The Thursby House, built on a mound of shells in 1872, is open Thursday through Sunday for a nominal fee and provides a look at life in the romantic steamboat days of the St. Johns River. Blue Spring has a boat ramp, camping, canoeing, fishing, nature trails, picnicking, restrooms, a refreshment stand, and swimming. ◆ Nominal fee. Daily 8AM-sunset. 2100 W. French Ave (take US 17-92 into Orange City and follow the signs to Blue Spring; it is 2 miles west of Orange City at the end of French St) 904/755.3663

De Leon Springs

2 Karlings Inn ★$$$ It is a relaxing ride away from the hubbub of the beach and city, and once you get to this old house and try one of the specialties, you'll be glad you did. Everyone raves over the lobster fricassee with cream cayenne pepper-scotch sauce. For an appetizer, try the escargots baked in garlic butter. For dessert the flan is a must. Karlings is one of the few places that does it properly. Traditional dishes from France, Spain, and other parts of Europe are served by women in peasant dresses. ◆ 4640 N. US 17. 904/985.5535

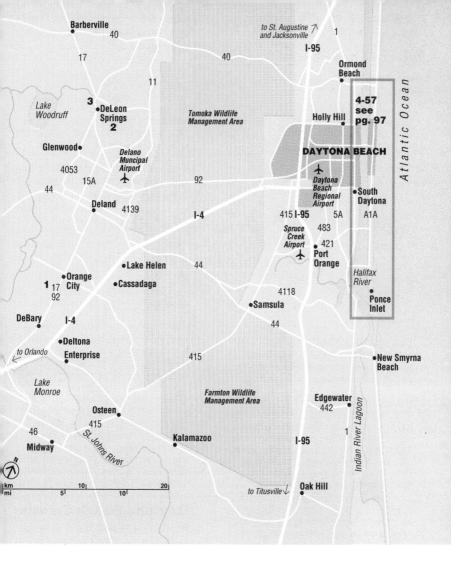

3 De Leon Springs State Recreation Area
The heart of this state park is a beautiful spring-fed pool good for swimming or snorkeling. Scuba tanks aren't allowed, however. ♦ Daily 8AM-sundown. 904/985.4212

Within the De Leon Springs State Recreation Area:

Old Spanish Sugar Mill & Griddle House
★$$ If you're in central Florida for a visit to Walt Disney World but want a non-Disney experience, put this at the top of your list. This homey restaurant, once an old stone waterwheel house, has specially built tables with big griddles in the middle. Guests order pitchers of marvelous pancake batter (don't miss the whole-wheat batter) and little bowls of goodies—such as maybe blueberries, bananas, or peanut butter, and cook their own flapjacks. Even folks who've forgotten how a kitchen works love it. Lines can be long if you arrive at midday. ♦ American ♦ M-F 9AM-5PM; Sa-Su 8AM-5PM; last seatings daily at

4PM. Closed Thanksgiving and Christmas. Reservations required for parties of 10 or more. 904/985.5644

Ponce Inlet

4 Lighthouse Landing $$ Dine on fresh mahimahi or farm-raised catfish inside, or eat shucked oysters outside under spreading oaks. Inside and out, you'll enjoy a sweeping view of the Halifax River and maybe spot fishers casting their nets at the water's edge. ♦ Seafood ♦ Daily 11:30AM-10PM Feb-Dec. 4940 S. Peninsula Dr (Lighthouse Dr-Robert A. Merrill Pkwy) 904/761.9271

5 Lighthouse Park Locals come here to get away from the crowded beaches. There is a playground, a picnic area, restrooms, a marina, and a beach.

At the Lighthouse Park:

JOANNE MARSH ZIMMERMAN

Ponce de Leon Inlet Lighthouse A lighthouse called Mosquito Lights was the first built in these parts in 1834, but it never opened. Indians vandalized it, then a storm swept it away. A more solid brick lighthouse was built to replace it across Ponce de Leon Inlet, north of the old structure. It first flashed its beacon on 3 November 1888. After years of using oil, the lighthouse was converted to electricity in the 1920s and a revolving lens made in Paris in 1867 was installed. It flashed six times every 26 seconds and could be seen as far away as 20 miles at sea. In 1970 the government decided it was too costly to maintain the lighthouse and closed it down, but the city of Ponce Inlet was deeded the lighthouse and has since fixed it up, along with the cottages on the grounds. The Coast Guard relit the lighthouse in December 1982, and it is once again in use. The new light can be seen for 16 miles out to sea. Visitors willing to climb 203 steps to the top of the 175-foot lighthouse are rewarded

with a great view of the area. Pass through a little white picket fence to the gift shop to start your tour. ♦ Admission. Daily 10AM-4PM (often later in the summer) 4931 S. Peninsula Dr (Lighthouse Dr) 904/761.1821

Head Lighthouse Keeper's House This building is now a sea museum.

First Assistant Keeper's Cottage After restoration and refurnishing, this cottage looks just as it would have at the turn of the century.

Second Assistant Keeper's Cottage The original lens is housed here, along with other

lighthouse artifacts, and you can read up on the history of Ponce Inlet.

6 Down the Hatch $ On a tree-shaded, residential street at the end of the peninsula, you will find this rustic, fishing-camp getaway. The chowder is terrific: follow it with one of the all-you-can-eat specials and a cold drink while taking in the river view. If it's a scorching day, dine indoors at big wooden tables, but the ideal way to enjoy this scenic outpost is to sit outside at one of the ceramic-tiled tables, chasing raw oysters with a brew. ♦ Seafood ♦ Daily noon-10PM. Timmons Fishing Camp, Front St (Beach St-Rains Dr) 904/761.4831

7 North Turn Restaurant ★$ The food isn't

anything to write home about, but the friendly service on the beach deck can't be beat. Inside, the atmosphere is casual and there's a convivial raw bar, but locals flock to the deck—for steamed crab legs and shrimp and the live, mellow sixties music on weekends. The name North Turn is a part of pre-Speedway folklore: drivers made the big turn here, after racing up the beach from the peninsula's southern tip, crossing over to Atlantic Ave, and zipping back down toward the lighthouse. Although the racing has ended here, the ambience and music has remained largely unchanged. ♦ American ♦ Patio deck: Daily 4-11PM indoors; dining room 4PM-midnight. 4511 S. Atlantic Ave (Seahaven Dr-Winterhaven Rd) 904/760.6467

Daytona Beach Shores

8 Royal Holiday Beach Motel $$ A basic, two-story motel, but with everything you need: efficiencies, suites, air-conditioning, color TV, wall-to-wall carpet, and a pool with an ocean view. ♦ 3717 S. Atlantic Ave (Phillips-Marcelle Aves) 904/761.5984

8 Captain's Quarters Inn ★$$$ Owner **Becky Sue Morgan** brings a touch of New England to the beach with her five-story, all-suites inn, complete with yellow clapboard exterior, white bedspreads, and oak furniture. Each suite has a living room with a queen-sized sofa bed, a bedroom with two double beds or one queen-sized bed, and a complete kitchen with dishwasher and coffeemaker. Wicker rocking chairs are on each of the private balconies. **The Galley,** the inn's coffee shop, serves fresh-baked goods and overlooks the heated swimming pool and the beach beyond. ♦ 3711 S. Atlantic Ave (Phillips-Marcelle Aves) 904/767.3119

Restaurants/Nightlife: Red	Hotels: Blue
Shops/ ♠Outdoors: Green	Sights/Culture: Black

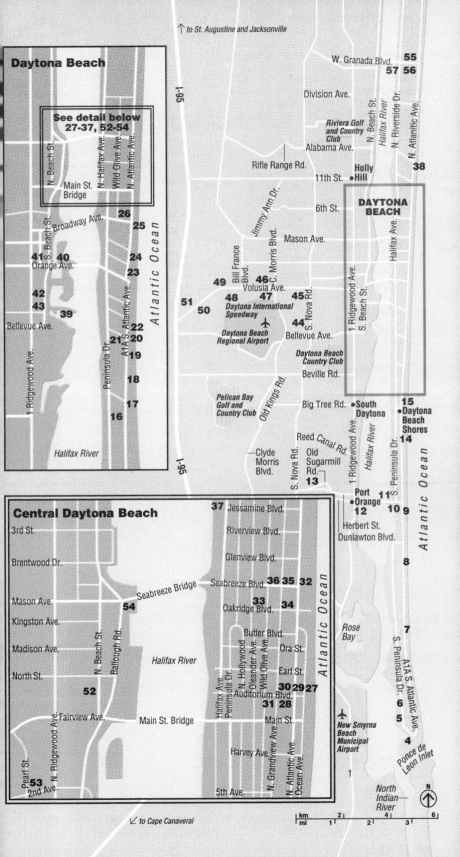

Daytona Beach

↑ to St. Augustine and Jacksonville

I-95

See detail below
27-37, 52-54

N. Beach St.
N. Halifax Ave.
Wild Olive Ave.
N. Atlantic Ave.

Main St.
Bridge

26

25

S. Beach St.
Broadway Ave.

24

41 S. 40
Orange Ave.

23

42

43

39

Bellevue Ave.

Atlantic Ocean

22
Peninsula Dr.
21 A1A S. Atlantic Ave. 20

19

1 Ridgewood Ave.

18

17

16

Halifax River

I-95

W. Granada Blvd. 55
57 56

Division Ave.

Riviera Golf
and Country
Club
Alabama Ave.

N. Beach St.
Halifax River
N. Riverside Dr.
N. Atlantic Ave.

38

Rifle Range Rd.

11th St.
Holly
• Hill

6th St.

Jimmy Ann Dr.

Mason Ave.

Halifax Ave.

DAYTONA
BEACH

C. Morris Blvd.

49

Bill France Blvd.

46
Volusia Ave.

47

45

1 Ridgewood Ave.
S. Beach St.

48

51

50

Daytona International
Speedway

S. Nova Rd.

44

Daytona Beach
Regional Airport

Bellevue Ave.

Daytona Beach
Country Club

Beville Rd.

Pelican Bay
Golf and
Country Club

Old Kings Rd.

Big Tree Rd. •South
Daytona

15
•Daytona
Beach
Shores

14

Reed Canal Rd.

1 Ridgewood Ave.
Halifax River
S. Peninsula Dr.

Atlantic Ocean

—Clyde
Morris
Blvd.

S. Nova Rd.

Old
Sugarmill
Rd.•

13

8

Port
•Orange

11
10 9

12

7

Herbert St.
Dunlawton Blvd.

Central Daytona Beach

37 Jessamine Blvd.

Rose
Bay

A1A S. Atlantic Ave.
S. Peninsula Dr.

6

3rd St.

Riverview Blvd.

5

Brentwood Dr.

Glenview Blvd.

4

Mason Ave.

Seabreeze Bridge

Seabreeze Blvd.

36 35 32

Kingston Ave.

54

Oakridge Blvd.

33

34

New Smyrna
Beach
Municipal
Airport

Ponce de
Leon Inlet

Madison Ave.

N. Beach St.
Ballough Rd.

Butler Blvd.

Ora St.

North St.

Halifax River

N. Hollywood
Oleander Ave.
Wild Olive Ave.

Earl St.

52

30 29 27

Halifax Ave.
Peninsula Dr.

Auditorium Blvd.

31 28

N. Ridgewood Ave.
Fairview Ave.

Main St. Bridge

Main St.

Harvey Ave.

N. Grandview Ave.
N. Atlantic Ave.
Ocean Ave.

Pearl St.
53
2nd Ave.

5th Ave.

North
Indian—
River

N

↙ to Cape Canaveral

km
mi
1   2   4   6
          2   3

9 Pirate's Cove Beach Lodge $$ This beachfront hotel offers refurbished rooms and efficiencies, each with a private balcony. The heated pool is on the ocean, and it is ringed by a pleasing deck. The **Ocean Terrace Restaurant** serves breakfast, lunch, and dinner, while **Rum Runner's** offers drinks and live entertainment. ◆ 3501 S. Atlantic Ave (Dunlawton Blvd) 904/767.8740 800/272.2683 (US) 800/233.2683 (Canada)

Port Orange

In these parts, "down under" refers to any location under the Port Orange Bridge.

10 Sinbad's Restaurant & Lounge $$ Hard by the Port Orange Bridge, right on the Halifax River sits this "down under" restaurant. Its specialty is seafood, but it also serves steak and prime rib. Don't pass up the deep-fried shrimp. ◆ American ◆ M-F 8AM-10PM, Sa-Su 7AM-10PM. 78 Dunlawton Blvd (Port Orange Bridge) 904/756.2921

11 JC's Oyster Deck $$ Another "down under" restaurant, this modest spot is well known among local folks as a great place to hit after a trip to the beach. Raw or steamed oysters, clams, shrimp and crab legs are available by the pound or the bucket. Beer, burgers, and seafood sandwiches, too. ◆ Seafood ◆ Daily 11AM-11PM. 79 Dunlawton Blvd (Port Orange Bridge) 904/767.1881

12 Aunt Catfish's ★★$$ It's rambling and rustic, and the cooking is down home and done right. The catfish is prepared just about every way you can imagine, but the flounder is also

excellent. Or try the Florida Cracker Sampler, a platter with crab fritters, catfish fingerlings and shrimp. For breakfast, don't miss the wonderful cheese grits. Sunday brunch is the talk of the town; stuffed flapjacks come flying hot off an iron stove. This light-blue wood-frame riverside restaurant has an air-conditioned, glass-enclosed room, along with open-air deck dining. ◆ Seafood ◆ Daily 11:30AM-10PM. 4009 Halifax Dr (Dunlawton Blvd) 904/767.4768

13 Sugar Mill Gardens The best preserved sugar mill in the country sits in a 12-acre Volusia County park surrounded by oak, holly, magnolia trees, and oddly enough, statues of dinosaurs. The people from the Botanical Gardens of Volusia, who now care for the 12 acres of Sugar Mill Gardens, never removed the dinosaurs. So keep your eyes open for them as you walk down the shady paths.

Besides the prehistoric animals you'll see the sugar mill building, vats, and machinery. The first sugar mill here was established by **Patrick Dean,** who received a grant of 995 acres in 1804 from the Spanish government. He was killed by the Seminole Indians. The plantation changed hands twice until it was burned down again in 1836 during the Second Seminole War. It was rebuilt in 1846 by **John Marshall,** who converted the refining process to steam. During the Civil War the Confederates used the big vats on the grounds to make salt from salt water. The gardens are open daily, but there aren't always people there to explain what you're seeing. A brochure helps, but you might call beforehand. ◆ Donation. Daily 8:30AM-5PM; gift shop: W, Sa 9AM-3PM. 950 Old Sugar Mill Rd (Herbert St-Bird Dr) 904/767.3812

14 Comfort Inn Oceanfront $$ Each room has a balcony in this L-shaped, eight-floor motel. A large sun deck surrounds a heated pool with stairs leading down to the beach. There is a restaurant, lounge, game room, and gift shop. ◆ 3135 S. Atlantic Ave (Van Ave) 904/767.8533, 800/228.5150

15 Daytona Beach Hilton ★★★$$$ Despite its rather forbidding exterior, this high-rise Hilton renovated in 1987 still gets the nod as the best hotel on the beach. Daytona Beach denizens say there is no better place to celebrate a special occasion. Dress casually and dine on a burger and fries in the **Sunroom Cafe,** or get dolled up for a gourmet meal at the top-floor **Roof Restaurant,** with its fine view of the beach and the Atlantic. Favorites are steak Diane and the Caesar salad, which are served by some of the most professional waiters in town. This full-service hotel also has room service, refrigerators in each room, a beachside pool, a putting green, lighted tennis courts, a sauna and exercise room, nonsmoking rooms, and suites. Beach bikes are complimentary. One small disappointment: those antique teddy bears in the gift shop's case are for show, not for sale. ◆ 2637 S. Atlantic Ave (Florida Shores Blvd-Ridge Rd) 904/767.7350, 800/525.7350; fax 904/760.3651

The last land speed record set on Daytona Beach was in 1935 when Sir Malcolm Campbell drove his rocket-powered car at 276 miles per hour.

16 Big Kahuna One of many surf shops that dot Atlantic Ave, this two-story, two-toned, bright aqua-blue store has a tropical grotto inside and sells everything you will need for a day at the beach—

from bikinis to baggy surfer shorts. ♦ Daily 9AM-10PM. 2540 S. Atlantic Ave (Sea Spray St) 904/760.5265. Also location at: 2739 N. Atlantic Ave. 904/672.1757; fax 904/673.3968

17 Sun Viking Lodge $$ Modest rates and a location on the beach are the biggest draws, but an indoor heated garden pool will keep water enthusiasts happy even if it is raining outside. The outdoor pool has a twisting, 60-foot waterslide. For sports fans, there is basketball, shuffleboard, and volleyball. The lodge has the **Viking Kafe,** nonsmoking rooms, and rooms for the physically disabled. ♦ 2411 S. Atlantic Ave (Milton-Dundee Rds) 904/252.6252

18 Aku Tiki Inn $$ Choose between rooms and efficiencies, all of which have ocean views and a private patio or balcony. **Trader's Restaurant** is open for breakfast, lunch, or dinner, and there is live entertainment every night. The large pool overlooks the ocean. ♦ 2225 S. Atlantic Ave (Bonner Ave) 904/252.9631, 800/258.8454

18 Perry's Ocean-Edge $$ One of the few hotels in Central Florida that has an "indoor solarium"—an indoor pool and spa topped with a retractable glass roof. There are two outdoor pools, as well as a putting green, and shuffleboard. All of the hotel's 204 rooms face the ocean. Morning begins with free doughnuts and coffee. ♦ 2209 S. Atlantic Ave (Bonner Ave) 904/255.0581, 800/447.0002 (US), 800/342.0102 (FL); fax 904/258.7315

19 El Caribe Resort and Conference Center ★★$$ While older rooms here continue to draw guests who have come for years, owner **Mary Ann Richardson** has recently added a new tower with huge suites suitable for family gatherings. Most are loaded with amenities including a Jacuzzi, wraparound balconies, and full kitchens. If you're in a romantic mood, ask for Suite 710 on the new tower's top floor: You will have a view of the ocean and the river, and the Jacuzzi is beneath a skylight in the bathroom. You can't miss the motel from the highway—look for the neon balloons on the building's walls. ♦ 2125 S. Atlantic Ave (Browning-Bonner Aves) 904/252.1550, 800/445.9889

Within the El Caribe Resort and Conference Center:

Third World Gift Shop This shop stocks clothing, jewelry, and handicrafts from artisans of 30 nations. ♦ Daily 7AM-10PM

20 Treasure Island Inn $$$ This high-rise beachfront hotel offers plenty of goodies, including in-room refrigerators, a whirlpool, two pools, a poolside bar, and a restaurant. Each room has an ocean view. ♦ 2025 S. Atlantic Ave (Botefuhr Ave-Sunrise Blvd) 904/257.1950, 800/874.7420; fax 904/253.9935

21 Sweet Luci's $ A down-home, country cookin' kind of place, with scattered tables and vinyl booths, serving up an all-you-can-eat breakfast buffet. Or you can order from the menu. No nonsmoking area. ♦ American ♦ Daily 7AM-2PM. 2006 S. Atlantic Ave (Botefuhr Ave-Sunrise Blvd) 904/255.7915

Daytona Beach

22 Nautilus Inn ★$$$ Each of the large, pastel rooms has a private balcony, a view of the ocean, a refrigerator, and a microwave. Rooms on the upper floors of this 10-story building offer terrific panoramas through floor-to-ceiling windows. Continental breakfast and evening cocktails are served in a spacious room overlooking the beach. Between the beach and the building is a pool and spa. There are shuffleboard courts, a whirlpool, rooms for the physically disabled, and kitchenettes. ♦ 1515 S. Atlantic Ave (Poinsetta-Old Trail Rds) 904/254.8600, 800/874.7420,

23 The Reef $$ Just 1.5 miles from the Boardwalk (see page 100), most of the rooms in this 236-room hotel have private balconies. Efficiencies are also available. There's a huge pool deck with a poolside bar, a casual deli, and a lounge. ♦ 935 S. Atlantic Ave (Lenox-Ribault Aves) 904/252.2581, 800/874.0136,

24 Texan Hotel This popular hotel for springbreakers has private balconies, a heated pool, and one of the hottest nightspots on the beach, **701 South,** with a sunken dance floor

Volusia County/Daytona Beach

in the middle of three bars. ♦ 701 S. Atlantic Ave (Lenox-Revilo Aves) 904/255.8431, 800/633.7010

25 Checkers Cafe A DJ spins top 40 hits from a booth built into an actual 1959 Edsel. There is a circular bar and, facing the ocean, a pool deck with an oyster bar. ♦ M-W, Su 7AM-10PM; Th-Sa 7AM-2AM. 219 N. Atlantic Ave (Broadway Ave) 904/252-3626

Grapefruit is Florida's second most important crop after oranges. But unlike the Florida orange business, which has been battered at times by Brazil's huge orange juice industry, the grapefruit has virtually no competition.

Restaurants/Nightlife: Red   Hotels: Blue
Shops/ 🌳 Outdoors: Green   **Sights/Culture:** Black

26 Daytona Beach International Youth Hostel $ You can't miss this bright-pink building that resembles a ship. Amenities are few but it's just a short walk to the Boardwalk. ◆ 140 S. Atlantic Ave (Kemp St-5th Ave) 904/258.6937

27 The Boardwalk Stretching from Main to Ora St, the once seedy Boardwalk has cleaned up its act, especially at the northern end where the Daytona Beach Marriott moved in. The south end retains some of its original flavor, with its bars and gondola and space needle rides. But "uptown," near the Marriott, there is a set of shops that make up the Clock Tower Plaza. Just past the hotel, at the end of the Boardwalk, sits the 4,500-seat, coquina-rock band shell, a local landmark since 4 July 1937. There are often free concerts here during the summer. Basketball courts are at the rear of the open-air auditorium. Another landmark is the Daytona Beach clock tower, which spells out "Daytona Beach" where the numbers should be. Between the band shell and the hotel the public bathhouse is a safe place to change clothes if you arrive at the beach by car and want to take a dip. The Boardwalk was begun in 1936 by WPA workers and completed in 1938. Most everything opens late in the morning and closes about midnight. ◆ Along Ocean Ave

On the Boardwalk:

The Ocean Pier stretches 1,000 feet out into the Atlantic from the end of Main St.

Surfside Bar This large, blue-and-white frame structure at the end of the pier has a bar on the left and a large dance hall on the right.

Space Needle A revolving ride to the top of the needle gives you an overview of Daytona Beach. ◆ Fee. Daily 11:30AM-midnight

Gondola This ride swings you out the length of the pier and back. ◆ Admission. Daily 11:30AM-midnight

Pit Stop A two-story, wooden bar that opens onto the beach.

Capt. Darrell's Oyster Bar Go through Capt. Darrell's and up the stairs. There are go-carts and a track on the roof.

28 Hog Heaven $$ A great location—A block from the Peabody Auditorium, the Ocean Center, and the Boardwalk—but short of its claim as far "World's Best Barbecue." Nevertheless, the barbecue sandwiches make a tasty lunch, and the ribs draw a dinner crowd. ◆ American ◆ Daily 9AM-9PM. 37 N. Atlantic Ave (Auditorium Blvd) 904/257.1212

29 Daytona Beach Marriott ★★$$$ This sleek, 17-story pink hotel with matching pink marble floors and decks trimmed with turquoise rails was an instant landmark when it opened in 1988, right on the beach and across from Ocean Center, the county's convention and civic center. Each room has an ocean view. The split-level decks are great places for soaking up sun, eating grilled sandwiches at the **Splash Pool Bar,** or watching people parade down the beach. You can swim from the indoor part of the heated pool—which begins in a rock grotto—to the sunlight outdoors. After dark, there's the **Clock Tower Lounge,** a piano bar that overlooks the beach, and dancing at **The Waves Lounge. Coquinas Restaurant,** the gourmet dining room, specializes in fresh fish including grouper, red snapper, and sole, served baked, poached, grilled, broiled, or Cajun style. The hotel has a concierge level and 25 suites. ◆ 100 N. Atlantic Ave (Earl St) 904/254.8200, 800/831.1000

Within the Daytona Beach Marriott:

Kokomos Known for its reggae music, the bar is on the beach with an outdoor deck.

Bernkastel Festhaus Bavarian Pub $$ The best of the hotel's Clock Tower Plaza eateries, serving breakfasts, snacks, salads, and sandwiches, along with imported beer and wine. The Danish Delight is a turkey-and-cheese sandwich served warm on a croissant with Havarti cheese. ◆ German ◆ M-Th 10AM-midnight; F-Sa 10AM-1AM; Sun 11AM-midnight 904/255.8300

Parkside Seafood Grill, Antoines Pizza, Aloha Sports, Nicole's Boutique, The Gold Mine, A1A Photo, Hair Options, Floral Emporium, Brick Shirt House.

OCEAN CENTER

30 Ocean Center A busy, functional center that hosts conventions, entertainment of all kinds, sporting events, and trade shows. ◆ Seats 10,000 for concerts, 8,400 for sporting events. 101 N. Atlantic Ave (Earl St-Auditorium Blvd) 800/858.6444. For schedules and tickets: 904/254.4545; for convention information: 904/254.4500

31 Peabody Auditorium Renovated in 1988, the auditorium is across the street from the Ocean Center. Many people prefer attending concerts at the Peabody over the more sterile Ocean Center. The Peabody plays host to the Daytona Beach symphony and ballet. ◆ 2,560 seats. Box office hours: M-F 9:30AM-5PM. 600 Auditorium Blvd (Wild Olive Ave) 904/255.1314

Daytona Beach is named after Mathias Day, a farm machinery manufacturer from Mansfield, Ohio, who purchased a 3,200-acre tract of land for $1,200 in April of 1870. The land was part of Orange Grove, an old sugar mill plantation owned by the Samuel Williams family. The name Daytona was selected in 1872 by three residents of the community, their choices were Daytona, Daytonia, and Daytown.

32 Howard Johnson Hotel and Conference Center $$ This big, white high rise has efficiencies, suites, a full-service restaurant, three lounges, and one of the largest pool decks on the beach. If you're not keen on ocean swimming, the hotel offers a heated pool, tennis, basketball, shuffleboard, beach volleyball, and a game room. A nightclub, **600 North,** rocks during spring break. ♦ 600 N. Atlantic Ave (Glenview-Seabreeze Blvds) 904/255.4471, 800/532.3224; fax 253.7543

32 The Whitehall $$ Each room has a private balcony and an ocean view. The hotel boasts one of the area's biggest pool decks. There's also a coin laundry. ♦ 640 N. Atlantic Ave (Glenview-Seabreeze Blvds) 904/258.5435, 800/874.7016; fax 253.0735

33 Seabreeze United Church One of the most beautiful buildings in the area, this church constructed of rock was known as Tourist Church for years. It was designed by **Harry M. Griffin** in 1930 in the California Mission style, and although the rock is sometimes passed off as coquina, it actually is bog rock, mined near the area where prehistoric fossils have been discovered. Coquina rock is made of limestone, usually mixed with sorted fossil debris. Bog rock, also call bog lime, is a soft, grayish or whitish calcium carbonate taken from the bottom of freshwater lakes or ponds. It hardens as it dries and is often used as a cover for dirt roads because it doesn't wash away. The colors on the church change as the sun plays off the rock at different times of the day. ♦ 501 N. Wild Olive Ave (Oakridge Blvd)

34 T.C.'s Top Dog $ No trip to the beach is complete without a hot dog. At T.C's you can have it any way you want it—and way past midnight, too. ♦ American ♦ Daily 10AM-4AM. 425 N. Atlantic Ave (Seabreeze-Oakridge Blvds) 904/257.7766

35 The Oyster Pub $$ Fans flock here to watch sports on big-screen TVs from little tables around a large horseshoe bar. The raw seafood bar is popular. ♦ Daily 11:30AM-3AM. 555 Seabreeze Blvd (Grandview Ave) 904/255-6348

36 St. Regis Hotel ★$$ This two-story, white-frame inn has an excellent restaurant on the ground floor. Rooms are decorated with antiques, and each has a private bath. ♦ 509 Seabreeze Blvd (Wild Olive-Grandview Aves) 904/252.8743

Within the St. Regis Hotel:

St. Regis Restaurant ★★$$$ Once a private residence—and some say a bawdy house—it is now a graceful setting for dining. Simple preparation is the rule here, and the favorite is catch of the day prepared to your request. If you don't care for seafood, try the filet mignon *au poivre* served with a rich green-peppercorn sauce. ♦ American ♦ M-F 11:30AM-2PM, 5:30-10PM; Sa 5:30-10PM. Reservations recommended. 904/252-8743

37 Daytona Playhouse This local theater has a regular schedule from September through June. The Playhouse is on the Halifax River. ♦ 100 Jessamine Blvd (Halifax Ave) 904/255.2431

Restaurants/Nightlife: Red **Hotels:** Blue
Shops/🌳Outdoors: Green **Sights/Culture:** Black

Seabreeze United Church

38 Best Western La Playa $$ This rooftop lounge with live entertainment is a pleasant evening escape after a day on the beach. The motel, directly on the beach, has an outdoor and indoor pool, hot tubs and a Jacuzzi, a new exercise room with aerobics equipment and rooms for the physically disabled. Located across the street from Belair Plaza, a large shopping center. ♦ 2500 N. Atlantic Ave (Plaza Blvd-Auburn Dr) 904/672.0990, 800/874.6996; fax 904/677.0982

38 Howard Johnson Oceanfront $$ A sprawling, oceanfront hotel that was refurbished in 1987, the rooms are basic but have private balconies facing the ocean. The motel has a restaurant and pool. ♦ 2560 N. Atlantic Ave (Plaza Blvd-Auburn Dr) 904/672.1440, 800/874.6996

38 Ramada Resort This oceanfront motel has two swimming pools overlooking the beach, a restaurant, a lounge, and a game room. ♦ 2700 N. Atlantic Ave (Plaza Blvd-Auburn Dr) 904/672.3770, 800/545.3030

Mainland

39 The Chart House ★★$$$ A wood-trimmed, skylit dining room overlooking the Halifax River that makes for an elegant dining experience. You can't go wrong with one of the tender steaks, or their creatively prepared fresh fish. End the evening in the convivial sunken lounge or on the outdoor deck watching the sun go down. ♦ American ♦ 1100 Marina Point Dr (Beach St) 904/255.9022

40 Jackie Robinson Statue A bronze statue of Jackie Robinson, the first black major league baseball player, was erected at the main entrance to old City Island Park, a baseball stadium that has been renamed Jackie Robinson Ballpark. Robinson, a member of the Montreal Royals, a Brooklyn Dodgers minor league team, played in Daytona Beach during a spring

training game in 1946. ♦ 105 E. Orange Ave (City Island Pkwy)

41 Halifax Historical Museum Should you choose the town over the beach for a day spend some time at this mainland museum, if only to see the interesting architecture and the wood-carved miniature of the Boardwalk circa 1938. The building, replete with an Ionic-pillared entrance, was designed by **W.B. Talley** in 1911 and first served as a Merchant's Bank. The two-story room is built of gray sandstone and smooth cement stucco. There are two stained-glass skylights in the ceiling of the main room, as well as stained-glass windows on the south wall. On the north wall are six large murals depicting local scenes by Florida artist **Don J. Emery** and his son, **Don W.** The lighthouse mural is particularly charming. The bank failed in 1929, and after a number of owners, the Halifax Historical Society purchased it in 1984. ♦ Free. Daily Tu-Sa 10AM-4PM. 252 S. Beach St (Magnolia-Orange Aves) 904/255-6976

42 Live Oak Inn $$$ This inn is actually two houses, each with great historical significance to Daytona Beach. The house at 444 S. Beach St, built around 1790 by Orange Grove Plantation owner **Samuel Williams,** was the first to go up along the Halifax River, but it was burned to the ground in the 1830s during the Seminole War. Williams' granddaughter sold the lot to Mathias Day, the founder of Daytona Beach, in 1870. The two-story frame house with gabled roof and wood and coquina ornamentation that stands now was built in 1871 by **Riley Peck,** who bought this house and the lot next door in 1871 from Day. The original five-room residence has been enlarged and the big, open porches enclosed. Peck sold the lot next door (448 S. Beach St) in 1881 to his brother, **Myron,** who built a three-story frame house with coquina foundation. The rooms are filled with antiques or period furniture, and each has a private bath with a Jacuzzi or Victorian-type soaking tub. This isn't a place for springbreakers, children, infants, or pets, but hosts **Sandra** and **Vinton Fisher** welcome boaters, who can dock across the street at the Halifax Harbor Marina for up to five days. Continental breakfast is served daily, as is afternoon tea and cocktails. Dinners are available. ♦ 444-448 S. Beach St (Live Oak-Loomis Aves) 904/252.4667, 800/253.4667; fax 904/254.1871

43 Coquina Inn $$ A comfortable B&B designed by **S. H. Grove** in 1912. Each room is furnished with antiques and has a private bath. ♦ 544 S. Palmetto Ave (Cedar St) 904/2524.4969

44 Museum of Arts and Science This interesting juxtaposition of art and science features some outstanding examples of Cuban folk art, a planetarium, and a skeleton of a 130,000-year-old giant ground sloth found only two miles from the museum. This center, on the grounds of the **Tuscawilla Nature Preserve,** is more than a rainy-day activity—that is, if you can find it (see specific directions at the end of this paragraph or call beforehand). Besides the planetarium, there are five galleries. As you enter the museum, the American Art and the Cuban Museum galleries are in the

Restaurants/Nightlife: Red   Hotels: Blue
Shops/ 🌳 Outdoos: Green   Sights/Culture: Black

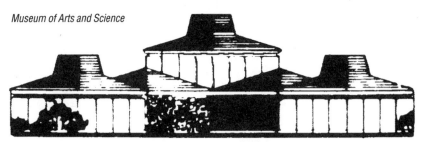

wing to your right. The museum's permanent Cuban collection was brought to Florida by **General Fulgencio Batista,** the dictator who was overthrown by **Fidel Castro.** The collection isn't all-encompassing, but it contains some ravishing pottery and beautifully detailed, mid-19th century lithographs that chronicle life on Cuba's great sugarcane plantations. Another room houses the museum's American Art collection. Notable here is a **Duncan Phyfe** silver serving set and Chippendale furniture once owned by **George Washington.** To the left of the main entrance is the original wing, which houses the main gallery and a science gallery; exhibits here change every four to eight weeks. The last gallery takes you through the prehistory of Florida. There is a viewing area where you can watch a short film about the giant ground sloth before walking through the gallery to see this mammoth, Pleistocene-era vegetarian that stood 13 feet tall and weighed more than 3 tons. Drawers in the gallery contain fossils and Indian artifacts, some for viewing and others for handling—for example, try to assemble the bones of a sloth's foot. The 260-seat planetarium has regularly scheduled programs, including musical laser light shows. In front of the museum is the **Frischer Public Sculpture Garden,** featuring large outdoor artwork. Behind the museum is Tuscawilla Nature Preserve, a 60-acre coastal hammock with nature trails. The trails are designed for 20-minute walks. ♦ Admission, free on W and F. Tu-F 9AM-4PM; Sa-Su noon-5PM; planetarium: Tu-Sa 12:30-3PM. 1040 Museum Blvd (turn off Nova Rd at South St and make a quick jog to your right onto Museum Blvd) 904/255.0285

45 Tarragona Arch Visitors driving into town on Volusia Ave just past the Speedway ride their brakes as they pass this 45-foot high octagonal tower that arches over Tarragona Way. The arch, inspired by one in Tarragona, Spain, was built of coquina rock with a red tile roof as an entrance to Daytona Highlands, a wealthy subdivision. Inside was the subdivision's sales office, complete with Spanish-style handmade furniture and tile floors. On top of the tower was a beacon. Today the arch is boarded up and used only during the Christmas season, when it is decorated by the city. Another arch was built across Volusia Ave. ♦ Along Tarragona Way (Volusia Ave)

46 Volusia Mall The largest mall in Volusia County is conveniently located near the intersection of two interstates on the main drag into town and across the street from Daytona International Speedway. There are more than 110 stores, including Belk Lindsey, Burdines, Dillard's, J.C. Penney, Maison Blanche, and Sears. ♦ M-Sa 10AM-9PM; Su noon-5:30PM. 1700 Volusia Ave (Midway Ave) 904/253.6783

47 Olive Garden $$ One of General Mills' new Italian restaurants that serves up fresh pasta specialties, including a very rich and creamy fettuccine Alfredo. Be forewarned: some Italian-Americans don't consider it authentic. ♦ Italian ♦ Daily 11AM-10PM. 1725 Volusia Ave (Midway Ave) 904/252.0639

48 Daytona International Speedway In 1959 racing moved off the beaches and into the high-banked speedway. Speed Weeks in February, Cycle Week in March, and the Pepsi 400 in July jam the city streets, beaches, and motels. **Speed Weeks** begins with the SunBank 24 at Daytona, a 24-hour endurance race over the track's 3 1/5-mile road course, and concludes two weeks later with the Daytona 500, the richest stock-car racing event in the country. The highlight during **Cycle Week** is the Daytona 200, which is the week's final event. The **Pepsi 400** marks the halfway point of the NASCAR Winston Cup Series and is always held on the first Saturday in July. In addition to these big events, the speedway plays host to a number of other races, including the World Karting Association's Enduro World Championships. Tours are offered daily except on racing or testing days. A 20-minute narrated tour in a minibus takes you down the stretch, on the

Volusia County/Daytona Beach

apron of a banked curve, and through the pits. ♦ Tours: nominal fee. Daily 9AM-5PM (except when track is in use) Volusia Ave (Williamson-Bill France Blvds) 904/254.2700

49 Daytona Beach Jai Alai Even if you're not the betting type, this fast-paced import from the Basque countries of Europe is fun to watch. Children must be 12 years old and accompanied by a parent, and they are not allowed near the windows. Programs explain the scoring and wagering pari-mutuel. ♦ Nominal admission. Tu, Th noon, 7PM; F 7PM; Sa noon, 7PM; Su 1PM. Feb-Aug.1900 Volusia Ave (Bayless Blvd across from the Daytona International Speedway) 904/255.0222

50 Daytona Beach Kennel Club In the shadow of the Daytona International Speedway Greyhound dog racing takes place daily year-round except on Sunday. Watch and bet from **The Pavilion,** which serves chicken, shrimp, and steaks. Buy a program when you come in; it explains the different wagers you can make and lists the racing record of each dog. Minors 12 and older can attend if accompanied by an adult. ♦ Nominal admission. M,W,Sa1PM, 7:45PM; Tu,Th-F 7:45PM. 2201 Volusia Ave (Williamson-Fentress Blvds) 904/252.6484

51 Hilton Indigo Lakes Resort & Conference Center $$$ Set among forests, gardens, and lakes, this resort caters to the leisure traveler as well as the businessperson and the conference set. It's big on sports, and offers archery, bicycling, golf, tennis, shuffleboard, swimming, and volleyball. It also has a fitness trail and a whirlpool. The rooms are large, each with a balcony or patio. Also at the complex is **Major Moultrie's** for seafood or steaks, and the **Atrium Lounge.** Nonsmoking rooms and rooms for the physically disabled. ♦ 2620 Volusia Ave (Indigo Dr) 904/258.6333, 800/874.9918 (FL) 800/223.4161

52 Main Post Office If you take a few minutes to drive down Beach St to marvel at the old buildings, don't miss the post office—especially if you are a gargoyle fan. This Spanish Renaissance-style WPA project, designed by **Harry M. Griffin** in 1932, has seven gargoyles near its red terracotta roof. Step inside and you will see marble floors and wrought-iron grillwork. ♦ 220 N. Beach St (3rd Ave-Bay St)

53 Mary McLeod Bethune Home On the Bethune-Cookman College campus, this two-story, white-frame 1914 house is where **Mary McLeod Bethune,** daughter of a freed slave, lived for about 50 years until she died in 1955. She is buried next to the house. Dr. Bethune began Daytona Normal and Industrial School for Girls in 1904 in order to give black women an opportunity for an education. The school merged with Jacksonville's Cookman Institute for Boys in 1924. Dr. Bethune's home was named a national historic landmark; it was

Florida's first site commemorating a black. The home is owned by the Mary McLeod Bethune Foundation and is open to visitors. In the front parlor there is a display case filled with mementos: medals, an invitation from **President Harry S. Truman,** and a letter from **Eleanor Roosevelt,** a frequent guest. Bethune's bedroom upstairs is just as it was when she lived there. Her hat and gloves are on a small table. The guest room is where Eleanor Roosevelt used to stay. ♦ Admission M-F 9AM-noon, 1-5PM Jan-May, Sep-Dec; M-F 9-10AM, 1-5PM June-Aug. 631 Pearl St (McLeod-2nd Aves) 904/255.1401 ext 372

54 Dixie Queen This stern-wheel paddleboat cruises the Halifax River. Its main deck is air-conditioned in summer and heated in winter. It offers a Sunday brunch with Caribbean music and a complimentary glass of champagne. The Dixie Queen also has luncheon, dinner, and weekend party cruises. For less money skip the buffet and just enjoy the sightseeing on the luncheon cruises. The dinner cruise is a buffet with a Dixieland band. Music on the party cruises has a preplanned theme, so if you don't want to be stuck with sounds you don't like, call ahead. Occasionally there is a special cruise to St. Augustine and back that takes almost seven hours and includes two buffet meals, live entertainment, two hours free in St. Augustine, and a return trip by bus. ♦ Admission. Party cruise: F-Sa 9:30AM-12:30AM April-Feb.; riverboat luncheon cruise: W, F, Sa noon-2:30PM; riverboat dinner cruise: W-Sa 5-7:30PM Feb-April; April-Feb W-Th 7-9:30PM, F-Sa 6-8:30PM; Sunday brunch cruise: 12:30-3PM; St. Augustine day trip cruise: call for dates and times. 841 Ballough Rd (Seabreeze Blvd) Reservations required. 904/255.1997

Ormond Beach

55 Amigos $$ If you're a Tex-Mex food lover, this is the place to go; the owners are transplanted Texans who know their stuff and serve some of the only decent chili con queso in Central Florida. Another must: enchiladas in a tangy green sauce. ♦ Tex-Mex ♦ Daily11AM-10PM. 255 E. Granada Blvd (Atlantic Ave) 904/677.5159

56 Birthplace of Speed Museum Here is a chance to see the Stanley Steamer that set a speed record of 27 mph in 1902. Located in a renovated old police garage, the museum briefly illustrates the area's role in the development of the automobile industry and car racing. Cars first raced on the beach in 1902. ♦ Nominal admission. Tu-Sa 1-5PM. 160 E. Grenada Blvd (Halifax Dr-Seton Tr) 904/672.5657

Restaurants/Nightlife: Red	Hotels: Blue
Shops/ 🌳 Outdoors: Green	**Sights/Culture:** Black

The Casements

57 The Casements Now a civic and cultural center, the white shingled 1912 mansion was the winter home of **John Rockefeller** from 1918 until he died in 1937. It is called The Casements because of the rows of hinged casement windows that open outward. The first floor is often the site of concerts and art exhibits. Upstairs is a Boy Scout historical exhibit; a display of Hungarian arts, crafts, and historic artifacts; and a room set up the way it was when Rockefeller lived in the house. Across Riverside Dr, sloping toward the Halifax River, are two acres of formal gardens that have been restored to their original design. The Casements is listed on the National Register of Historic Places. ♦ M-Th 9AM-9PM; F 9AM-6PM; Sa 9AM-noon. Tours every half hour: M-F 10AM-2:30PM; Sa 10AM-11:30AM. 25 Riverside Dr (Granada Blvd) 904/673.4701

Meet the Manatee

The West Indian manatee (or Florida sea cow) has almost a cult following in Florida. And these days, you can buy a license plate for your car that bears the manatee's likeness and have part of your license fee contributed toward the manatee's protection.

The manatee makes its home in warm, shallow coastal waters and the rivers and springs of Florida. The creature is found all the way from the St. Johns River around Jacksonville, down to Miami, and back up the west coast of Florida past St. Petersburg and Tampa to the Homosassa River area. The bulbous-faced manatee can usually be found munching on its favorite underwater sea plants.

Why all the fuss over the manatee? These huge, water-dwelling and plant-eating mammals appear sweet, gentle, and vulnerable. All too vulnerable, unfortunately—so much so that they have become an endangered species, and often are fatally crushed by big boats or barges in shallow water where there is no escape route. Small boats kill manatees, too: they die from wounds inflicted by propellers of motorboats. In fact, most manatees in Florida bear scars or deformities from being run over by boats. And 80 percent of all manatee deaths from boat or barge collisions occur in eastern Florida, particularly in Brevard County and the St. Johns River.

Manatees also die from cold temperatures. When Florida has bad freezes (as it did during 1984), some sea cows don't make it. Scientists have observed that the young manatees are most susceptible to cold temperatures because they have less body fat and they aren't experienced in migrating to warmer waters.

From November to March every year, manatees migrate to warmer water, and one of the best places to get a glimpse of them is at **Blue Spring State Park,** two miles west of Orange City. In addition to the waters of Blue Spring, manatees cluster near the Crystal River Power Plant about 80 miles north of Tampa,

Volusia County/Daytona Beach

where discharged, treated water keeps them warm.

If you spot a dead or injured manatee, or see one being harassed by boaters, divers, or just general mischief-makers, contact the Florida Department of Natural Resources by calling its manatee hot-line at 800/342.1821 (a Florida number only).

For more information about the manatee, contact the Save the Manatee Club, 500 N. Maitland Ave, Maitland FL 32751; 647.2615. Or request a copy of "The West Indian Manatee in Florida," written by Victoria Brook van Meter and commissioned by the Florida Power & Light Co., by writing to: Florida Power & Light Co., Corporate Communications, Box 029100, Miami FL 33102.

MICHAEL BLUM

St. Augustine

This city is the perfect antidote to Walt Disney World and Florida's other theme parks. Although St. Augustine has more than its share of tourist kitsch, its enthralling past and varied architecture make for the kind of fun that's different from the mechanical thrills of the amusement parks. The city does have one thing in common with the big theme parks, though: the requirement to spend a lot of time walking. Almost every door beckons in the downtown historic district. And the best way to see it is by foot or by bicycle. Avoid driving, because you'll just end up in many nerve-racking traffic jams.

Unlike most of Florida's cities, which have sprung up in this century, St. Augustine is more than 400 years old. In fact, it's the nation's oldest city. Native Americans, of course, were the first to inhabit the area, although **Juan Ponce de León** is given credit for having discovered Florida and St. Augustine in 1513, even though there is evidence of prior European exploration. Some historians contend that de León wasn't seeking the Fountain of Youth when he landed here, but rather any gold or land he could claim for Spain. Other historians disagree, insisting that he was indeed in search of the charmed spring, which medieval legend placed in the Garden of Eden—then thought to be somewhere far to the east of Europe.

Whatever de León's motive, he came ashore between St. Augustine and the Saint Johns River around Easter. After naming the land "Florida," from **Pascua Florida** —the Feast of Flowers—he sailed down the coast and didn't return until 1521.

By 1562, **King Philip II** of Spain had decided to abandon Florida—that is, until the arrival of a French expedition of 150 Huguenots led by the French admiral, **Gaspard de Cologyn.** Philip II ordered **Pedro Menendez de Aviles** to drive them out. In 1565 de Aviles amassed the largest armada of ships and colonists ever sent to Florida, and on 4 September, after all the Spanish colonists were ashore, mass was said and St. Augustine was officially born. Then the king's enforcers went about the business of attacking the French. In the course of two different raids, they executed all captured French soldiers who said they were not Catholic. The pretty Spanish word *matanza* (which you see everywhere in St. Augustine) means "slaughter," and in this city refers to the massacre of the French, many of whom are buried in a small cemetery next to the **St. Augustine Visitors Information Center.**

Twenty-one years later, in 1586, the thriving Spanish settlement had a visitor: **Sir Francis Drake.** The Englishman had sailed to the New World to capture Havana, but illness among his men forced him to give up that adventure. Instead, he sailed up the coast of Florida and attacked St. Augustine with 23 warships and 2,000 men. Drake eventually withdrew, but before he did, he burned the city to the ground.

The next century didn't get any easier for the citizens of St. Augustine. A plague epidemic from 1613-17 nearly wiped

out the town, killing thousands of settlers and Native Americans. Famine ravaged the area in 1640. But natural calamities weren't the only concern. Ever fearful of attacks by the English and pirates, the Spanish decided to build a fort that could defend the city. In 1672 they began mining coquina, or shellstone, from a quarry on Anastasia Island to build **Castillo de San Marcos** (see page 114). Some of the workers who helped build the fort were skilled stonemasons from Havana, but Native Americans and black slaves were also conscripted. The fort dominated the northern entrance to the harbor from its vantage point on the west bank of the Matanzas River, opposite the north end of Anastasia Island. In 1740 the British shelled the fort for 27 days, but it didn't fall.

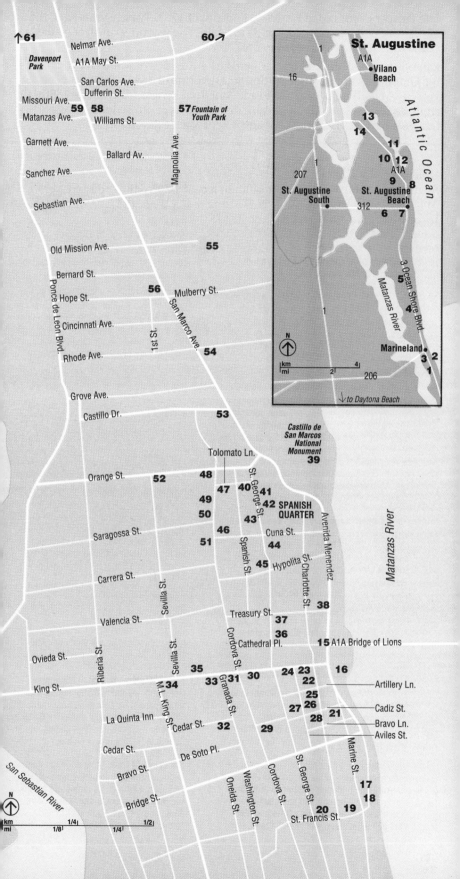

↑61 Nelmar Ave.
60↗

Davenport Park

A1A May St.

San Carlos Ave.
Dufferin St.

Missouri Ave.
59 58 57 Fountain of Youth Park
Matanzas Ave. Williams St.

Garnett Ave.

Ballard Av.

Sanchez Ave.

Magnolia Ave.

Sebastian Ave.

Old Mission Ave. 55

Bernard St.

Hope St. 56 Mulberry St.

Ponce de Leon Blvd.

Cincinnati Ave.

San Marco Ave.

1st St.

Rhode Ave. 54

Grove Ave.

Castillo Dr. 53

Orange St. 52 48
Tolomato Ln.
47 40
49 St. George St.
50 41
46 42 SPANISH QUARTER
Saragossa St. 43
51 Cuna St.
Spanish St. 44
Carrera St. 45 Hypolita St.
Charlotte St.
Avenida Menendez

Sevilla St.

Valencia St. Treasury St. 38
37
Ovieda St. Cathedral Pl. 36
Riberia St. 15 A1A Bridge of Lions

King St. 35
M.L. King St. 33 31 30 24 23 16
34 Granada St. 22 Artillery Ln.
Cordova St. 25
La Quinta Inn 27 26 Cadiz St.
Sevilla St. Cedar St. 32 28 21 Bravo Ln.
29 Aviles St.
Cedar St.
De Soto Pl. Marine St.

Bravo St.
Washington St.
Cordova St.
St. George St. 17
Bridge St. Oneida St. 18
20 19
San Sebastian River St. Francis St.

N
km
mi
1/8 1/4 1/4 1/2

St. Augustine (inset)

St. Augustine
1
16
A1A
Vilano Beach
Atlantic Ocean
13
14
11
10 12
207 A1A
9
St. Augustine South 8
312 St. Augustine Beach
6 7
5
Matanzas River
4
3 Ocean Shore Blvd.
1
N
km
mi 2 4
206
Marineland
3 2
1
↓to Daytona Beach

Castillo de San Marcos National Monument 39

Matanzas River

The Treaty of Paris ceded Florida to England in 1763. Twenty years later, the Second Treaty of Paris returned Florida to Spain. The second Spanish era ended in 1821, when Florida was ceded to the US.

Railroad tycoon **Henry Flagler** ushered in the modern era and changed much of the Oldest City's look. After visiting St. Augustine in 1883, Flagler was convinced he could transform it into an "American Riviera." By the late 1880s, the city's skyline had been dramatically altered by his construction of massive hotels and churches, built in the Spanish Renaissance Revival style.

1 Marineland of Florida The world's first oceanarium, Marineland is 18 miles south of St. Augustine on scenic SR A1A. The dolphin show is the star attraction, but viewing sea life through underwater portholes is also a kick. The park has a motel, campground, and restaurant, along with plenty of snack bars. ♦ Admission. Daily 9AM-5PM. 9507 Ocean Shore Blvd (Burden Dr) 904/471.1111

Within Marineland of Florida:

Aquarius Theatre Coming up SR A1A from the south, you pass the Marineland Camping Resort on the left and Quality Inn on the right. The main entrance to the park is on the left at Burden Dr. Cross the highway to the oceanariums or begin at the theater, which features a dozen showings daily of *Sea Dream,* a 22-minute, 3-D movie of underwater scenery and sea life. There is a snack bar at the theater. Follow the path from the theater past the otters, electric eels, toucans, and wading birds to the **Herrick Shell Museum,** with its **Beachcomber Shop.** Farther down the path is another souvenir stop, the **Shell Shop.** It is next to the high-dive area, which is open to swimmers in spring and summer, and across from **Playport,** a children's playground. The path continues to the **Sandpiper Grille** and then over the highway.

Oceanariums Most of the action is on the ocean side of the highway. **Wonders of the**

Sea is on the west side of the circular oceanarium, and **Secrets of the Reef** is between the circular and rectangular tanks. Both exhibit colorful tropical fish. **Dolphin's World** offers two underwater feedings daily at the circular oceanarium, and five 10-minute *Jumping Dolphins* shows performed at the **Top Deck** at the circular aquarium. At the rectangular tank, there are four underwater feedings daily. Between the oceanariums and the Atlantic Ocean, there is **Ocean Shore Gifts** and **Wonders of the Spring,** where Florida fish frolic in a 35,000-gallon tank that represents a native freshwater spring.

Stadium Past the oceanariums is the park's most popular show, *Educated Dolphins.* Twenty minutes long, it is performed five times daily.

Whitney Park This is the dolphin training area, but there are other events as well: The sea lions perform three times daily, and the penguins are fed twice daily.

Boardwalk This snack bar is right on the ocean.

Marina Directly across the highway from the oceanariums is the Marineland Marina, which provides a boat ramp, docks, and access to the Matanzas River and the rest of the Intracoastal Waterway.

1 Marineland Camping Resort $ There are 120 hookups, plus beach access, a pool, a supply store, a playground, tennis courts, fishing, and laundry facilities. The park has room for tent camping; pets are allowed, but must stay on leashes. You may enter the park through Marineland's main entrance (Burden Dr) and cut through the parking lot. ♦ 9741 Ocean Shore Blvd. 904/471.4700

2 Quality Inn Marineland $$ This new 121-room motel is built right on the beach and offers an ocean view from every room. Children stay for free. There is a pool, lighted tennis courts, a dining room, and a gift shop. Rooms for the physically disabled. Pets allowed. ♦ 9507 Ocean Shore Blvd (Burden Dr) 904/471.1222

2 Dolphin Restaurant $$ A few steps up the beach from the Quality Inn motel, this seafood and steak restaurant is convenient if you are staying at the park. The **Moby Dick Lounge** provides a view of the Atlantic. ♦ American ♦ Daily 7AM-9:30PM 9507 Ocean Shore Blvd (Burden Dr) 904/471.1222

3 Fort Matanzas National Monument Between 1740 and 1742 the Spanish built this fort to protect St. Augustine from attack. The Intracoastal Waterway is called the **Matanzas River** here—*matanza* is the Spanish word for "slaughter"—because of a bloody incident that took place in 1565 near this spot. Having captured 276 French soldiers, Menendez de Aviles executed all who were not Catholics—245 in all. A free ferry shuttles you out to the fort on **Rattlesnake Island** in the Matanzas River, and a ranger recounts its history. At the fort you will see the gundeck, the enlisted men's quarters, the officers' quarters, and an observation deck. Although it was never conquered, the fort wasn't used after 1821. It became a national monument in 1924. The 298-acre park, which is about 14 miles south of St. Augustine, has clean restrooms, hiking trails, and a beach. ◆ Free. Daily 8:30AM-5:30PM; ferryboat 9AM-4:30PM; closed Christmas. SR A1A (Marineland-SR 206) 904/471.0116

4 Salt Water Cowboys ★★$$ Built out over a saltwater marsh, this rustic restaurant (pictured above) with its wooden deck, tin roof, exposed beams, and planked floors will make you feel as if you stepped into a fishing camp. Best known for its soft-shell crabs, the restaurant also serves a tasty redfish chowder. But while appetizers such as the Florida Cracker combo sound tempting, the frog legs, gator, and turtle are buried beneath too much breading, and the snapper is overwhelmed by cucumber sauce. You can enjoy a drink on the deck and watch the birds, fish, and turtles beyond the railing. The restaurant doesn't take reservations and parking is limited, but the scenery and much of the food are great. At night, outside lights illuminate the marsh near the restaurant. ◆ Seafood ◆ Daily 5-10PM. 299 Dondanville Rd (SR A1A) 904/471.2332

5 Comfort Inn $$ They answer the phone, "Comfort Inn on the Beach." But don't be misled. The hotel is new, clean, has comfortable beds and 25-inch TVs in each room, a Jacuzzi, and a pool, but it's not on the beach. You must cross busy SR A1A and walk a bit before getting to a sandy shore. ◆ 3401 A1A. 904/471.1474, 800/221.2222

6 Antonio's Italian Restaurant $$ Watch the chef make the pasta, then dig in. The cheese ravioli and the fettuccine Alfredo are both good. You might want to finish your meal with a drink on the open porch. ◆ Italian ◆ Daily 4-9PM. 1915 SR 3 (SR 312) 904/824.0971

7 Sunset Grille $ This popular hangout across the street from the ocean serves steaks, oysters, seafood, omelets, and French toast rolled in Rice Krispies. Order from a walk-up window and eat on a picnic table, or sit in an open-air lounge. There is also an air-conditioned dining room, a big-screen TV, and live entertainment occasionally. ◆ American ◆ Daily 7AM-11PM (kitchen closes at 9:30PM) 2295 SR A1A (First St) 904/471.5555

8 Howard Johnson-St. Augustine Beach $$ Formerly the Anastasia Inn, this oceanfront motel is just a hundred yards from the beach. The poolside rooms have views of the ocean and the pool, and each room has two double beds. The motel has a dining room, a lounge, some efficiencies, and rooms for the physically disabled. ◆ 2050 SR A1A (Pope Rd) 907/471.2572

9 Cross and Sword This outdoor drama about the founding of St. Augustine in 1565 has been running since 1965. It is performed at the St. Augustine Amphitheatre during the summer, and was written by Pulitzer Prize-winning playwright **Paul Green.** It was designated Florida's Official State Play by the state legislature in 1973. ◆ Admission. M-Sa 8:30PM, June-Aug. SR A1A (SR 312-Anastasia Blvd) 904/471.1965

10 St. Augustine Alligator Farm In 1893 there was a pen of alligators at an attraction known as the Museum of Marine Curiosities, about a mile south of the St. Augustine lighthouse. The pen soon became an alligator farm, and as the area deteriorated, was moved to its present location. The entrance is a white-washed, Mediterranean-style building with a red-tiled roof. Visitors walk through most of the lushly landscaped park on elevated, wooden bridges. The hourly Florida Wildlife Show is entertaining, plus you get the opportunity to feed and pet a number of animals—goats, deer, and farm animals. Not the alligators, however. Snack bar and gift shop. ◆ Admission. Daily 9AM-5PM. SR A1A (across from Old Beach Rd) 904/824.3337

11 Lighthouse Museum of St. Augustine St. Augustine's inlet to the sea was so treacherous that its shifting sands were called "crazy banks" by generations of sailors. Today, you can pay for the privilege of climbing to the top of this lighthouse, but it's a lot more relaxing to walk through the **Keeper's House**—which is now the **Lighthouse**

Museum of St. Augustine—and it's free. The lighthouse keeper, his assistant, and their families occupied the two-story, Victorian coquina-and-brick structure from 1875 to 1955. Inside, a curving staircase leads down into the basement, where nautical artifacts, including beacons that once shone from the lighthouse, are on display. ◆ Daily 10AM-5PM. 81 Lighthouse Ave (Old Beach Rd) 904/829.0745

12 Lighthouse Park Restaurant $ Drive under large oak trees to the wooden gray building by the boat ramp. Inside you can sit in the air-conditioned, wood-paneled diner and order something off the grill. If you are heading out for a day of fishing, bait and tackle are also available. ♦ American ♦ Daily 9AM-7PM. 442 Ocean Vista Dr (Old Beach Rd) 904/825.1164

13 Conch House Marina Resort $$$ This 21-room resort has a great bar, fun places to dine, and boring but functional rooms. There is a pool, as well as rooms for the physically disabled and a 60-slip marina, from which you can charter fishing or pleasure cruises. Dine in,the **Captain's Room,** with its romantic, secluded upstairs rooms, or in the **Seminole Room,** under a palm-thatched structure on one of the decks stretching out into Salt Run. Both have similar menus of chicken, seafood, and steak. But the real reason to come is to have a drink in the **Conch House Lounge,** an octagonal, cypress shanty on pilings at the end of the pier. The brass doors of the lounge are said to be from the **Hotel Alcazar** (see page 113). The view from the **Crow's Nest,** up a narrow spiral staircase, is great. ♦ 57 Comares Ave (Anastasia Blvd) 904/829.8646, 800/940.6256

14 Anchorage Motor Inn $ Although many visitors prefer to stay in bed-and-breakfast inns or on the beach, this little two-story, blue-and-white motel should not be overlooked. It is at the east end of the Bridge of Lions, right on the Matanzas River. Ground-floor rooms have patios, and second-floor rooms have balconies with an outstanding view of the city. It has a fishing pier and a pool. Pets allowed. ♦ 1 Dolphin Dr (Anastasia Blvd) 904/829.9041

15 Bridge of Lions This is the perfect way to enter town, traveling over a drawbridge designed in 1926 by **J.E.Greiner** that complements the Spanish Renaissance Revival-style architecture that prevails downtown. Four towers with tile roofs flank the drawspan. The two marble lions standing on the city side of the bridge were gifts from **Dr. Andrew Anderson,** a local physician. The current bridge replaced a wooden structure that connected St. Augustine with Anastasia Island over the Intracoastal Waterway from 1895 to 1925.

16 Scenic Cruise Four generations of the **Usina** family have been taking tourists for

cruises on Matanzas Bay since the early 1900s. *Victory II* is a double-decker built in 1917. Once used as a passenger ferry and for river fishing, it's now strictly for sightseeing. Both decks are covered. *Victory III,* purchased in 1988, has an open upper deck and an enclosed lower deck. Tours take about an hour and 15 minutes. Both ships have refreshments and restrooms aboard. ♦ Fee. Daily 1, 2:45, 4:30, 6:15PM, 16 Mar-14 May and Labor Day-15 Oct ; 1, 2:45, 4:30, 6:15, 8:30PM, 15 May-Labor Day; 1, 2:45, 4:30PM 16 Oct-15 Mar.

4125 Coastal Hwy (cruises depart from City Yacht Pier, one block south of the Bridge of Lions) 904/824.1806

17 Villas de Marin $$ Rooms are rented by the week here, making this a good choice for families. Some of the villas in this two-story, wooden-frame building retain original features, including coquina (shellstone) walls, window seats, high ceilings, and porches. All have views of Matanzas Bay. ♦ 142 Avenida Menendez (St. Francis-Bridge Sts) 904/829.1725

18 Westcott House $$$ Because it offers some of the nicest rooms along with one of the very best locations for exploring the city, this bed-and-breakfast inn (pictured above) is often booked six to eight weeks in advance on weekends. The nine rooms are warm and welcoming, with high-quality linens and beautiful furniture. Some have working fireplaces. Two rooms, Nos. 204 and 205, are in a small separate building, offering complete privacy. There's also a charming attic room with a double bed and a full bath, but the stairs are steep. A Continental breakfast is served in your room, on a side porch, or in a courtyard. Matanzas Bay is visible from the front and side porches. ♦ 146 Avenida Menendez (St. Francis-Bridge Sts) 904/824.4301

19 Oldest House It's worth taking the time for a tour of this house, the oldest structure built by settlers in the New World. The house ably illustrates much of the city's history, showing both Spanish and British influences. The first structure, begun in about 1650 as a thatched wooden cottage, was replaced by coquina stone soon after the English burned St. Augustine to the ground in 1702. **Tomas Gonzales y Hernandez,** an artilleryman at the **Castillo de San Marcos** (the fort), first lived here with his family. After Gonzales left, a British major named **Peavetz** and his wife purchased the house. The Peavetzes added a second floor and turned the ground floor into a tavern, a shrewd move since there was (and still is) a barrack across the street. **Maria Peavetz** was widowed, then remarried, and lost the house when her young, wild Irish husband was imprisoned in 1790 for gambling debts. **Eugenia Price's** romance novel *Maria,* displayed all over town, is based on her story. Beautiful grounds for picnicking. ♦ Admission. Daily 9AM-5PM; closed Christmas. 14 St. Francis St (Charlotte-Marine Sts) 904/824.2872

Restaurants/Nightlife: Red	Hotels: Blue
Shops/ Outdoors: Green	Sights/Culture: Black

20 St. Francis Inn $$ This 200-year-old bed-and-breakfast offers a homey atmosphere complete with a piano in the small parlor, but its tattered appearance isn't likely to please even the purists. Some rooms have kitchenettes, others have fireplaces, and there is a separate cottage that can accommodate up to two couples. The two-bedroom suite has a double-sized bed for adults and twin-sized beds for kids. Breakfast includes fresh fruits, bagels, and a variety of pastries. ◆ 279 St. George St (St. Francis St) 904/824.6068

21 Kenwood Inn $$ Guests will know they made a wise choice when they step inside this inn's spacious and immaculately kept common rooms. Guest rooms are also large and comfortable: The Old English Room has a king-sized bed and a working fireplace, and all rooms have private baths. The inn (pictured above) has two suites, including one with a view of the water. Period furnishings are found throughout, but the inn isn't cutesy or overdone. There is a swimming pool within a walled-in courtyard. Owners **Mark, Kerianne,** and **Caitlin Constant** serve a Continental breakfast that includes homemade breads and cakes. ◆ 38 Marine St (Bridge St-Bravo Ln) 904/824.2116

All lighthouses have distinguishing "daymarks" and "signatures" to help a mariner determine his or her location. The daymark of the St. Augustine lighthouse is the red top and black and white spiral stripes. Its signature, or pattern of light, is a short, white flash every 30 seconds.

22 Denoël French Pastry Forget the junk food and try a juicy shrimp-salad sandwich on a buttery croissant. The pastries here attract crowds: dense cheesecake, flaky chocolate éclairs, and blueberry tortes are the best in town. ◆ M, W-Su 10AM-5PM. 212 Charlotte St (Artillery Ln-King St) 904/829.3974

23 The Lyons Maritime Museum This new museum has floor-to-ceiling shelves loaded with deep-sea diving helmets—close to 200 in all—dating back to 1850. Owner **Leon Lyons** has filled this museum with maritime artifacts ranging from a 1786 English bosun's pipe to a collection of deep-sea divers' communication boxes. You can take just about anything off the walls and examine it, blow the foghorn and ring the bells, but Lyon's pride and joy are his helmets. Three of them were in movies, worn by **John Wayne** (*Wake of the Red Witch*), **Ray Milland** (*Reap the Wild Winds*), and **Bob Hope** (*Road to Rio*). ◆ Admission. Daily 10AM-8PM. 9 King St (Aviles St) 904/825.0184, 904/825.0286

23 Spanish Military Hospital This building was recently reopened as a living history museum in conjunction with the restored **Spanish Quarter.** Enter through the side door, where a plaque explains that the building stands on a site which originally housed stables. When the English took over, **William Watson** converted the stables into a residence. When the Spanish returned in 1784, they turned the building into a hospital and pharmacy. You can tour the apothecary, to look at old instruments; the administrative office, to see how the records were kept; and the herbarium, to learn about the local herbs used in developing medicine. Before leaving, stop at the five-bed ward (with the flowered chamber pot) that looks like

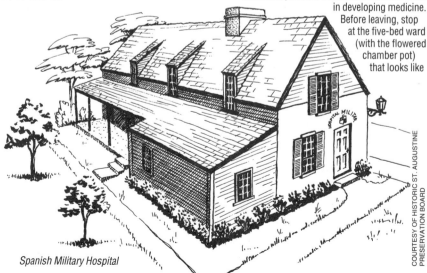

Spanish Military Hospital

it did more than 200 years ago, when this hospital was known as the **Hospital of Our Lady of Guadalupe.** ♦ Nominal charge. If you pass through the restored Spanish Quarter first, show your receipt here and get in free. Daily 9AM-5PM. 3 Aviles St (Artillery Ln-King St) 904/825.6808

24 Potter's Wax Museum Opened in 1949 by **George L. Packer,** this wax museum claims to be the oldest in the country. Whether it's true or not—and despite the fact that it has very little to do with St. Augustine—it is still fun to duck into the air-conditioning and, without peeking at the names, see if you can recognize the figures as you wind through the museum. The costumes are spectacular. Among the more than 170 figures: **King Henry VIII** with all six of his wives; **Ulysses S. Grant,** regal in uniform; **Thomas Jefferson** seated behind a desk, presumably writing the *Declaration of Independence;* writers **Henry Wadsworth Longfellow, Alfred Lord Tennyson,** and **George Washington Carver** sitting proudly amid other inventors; **Louis Pasteur** behind a desk in a lab coat; and **Leonardo da Vinci** with his long beard and flowing robe. A short theater presentation is shown periodically throughout the day. The newest attraction, **Wax Works,** features a craftsperson designing wax figures. ♦ Daily 9AM-8PM 15 June-2 Sep; daily 9AM-5PM 3 Sep-14 June; closed Christmas. 17 King St (Aviles St) 904/829.9056

25 Oldest Store Museum You'll know this place by the cigar-store Indian out front. While a player piano tinkles turn-of-the-century hits such as "Peg O' My Heart," you can look at some of the store's original stock, including century-old buttonhook shoes and 1890s-era bathing suits. Another curious item is "The Bonebreaker," a massive 1850 bicycle with a heavy steel frame and large wooden-spoke wheels. Clean public restrooms inside.
♦ Admission. M-Sa 9AM-5PM; Su noon-5PM; closed Christmas. 4 Artillery Ln (Aviles-Charlotte Sts) 904/829.9729

26 Casa de Solana $$$ One of the oldest houses in Florida, the **Don Manuel Solana House** was built in 1763. Each of Casa de Solana's four rooms are suites, some with fireplaces and others with balconies overlooking a lush garden. Innkeeper **Faye McMurry**

serves a full breakfast and lends guests bicycles for touring. ♦ 21 Aviles St (Cadiz St) 904/824.3555

27 Ximenez-Fatio House Built in 1798 by **Andreas Ximenez,** a Spanish merchant, this house was originally split into a general store and tavern on the first floor and living quarters above it. In 1830 **Margaret Cook** enlarged the house and turned into a boarding house. **Louise Fatio** acquired the house in 1855 and rented rooms to rich northerners who visited for the winter. The fine reputation of the

boarding house soon grew. The three-story coquina-and-wood structure, with its gabled roof and wooden balcony over what was once the front door, has a distinctive appearance. It is now a boarding-house museum, set up to look just as it did in the mid-1800s, and run by the Florida chapter of the **National Society of the Colonial Dames of America.** ♦ Free. M, Th-Sa 11AM-4PM; Su 1-4PM, 1 Mar-30 Sep. 20 Aviles St (Cadiz St) 904/829.3575

28 Victorian House $$ This two-story, yellow-frame house dating from 1890 has eight rooms, each very different. The room most in demand has a queen-sized canopy bed. A few rooms offer a double- as well as a twin-sized bed. ♦ 11 Cadiz St (Aviles-Charlotte Sts) 904/824.5214

29 Old City House Inn $$ This two-story brick, stucco, and wood building was built in 1873 originally as a stable; it was converted to guest rooms at the turn of the century. It then served as shops and offices until becoming a guest house again in 1991. Each of its five rooms is decorated differently and filled with modern conveniences such as TVs, updated bathrooms, and queen-sized brass beds. Breakfast is served downstairs in the restaurant, and there is complimentary cheese and wine in the afternoon. ♦ 115 Cordova St (Cadiz St) 904/826.0113

Within Old City House Inn:

Old City House Restaurant ★$$$ The restaurant is open for lunch and dinner and the rack of New Zealand lamb is always a big hit. ♦ American ♦ Tu-Th 11:30AM-2:30PM, 5-9PM; F 11:30AM-2:30PM, 5-10PM; Sa 5-10PM; Su 8:30AM-3PM. Reservations recommended. 904/826.0781

30 County Courthouse This building was remodeled and turned into a courthouse in 1961. Originally the **Casa Monica Hotel,** it was designed and built in 1888 by **Franklin W. Smith,** who already built the outrageous **Zorayda Castle** up the street as a winter home. Smith's medieval, Spanish-style hotel was a fine match for **Henry Flagler's** magnificent Hotel Ponce de León across the street, but Smith found himself overextended and sold his hotel to Flagler, who changed its name to the **Cordova Hotel.** Flagler then connected it with his Hotel Alcazar across Cordova St. The Cordova closed in 1932, and the Florida East Coast Hotel Co. sold it to the St. Johns County Commission in 1961.

St. Augustine was founded in 1565, 42 years before the English created Jamestown and 55 years before the Pilgrims landed at Plymouth Rock.

31 Lightner Museum Built in 1888 by **Henry Flagler** as a retreat from cold northern winters and christened the **Hotel Alcazar,** the building was converted to a museum in 1948 by **Otto C. Lightner,** editor of *Hobbies* magazine. Like many smaller museums in Florida, the collection is an entertaining hodgepodge: grand furniture sits near the entrance, including a mahogany-and-satinwood bureau built in the 1860s; nearby musical instruments, such as a player piano capable of mimicking an entire orchestra, are demonstrated daily at 11AM and 2PM. For those interested in the exotic, shrunken heads are displayed on the second floor. An intact but nonfunctional turn-of-the-century steam room hark back to when the building was a bustling hotel that also boasted shops, a casino, a large indoor swimming pool, a dance floor, a gym, and a bowling alley. The casino and swimming pool area is now the **Lightner Antique Mall** selling antique furnishings, glassware, china, coins, and books. The city hall offices are also housed in the building. ♦ Museum daily 9AM-5PM; antique mall daily 10AM-5PM; closed Christmas. 75 King St (Granada-Cordova Sts) 904/824.2874

32 The 1890 Inn This tiny, four-room B&B is a bit off the beaten path, but that's part of its charm. Each room in this turn-of-the-century house has a separate entrance, a private bath, and cable TV. The inn is just half a block from the Lightner Museum. ♦ 83 Cedar St (Granada St) 904/826.0287

33 Museum of Weapons and Early American History Gun lovers and Civil War buffs will find this museum worthwhile. It's essentially one big room with antique rifles hung on the walls and small firearms, antique coins, newspapers, and Civil War memorabilia enclosed in display cases. Even non-gun enthusiasts will appreciate the beautiful flintlock pistols dating back to 1770, and there are several touching letters home from Civil War soldiers. One anomaly in the collection: **President John Tyler's** piano, circa 1830. ♦ Admission. Daily 10AM-5PM. 81-C King St (Granada-Martin Luther King Sts) 904/829.3727

34 Zorayda Castle Much of Henry Flagler's inspiration for transforming St. Augustine into the "American Riviera" came from a Boston millionaire **Franklin W. Smith,** famed for his interest in exotic architecture. In 1883, after his trip to Spain, Smith modeled his winter home from a wing of the Alhambra in Granada, thus making it one of the first all-concrete buildings in the US. Now it contains rare artifacts from around the world collected by the home's second owner, **Abraham S. Mussallem,** an Egyptian consul, who bought the house in 1913 and opened it as a gambling casino some 10 years later before turning it into a museum in 1936. Highlights downstairs include the **Harem's Prayer Room** with a Chinese teakwood fountain; an eye-catching damascene brass lamp in the **Second Prayer Room;** and displayed in the **Hall of Justice,** a game table made up of thousands of pieces of sandlewood, satinwood, rosewood, mother of pearl, and ivory. It took nine years and five men to fashion the table. Also downstairs is a scaled-down **Court of Lions,** similar to the one in Granada, but without the lions. Floor tiles are from Valencia, and wall mosaic tiles are 12th-century Egyptian. Upstairs is the **Egyptian Room,** the **Harem Room,** the **Sultan's Den,** the **Tower Alcove,** and the **Tower of the Princesses.** Here you learn that **Zorayda** was one of three daughters of **King Mohammed el Hazare.** You exit through the Hall of Justice into the gift shop. ♦ Admission. Daily 9AM-5:30PM, closed Christmas. 83 King St (Martin Luther King Ave-Granada St) 904/824.3097

35 Flagler College It was Henry Flagler's dream of making St. Augustine into the "American Riviera" that began here in 1888. Flagler chose architects **John M. Carrere** and **Thomas Hastings,** the 25-year-old son of an old business acquaintance, to build his hotel. Hastings and Carrere went on to establish themselves among the top architects of the early 1900s, and the project that brought them to prominence was Flagler's hotel. They dubbed their style "Spanish Revival Renaissance," and the **Ponce de León Hotel,** as it was then called, was the first major building in the country to be constructed of poured concrete—a mix of cement, native coquina shell, and sand. The exterior's soaring spires were matched by the elegance within: murals by **George W. Maynard,** and a canvas on the ceiling of the grand parlor painted in France by **Virgilio Tojetti** and stretched into place at the hotel, complement imported marble and carved oak. Windows are stained glass from

Louis Tiffany. In 1968 the building became Flagler College, an independent, coeducational liberal arts school. A statue of Flagler marks the entrance. ♦ 74 King St (Sevilla-Cordova Sts) 904/829.6481

36 Basilica Cathedral of St. Augustine The church dates back to 1791, although its parish registers go back to 1594 and are said to be the oldest written records in the US. After a fire in 1887, a bell tower and transept were added. ♦ Daily 7AM-5PM. 40 Cathedral Pl (St. George-Charlotte Sts) 904/824.2806

37 Dr. Peck House Also known as the **Pena-Peck House,** it was built for the Royal Treasurer of Spain, **Estevan de Pena.** During the British Period, it was the home of **Governor Moultrie.** In 1837 **Dr. Seth Peck** bought it and renovated it, adding a second story. His granddaughter, **Anna Burt,** left the house to the city in 1931. The Women's Exchange conducts tours of the house, filled with antebellum furnishings. ♦ Donation. M-Sa 10AM-4PM. 143 St. George St (Treasury St) 904/829.5064

38 Casa de la Paz $$$ This inn (pictured above) is a fine example of Spanish Renaissance Revival architecture, and the sweeping Matanzas River is visible from its rooms and the veranda. Rooms are extremely well-outfitted with high-quality linens and antiques. ♦ 22 Avenida Menendez (Treasury-Hypolita Sts) 904/829.2915

39 Castillo de San Marcos National Monument Walking around this imposing, gray-walled fort is reason enough to visit St. Augustine. After crossing a bridge over a shallow moat and as you enter into the fort, there are displays that explain its history. From the promenade, volunteers clad in Spanish colonial uniforms fire cannons at various times throughout the day.

The Spanish needed an outpost in North Florida as a way station for their treasure-filled ships bound home from the Caribbean; the St. Augustine harbor was one of the few operating harbors along the southern Atlantic Coast. Early forts built by the Spanish were made of wood, but after pirates sacked St. Augustine in 1668, Spanish engineers constructed the sturdy Castillo out of coquina. Wars between Spain and England resulted in two serious sieges in 1702 and 1740, but the fort was

never captured. The exhibits also chronicle some of the fort's less illustrious history: during the 1835 Seminole wars, the US Army kept more than 300 Indians imprisoned here, and Great Plains Indians were incarcerated at the fort after the Civil War. In 1924 the Castillo was declared a national monument. ♦ Nominal fee. Free for children under 16 and senior citizens over 61. Daily 9AM-6PM, 9AM-5:15PM Labor Day-Memorial Day; closed Christmas. 1 Castillo Dr (entrance is on Avenida Menendez at Charlotte St) 904/829.6506

40 The Oldest Wooden Schoolhouse This schoolhouse, built more than 225 years ago, of cypress and red cedar joined by wooden pegs, stands on its original site despite the wars, fires, and hurricanes that St. Augustine has endured. It was only in recent years that a heavy chain was placed around the top of the building (look up near the roof) and anchored to the ground to protect it from being blown away by hurricanes. Before entering the building, walk into the garden out back to see the one-seat outhouse. Also behind the school is the kitchen, which was situated away from the main building in case of fire and excess heat in the summer. The trees and plants are all identified, and there is an old school bell you can ring. During the Seminole Indian Wars from 1834-41, the schoolhouse was turned into a guardhouse and shelter for the sentries at the City Gate. Fifteen years later it was converted back into a school. Inside, the floors are the original tabby (a concrete made of crushed oyster shells and mortar). When you push a button, life-sized mannequins, dressed in original costumes, describe what school was like back in the olden days. For insurance reasons, visitors can no longer visit the schoolmaster's residence, but a mirror placed at the top of a steep flight of stairs provides a substantial view inside. As you leave through the gift shop, pick up a complimentary diploma. ♦ Nominal fee. Daily 9AM-5PM. 14 St. George St (Fort Alley-Orange St) 904/824.0192

How Sidney Lanier Spread the Word

In 1875 the American poet **Sidney Lanier** helped turn a deplorable condition into a profitable St. Augustine tourist attraction.

US Army troops held prisoner about 75 western Indians who had been removed from the path of America's westward expansion. Determined to make the best of a bad situation, the Indians who were locked up in the old fort – the **Castillo de San Marcos** (see entry no. 39, at left) – began painting depictions of their lost culture and homelands. In his widely circulated Florida travelogue, Lanier lamented the severe conditions under which the Indians were held captive, declaiming the old fort "as unfit for them as they are for it." Word spread quickly to the north, and when visitors to the Ancient City came home with elaborate, authentic Indian paintings and colorful stories to match, others followed.

The Indians were soon the city's most popular tourist attraction, performing tribal dances and other ceremonies before paying audiences, and filling their sketchbooks with drawings and paintings. It was with regret that many St. Augustine residents eventually watched the Indians return to the west.

The construction of the Castillo de San Marcos in St. Augustine was completed in 1695, and it's the oldest masonry fortification in the US and the only original fort in the country that's still standing.

Casa de Martin Martinez Gallegos

41 St. Augustine's Restored Spanish Quarter Based on archaeological and historical research, this state museum re-creates life as it was back in the mid-1700s, successfully mixing education and entertainment without being hokey. Guides and craftspeople are dressed in period costumes, and you will see how ordinary citizens and soldiers lived, along with demonstrations from weavers, blacksmiths, and woodworkers. Enter the museum at the **Triay House.** Keep your receipt; with it you're admitted in free to the Spanish Military Hospital museum. ♦ Admission. Daily 9AM-5PM; closed Christmas. 29 St. George St (Cuna St-Fort Alley) 825.6830

Within St. Augustine's Restored Spanish Quarter:

Casa de Maria Triay This reconstructed two-room Spanish colonial home is typical of those owned by families from the island of Minorca in the late 1700s.

Casa de Lorenzo Gomez In 1740 this was the home of a foot soldier. One corner of the small house served as a store to help the family supplement their income.

Casa de Martin Martinez Gallegos Next door to the Gomez House is the reconstructed home of Artillery Sergeant Martin Martinez Gallegos. It is only slightly larger than the Gomez House.

Blacksmith Shop You'll have to backtrack through the yards of the first three homes to get here. As you do, look to the left and notice how close you are to the fort that protected these people. The blacksmith produced whatever metal objects are needed for the Spanish Quarter; some replicas are sold at The Museum Store. His techniques are strictly 18th century.

Casa de Bernardo Gonzalez Gonzalez was a cavalryman, whose small home is now used for 18th-century crafts such as spinning and weaving.

Restaurants/Nightlife: Red   Hotels: Blue
Shops/ 🌳Outdoors: Green   **Sights/Culture: Black**

Casa de Geronimo de Hita y Salazar Another typical soldier's home of the mid-18th century, this one is a bit larger to house a big family. After leaving this house, pass through the gate to return to St. George St. The next building on your left is **St. Photios Chapel.** Walk past the chapel and turn into the next yard, with The Museum Store on the right.

Casa de Antonio de Mesa This was originally a two-room house owned by **Antonio de Mesa** in the mid-1700s. A second story was built during the second Spanish Period (1783-1821), when it was owned by **Juan Sanchez.** However, the home is furnished as it was in the early 1800s and exhibits how a middle or upper-middle class American family lived in St. Augustine then. Tours every 30 minutes.

The Museum Store This is the gift shop, where you will find works from blacksmiths and weavers as well as some history books about the area. The shop is housed in a building that was built as a duplex in the late 1700s. On one side lived **Jose Peso de Burgo,** a Corsican merchant and shopkeeper, and on the other lived **Francisco Pellicer,** a Minorcan carpenter.

42 St. Photios Chapel The chapel is part of the **St. Photios National Greek Orthodox Shrine** housed in **Casa Avaro** and built in 1749. The first Greeks arrived in St. Augustine in 1768, and later most of them moved 65 miles down the coast to New Smyrna. But after several dif-

St. Augustine

ficult years of hurricanes and other disasters, the survivors returned to St. Augustine and used the Avaro House for worship. The house was bought in 1965 by the Greek Orthodox Archdiocese of North and South America partially because of its significance to St. Augustine's Greek community. Reconstruction of the chapel began in 1979 and was completed in 1982. While the outside is Spanish design, the interior is filled with Byzantine-style frescoes highlighted with gold that depict scenes from the life of Christ. The museum

St. George Street Shopping Map

ORANGE ST.

ST. GEORGE ST.

Huckleberry's
One Stop Fun Shop
Fudge Kitchen
rag dolls The Colonial Shop
Oldest Wooden School House
Old School Gifts
glass prisms Sunburst
stained-glass lamps Faraway Places
Kennedy Studios
Public Restrooms
The Candy Kitchen
Spanish Bakery
Panama hats San Agustin Imports Inc.
Venetian glass necklaces Casa Rodriguez
St. Agustine Art Glass and Craft Gallery
The Monk's Vineyard
European arts and crafts Spanish Dutch Convoy

The Shell Co.
Hot Dogs of the World
City Cafe
Mill Top Tavern
B. Lee Bird *handcrafts, wooden toys*
Grist Mill
Grist Mill Gifts

FORT ALLEY

Casa de Martin Martinez Gallegos
part of Living History Museum
Casa de Lorenzo Gomez
part of Living History Museum
Casa de Maria Triay
entrance of Living History Museum
Spanish Q Cafe
Casa de Bernardo Gonzalez
part of Living History Museum
Casa de Geronimo de Hita
part of Living History Museum
Casa Avaro *St. Photios*
Casa de Antonio de Mesa
part of Living History Museum
Casa de Peso de Burgo-Pellicer
the museum store
Oliveros House *cigar factory*

CUNA ST.

T-shirts J. R. Benet
hand-made rugs Dreamweavers
exotic earrings The Pirate and His Lady
metal sculpture The Secret Cove
The Columbia Gift Shop
Columbia Restaurant and Bakery

Ice Cream parlor
Art to Wear
Mi Casa Cafe
Florida Cracker Cafe
Savannah Sweets
Sea Gems of St. Agustine
The Pink Petunia *handcrafts*
Kite Shop

HYPOLITA ST.

sangria Rendezvous Restaurant
earrings Unique by Edith
purses The Bay Lady
trendy youth wear Bags and Boards
St. George Souvenir Shop
St. George Tavern
The Vagabond's House
The Chantilly Cottage
Cuzzins Sandwich Shop
Moeller's Jewelers
Sonico Tourist Shopping Spot
Leonardi's Jewelry and Gifts
World of Flags
sportswear East Coast-West Coast

Casa de Hidalgo *Spanish tourist office, gifts*
Old Tyme Photo
The Bunnery
Far East Traders *inside Sanchez House*
Sunburst Crystal
The Ancient Mariner *nautical gifts*
Akras *women's clothes*
St. George Dinnerware
St. George Pharmacy and Restaurant
Calle Real Shops
Treasure Hall
Donna's
St. Agustine Men's Shop
P. K.'s Cafe
The House of Ireland

TREASURY ST.

ST. GEORGE ST.

The Shell Shop
The Lucille Shop
Sun 'n Surf Shop
casual wear Materialistic
JR Department Store
McCrory's

Pena-Peck house
Churchyard

CATHEDRAL PL.

offers an audio/visual presentation with exhibits illustrating the struggle of Greek immigrants in the US. ◆ Donation. Daily 9AM-5PM. 41 St. George St (Cuna St-Pirate Alley) 904/829.8205

43 The Monk's Vineyard ★$ One of the most inviting places to eat along touristy St. George St, this restaurant serves up a cool, tangy gazpacho, hearty salads (the usual ubiquitous iceberg lettuce thankfully absent), and big burgers. You can eat or drink in the air-conditioned dining room, or dine outside on little wooden tables. The helpful servers are dressed as monks. ◆ American ◆ Daily 11AM-9:30PM. 56 St. George St (Cuna-Orange Sts) 904/824.5888

44 Florida Cracker Cafe ★$ Enjoy lemonade

made from freshly squeezed lemons, juicy burgers, light sandwiches, garden salads, conch fritters, Jamaican Red Stripe beer, and frozen yogurt.
◆ American
◆ M-Th, Su 11AM-5PM; F-Sa 11AM-8PM. 81 St. George St (Hypolita-Cuna Sts) 904/829.0397

45 Columbia Restaurant ★$$ Diners are surrounded by stone fountains, handpainted ceramic tiles, and handcrafted furnishings as they feast on black bean soup, *arroz con pollo* (yellow rice and chicken), and paella *à la Valenciana*. Huge crowds line up for the fiesta brunch served every Sunday from 11AM to 2:30PM. ◆ Spanish ◆ Daily 11AM-10PM. 98 St. George St (Hypolita St) 904/824.3341

46 Carriage Way Bed & Breakfast $ Brass and four-poster canopied beds add to the Victorian ambience in this nine-room inn. Bicycles are available for exploring the district. ◆ 70 Cuna St (Cordova-Spanish Sts) 904/829.2467, 800/648.2888

47 Museum-Theater Two films are shown on the founding and settling of St. Augustine. *Dream of Empire* is the story of **Pedro Menendez de Aviles** beginning with King Philip II's order to kick the French out of Florida and ending with Menendez de Aviles death in Spain. A second film, *Struggle to Survive,* is about the early settlement of St. Augustine. It's a cool and comfortable place to take a break. ◆ Daily 9AM-5:30PM. 5 Cordova St (Cuna St-Tolomato Ln) 904/824.0339

48 Oldest Drugstore This is a don't-miss tourist spot. The drugstore displays some of its original stock, including a concoction that was guaranteed to cure a "loose operation" (diarrhea). People over the age of 50 will cackle at the bottles of Hadacol, recalling how it was hawked relentlessly by a Louisiana entrepreneur: It didn't really cure anything, but the 12-percent solution helped patients forget their aches and pains. The drugstore began as a trading post, but grew into a general store and

by 1872 had become a pharmacy. ◆ Daily 8:30AM-6PM. 31 Orange St (Cordova St) 904/824.9898, 800/332.9898

49 Cordova House $$ This bed-and-breakfast inn has five rooms filled with antiques, but it also has a luxury the competition doesn't: a hot tub. Innkeepers **Carole** and **Hal Schroeder** serve a full breakfast, complimentary wine and iced tea, and an evening snack. The sprawling verandas are a great place to unwind. ◆ 16 Cordova St (Orange-Cuna Sts) 904/825.0770, 800/247.8284

50 Southern Wind Inn $$$ Owners **Dennis** and **Jeannette Dean** make you feel at home in this two-story, Victorian bed-and-breakfast inn (pictured above). Rooms are furnished with antiques, but each room also has a cable TV and queen-sized bed. In addition, there is a charming guest cottage a block and a half from the main inn with pine floors, TV, outside decks, and a kitchen with a microwave, coffee maker, and small refrigerator. The inn furnishes bicycles for touring the historic district. ◆ 18 Cordova St (Orange-Saragossa Sts) 904/825.3623

51 Old Powder House Inn $$ This fancy, six-room bed-and-breakfast inn under towering pecan trees offers big breakfasts, high tea in the afternoon, and complimentary wine and hors d'oeuvres. It has a Jacuzzi, cable TV, and bicycles for exploring. ◆ 38 Cordova St (Cuna-Hypolita Sts) 904/824.4149, 800/447.4149

52 Memorial Presbyterian Church Built in 1889, it is another fine example of Henry Flagler's preferred architecture for St. Augustine: Spanish Renaissance Revival. St. Mark's Basilica in Venice, Italy, with its dome, elaborate ornamentation, rounded arches, towers, and re-tiled roof was the inspiration for its design. ◆ M-F 8:30AM-4:30PM. 36 Sevilla St (Valencia St) 904/829.6451

Restaurants/Nightlife: Red   Hotels: Blue
Shops/ 🌳 Outdoors: Green   Sights/Culture: Black

53 Visitors Information Center This is a good place to start your day. Come early, when there is plenty of free parking. Before walking east to the fort or south to most of the sights, stop in and pick up your brochures, or watch the 28-minute orientation film for a nominal charge. Next door is a half-acre public burial ground, set aside for residents who died in 1821 from a yellow-fever epidemic. ♦ Daily 8:30AM-5:30PM. 10 Castillo Dr (San Marco Ave) 904/824.3334

54 Ripley's Believe It or Not Museum This museum recalls the days when people were dazzled by giants, sword-eaters and tightrope walkers. Videos briefly extol Ripley's curiosities; less interesting are the matchstick London Tower Bridge and the toothpick model of the Eiffel Tower. The museum ends with a nifty trick involving a nude woman and mirrors (see it for yourself) and a walk through a revolving tunnel—guaranteed to give you vertigo. The house was built as a private residence by a business associate of Henry Flagler and known for years as **Warden Castle.** Later it became a hotel owned by novelist **Marjorie Kinnan Rawlings.** ♦ Admission. Daily 9AM-8:30PM June-Labor Day; daily 9AM-6PM May-Labor Day. 19 San Marco Ave (Grove Ave) 904/824.1606

54 Le Pavillon $$ This Victorian house was transformed into a restaurant instead of a bed-and-breakfast inn and serves a short menu in an intimate setting. A couple of their chicken meals are tasty: chicken curry Bombay is boneless chicken breast served with rice pilaf and sprinkled with bananas, chutney, coconut, and raisins; chicken Pavillon is boneless chicken breast sautéed and topped with a fresh mushroom sauce. They also serve a rack of lamb for one. Lunches are light: The onion soup hits the spot, and crepes are delicate and flavorful. A special crepe is stuffed with minced beef and mushrooms. Another good bet: bouillabaisse with fresh fish, crabmeat, mussels, shrimp, and vegetables. ♦ American ♦ Daily 11:30AM-2:30PM, 5-10PM. 45 San Marco Ave (Joiner-Mulberry Sts) Reservations recommended. 904/824.6202

Shrine MISSION

55 Mission Nombre de Dios This pretty little mission, set on tranquil grounds, was founded in 1565 by Spanish explorer **Pedro Menendez de Aviles,** who landed nearby with a group of settlers and priests. Early missions built on the site were destroyed by pirates, hurricanes, and English gunfire. The present mission was built in 1915 and is a reconstruction of the original. Inside is a statue of the Virgin Mary brought from Spain in the 17th century. Nearby is a 108-foot-high stainless-steel cross that was erected in 1965 to celebrate the city's 400th birthday. ♦ Donations. Daily 7AM-8PM summer; 8AM-6PM winter. San Marco Ave and Old Mission Ave. 904/824.2809

56 Raintree ★★★$$$ When the **MacDonald** family immigrated from England in 1981, they opened a restaurant in a stately Victorian house. Since then, Raintree (named for the tree-shaped fountain out front) has become perhaps St. Augustine's best restaurant. Many selections on the menu change each month, but the catch of the day is always good, especially when served à la Raintree, in white wine, mushrooms, and cream. Another favorite is the flaky Florida grouper, whose delicacy isn't overwhelmed by the rich crawfish cream sauce. ♦ American ♦ Tu-Th, Su 5-9:30PM; F-Sa 5-10PM. 102 San Marco Ave (Hope-Bernard Sts) Reservations recommended. 904/824.7211

57 Fountain of Youth Park Legend has it that in 1513, **Juan Ponce de León** came ashore here in search of the Fountain of Youth, but what he really wanted was to claim the land for Spain. Besides "discovering" North America, he came across the **Timucuan Indians,** who archaeologists say lived in a settlement here called **Seloy.** At the ticket booth, visitors are ushered into a cavelike structure, where drinks are free from a spring that purports to be the one de León believed was the Fountain of Youth. A diorama of his landing and several Fountain of Youth-related items, such as old cartoons and letters, are displayed behind glass. Near the spring are 27 rocks, laid out in the shape of a cross—15 down and 13 across—supposedly placed by de León to mark the fountain and the year (1513) it was discovered. A ranger explains the history of the area in a brief lecture. Artifacts such as Indian dugout canoes and Spanish anchors are labeled and placed around the grounds of the park. A path leads to the site where de León is thought to have landed. In1976 archaeologists discovered hut foundations of the Timucuan Indians, evidence that they were here a thousand years before the Spaniard's arrival. There are two short shows at the park: the *Discovery Globe,* inside a

PATRICIA KEELIN

Juan Ponce de León

small auditorium, is a movie about the first hundred years of European exploration in America; the other is presented in the **Navigator's Planetarium,** where you walk past ship models and into a planetarium showing astronomical sailing techniques used by the early explorers. The constellations are the same ones de León would have seen when he landed. ♦ Admission. Daily 9AM-5PM; closed Christmas. 155 Magnolia Ave (Williams St) 904/829.3168

58 Old Jail This is the old St. Johns County jail, built in 1890 on land purchased by **Henry Flagler** because an older jail was too close to his fancy Ponce de León Hotel, and used until 1953. To begin your self-guided tour follow the big yellow footprints painted in the prison yard. They lead to the jailhouse, an imposing Queen Anne-style house that served as living quarters for the jailer and his family. Weapons used in murders and other crimes are displayed at the entrance to the jail itself. The building is creepy enough, but the jail cells are downright eerie. ♦ Admission. Daily 8:30AM-5PM. 1676 San Marco Ave (Williams-Dufferin Sts) 904/829.3800

59 Sightseeing Trains Although it's just as easy to devise your own walking tour of St. Augustine's historic area, these open-air trolley tours are worth considering for a narrative history of the district. There are eight tours to choose from, ranging from one to six hours in various price ranges. Trains leave from sites all over town, but there is plenty of parking across the street from the Old Jail. ♦ Daily 8:30AM-5PM. 170 San Marco Ave (Matanzas Ave) 904/829.6545

60 Fiddler's Green $$$ Large windows offer a fabulous view of the Atlantic Ocean, and a cozy, stone fireplace sets the mood here. Delicate snails baked in butter and herbs with garlic and two cheeses, or juicy oysters Rockefeller are the perfect accompaniment to crabs fried in a light tempura batter. ♦ American ♦ M-Th 5-10PM; Sa-Su 5-11PM. 50 Anahma Dr (east of Vilano Bridge) Reservations recommended. 904/824.8897

61 Days Inn Downtown $$ Minutes away from the action, this inn is a quiet oasis after a hectic day of sightseeing. A large pool, a playground, and a flower garden, all shaded by large oak trees, can be found behind the motel. Sightseeing trams leave from the motel. Rooms are furnished with double- or king-sized beds, and there are nonsmoking rooms and rooms for the physically disabled. ♦ 2800 Ponce de León Blvd (SR 16) 904/829.6581, 800/325.2525

61 St. Augustine Outlet Center This outlet mall, right off the interstate, has 40 stores, with plans to add about 10 stores to increase its size to 232,000 square feet. Anchoring the mall is **West Point Pepperell Mill Store,** a linen outlet featuring **Lady Pepperell, Martex, Stevens,** and **Utica.** You will also find **Jordache, Harve Benard, London Fog, Polly Flinders, Stone Mountain Handbag, Van**

Heusen, American Tourister, Corning/ Revere, Toy Liquidators, and housewares, shoe stores, and bookstores. A tourist information booth is located in the small food court, where there are restrooms and telephones. ♦ M-Sa 9AM-9PM; Su 10AM-6PM. SR 16 (I-95, exit 95)

A Concrete Idea

Until the turn of the century, a building's height was restricted by materials. Brick and mortar, the most dependable of materials, could only accommodate limited heights before their weight caused foundations to crack.

St. Augustine's **Franklin Smith,** a transplanted Boston millionaire, changed high-rise construction forever, establishing an architectural style by which St. Augustine, then the jewel of Florida cities, is still defined today.

Smith was a successful hardware merchant. But his passion was architecture. He visited Paris, Rome, Athens, Cairo, and Constantinople, wondering how he might share the architectural treasures he saw with the less-cultured masses back home. Florida gave him that opportunity.

Smith acquired a plot of land in St. Augustine and focused his energies on the design and construction of a winter home. He was inspired by the Alhambra in Granada, Spain, with its architectural style known variously as Islamic, Hispano-Moresque, Oriental, or, most commonly, Moorish Revival, but he bemoaned the lack of substantive building products in Florida. Most homes were designed in the Victorian style and were constructed of the most readily available material, heart of pine.

Then one day he watched as workers in Rome crafted a two-story building of poured concrete, mixing cement with sand and crushed stone. Florida might lack granite or marble, he thought, but the beautiful coquina stone was abundant. So he began construction with cement immediately.

Residents thought his concrete forms were a bit ridiculous, but he persevered, and the result was a magnificent castle that endures to this day.

Smith and his wife scoured Europe and the mid-East for furnishings and bric-a-brac to decorate the palace. Floor tiles and wainscoting were crafted in Valencia, window lattices and balustrades came from Cairo, and a fireplace was hauled over from Constantinople. The intricate arabesque traceries on the walls of the

Alhambra were not for sale, but Smith found their original molds in the Kensington Museum, bought them, and shipped them to Zorayda.

In the end, Smith had single-handedly fashioned an architectural style that has been duplicated throughout Florida, from mansions in Miami to Henry Plant's magnificent Tampa Bay Hotel. But more important, perhaps, was his introduction of poured concrete; its success led immediately to the design and construction of buildings taller than had ever been contemplated. And when coupled with steel reinforcement, Smith's technique resulted in the skyscrapers we see today.

Cassadaga/Mt. Dora/ Ocala/Gainesville

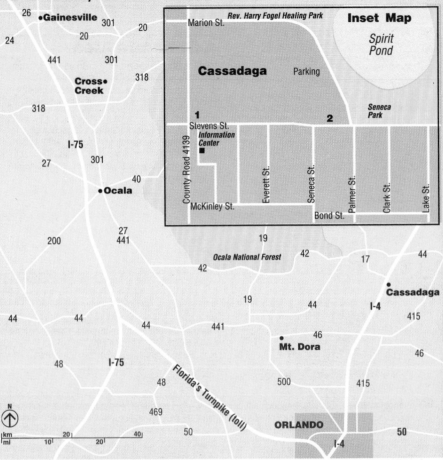

Gainesville
26
301
20
20
24
441
301
318
Cross• Creek
318
I-75
301
27
40
•Ocala
200
27
441
42
Ocala National Forest
42
19
44
44
44
44
441
48
I-75
48
469
50

Marion St.
Rev. Harry Fogel Healing Park

Inset Map

Spirit Pond

Cassadaga
Parking

Seneca Park

1
2

Stevens St.
Information Center ■
County Road 4139
Everett St.
Seneca St.
Palmer St.
Clark St.
Lake St.
McKinley St.
Bond St.

19
42
17
44
19
44
I-4
Cassadaga
415
46
• Mt. Dora
46
500
415
ORLANDO
50
I-4
50

N

km 20 40
mi 10 20

Area code 407 unless otherwise indicated.

Cassadaga

Walt Disney World may have fun with fantasy and the future, but Cassadaga, which lies about 45 minutes north of the giant theme park, takes these matters seriously. The little Florida village is home to the **Southern Cassadaga Spiritualist Camp,** a group of about 40 spiritualists who classify themselves variously as seers, mediums, and clairvoyants. They attract a steady clientele of the faithful and curious, who trek up Interstate 4

Cassadaga/Mt. Dora/Ocala/Gainesville

to Exit 54, where a small road leads into town. Cassadaga has been a haven for spiritualists since 1875, when **George Colby** left Dale, New York, to seek a winter home for his fellow mediums. Colby said spirits led him to the piney woods of northcentral Florida. Today, the hamlet is an odd, somewhat eerie collection of small, wooden-framed, New England-style houses.

1 Southern Cassadaga Spiritualist Camp Bookstore & Information Center The friendly behind-the-counter help here will suggest you use their phone to make an appointment with a medium—a person who claims to act as a conduit for messages from the dead. If that doesn't feel right, you can walk around the tranquil town until the vibrations from the *right* house beckon you inside. If you prefer not to go inside someone's home for a reading, a medium is available in a room adjacent to the information center daily except Sunday. As you enter the bookstore, also called the **Andrew Jackson Davis Building,** you'll find a community bulletin board to your left where mediums who are available for readings sign in daily. ♦ M-Sa 9:30AM-5PM; Su noon-4PM. 1112 Stevens St (Everett Ln-County Rd) 904/228.2880

2 Colby Memorial Temple On the Sabbath, there are weekly spiritualist services in this small, wooden church that was built in 1923. ♦ Stevens St (Palmer-Seneca Sts)

Mt. Dora

There isn't really a mountain in Mt. Dora, but this charming small town, situated 184 feet above sea level, does have rolling hills, beautiful public parks, gorgeous lakes, and plenty of charm. The town sits on the northeastern shore of Lake Dora, named for **Dora Ann Drawdy,** who moved here with her husband in the mid-1800s. The lake was named for her by government surveyors after she allowed them to camp on her property. The town, born in 1880, was first known as **Royellou,** after the three children of postmaster R.C. Tremain—Roy, Ella, and Louis. The name was changed to Mt. Dora in 1883. Visitors come to Mt. Dora to enjoy the turn-of-the-century architecture (a rarity in modern Florida), a hotel where President Calvin Coolidge and his wife vacationed in 1930, and a number of weekend festivals celebrating art, antiques, and bicycle-riding.

3 Lakeside Inn Listed on the National Register of Historic Places, this 1883 hotel tries hard to re-create the ambience of an elegant, romantic New England lakeside inn, although sometimes with too few employees. Still, minor renovations underway should spruce up the weather-beaten exterior, returning the inn to its glory days of the 1920s.

The hotel began as the 10-room **Alexander House** in 1883 and soon became the social hub of the community. This two-story, cream-colored building now houses a spacious lobby with polished hardwood floors and high ceilings; the Beauclaire dining room; the Tremains Lounge; a formal ballroom; and the inn's best rooms, including the Edgerton Suite, which have large windows that overlook the lake. **Charles Edgerton** headed the group of investors that saved the inn in 1924, and his son **Dick** who managed the Lakeside Inn. He eventually bought the hotel. It ran into financial trouble again in 1985, but was saved once more—this time by new owners from the Management Development Group of Orlando and Horizon Builders of Winter Park.

Today the renovation is most evident in the rooms and the main building, as well as in the redbrick driveway that separates the inn from two of the outlying buildings: the **Gables** (located on the right side when viewed from the inn's porch) and the **Terrace.** When these two buildings were constructed in 1930, **Calvin Coolidge** was invited to dedicate them; he and his wife were spending a month relaxing at the inn after he'd finished his term as president. Between the buildings is a lawn that runs down to a lakeside pool (which will be replaced by a new pool in mid-1992). The third outlying building, to the left of the Terrace, is the **Sunset,** which sits back on the lawn. The hotel offers croquet, lighted tennis courts, a putting green, shuffleboard, and a small boat dock, where visitors can call a water taxi. A large, covered wooden porch with ceiling fans and rocking chairs stretches out along the front of the inn. Afternoon tea is served here, and it's a great place to enjoy a sunset over the lake. ♦ 100 S. Alexander St (Third Ave) 904/383.4101, 800/556.5016

Within Lakeside Inn:

The Beauclaire ★★$$ A wall of windows overlooking a well-manicured floral garden sets off this formal dining room. Crabmeat-stuffed filet of turbot is a good choice, as is the boneless breast of duck gently charbroiled and topped with raspberry and brandy sauce. The fruit-and-nut waffles are a favorite of bicyclists who love to test their skills in the Mt. Dora hills (see page121). ♦ American ♦ M-Th, Su 11:30AM-2:30PM, 6-9PM; F-Sa 11:30AM-2:30PM, 6-10PM. 904/383.4101

Tremains Lounge Overstuffed furniture makes this lounge cozy. A fine place to have a few drinks with friends and watch televised sports.

When Lightning Strikes

Scientists say there are lightning storms more than a hundred days a year in Central Florida, making it one of the lightning capitals of the world. The frequent storms that are accompanied by lightning are spawned by the sea breezes and high humidity that are especially common during Florida's warmest months.

But those beautiful bolts can be deadly. Lightning killed 74 people in the US last year, and 15 of the deaths occurred in Florida; another 252 people were hurt by lightning, 29 of them in Florida.

Cassadaga/Mt. Dora/Ocala/Gainesville

The best way to protect yourself from lightning is to stay indoors when a storm is approaching. The most dangerous places to be during a lightning storm are in water, standing by a car or truck, or huddling under a tree. If you're outdoors and can't get inside, lie down in a ditch or even a shallow depression in the ground.

Restaurants/Nightlife: Red   **Hotels:** Blue
Shops/ 🌳Outdoors: Green   **Sights/Culture:** Black

4 Eduardo's ★$ Large wooden shutters are pulled back to give this Mexican restaurant the feel of an open courtyard. It also has a small indoor bar. Choose from 40 imported beers. ◆ Mexican ◆ Daily 11AM-2AM. 100 E. 4th Ave (Donnelly St) 904/735.1711

5 Royellou Museum Originally a fire station with jail cells in the back. The old cells are now home to an odd assortment of exhibits reflecting the city's history: bayonets, a telephone from 1879, the first edition of the city's newspaper, the *Mount Dora Voice,* and a collection of Depression glass. Cell No. six features a hole in the wall (now patched), that was knocked out by an escaping prisoner. Because he left a note behind telling the jailers where he was having dinner, they decided not to round him up. The escapee, good as his word, returned after dinner. Hours vary, but the museum is generally open a few hours a week in winter. For more information, call the Chamber of Commerce. ◆ Donation. Alley between 4th and 5th Aves. 904/383.2165

6 Cafe Dora ★$ You won't get the usual iceberg lettuce salad or dull sandwich at this unassuming restaurant with a cool blue interior and pressed-tin ceiling. Light lunches of quiche or tangy chicken salad with curry are accompanied by a romaine-and-green lettuce salad, orange slices, and spicy black bean soup served with corn bread. ◆ American ◆ M-F/11AM-3PM; Sa-Su 11AM-8PM. 442 N. Donnelly St (4th-5th Sts) 904/735.3002

7 The Lamp Post $$ A New Orleans-style French Quarter building in a New England-style downtown. The Lamp Post serves beef, seafood, and veal with a French flair. For a terrific tableside presentation, order steak Diane—filet mignon sautéed in butter and flamed with cognac. It's tough to pass up bananas Foster, a dessert, but the homemade pies are tops. Above the restaurant is the **Top of the Post,** a dance hall where popular

Cassadaga/Mt. Dora/Ocala/Gainesville

music is played. ◆ French ◆ M-Sa 11:30AM-4PM, 5-10PM. 523 Donnelly St (5th Ave) 904/383.6118

8 Donnelly House This is an excellent example of steamboat-Gothic architecture, and was named "J.P.'s Gingerbread House" by townsfolk when **John Phillips Donnelly** built it in 1893 for his bride, **Annie Stone.** He became Mount Dora's first mayor when

the city was incorporated in 1910. The Donnelly House is now owned by the Mount Dora Masonic Lodge and is open on special occasions. ◆ Corner of Donnelly St and 5th Ave

9 Captain Abbleby's Inn ★★$$ A funky family restaurant loaded with antiques and collectibles. As you walk in the room on your right houses an old icebox, a player piano, and old typewriters. The food isn't particularly memorable, but the well-stocked, all-you-can-eat salad buffet is included with your meal. Locals favor the cinnamon sticky buns. Water comes from a pump-it-yourself well and is served in mason jars. If you're visiting Florida for the first time, try the traditional Florida Cracker sampler platter, which includes baked chicken, crab cakes, fried petite shrimp, and fried catfish fingerlings. ("Cracker" is a term used to describe old-time Floridians, not the crunchy stuff you get with your soup.) If you're a hearty eater, try the split-king crab legs, snowcrab clusters by the pound, or rib eye steak with shrimp. For dessert, fried alligator and fried honey ice cream are available for the adventurous. ◆ American ◆ M-Th 11:30AM-9:30PM; F-Sa 11:30AM-10PM; Su 11:30AM-8PM. US 441 (west of Donnelly St) Reservations Su only. No personal checks. 904/383.6662

10 Renninger's Twin Markets As you leave the highway at Renninger's entrance, you will come immediately to a fork in the road. The left fork goes up a small hill and leads to the **Farmers and Flea Market;** the right fork goes to the **Antique and Collectible Center.** At the latter, there are about 200 dealers, but not all have antiques. The selection is wide, ranging from antique furniture and toys to old coins and glass by Steuben and Lalique. The flea market has the same wide variety, which might include a pair of blue lovebirds, homemade moccasins, tapes and compact discs, records from the forties and fifties, cut flowers, and old baseball cards. The markets' 72 acres are packed on the first weekend of each month (except July and December) when Renninger's holds its **Antique Fairs,** attracting dealers and collectors primarily from the southeast. On the third weekend of November, January, and February, Renninger's **Extravaganzas** bring in nearly a thousand dealers from around the country. ◆ Sa-Su 8AM-5PM. US 441 (north of SR 46) 904/383.8393

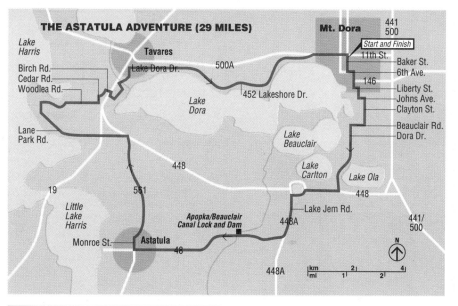

THE ASTATULA ADVENTURE (29 MILES)

Mt. Dora
441
500

Start and Finish

Lake Harris
Tavares
Birch Rd.
Cedar Rd.
Woodlea Rd.
Lake Dora Dr.
500A
11th St.
Baker St.
6th Ave.
146
452 Lakeshore Dr.
Liberty St.
Johns Ave.
Clayton St.
Lake Dora
Lane Park Rd.
Lake Beauclair
Beauclair Rd.
Dora Dr.
448
Lake Carlton
Lake Ola
19
551
448
Little Lake Harris
Lake Jem Rd.
441/500
Apopka/Beauclair Canal Lock and Dam
448A
Monroe St.
Astatula
48
448A
N

Mt. Dora by Bike

Every October, bicyclists from all over Florida gather for the **Mt. Dora Bicycle Festival,** a weekend of well-organized rides, complete with easy-to-read map routes and a bike fair. Inexperienced riders may rent bikes and enjoy a ride during the festival; although Mt. Dora has some gentle hills, you won't have to huff and puff through a ride if you pick the right one. Organizers of the festival have thoughtfully chosen some routes that are mostly flat, and rental bikes have gears that will help maneuver around the small hills.

If you're a more serious biker and arrive with your 10-speed, Mt. Dora is well worth the 45-minute car trip from Orlando. Scenic bike routes take you past orange groves and freshwater lakes, where bright green cypress trees line the lakefront and moss-hung oaks shade the street. One popular tour, the Lake Ola Loop (see map below), passes Lake Ola, the head-waters of a chain of lakes that drain into the Atlantic Ocean more than 55 miles east. (Lake Ola's 442 square acres contain some of the purest water in Lake County, so take a dip if you have time.)

Another route leads past the Apopka-Beauclair canal lock and dam. The lock, basically an elevator that enables recreational boats to get from one lake to another, was built in 1957. The accommodating lockkeeper will answer all your questions about how the lock works. Serious bicyclists usually forego the swimming and a stop at the locks; what keeps them

coming back to Mt. Dora is the pure air, the varied terrain, and the lack of heavy auto traffic. This is Florida bicycle-riding at its best.

LAKE OLA LOOP (11 MILES)

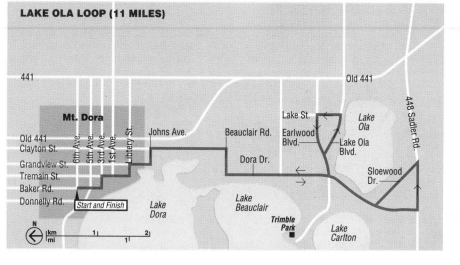

441
Old 441
Mt. Dora
Old 441
Clayton St.
6th Ave.
5th Ave.
3rd Ave.
1st Ave.
Liberty St.
Johns Ave.
Beauclair Rd.
Lake St.
Earlwood Blvd.
Lake Ola
448 Sadler Rd.
Lake Ola Blvd.
Grandview St.
Tremain St.
Baker Rd.
Donnelly Rd.
Dora Dr.
Sloewood Dr.
Start and Finish
Lake Dora
Lake Beauclair
Trimble Park
Lake Carlton
N

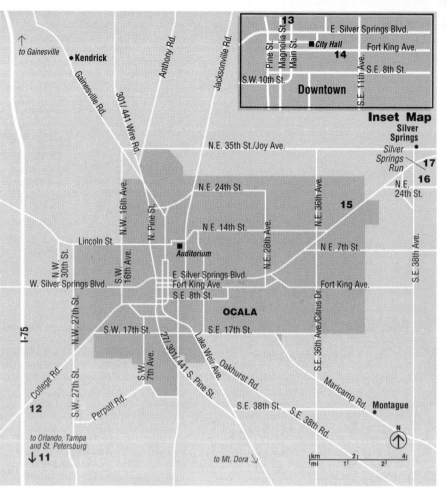

Ocala

Ocala is synonymous with horse country. A drive through Marion County will take you past more than 400 purebred horse farms. Some are open to visitors, but only by appointment. Pick up a list of farms that welcome guests from the Ocala/Marion County Chamber of Commerce at 110 E. Silver Springs Blvd, Ocala, 904/629.8051; fax 904/629.7651. If you're looking for a scenic ride, take 27th Ave (also called Shady Rd) south out of town to see tidy farms in picture-postcard settings.

11 Museum of Drag Racing This shrine to car racing lies 10 miles south of Ocala. "**Big Daddy" Don Garlits,** the "Babe Ruth" of drag racing, started putting together the museum in 1976, first with his trophies and memorabilia, then acquiring more and more cars until he had enough to open a 25,000-square-foot museum in 1984. In addition to a display of race cars, look for the collection of old Fords, including a 1932 roadster and a 1940 convertible coupe. ♦ Admission. Daily 10AM-5PM. 13700 SW 16th Ave (County Rd 484 at exit 67 off I-75) 904/245.8661

12 Ocala Hilton $$ This 200-room hotel sits quietly back from the highway on tastefully landscaped grounds that include a swimming pool and lighted tennis courts. ♦ SW 36th Ave (at exit 68 of I-75) 904/854.1400; 800/843.3756 (FL), 800/922.5155 (US)

Within the Ocala Hilton:

Arthur's ★$$ An upscale restaurant with a cool, pastel decor. Meals are served without pretense and lean toward regional favorites such as conch chowder and gator-tail *rémoulade.* ♦ American ♦ M-Sa 6:30-11AM, 11:30AM-2:30PM, 5:30-10PM; Su 7-11AM, 11AM-2:30PM, 5:30-10PM. 854.1400

No dinosaur bones have been found in Florida because dinosaurs were extinct several million years before the formation of Florida's landmass.

13 WMOP Broadcasting since 1953, WMOP (900 AM) is the oldest country music station in Florida. It also has another claim to fame: a **Radio Museum.** Owner **Jim Kirk,** a former Ocala mayor, collects antique radios as a hobby, and they're all on display in this spic-and-span museum, which houses everything from early Edison gramophones, circa 1898, to plastic Charlie McCarthy radios from the 1930s. While viewing the museum, you can watch the DJ in WMOP's control room. ♦ M-F 9AM-5PM; Sa 9AM-noon. 343 NE 1st Ave. 904/732.2010

14 Seven Sisters Inn $$ (1888) Owners **Bonnie Morehardt** and **Ken Oden** work as commercial pilots, but they also know what it takes to run a successful bed-and-breakfast (pictured above). Each of the five rooms, named for sisters of a former owner, has its own distinct personality. The king-sized bed in Sylvia's Room is backed by a graceful bay window; Judy's Room has a charming, handpainted armoire; Lottie's Loft, which sleeps four, is a sunlight-filled space with white, eyelet-lace pillow covers. Loretta's Room has cozy quilts on the four-poster double bed, and Norma's Room contains a graceful four-poster bed and adjacent sitting room with white wicker furniture. All rooms have baths. The generous breakfast usually includes homemade muffins, blueberries, and French toast. ♦ 820 SE Fort King St. 904/867.1170

15 Appleton Museum of Art African, pre-Columbian, and Mayan artworks are among the hodgepodge of artifacts here. You'll also find a Louis XVI desk decorated with more than 100 pieces of Limoges china and enamel medallions of mythological figure, a Colt third model dragoon revolver owned by **General Joseph Hardee,** after whom a Florida county was named, **Marie Antoinette's** hunting rifle, and, tucked into a corner, etchings by **Rembrandt.** For history buffs, there is the Louis XIV table on which the peace treaty ending WWI was signed at the Palace of Versailles. The museum was a gift from **Arthur I. Appleton,** the president of Appleton Electric Company of Chicago, who owned a thoroughbred farm in the area. ♦ Admission. Tu-Sa 10AM-4:30PM; Su 1-5PM. 4333 E. Silver Springs Blvd. 904/236.5050

16 Silver Springs This venerable Florida attraction may have been upstaged by Walt Disney World, but for natural beauty, it hasn't been outclassed. The park's most famous attraction is glass-bottom boats that ply the Silver River, and home to 14 fast-flowing springs. Some *Tarzan* movies were filmed here, as was **Lloyd Bridges'** *Sea Hunt* TV series. The water is so clear that park managers say you can often see to a depth of more than 80 feet. The water safari, *Jungle Voyage,* takes you through an area stocked with exotic animals, including giraffes and antelopes; at one stop children can feed friendly spider monkeys. A new attraction is **Jeep Safari,** where you ride four-wheel drive jeeps deep into the park's interior for close-up looks at deer, zebras, wild boar, alligators, and monkeys. For a longer look at the Silver River, take the *Lost River Voyage,* a 30-minute tour aboard a glass-bottom boat. The park also has an antique car museum, a petting zoo, and gift shops. ♦ Admission. Daily 9AM-6:30PM. State Rd 40 (one mile east of Ocala) 904/236.2121, 800/274.7458

17 Wild Waters This six-acre water park is a sister attraction to **Silver Springs.** Highlights include a 450,000-gallon wave pool, eight flume rides, a play area for children, a nine-hole miniature golf course, a video game arcade, and a gift shop. Handy lockers are available for a change into dry duds. Free parking and pet kennels are available. Volleyball and picnic areas. ♦ 904/236.2121, 800/342.0297 (FL only)

Gainesville

This is a typical university town with a tolerant atmosphere, cheap eats, oak-shaded neighborhoods, and a lively campus scene. Peaceful Gainesville was named after **General Edmund Gaines,** a hero of the Seminole Wars. The town started as a tiny community of 250, and now it's home to the University of Florida, the largest university in the state. Its 34,000 students come from all corners of the nation and from more than a hundred countries, lending the city a sophisticated and lively air. Competition to get into the university (once known as a party school) has grown increasingly difficult, and today's students aren't just here for a suntan: A recent freshman class entered with a GPA of 3.5 and SAT scores 200 points above the national average.

Although Gainesville isn't huge, you'll probably need a car unless you stay on campus. There are traffic snarls when the Florida Gators football team is playing at home, but

the rest of the time you can breeze through town because it doesn't really cater to a big tourist market. Yet many people come here to meet on university business and to visit students, so there are plenty of upscale hotels and restaurants for visitors.

Restaurants/Nightlife: Red **Hotels:** Blue
Shops/ Outdoors: Green **Sights/Culture:** Black

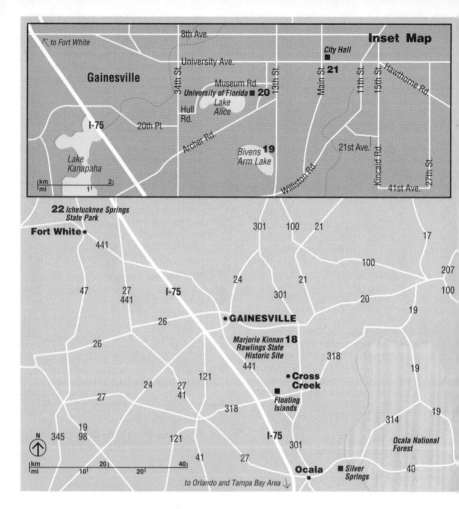

Inset Map

Gainesville

8th Ave.

University Ave.

City Hall
■ **21**

34th St.

Museum Rd.
University of Florida ■ **20**

13th St.

Main St.

11th St.

15th St.

Hawthorne Rd.

↖ to Fort White

I-75

20th Pl.

Hull Rd.

Lake Alice

Archer Rd.

Lake Kanapaha

Bivens Arm Lake **19**

Williston Rd.

21st Ave.

Kincaid Rd.

27th St.

41st Ave.

km / mi

22 *Ichetucknee Springs State Park*

Fort White•

441

301 100 21

17

100

207

100

24

21

47 27
441

I-75

301

20

19

26

•GAINESVILLE

19

26

Marjorie Kinnan **18**
Rawlings State Historic Site

441

318

19

24 27
41

121

•**Cross Creek**

318

■
Floating Islands

314

19

19
98

345

121

41   27

I-75

301

Ocala•
•

■ *Silver Springs*

Ocala National Forest

40

N ↑

km / mi

to Orlando and Tampa Bay Area ↓

18 Marjorie Kinnan Rawlings State Historic Site, Cross Creek The former home of Pulitzer Prize-winning author Marjorie Kinnan Rawlings, Cross Creek, 15 miles south of Gainesville, lies beyond "open pine woods and gallberry flats," as Rawlings wrote in the 1940s. When you arrive, look for a sign-up sheet; tours of the author's little Florida Cracker house although given every

behind the volumes. Docents sometimes arrive early to whip up recipes from Rawlings' *Cross Creek Cookery* at her black, wood-burning stove. There's an adjacent picnic area on Orange Lake. ♦ Admission. M, Th-Su 10-11:30AM, 1-4:30PM. Alachua County Rd 325. 904/466.3672

19 Gainesville Hilton $$ This efficiently run hotel lies on tranquil Bivens Arm Lake. It offers free shuttle service to the university and has a conference center that can accommodate up tp a thousand people. ♦ 2900 SW 13th St (Williston Rd) 904/ 377.4000, 800/344.5866; fax 904/371.1159

Cassadaga/Mt. Dora/Ocala/Gainesville

half-hour, are limited to 10 people and fill up fast. Rawlings based the 1942 classic, *Cross Creek,* on her experiences in the then-remote Florida hamlet. Born in Washington DC, she moved to Cross Creek at age 32. A glass bookcase—the only item added since Rawlings' time—holds many of her works in various languages. Her framed Pulitzer Prize, received for *The Yearling*, sits modestly

The crystalline waters at Florida's Silver Springs have lured many filmmakers and TV producers. Everything from famous movies to TV commercials have been filmed there, including six of the Tarzan movies that starred Johnny Weismuller and Maureen O'Sullivan. Whenever Lloyd Bridges dove underwater in the sixties hit TV series "Sea Hunt," he swam in Silver Springs waters. Robert Culp and Bill Cosby starred in an "I Spy" episode filmed at the park, and the US Army, Navy, and Marines have used the densely forested area to film jungle warfare survival films.

FLORIDA MUSEUM OF NATURAL HISTORY

20 Florida Museum of Natural History
Located on the University of Florida campus, this is the largest natural history museum in the South and is well worth a visit. You can walk through a replica of a large Florida limestone cave or a seventh century Mayan palace display. The **Object Room** contains large drawers that house a variety of Florida flora and fauna, including stuffed birds and snakes. However, portions of the museum suffer from a lack of attention to detail—for example, in some cases there are no explanatory notes to guide you. With the exception of the Apple computers that allow you to play fossil hunter, the older exhibits are the better ones. ♦ Free. Tu-Sa 10AM-4PM; Su and holidays 1-4PM. Museum Rd and Newell Dr (University of Florida) 904/392.1721

21 The Sovereign ★★★$$$ Housed in a warehouse (in the warehouse district), this restaurant serves the best meals in Gainesville. Students and locals rave about the chateaubriand *bouquetiere* for two, which is sliced tableside.

Other favorites are baked moussaka with cheese, eggplant, herbs and chopped lamb, and *scallone a la Sovereign* sautéed with mushrooms and scallops. Chef/owner **Elmo Moser** whips up a special Mexican menu twice a month. ♦ American ♦ M-Th 5:30-10PM; F-Sa 5:30-11PM. Closed two weeks every Aug. 12 SE 2nd Ave (2nd Ave-Main St) Reservations recommended. 904/378.6307

22 Ichetucknee Springs State Park The Sunshine State's manufactured attractions don't hold a candle to the simple pleasure of sitting in an inner tube and effortlessly floating down the cold, crystalline Ichetucknee River. Enter the spring-fed river at its northern end in Ichetucknee Springs State Park, about 20 miles northwest of Gainesville. Arrive early because the state has set limits on the number of tubers on the river. The trip takes about three hours and is a wonderful way to see Florida's native waterfowl. A concessionaire operates a shuttle bus that meets tubers at the end of the river and ferries them back to the parking lot. ♦ Admission. Daily 8AM to sunset. For more information, write to: Ichetucknee Springs State Park, Route 1, Box 173, Fort White FL 32038; or call 904/497.2511

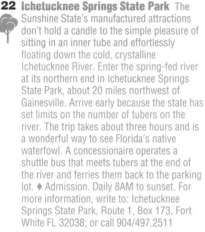

Bests

Steven G. Janicki
Executive Director, Maxwell C. King Center

Space shuttle launches at **Kennedy Space Center**—especially at night.

Meritt Island Wildlife Preserve—Florida in its natural state.

The ugly but fascinating manatees in **Blue Springs**, Orange City.

The smell of orange blossoms in the citrus groves in the spring.

Mark Rodriguez
Owner, Jordan's Grove Restaurant

Spending a day at the National Seashore Park at **Playlinda Beach** near Titusville.

Strolling through the Winter Park Art Festival in Winter Park in the spring.

Gamefishing for wahoo and marlin off **Port Canaveral** in Brevard County; bass fishing on **St. Johns River** in St. Augustine.

Watching the eagles soar off **Marco Isle** in the Lee Barrier Islands while the sun sets.

Sitting behind home plate with a hot dog, a Coke, and a scorecard during spring training at **Tinker Field** in Orlando.

Cheering at an Orlando Magic basketball game when we beat the socks off our archrival team, the Miami Heat.

Going to Winter Park's Park Avenue for a glass of wine at the **Wine and Cheese Cellar,** a walk down the avenue, and window-shopping at dusk.

Watching thunderheads gather above the Orlando skyline, just before a torrential summer shower.

Reading *Sunday at Bob's* by Bob Morris in the *Orlando Sentinel* while sipping a cup of freshly brewed coffee.

Taking in a Seminole Pony League baseball game at **Five Points Field** in Winter Springs.

Observing the birds and gators at **Meritt Island Wildlife Refuge** in Titusville.

Eating silver queen corn until you bust at the **Zellwood Corn Festival.**

Bicycling the **Killarney Loop** in Clearmont (a 30-mile ride through lakes, hills, graves, and pastures).

Charles D. Ragland
General Manager, Bernard's Surf

Kennedy Space Center, Spaceport USA.

King Center for Performing Arts in Cocoa Beach.

Cassadaga/Mt. Dora/Ocala/Gainesville

Eating oysters at **Rusty's Raw Bar** in Cocoa Beach.

Playing at the world-famous **Cocoa Beach Pier.**

A cruise from **Port Canaveral.**

Orlando suffered its first population decline following the big February freeze of 1895 that destroyed the citrus industry. In one night, the temperature dropped from 85 to 17 degrees Fahrenheit.

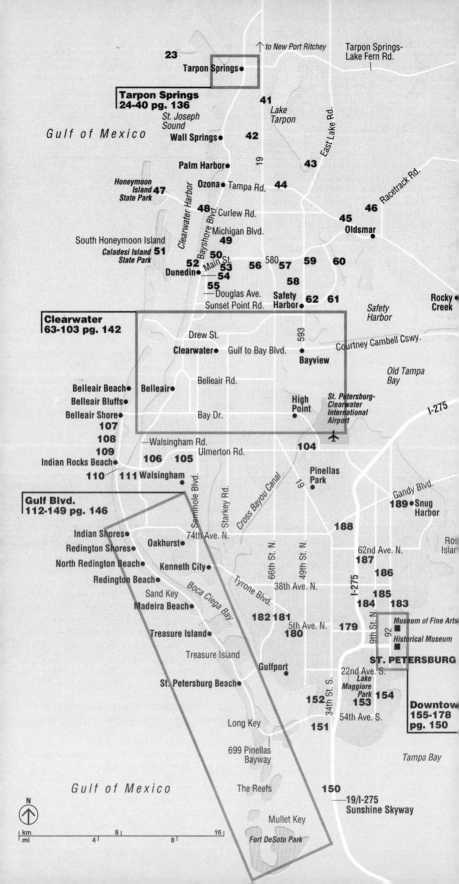

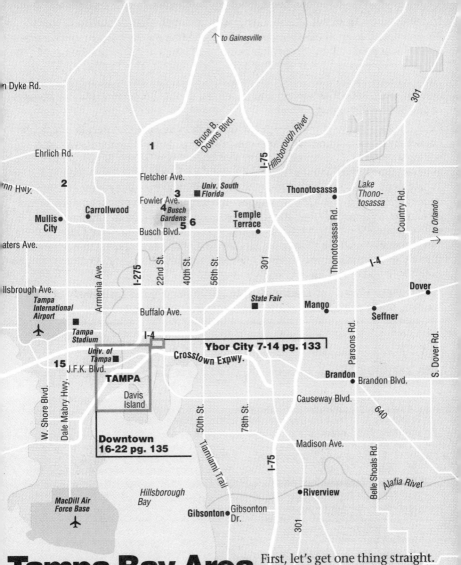

↑ to Gainesville

n Dyke Rd.

Ehrlich Rd.

nn Hwy.

1

2

Fletcher Ave.

Bruce B. Downs Blvd.

Hillsborough River

I-75

Thonotosassa

Lake Thonotosassa

Country Rd.

→ to Orlando

301

Carrollwood

Mullis City

Fowler Ave.

3

Univ. South Florida

Busch Gardens

4

5

6

Temple Terrace

Busch Blvd.

Thonotosassa Rd.

I-4

Dover

aters Ave.

llsborough Ave.

Tampa International Airport

Armenia Ave.

I-275

22nd St.

40th St.

56th St.

Buffalo Ave.

301

State Fair

Mango

Seffner

S. Dover Rd.

Tampa Stadium

Univ. of Tampa

J.F.K. Blvd.

15

I-4

Crosstown Expwy.

Ybor City 7-14 pg. 133

Parsons Rd.

Brandon

Brandon Blvd.

TAMPA

Davis Island

Causeway Blvd.

640

W. Shore Blvd.

Dale Mabry Hwy.

Downtown 16-22 pg. 135

50th St.

78th St.

Tiamiami Trail

I-75

Madison Ave.

Belle Shoals Rd.

Alafia River

MacDill Air Force Base

Hillsborough Bay

Gibsonton

Gibsonton Dr.

Riverview

301

Tampa Bay Area

First, let's get one thing straight. **Tampa Bay**, the name of a National Football League team, isn't a city. Tampa Bay is a body of water that separates Tampa from St. Petersburg. Tampa is also a name associated with cigars, but the city had a colorful history even before the smokes made it famous. The city began as a military fortification: **Fort Brooke** was established on Tampa Bay in 1824 to keep watch on the **Seminole Indians**, whom the US government feared would receive arms and ammunition from Cuba or other foreign nations. Thirty-eight years later, however, it was Union gunboats that shelled the town. The locals refused to surrender, but Tampa was burned to the ground a year later when Union sympathizers on Florida's west coast mounted a force that destroyed the Tampa Confederates' saltworks and captured all of their cattle and supplies.

Tampa remained primarily a military base until 1868, when thousands of Cuban cigarmakers migrated here and to Key West. Most of the tobacco was imported from Cuba, and some of the cigarmakers were political refugees who fled the island nation at the outbreak of Cuba's Ten Years' War with Spain (1868-78).

In 1884, when **Henry B. Plant** connected the **South Florida Railroad** line to Tampa Bay, the small town began to change. Tampa grew quickly for two reasons: It was an excellent deepwater port, and Plant's hotel, which he called "the greatest in the world," was gaining quite a reputation. The **Tampa Bay Hotel** was an instant landmark when it opened in 1891. Guests and residents were awed by its 13 Moorish towers and minarets, and its broad verandas with views of the little Hillsborough River.

Even so, Tampa was unable to escape its military destiny. Soldiers (some accompanied by anxious parents), war correspondents, Army officers, and foreign military advisors all descended upon Tampa and the Tampa Bay Hotel in 1898. William Randolph Hearst's *New York Journal* and Joseph Pulitzer's *New York World* were pushing the country toward war with Spain. But many Tampa residents were cool to the idea. By the 1890s tourism had become a good business in Tampa, and some feared that if the war were won, Cuba would become part of the United States, and tourists would bypass Tampa in favor of Cuba. But war came anyway, leading to another storied part of the city's past when **Theodore Roosevelt** recruited some of his Rough Riders from **Ybor City**, a colorful Tampa neighborhood of restaurants and shops.

Today, Plant's hotel is the administration building for the **University of Tampa**, and Tampa is one of the nation's fastest-growing cities.

Area code 813 unless otherwise indicated.

1 Skipper's Smokehouse and Oyster Bar
$ Alligator, catfish, Jamaican chicken, and seafood are served on an outdoor wooden deck under spreading oaks. Regulars rave about the oyster bar and Key lime pie. Management brings in big-name musicians for blues (Su 6-11PM) and reggae (W, F-Sa 8-11PM). Cover. ♦ Seafood ♦ Tu, Th 11AM-10PM; W, F 11AM-11PM; Sa noon-11PM; Su 1-11PM. 910 Skipper Rd (Nebraska Ave) 971.0666

2 Kaoribana Japanese Restaurant
$$ Authentic sushi, sashimi, yakitori, and tempura. ♦ Japanese ♦ M-Th, Su 5:30-10PM; F, Sa 5:30-11PM. 13180 N. Dale Mabry Hwy (In the Village Center, Fletcher Ave-Ehrlich Rd) 968.3801

3 Museum of Science and Industry
Purportedly the largest hands-on museum in the state. ♦ Admission. 4801 E. Fowler Ave (30th-50th Sts) 985.5531

4 Embassy Suites USF/Busch Gardens
$$ A good value for families visiting Busch Gardens. The suites have a kitchen and living area, pool table, heated pool, and Jacuzzi. Breakfasts and afternoon cocktails are included in the rate. Up to two children younger than 12 may share their parents' room free. There is a complimentary shuttle to Busch Gardens. Prices go down on the weekend. ♦ 129 rooms. 1310 N. 30th St (E. Fowler-E. Busch Blvds) 971.7690

5 Busch Gardens-The Dark Continent One of the top five theme parks in Florida and the number one show on the state's west coast, Busch Gardens combines fine animal displays with thrill rides on 300 acres. As an accredited member of the American Association of Zoo-

logical Parks, Busch Gardens does a splendid job of displaying animals, and sometimes has special guest appearances by animals on loan, such as Chinese pandas. To see Busch Gardens, arrive early and go straight to the newest attraction, Questor, a thrill ride using flight-simulator technology. Next, hop on the monorail around Serengeti Plain to view the roaming animals. The African animals are more active in the morning. Then go to Nairobi Train Station and climb aboard the train, which circles the park. Get off at Stanleyville Train Station and walk back to the front, passing through Congo, Timbuktu, and Nairobi. You will then be ready for the brewery tour, which is next to the children's play area. This is also one of the few places in the country to see koalas, who live in the Bird Gardens area. ♦ Admission. Parking. Daily 9:30AM-6PM. 3000 Busch Blvd (40th St) 987.5000

Within Busch Gardens-The Dark Continent:

Morocco Here, at the main entrance to the park, visitors can watch Moroccan craft demonstrations and snake charmers in the "Sultan's Tent" section. This area also contains a 1,200-seat Moroccan Palace indoor theater where the "Around the World on Ice" show is presented. Lockers, a bank machine, guest relations, restrooms, and lost and found are located here. For snacks there is the **Boujad Bakery, Zagora Cafe,** and an ice cream parlor.

Restaurants/Nightlife: Red	Hotels: Blue
Shops/ ♠Outdoors: Green	Sights/Culture: Black

Busch Gardens, The Dark Continent

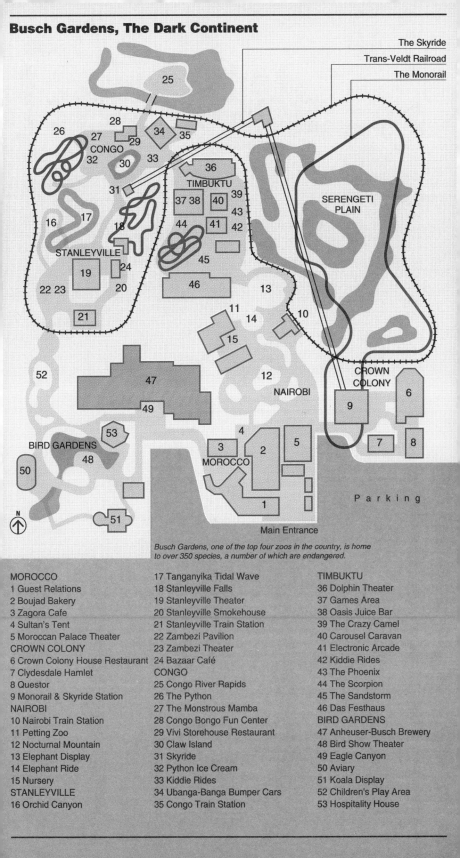

The Skyride
Trans-Veldt Railroad
The Monorail

25

28
26 27 29
34 35
CONGO
32 30 33
36
TIMBUKTU
31
37 38 40 39
43
44 41 42
16 17
18
45
STANLEYVILLE
24
19
46
13
22 23 20
21
11
14 10
15
52
47
12
49
NAIROBI
53
4
BIRD GARDENS
3 2 5
48
MOROCCO
50
1
51
Main Entrance

SERENGETI PLAIN

CROWN COLONY
9 6
7 8

Parking

N

Busch Gardens, one of the top four zoos in the country, is home to over 350 species, a number of which are endangered.

MOROCCO
1 Guest Relations
2 Boujad Bakery
3 Zagora Cafe
4 Sultan's Tent
5 Moroccan Palace Theater
CROWN COLONY
6 Crown Colony House Restaurant
7 Clydesdale Hamlet
8 Questor
9 Monorail & Skyride Station
NAIROBI
10 Nairobi Train Station
11 Petting Zoo
12 Nocturnal Mountain
13 Elephant Display
14 Elephant Ride
15 Nursery
STANLEYVILLE
16 Orchid Canyon

17 Tanganyika Tidal Wave
18 Stanleyville Falls
19 Stanleyville Theater
20 Stanleyville Smokehouse
21 Stanleyville Train Station
22 Zambezi Pavilion
23 Zambezi Theater
24 Bazaar Café
CONGO
25 Congo River Rapids
26 The Python
27 The Monstrous Mamba
28 Congo Bongo Fun Center
29 Vivi Storehouse Restaurant
30 Claw Island
31 Skyride
32 Python Ice Cream
33 Kiddie Rides
34 Ubanga-Banga Bumper Cars
35 Congo Train Station

TIMBUKTU
36 Dolphin Theater
37 Games Area
38 Oasis Juice Bar
39 The Crazy Camel
40 Carousel Caravan
41 Electronic Arcade
42 Kiddie Rides
43 The Phoenix
44 The Scorpion
45 The Sandstorm
46 Das Festhaus
BIRD GARDENS
47 Anheuser-Busch Brewery
48 Bird Show Theater
49 Eagle Canyon
50 Aviary
51 Koala Display
52 Children's Play Area
53 Hospitality House

Crown Colony This section of the park recently added a hospitality center and the **Crown Colony House Restaurant.** For a close-up look at the massive draft horses known as Clydesdales, visit the **Clydesdale Hamlet.** Nearby **Questor** provides a different kind of ride and is the newest thrill at Busch Gardens. The 59-seat Questor is a computer-controlled flight simulator that takes you from a Victorian-era carriage house on a fantasy journey to find the magical Crystal of Zed. On your trip, you'll zoom through caverns with jutting stalactites and stalagmites, plunge over a waterfall, survive a close call with boiling lava, and take an eerie trip underwater. Children love the ride—and although it lasts only six minutes, it's wild enough to please thrill-seeking teens and jaded adults, too.

Serengeti Plain A well-planned part of the park that allows visitors a good look at nearly 500 different African animals, including hippos, giraffes, antelope, Nile crocodiles, dromedary-camels, flamingos, and ostriches. This veldt-like plain also serves as a breeding ground for several endangered species, including the black rhino and Asian elephant. If the Florida heat's getting you down, see this area from air-conditioned monorail, steam locomotive, skyride, or walkway.

Nairobi A great place to take children, the Nairobi Field Station nursery is home to baby birds and other infant animals. The nursery looks like a Dr. Livingston-era African hospital, but inside, modern equipment provides tender loving care to diapered baby chimpanzees, young gazelles, cape buffalo, and other animals. Nairobi Train Station, also in this section, is a petting zoo with reptile displays. Elsewhere in the Nairobi section Nile perch, turtles, and American alligators float in a pond crossed by a suspension bridge. Feed is available. You will also find the Latin American capybara (the largest living rodent), playful American river otters, greater white-nosed monkeys, and a spacious pit with a central is-

land for active chimps. Reptiles include many varieties of nonpoisonous Florida water snakes, and legions of crocodiles and alligators, including 13-foot-long Big Joe, which was captured in a lake at Kennedy Space Center. An unusual and fascinating feature is

Nocturnal Mountain, where creatures of the night are exhibited inside a cavelike environment. Here reside bushbabies, sloths, fruit bats, hedgehogs, and an assortment of poisonous American snakes as well as pythons and boa constrictors. Near the entrance to Nocturnal Mountain is an area with Aldabra tortoises, the last survivors of their species. The huge creatures can weigh up to 300 pounds and live more than 100 years. Up to 12 elephants share the new one-acre **Elephant Display** that opened in 1990 in Nairobi's northernmost sector just above the train station. Elaborate rock work against a backdrop of verdant landscaping surrounds the display, which is circled with pedestrian walkways. The rocks act as a privacy barrier for the elephants and as a source of shade from the Florida sun. Two waterfalls cascade over the rocks into shallow ponds used for impromptu showers. The closest possible view of the world's largest land mammal is provided. Elephant washes are scheduled daily at 10:45, 11:30AM, and 3PM for spectators. Zoo education aides are available at these times to answer questions. Both Asian and African elephants are featured. The African species is threatened; the Asian species, endangered.

Stanleyville Skip the shopping bazaar here and head for the two water rides, **Tanganyika Tidal Wave** and **Stanley Falls.** The Tidal Wave, a boat ride, concludes with a big splash, while Stanley Falls is an outstanding water-flume ride. Snack stops include **Stanley Smokehouse** and **Bazaar Cafe,** where you can grab a barbecued beef sandwich.

Congo Here, **Congo River Rapids** is the crowd-pleaser. The white-water thrill ride has spawned a host of imitators, but it's still the favorite. For roller coaster fans there's also the **Python,** which sends you zooming along 1,200 feet of track. **Claw Island** displays rare white Bengal tigers in a natural setting; with luck the tigers will be in a playful mood, cooling off in the waterfall. Strawberry waffle cone sundaes are specialties at **Python Ice Cream.**

Timbuktu You can't miss the wild, swinging **Phoenix** boat ride here—a thrill for the hardiest of ride lovers—as well as the **Scorpion,** a looping roller coaster. Also in Timbuktu are African craftsmen at work in a shopping bazaar. **Das Festhaus** is a large German beer hall serving up corned-beef sandwiches and cold beers.

Anheuser-Busch Brewery Tours
Busch Gardens is owned by giant bräumeister Anheuser-Busch of St. Louis, and if you're hankering to see how brews get brewed, the company will oblige year-round. You'll see the ingredients that produce beer, as well as helpful displays that explain the brewing process. It's fun—and free, as are the Buds at the end of the tour. ♦ Daily 10AM-6PM

Bird Gardens This area was a hit when Busch Gardens opened in 1959 and the park has improved it every year since. Today, there are more than 2,000 exotic birds on display; some perform in the park's World of Birds show, others can be seen in Eagle Canyon, a natural habitat display that is home to American bald eagles. The free-flight aviary is full of exotic birds and greenery. Also in this section is a koala exhibit featuring Australian wallabies and rose-breasted cockatoos. Within Bird Gardens there is a children's play area and the Anheuser-Busch Hospitality House, serving pizza and sandwiches.

6 Adventure Island This 19-acre waterpark has the best water thrill rides on Florida's west coast. The newest is the **Calypso Coaster,** where riders climb a 45-foot tower to a twisting flume that ends in a splash pool. Take the serpentine plunge on either a one-person tube or a two-person raft. Other favorites are the **Caribbean Corkscrew,** a four-story ride through a 240-foot, enclosed translucent tube that crisscrosses over another tube, and the **Everglides,** a 35-foot drop on a surfboggan that zips you down a 72-foot slide and then skims across a hundred feet of water. There are snack bars, picnic areas, a surf shop, video games, and locker rooms. ♦ Admission. Daily 10AM-5PM, extended hours in the summer and on holidays. Closed late Oct-late Mar. 4500 Bougainvillea Ave (Malcolm McKinley Dr-46th St) 987.5660

Ybor City (Nos. 7-14)

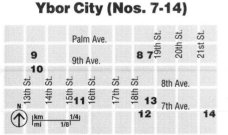

Don Vicente Martinez Ybor created Ybor City (pronounced "Ee-bor") in 1886 in an effort to avoid labor unions. His idea was to create a planned industrial community based on cigar manufacturing. Between 1886 until the city's decline in the 1930s, one fifth of Ybor City's 20,000 residents were employed at the cigar factory. But the Depression, the new popularity of cigarettes, and cigar-rolling machines hit Ybor City hard. Ybor City has sputtered ever since: As new shops come in, others go out of business; buildings are refurbished as neighboring structures cry out for paint. During the day tourists and locals alike shop and dine on Seventh Ave, Ybor City's main street, or in Ybor Square, the upscale shopping area in the old cigar factory, but at night the dim lighting and shabby shops keep potential tourist dollars out.

Within Ybor City:

7 Ybor City State Museum The first stop in Ybor City should be the state museum housed in the **Ferlita Bakery** building where you will see the original oven from 1896, which survived the 1922 fire that burned down the original building. There are also historic pictures of the founding of Ybor City and the rise and fall of the cigar industry. ♦ Nominal admission. Tu-Sa 9AM-noon, 1-5PM. 1818 9th Ave (18th-19th Sts) 247.6323

A small formal garden connects the museum with the Cigar Worker's Cottage.

8 Cigar Worker's Cottage Three cottages built around 1895 in the 1500 block of 5th Ave were moved here to re-create a turn-of-the-century streetscape. The Cigar Worker's Cottage with its shingle roof has been restored to its original appearance; helpful docents will give you as brief or as long a tour as you wish. Enter the cottage through a picket gate. The front room extends the width of this narrow home, and the hallway leads back to the kitchen, passing two bedrooms on the right. Water comes from a pump, but when the houses were originally built there was no electricity, heat, or water. Window shutters were pulled closed to keep the house as cool as possible, and cheesecloth was used for screens. ♦ Voluntary contribution. Tu-F 10AM-3PM. 1804 E 9th Ave (18th-19th Sts) 247.1434

9 Cafe Creole & Oyster Bar $$ Gumbo, Louisiana oysters, and crawfish. There is dining available in an outdoor courtyard, and live jazz W-Sa evenings. ♦ Cajun/Creole ♦ M-Th noon-11PM; F-Sa noon-1AM. 1330 E 9th Ave (13th-14th Sts) 247.6283

10 Ybor Square Restaurants and shops are squeezed into Don Vicente Martinez Ybor's original cigar factory, which consisted of three buildings. Note the five-globe light posts that are prevalent in Ybor City. ♦ M-Sa 9:30AM-5:30PM; Su noon-5:30PM. 1901 13th St (8th Ave) 247.4497

When cigarmakers worked by the hundreds in Ybor City, they were entertained by a "reader"—a well-paid individual with a fine voice and some acting ability who read aloud everything from newspapers to novels to keep the staff entertained.

At Ybor Square:

The Stemmery A three-story, redbrick building. It was here that the stems were removed from the tobacco.

Among the first-floor shops:

Chevere Colorful cotton clothes imported from Guatemala and Mayan folk art. ♦ M-Sa 9:30AM-5:30PM; Su noon-5:30PM. 247.1339

Rough Riders Restaurant $$ The name of the restaurant recalls the days when **Teddy Roosevelt** and his Rough Riders were in town before they invaded Cuba. Fascinating photos from that time hang on the walls. Some say this place makes the best hamburger in town. ♦ American ♦ Daily 11:30AM-2AM. 248.3756

Among the second-floor shops:

Don Quijote Restaurant ★★$$$ Exposed beams and hardwood floors lend to the charm of this restaurant. The menu is ambitious, but you might just want to rest your feet here and order seasoned and grilled scallops and a glass of wine. ♦ Spanish ♦ M-Th 11AM-2:30PM; F, Sa 11AM-2:30PM, 5:30-10PM. 247.9454

Tampa Rico Cigar Co. The sign in here says it all: "Thanks for smoking." Notice the cigar-store Indian on the right as you walk in; on the left a cigarmaker rolls cigars behind a counter. He works until 3PM weekdays. In this little shop, a cigar is completely handmade. ♦ M-Sa 9:30AM-5:30PM; Su noon-5:30PM. 247.6738

The Warehouse Left of the entrance to the Stemmery is a staircase and doorway leading to what was once the Warehouse. The first floor is now **The Spaghetti Warehouse,** a large Italian restaurant that is part of an international chain. ♦ M-Th 11AM-10PM; F 11AM-11PM; Sa noon-11PM; Su noon-10PM. 1911 13th St (9th Ave) 248.1720

The Factory The Factory is across a courtyard. The first floor houses shops; offices are located on the second floor.

11 Three Birds Bookstore and Coffee Room A bookstore-cafe run by three British women. The eclectic selection ranges from modern poetry to hard-to-find novels. You can browse

while drinking coffee. ♦ M-Th 11AM-6PM; F-Sa 11AM-10PM. 1518 E 7th Ave (15th-16th Sts) 247.7041

Restaurants/Nightlife: Red   Hotels: Blue
Shops/ 🌳 Outdoors: Green   Sights/Culture: Black

12 Silver Ring $ For an inexpensive but authentic Ybor City experience that will fill you up, try a Cuban sandwich at this little storefront cafe. Ham, cheese, salami, and sometimes turkey are stuffed into crusty Cuban bread. The Silver Ring has been around since 1947. ♦ Cuban ♦ M-Sa 6:30AM-5PM. 1831 E 7th Ave (18th-19th Sts) 248.2549

13 La Tropicana Cafe This informal restaurant has been a hotbed of political activism ever since the Spanish American War, and it is still the place to be seen and make deals if you're a local politician. In a back corner is a table set apart from the others with a nameplate on it: "Reserved for **Roland Manteiga.**" Manteiga is the editor of *La Gaceta,* an Ybor City weekly, which is printed in Spanish and English, and includes a page of news in Italian. (There is a painting of him in his trademark white-linen suit hanging on the restaurant wall.) The paper was begun by his father as a Spanish-language daily in 1922. It would be worth it to poke your head in just for the atmosphere, but the cafe also serves up great Cuban sandwiches, spicy crab cakes, and stuffed potatoes. ♦ Cuban ♦ M-Sa 8AM-4PM. 1822 E 7th Ave (19th St) 247.4040

14 Columbia Restaurant ★★★$$$ Billed as "America's Oldest Spanish Restaurant," the Columbia dates from 1905 and is a favorite of tourists. The architecture alone is worth a peek; it grew from **The Corner Cafe** to a restaurant that now occupies a whole city block and has 11 separate serving rooms. Ornate chandeliers hang from the ceiling; the walls are brightly colored Spanish tiles. Waiters wear dinner jackets, even at lunch. In the evening there is live entertainment, including a flamenco show M-Sa at 8:30PM. Cuban black-bean soup and Spanish bean soup are recommended, as are the 1905 salad, paella, red snapper *alicante*, and flan. Inconsistent service and food quality. ♦ Spanish ♦ Daily 11AM-11PM. 2117 E 7th Ave (21st-22nd Sts) 248.4961. Also at: Harbour Island. 229.2992

15 Donatello ★★$$$$ This plain, white stucco building doesn't give a hint of the elegance inside. The red rose on each table sets off the sophisticated main dining room where diners enjoy northern Italian dishes prepared by Italian chefs and served by tuxedo-clad waiters. The desserts and pasta are homemade. If you have room for dessert, spend your calories on the amaretto cake. Each woman is presented with a long-stemmed red rose as she leaves. ♦ Italian ♦ Daily noon-2:30PM, 6-10:30PM. 232 N. Dale Mabry Hwy (Kennedy Blvd) Reservations recommended. 875.6660

Downtown Tampa (Nos. 16-22)

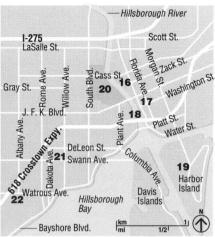

16 Tampa Museum of Art This pretty museum has a glass-walled gallery overlooking the Hillsborough River and the University of Tampa campus. There are six galleries with changing exhibits ranging from classical antiquities to contemporary art. Stairs lead down to a river walk. ◆ Admission. Tu-Sa 10AM-5PM; W 10AM-9PM; Su 1-5PM. 601 Doyle Carlton Dr (Gasparilla Pl-Madison St) 223.8130

17 rg's Downtown ★★$$$ Elegant marble surroundings set the mood for finely prepared seafood and fowl dishes such as charcoal-grilled duck, scallops Jack Daniels, and lobster mousse *en croûte*. Don't pass up the cheesecake or chocolate pecan toffee mousse. ◆ Seafood/American ◆ M-Th 11:30AM-2PM, 5:30-10PM; F 11:30AM-2PM, 5:30-11PM; Sa 5:30-11PM. 110 N. Franklin St (In Tampa City Center, Jackson-Washington Sts) Reservations recommended. 229.5536. Also at: 3807 Northdale Blvd. 963.2356.

18 Hyatt Regency Tampa $$$ Tampa's largest hotel, it's conveniently located near the Franklin Street Pedestrian Mall and the People Mover Monorail Station. The focal point of the striking atrium lobby is a graceful waterfall. The recently renovated hotel has a pool, a health club, in-room movies, two lounges, and two restaurants. Rooms for the physically handicapped are available. Within the hotel is **Saltwaters Bar and Grille ($$$)**. ◆ 519 rooms. 211 N. Tampa St (Jackson-Washington Sts) 225.1234, 800/233.1234

19 Harbour Island This little island is connected to the mainland by the People Mover Monorail and a bridge. The island was used until 1972 as a railroad terminus, where freight trains were loaded with cargo brought in by ship. The island now consists of shops and restaurants and offers entertainment. ◆ M-Sa 10AM-9PM; Su 11AM-6PM. 777 S. Harbour Island Blvd (Water St) 223.0876

At Harbour Island:

The Columbia ★★$$$ Definitely lacks the atmosphere of the original Columbia in Ybor City (see page 134) but it serves up tasty Spanish dishes and seafood platters, along with choice-cut steaks. There is entertainment in the evenings; flamenco dancing is often featured. ◆ Spanish ◆ Daily 11AM-11PM. 229.2992. Also at: 2117 E 7th Ave (21st-22nd Sts) 248.4961

Parkers' Lighthouse $$$ With a view that overlooks the water and the Tampa skyline, this restaurant specializes in fresh fish, prepared to your taste. There is patio dining and live entertainment. ◆ Seafood ◆ M-Th 11:30AM-2PM, 5:30-10PM; F-Sa 11:30AM-2:30PM, 5:30-10:30PM; Su 10:30AM-1:30PM, 4:30-9PM. 229.3474

Cha Cha Coconuts $$
Try the peel-and-eat shrimp or the spicy chicken wings for an appetizer, and the lightly grilled lime-garlic grouper sandwich for lunch. Well known for its tropical drinks. ◆ American ◆ M-Th 11AM-midnight; F, Sa 11AM-1PM; Su noon-10PM. 223.3101. Also at: The Pier, St. Petersburg. 822.6655; Sand Key, Clearwater Beach. 596.6040

Wyndham Harbour Island Hotel $$$ If you wish, arrive by boat and dock at the hotel marina. Each room has a waterfront view, and amenities include tennis, racquetball, squash, swimming, exercise room, and spas, as well as a jogging trail along five miles of Bayshore Blvd. Suites are available. ◆ 725 S. Harbour Island Blvd. 229.5000, 800/631.4200 (US), 800/822.4200 (Canada)

20 Henry B. Plant Museum The silver onion-shaped minarets on this building have been a Tampa landmark since it was built by Henry Plant as the Tampa Bay Hotel in 1891. Since 1933 it has been the main building of the University of Tampa. A museum in the south wing has cabinets once owned by Queen Isabella of Spain and chairs that belonged to Marie Antoinette. ◆ Admission. Tu-Sa 10AM-4PM. 401 W. Kennedy Blvd (Hyde Park Ave) 254.1891

21 Old Hyde Park Village Tampa's upscale shopping area. There are about 60 stores and restaurants, including Jacobsen's and

Ann Taylor, AMC movie theaters, and places to grab a bite. ◆ M-W, Sa 10AM-6PM; Th, F 10AM-9PM. Some establishments are open on Sunday. 1509 W. Swann Ave (Rome-Willow Aves) 251.3500

Cactus Club ★$$ Try its unusual thin-crust Texas pizzas. One comes with avocado and red chili sauce, another with red and green peppers, spicy chorizo sausage, and Monterey jack cheese. Burgers and Mexican platters are the favorites here, including the *chiles rellenos*, an Anaheim pepper stuffed with cheese, covered with a light batter, and fried. ◆ Tex-Mex ◆ M-Sa 11:30AM-midnight; Su noon-midnight. 251.4089

Selena's ★$$$ A pretty restaurant with a pleasing but split personality. It serves zesty Creole and hearty Italian fare in several antique-filled dining rooms. Spicy red beans and rice served with sausage won't leave you hungry. For a lighter meal try the catch of the day prepared Creole style and laced with plenty of garlic and lemon butter. You can't go wrong with any of the delicate pasta dishes. There is live music M-W 8PM; Th 9PM; F, Sa 9:30PM. ◆ Creole/Italian ◆ M-W 11AM-10PM; Th 11AM-11PM; F, Sa 11AM-midnight; Su 11AM-3PM, 4:30-9PM. 251.2116

Joffrey's Coffee & Tea Co $ This gourmet coffee house has wonderful desserts as well as a Sunday brunch. ◆ Coffee house ◆ M-Sa 8AM-midnight; Su 9AM-11PM. 251.3315

22 **Bern's Steak House** ★★★$$$$ Tampa's famous 300-seat steakhouse has a telephone book-sized wine list with more than 6,000 selections. Beef is ordered from a chart according to cut, thickness, and weight. Vegetables are grown on owner **Bern Laxer's** own organic farm. Don't let the garishness of red velvet, antiques, and assorted statuary put you off—the restaurant is worth at least one visit, and more if you are a steak purist. You can select your seafood from live seafood tanks. There are private rooms upstairs for dessert. ◆ American ◆ Daily 5-11PM; dessert room open until 1AM. 1208 S. Howard Ave (Watrous-Marjory Aves) Reservations recommended. 251.2421, 800/282.1547 (FL only)

Tarpon Springs

This town was founded in 1876, but it wasn't until 1905 that Greek sponge divers from Key

West settled in the area, giving this little community its ethnic identity. Today visitors can walk along Dodecanese Blvd among heaps of newly harvested sponges drying on the docks. You can buy the soft, natural sponges in every imaginable size in nearby shops or enjoy a

Greek dessert in one of the small cafes. The biggest and most colorful festival in town, Epiphany, occurs on 6 January, and is celebrated by a procession that marches to the Anclote River where a bishop blesses the river and throws a cross into the water. Youngsters then dive into the river to try to find the cross. A gold cross was used in the past, but a white, wooden cross has been substituted because it is easier to find in the sometimes muddy water. The one who retrieves the wooden cross receives a gold cross in exchange and, legend has it, a year of good luck. The afternoon is given over to a party with traditional Greek dancing, food, and music. In the evening there is the Epiphany Ball, the only event requiring reservations.

(Nos. 24-40)

23 **Fred Howard Park** Tarpon Springs' best beach can be reached by a mile-long causeway. There are facilities for picnics, barbecues, fishing, and boating as well as a children's playground. ◆ Sunset Dr (Gulf of Mexico-Seaside Dr)

24 **Louis Pappas' Riverside Restaurant** ★$$ Long a tradition here, the 40,000-square-foot restaurant spawned from a roadside cafe in the 1920s has become a slick commercial emporium with inconsistent food and service. Pappas' unusual Greek salad with chunks of potato is a meal in itself. But the wines, moussaka, *pastitsio,* and kebabs are authentic. ◆ Greek ◆ M-Th, Su 11:30AM-10PM; F-Sa 11:30AM-11PM. 10 W. Dodecanese Blvd (US 19A) Reservations recommended. 937.5101

25 **Spongeorama** This complex includes a gift shop, a movie theater, and a museum in an old sponge factory on the area's main tourist strip. Although the film and display are nothing fancy, the tour is the best way to understand the Greek community's roots and learn about sponge diving. ◆ Admission for theater, daily 10AM-5PM; factory daily 10AM-9PM. 510 Dodecanese Blvd (Arfaras-Athens Sts) 942.3771

25 Casablanca Cruises Passengers on this 85-foot catamaran cruise the Anclote River and the Gulf of Mexico, often seeing dolphins, manatees, and several species of birds, including eagles. The boat passes Anclote Park and Fred Howard Park as well as several mansions, Anclote Key Island and its historic lighthouse, and Honeymoon Island. The catamaran holds 150 passengers and makes no stops. There is no live entertainment, although dinner passengers can dance to recorded music. Lunch and dinner cruises. Boarding is behind the Spongeorama. ♦ Admission. Schedule varies according to season. 510 Dodecanese Blvd (Arfaras-Athens Sts) 942.4452

25 Golden Docks ★$ Simple but good food is offered in a wharfside outdoor taverna adjacent to the Sponge Docks. Try the combination platter for a sampling of Aegean dishes. ♦ Greek ♦ Daily 7:30AM-11PM. 698 Dodecanese Blvd (Arfaras-Athens Sts) 938.5155

26 St. Nicholas Boat Line These 30-minute rides take visitors down the Anclote River for a simulation of sponge harvesting complete with a diver in an old-time orange suit. After all the hype from streetside barkers, this adventure proves rather disappointing. ♦ Admission. Daily 10AM-4:30PM. 693 Dodecanese Blvd (Athens St) 937.9887

27 Hellas Bakery ★$ This is the best place to adopt the Greek custom of an afternoon treat of sweet pastry and hair-raising Turkish coffee. The *filo*-dough pies, baklava, and apple turnovers are sinfully delicious. ♦ Greek ♦ Daily 10AM-10PM. 785 Dodecanese Blvd (Athens-Hope Sts) 934.8400

27 Sponge Exchange This original trading post for sponges has been restructured into a stylish open-air shopping center with a typically touristy offering of shops and restaurants. The merchandise consists mostly of women's clothing, souvenirs, and gifts. At the front is a walk-in exhibit on sponge auctions. ♦ 735 Dodecanese Blvd (Athens-Hope Sts)

28 Konger Coral Sea Aquarium This latest addition to the Dodecanese lineup features a 100,000-gallon tank filed with fish found in the waters off Florida, including lemon, bonnet-head, and nurse sharks, spiny lobster, grouper, bluerunner jack, and redfish. The twice-daily feeding is a major attraction. Three smaller tanks showcase other marine life, including lionfish, eels, small damsels, and sea anemones. ♦ Admission. M-Sa 10AM-6PM; Sun 11AM-6PM. 852 Dodecanese Blvd (Roosevelt Blvd) 938.5378

29 Bill's Lighthouse ★★$$ Greek meatballs, dolmas (stuffed grape leaves), flaming shish kebab, souvlakia (a lamb and beef kebab), assorted seafood, and baklava are served amid Greek sponge-diving decor. This small cafe is at the lower end of the Sponge Docks. ♦ Greek ♦ M-Sa 11AM-9:30PM; Su 11AM-9PM. 813 Dodecanese Blvd (Roosevelt Blvd) 938.4895

30 Paul's Seafood ★★$ Some of the best boiled shrimp in the bay area is seasoned with lemon juice, olive oil, and Greek spices. Other specialties are conch salad, Greek salad, broiled octopus, and fried squid. The menu is limited, but each item is prepared with care. ♦ Greek ♦ M-Sa 11AM-10PM; Su 11AM-9:30PM. 630 Athens St (Dodecanese-Grand Blvds) 938.5093

31 Shrine of St. Michael In 1939, an 11-year-old boy, Steve Tsalichis, became ill with a high fever. Efforts by 15 physicians to diagnose the child's condition failed, and his condition worsened. Hospitalized, in a coma, and with virtually no hope of recovery, Steve suddenly awoke one day and told his mother that a vision had appeared to him through an icon in the family's possession (icons are pictures representing holy people and objects). The vision told the boy that he would be completely healed if his mother would promise to construct a shrine to St. Michael. The promise was made, young Steve recovered from his illness, and the shrine was built next to the family's home. People of all faiths visit the shrine, and many have claimed miraculous healings. ♦ 113 Hope St (Dodecanese Blvd-Park St)

32 Inness Paintings The largest collection of works—11 in all—by **George Inness Jr.**, the American landscape artist, are on display in the Universalist Church. Inness had a home nearby and painted numeous scenes of Tarpon Springs between the 1890s and 1920s. Themes of spirituality and love of nature predominate. ♦ Tu-Su 2-5PM. Closed June-Sep. 57 Read St (Grand Blvd) 937.4682

33 Safford House **Anson Safford** was an early developer of Tarpon Springs. His home began as a simple one-story frame cottage when first constructed in 1883. In 1887 the house was expanded to two stories, and by 1890 several elaborate Victorian touches were added. The house was moved from its original location on North Spring Blvd to its present location in 1903. Originally called The Miramar, it is a prime example of wood-frame Vernacular Domestic architecture in Central Florida. Rectangular in shape, the house consists of a balloon structure and a pier-type foundation. Hip-roofed porches with post supports and balustrades are attached to the southern, eastern, and western sides of the house. The gabled main roof is partly shingled and partly tin. Its current owner, **Nausse're Zadeh,** is in the midst of a painstaking restoration. It's the only private residence in Tarpon Springs that is listed on

the National Register of Historic Places. It is not open to the public. ♦ Parkin Court (Grand Blvd)

Restaurants/Nightlife: Red   Hotels: Blue

Shops/ ♥Outdoors: Green   Sights/Culture: Black

34 Spring Bayou Epiphany, a holy day on the Greek calendar, is celebrated here on 6 January. A morning service at the cathedral is followed by a procession to the bayou where a lead-weighted white wooden crucifix is cast into the water. Greek youths dive to retrieve it and receive the church's blessing for the next year (see "Tarpon Springs" on page 136). ♦ Spring Blvd-W. Tarpon Ave

35 Golden Crescent During the late 1800s, Tarpon Springs flourished as an exclusive retreat for the wealthy who came to escape the harsh Northern climate. Many built lavish mansions along Spring Bayou. North and South Spring Blvds form a horseshoe, or crescent, around this community. The houses, which date from 1885 to 1905, may be viewed from the outside. A detailed booklet for a walking tour is available from the cultural center. ♦ Spring Blvd (Lemon St-Riverside Dr)

36 Spring Bayou Inn $$ This two-story clapboard building with five guest rooms, built in 1905, has been converted into a B&B with an inviting portico and a dramatic rotunda tower. Featured is an eclectic assortment of modern and antique furnishings. Vintage clothing is draped in closets or on armoires. Two of the rooms share a bath. A Continental breakfast is served in the dining room on china and lace. ♦ 32 W. Tarpon Ave (Grand Blvd-US 19A) 938.9333

37 St. Nicholas Greek Orthodox Cathedral This structure is a scaled-down reproduction of St. Sophia's in Istanbul and is an outstanding example of New Byzantine architecture. The present cathedral was built in 1943; the original wooden structure burned to the ground in the late 1930s. The architect, **P. Pipinos,** died shortly before the building was completed. The interior contains stained glass and elaborate icons placed within sculptured Grecian marble that fronts the altar. The marble came from the Greek exhibit at the 1939 New York World's Fair. Although all the icons have religious significance, the weeping icon of St. Nicholas is the most famous. On 5 December 1970 (the day before the name day of St. Nicholas), drops of moisture were noticed around the halo and on the eyes and cheeks. The church, which is open to the public, does not conduct its own scheduled tours, but is included in tours conducted by the Tarpon Springs Cultural Center. Tour groups are encouraged to contact the church to make special arrangement to visit. ♦ 36 N. Pinellas Ave (Orange-Cypress Sts)

Tampa Bay Area

According to *The Wall Street Journal,* Orlando is an "immaculate" city where public telephones are sprayed with Lysol every week.

38 Oxford House ★$ This tearoom doubles as a gift shop with homemade—and non-Hellenic—accessories and crafts. Sandwiches, salads, muffins, and scones are served in the best British tradition. A nice spot to stop after touring the cathedral. ♦ British ♦ M-Th 11AM-2PM; Sa 11AM-4PM. 118 E. Orange St (Center St-E. Tarpon Ave) 937.0133

39 Tarpon Springs Historical Society Museum This renovated downtown railroad station displays historic photos and memorabilia of the area. It is surrounded by antique shops and restaurants. Fresh produce is sold in the farmers market at the rear of the building. ♦ Tu 2-4PM; Sa 10AM-noon. 160 E. Tarpon Ave (US 19A-Safford St) 937.2712

40 Tarpon Springs Cultural Center Puppet workshops and seminars on Greek culture often take place in this brick building built in 1914 to serve as city hall. There is a 100-seat theater, and the gallery has exhibits pertaining to the town's culture and history. ♦ Tu-F 9AM-4PM; Sa 1-4PM. 101 S. Pinellas Ave (Lemon St) 942.5605

Refer to map on page 128 for numbers 41-74

41 A.L. Anderson Park This 128-acre park on Salmon Bay and the shores of Lake Tarpon has barbecue grills, a boat ramp, a playground area, and covered picnic tables on hills that overlook the lake. ♦ US 19N (Woodhill Dr)

42 Innisbrook $$$$ Even if golf and tennis

aren't your games, this heavily wooded, 1,000-acre, self-contained sports resort is one of Florida's best. The three golf courses and the 18-court Australian Tennis Institute consistently rank high on national and state sports lists. The mansard-roofed lodges contain 1,000 handsome suites with kitchens. This $100 million complex also provides racquetball courts, a fitness center, fishing, cycling, a regular beach shuttle, children's programs, and jogging trails. Money-saving packages are available; rates are least expensive during the summer. ♦ 1,000 rooms. 36750 US 19N (Old Post Rd) 942.2000, 800/456.2000

43 John Chesnut Sr. Park The park's 400 feet of sand is the only freshwater beach in Pinellas County. Other features are a bathhouse, a 30-foot lookout tower, canoe trails, boat dock, and over a mile of boardwalks. Nearly two miles of nature trails wind through the park. ♦ E. Lake Rd at Pasado Dr

44 Shoppes at Cloverplace Stores and two notable eateries in a mall on the strip. ♦ Tampa Rd (Lake St-George Dr) Palm Harbor

Within the Shoppes at Cloverplace:

Sea Grill ★★$$ You won't go wrong if you choose calamari, grouper, or catch of the day. A fine wine list, too. ◆ Seafood ◆ M-Th 5-10PM; F-Sa 5-11PM; Su 5-9PM. 3253 Tampa Rd (Lake St-George Dr) 787.6129

The Blue Heron ★★★$$
Thai, Latin, and Jamaican spices are blended to near-perfection here in unusual seafood and pasta dishes. The roast chicken and the pork chops are good for less adventurous diners. ◆ American ◆ M, Sa-Su 5-9PM; Tu-F 11:30AM-2PM. 3285 Tampa Rd (Lake St-George Dr) Reservations recommended. 789.5176

45 The Boston Cooker ★★★$$ New England dishes and other seafood served with Southern hospitality. Fresh scrod and big-belly Ipswich clams, unusual for Florida, are served, as is lobster. Unlimited refills of salad and hot rolls. ◆ Seafood ◆ M-Th 11:30AM-10PM; F, Sa 11:30AM-11PM. 3705 Tampa Rd (In Forest Lakes Plaza, Forest Lakes Blvd) Oldsmar. Reservations recommended. 855.2311

46 Tampa Bay Downs The only horse-racing course on Florida's west coast, its season normally runs from December to early May. The course is the home of the **Tampa Bay Derby,** a qualifier for the Triple Crown. There are as many as 10 races a day. A restaurant, a lounge, and a gallery with big screens for replays. ◆ Nominal admission, free for women and seniors one day a week. Daily except M, W-Su 1PM. 11225 Racetrack Rd (Tampa Rd) Oldsmar. 855.4401

47 Honeymoon Island State Park A state recreation area suited for swimming, shelling, fishing, picnics, or nature study. ◆ Nominal admission. Daily 8AM-sunset. 1 Causeway Blvd (Curlew Rd-US 19A) Oldsmar. 469.5942

48 Classic Boutique Gallery An authorized dealer for collectors' clubs such as Hummel and Lladro, featuring an extensive assortment of plates, figurines, silver, crystal, and other collectibles. ◆ M-Sa 9AM-5PM. Open Sundays in winter months. 2636 Bayshore Blvd (Curlew Rd-US 19A) Oldsmar. 736.1444

49 Dunedin Fine Arts Center The bright, open gallery features exhibits of proven and emerging artists in two galleries, the first built in 1974 and the second in 1990. ◆ M-F 9AM-4:30PM; Su 1-4PM. 1143 Michigan Blvd (Ed Eckert Ave) Dunedin. 738.1892

50 Andrews Memorial Chapel The church was built in 1888 at a site several miles south, but was displaced in 1926 by the First Presbyterian Church. The chapel was saved by the local historical society in 1970 and underwent a difficult relocation to Hammock Park where it was subsequently restored. It remains a fine example of Florida Gothic architecture, most evident in the tall, pointed windows and wood framing. The chapel is listed on the National Register of Historic Places. ◆ 1899 San Mateo (San Salvador Dr) Dunedin

51 Caladesi Island State Park One of the state's few remaining undisturbed barrier islands, this park lies off the coast of Dunedin in the Gulf of Mexico. It's an ideal setting for shelling, fishing, picnicking, or beachcombing. A three-mile nature trail winds through the interior. The park can be reached only by boat. A ferry departs hourly from nearby Honeymoon Island and downtown Clearwater. ◆ Admission. Daily 8AM-sunset. 443.5903

52 Bon Appétit ★★★$$$ This award-winning waterfront restaurant presents the classics—rack of lamb, veal, and Dover sole—as well as German specialties. The cuisine and service never fail to please, and there is an extensive wine list. ◆ French ◆ Daily 7AM-10PM. 148 Marina Plaza (US 19A) Dunedin. Reservations recommended. 733.2151

53 Sabals ★★$$ An old storefront has been transformed into an Art Deco cafe. The pâté and hot shrimp appetizers are recommended, as are the homemade soups and breads. Entrées include black pepper linguine with pesto sauce, swordfish, and filet mignon. ◆ American ◆ Daily 6-10PM. 315 Main St (US 19A) Reservations recommended. 734.3463

54 J.O. Douglas House (1878) Dunedin's oldest house, remarkably unaltered considering its age, is one of the few remaining original homesteads along Edgewater Drive, and is the first house constructed of milled lumber rather than logs in Dunedin. The house is a fine example of a typical late 19th century dwelling in Central Florida. Douglas, along with other men of Scottish ancestry, petitioned the government, asking for a post office to be named Dunedin, which is Gaelic for Edinburgh, Scotland's

Tampa Bay Area

capital. Listed on the National Register of Historic Places. ◆ 209 Scotland St (US 19A)

Restaurants/Nightlife: Red **Hotels:** Blue
Shops/ 🌳Outdoors: Green **Sights/Culture:** Black

55 Grant Field The expanded field in Dunedin is the spring training site for the Toronto Blue Jays from mid-February to April. It then becomes home to the Dunedin Blue Jays, a member of the Class A Florida State League. ♦ Ballpark seats 6,200. 373 Douglas Ave (Beltrees St) 733.9302

56 Paperback Palace Huge selection of used paperbacks, some of which are out of print. ♦ M-Th 9AM-8PM; F 9AM-9PM; Sa 9AM-6PM; Su noon-5PM. 26948 US 19N (In Countryside Plaza Shopping Center, SR 580) 796.1322. Also at: 1293 Missouri Ave. 461.2160; 12987 Walsingham Rd, Largo. 596.9049

57 Countryside Mall This 155-store mall is one of the area's largest, with an eye toward the middle-income and affluent shopper. Upscale shops like **Victoria's Secret** are represented, as well as gourmet food outlets such as **Schnickel Fritz,** which sells 180 kinds of cheese and 60 types of smoked meats and sausages. But there is also a McDonald's for a quick, inexpensive bite. An ice-skating rink in the middle of the mall is a fun diversion. ♦ M-Sa 10AM-9PM; Su 12:30-5:30PM. US 19-SR 580. 796.1079

58 Countryside Village Square A shopping center with a wide array of specialty shops. ♦ M-Sa 10AM-9PM; Su noon-5PM. 2569 Countryside Blvd (Village Dr-Enterprise Rd)

Within Countryside Village Square:

Amy Stoudt A discount outlet for large women's fashions with excellent quality and selection. ♦ 799.4027

The Petite Shop Fashions for petite women at reduced prices. ♦ 799.4703

59 Get Personal Almost everything sold here can be personalized, from stationery to gifts and toys. Paper may be purchased by the pound, but it's expensive. ♦ 2510 McMullen-Booth Rd (SR 590) 791.6804

60 Philippe Park The park, which overlooks Old Tampa Bay, is named for **Count Odet Philippe,** a Frenchman who was the first white settler on the Pinellas peninsula. He settled at this site in the 1830s and is credited with introducing the first grapefruit trees to the New World. Before Philippe settled here, the site was occupied by Indians, and a sizable ceremonial mound from the ancient Indian inhabitants can be

viewed today. Facilities include picnic shelters (reservations available), picnic tables, and a children's playground. The archaeological site is listed on the National Register of Historic Places. ♦ Daily 7AM-sunset. 2355 Bayshore Blvd (SR 590) Safety Harbor. 726.2700

SAFETY HARBOR

61 Safety Harbor Spa & Fitness Center $$$ This full-scale, 35-acre fitness center is on the Espiritu Santo Springs, said to have been discovered by **Hernando DeSoto** in 1539. The "springs of the Holy Spirit" consist of five mineral springs that figure in the spa's treatments for guests. Although the spa has been in existence since 1926, it was revamped to accommodate a younger clientele in the late 1980s. There are 35 fitness activities for spa guests, including specialized exercises designed for professional boxers training here. Facilities include heated indoor and outdoor pools, seven clay tennis courts, a Lancôme Skin Institute, a driving range, saunas, steam baths, and a full range of health and beauty treatments. The hotel rooms are decorated in a tropical motif. Three nutritional spa meals daily are usually included in rates. ♦ 212 rooms. 105 N. Bayshore Dr (SR 590) Safety Harbor. 726.1161, 800/237.0155

62 Three's Company Tucked into a downtown block next to the post office, this boutique offers unusual fashions and some fashionable resort wear. Custom-made T-shirts and T-shirt/leggings sets are made by local artists; some fashions are appliquéd and painted. There are frequent sales on trendy items. ♦ M-F 10AM-4:30PM; Sa 10AM-3PM. 319 Main St (2nd-3rd Aves North) Safety Harbor. 725.4223

63 Forbidden City ★$$ Chicken with broccoli, and steamed, Mandarin-style fish are treats for dieters. Seven Stars Around the Moon, which is fresh jumbo shrimp dipped in batter, wrapped in bacon, and fried with sautéed Chinese vegetables, lobster, chicken, and scallops, is only for those who aren't counting calories. Another good bet is the Kung-Fu Twins *au poivre,* which is peppersteak with a Chinese twist. The food not only looks good but tastes good, too. ♦ Chinese ♦ M-Th, Su 11:30AM-10PM; F-Sa 11:30AM-11PM. 25778 US 19N (SR 588) 797.8989

64 Loehmann's Women's designer clothes can be purchased here at a great reduction in price—but they still aren't inexpensive. And there's a communal dressing room. ♦ M-F 10AM-9PM; Sa 10AM-5:30PM; Su noon-5PM. 23148 US 19N (NE Coachman Rd) 799.4300

65 Moccasin Lake Nature Park: An Environmental and Energy Education Center Among the plants you will see are wax myrtle, laurel oaks, water oaks, live oaks, cypress, slash pine, and wildflowers. The animals include alligators, bald eagles, barn owls, screech owls, burrowing owls, flying squirrels, possums, snapping turtles, and wild armadillos. A one-mile nature trail winds through the 50-acre park. ♦ Admission. Tu-F 9AM-5PM; Sa-Su 10AM-6PM. 2750 Park Trail Ln (Drew St-Fairwood Ave) 462.6024

66 Ruth Eckerd Hall This performing arts center is home to the Florida Orchestra and the Florida Opera. Concerts, ballet, Broadway shows, and other events are staged year-round. The efficient, modern design has an inconvenience—no center aisle. ♦ Seats 2,100. 1111 McMullen-Booth Rd (McFarland Dr) 791.7400

67 Tio Pepe's ★★★$$ This lovely hacienda is always jammed with customers. Excellent Spanish cuisine, including Spanish bean soup, black bean soup, and a spectacular 22-ounce pork chop that goes well with rich black bread and a salad mixed at your table. There is a good choice of wines, including red and white sangria. The bakery in the foyer makes bread and apple tarts. To avoid the crowds and noise, ask for the front room. ♦ Spanish ♦ M 5-11PM; Tu-Th 11AM-2:30PM, 5-11PM; F 11AM-2:30PM, 5-11:30PM; Sa 5-11:30PM; Su 4-10PM. 2930 Gulf-to-Bay Blvd (US 19-Bayview Ave) 799.3082

68 Hooters ★$ This is the original of the finger-food chain where the female serving staff is clothed in brief T-shirts and shorts. The menu consists mostly of chicken wings, steamed shrimp, and sandwiches. It's quick and inexpensive. ♦ American ♦ M-Th 11AM-midnight; F-Sa 11AM-1PM; Su noon-10PM. 2800 Gulf-to-Bay Blvd (Hampton Rd) 797.4008

69 Key West Grill ★$$ Another first of a chain, but this one feels like a cozy Key West restaurant. The fish of the day is grilled or blackened and served in a casual atmosphere. Servings are generous, and the muffins are fresh. Start with the luscious shrimp bisque and munch on tiny homemade rolls and strawberry butter. The conch fritters are flavorful but tough. ♦ Seafood ♦ M-Th 11:30AM-11PM; F-Sa 11:30AM-midnight; Su 11:30AM-10PM. 2660 Gulf-to-Bay Blvd (US 19-Hampton Rd) 797.1988

70 Hops Grill & Brewery ★★$$ Of the four beers brewed here, the British-style pale ale is a standout. Pastas, soup, and steaks are excellent. For those interested in home brewing, a miniature brewery is on display. ♦ American ♦ M-Th 11:30AM-11PM; F, Sa 11:30AM-midnight; Su 11:30AM-10PM. 1451 US 19S (Nursery Rd) 531.5300

71 Bay Area Outlet Mall Everything from paper goods and books to clothes from **Laura Ashley** and **Aileen** are available at bargain prices in this 80-store emporium for careful shoppers. ♦ M-Sa 10AM-9PM; Su noon-6PM for most stores. Roosevelt Blvd at US 19. 535.2337

72 Boatyard Village A re-created 1890s fishing village nestled in a cove on Old Tampa Bay next to St. Petersburg-Clearwater International Airport. Restaurants, boutiques, and galleries with tin roofs and weathered wood exteriors are meant to attract the tourist crowd. **The Boatyard Stage,** a 176-seat theater, holds performances year-round. ♦ M-Th 10AM-7PM; F-Sa 10AM-9PM; Su 10AM-6PM for most stores. 16100 Fairchild Dr (Roosevelt Blvd) 535.4678

73 Florida Military Aviation Museum The exhibits of restored aircraft, aviation artifacts, vehicles, and weapons, dating from WWII to the present, are a treat for war and aircraft buffs. ♦ Admission. Tu, Th, Sa 10AM-4PM; Su 1-5PM. 16055 Fairchild Dr (Roosevelt Blvd) 535.9007

74 Flightshops Aviation books and charts may be purchased at this store near the St. Petersburg-Clearwater International Airport. ♦ M-F 9:30AM-6PM; Sa 10AM-5PM; Su noon-5PM. Roosevelt Blvd at Terminal Pkwy. 530.1415

Clearwater

Long, sandy beaches and warm gulf waters combine with a wide variety of reasonably priced hotels and ethnically diverse restaurants to make this area popular with visitors.

75 A Blue Moon Rare and old books, decorative maps, prints, records, and posters. Appraisals are also available. ♦ M-Sa 9AM-8PM. 1415 Cleveland Ave (Hillcrest Ave) 443.7444

76 Jack Russell Stadium The Philadelphia Phillies hold their spring training here from mid-February to April. Then it becomes home to the Clearwater Phillies, a Class A Florida State League team. ♦ Seats 7,000. 800 Phillies Dr (Palmetto St-Greenwood Ave) 441.8638

77 Bill Irle's ★★$$ Irle's native German touch is evident in the dishes served—sauerbraten, Wiener schnitzel, potato pancakes, and Black Forest cake. The salads are fresh, and the

desserts are homemade. ♦ German ♦ Daily 11:30AM-8PM. 1310 N. Fort Harrison Ave (Engman St) 446.5683

Restaurants/Nightlife: Red   **Hotels:** Blue
Shops/ 🌴Outdoors: Green   **Sights/Culture:** Black

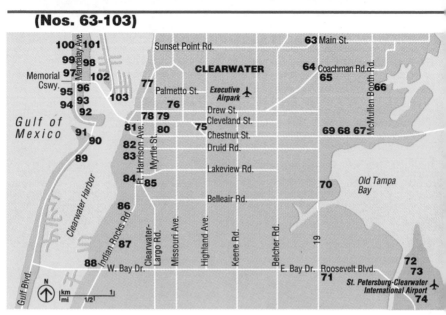

78 Ottavio's Place ★★$$$ Fireplaces, bookshelves, and wine bottles decorate this intimate eatery in downtown Clearwater. Veal is a specialty. Pasta, desserts, and bread are homemade. ♦ Italian ♦ M-F 11:30AM-2:30PM, 5-10PM; Sa 5-10PM. 45 N. Fort Harrison (Drew-Cleveland Sts) 442.6659

79 Cleveland Street Post Office This Mediterranean Revival building is representative of the 1929-39 federal public works program that commissioned local professionals and industries. Listed on the National Register of Historic Places, it is still in use. ♦ 650 Cleveland St (Garden Ave-Myrtle St)

80 Bilgore Groves A fine selection of fruit, especially citrus, for shipment only; you don't take any with you. There are no groves attached to this storefront; they are in Indian River County. ♦ M-Sa 9AM-5PM; M-F 9AM-3PM in summer. 807A Court St (Myrtle St-Prospect Ave) 442.2171

81 Pinellas County Courthouse The second Pinellas County Courthouse, built in 1917 and representing the Neo-Classical style, served the county's needs until 1960. It is still used along with a third courthouse. ♦ 324 S. Fort Harrison Ave (Court St)

82 South Ward School (1906) This elementary school is listed on the National Register of Historic Places and has the distinction of being Florida's oldest county

school continuously operating in the same building. ♦ 610 S. Fort Harrison Ave (Chestnut-Turner Sts)

Restaurants/Nightlife: Red
Shops/ ♠Outdoors: Green
Hotels: Blue
Sights/Culture: Black

83 Clearwater Harbor Oaks Historical District This district, overlooking Clearwater Harbor, was developed in the 1920s. Many fine old homes of various architectural styles are still standing in this six-square-block area. A pleasant detour on the way to the beaches. ♦ S. Fort Harrison Ave (Lotus Path-Druid Rd)

84 Louis Ducros House The house was built in the 1890s for railroad tycoon **Henry Plant,** who had a number of cottages constructed along a railroad spur for men working on his grand Bellview Hotel nearby. The structure, listed on the National Register of Historic Places, is a rare example of Carpenter Gothic architecture with its gable roof, bay windows, and veranda stretching across the front of the house. Ducros was Plant's official photographer, and possibly the first resident in Clearwater. ♦ 1324 S. Fort Harrison Ave

85 A Place for Cooks An exhaustive collection of bakeware, gadgets, and unusual specialty foods. ♦ M-F 10AM-6PM; Su 10AM-5PM. 1447 S. Fort Harrison Ave (Belleview Rd) 446.5506

86 Florida Gulf Coast Arts Center This regional arts center on 12 wooded acres shows contemporary works by nationally recognized artists. Visitors can wander through the studios and watch potters, sculptors, and painters at work. ♦ Tu-F 10AM-4PM; Sa noon-4PM. 222 Ponce de Leon Blvd (Indian Rocks Rd) Belleair. 584.8634

87 Belleair Consignment Boutique The Belleair area is Clearwater's poshest, which is reflected in this shop's merchandise: Beaded dresses, designer clothes, and jewelry from a wealthy clientele are among the estate items sold here. ♦ M-Sa 10AM-4:30PM. 2617 Jewel Rd (Indian Rocks Rd) Bellair Bluffs. 585.9351

88 Eugen's ★★$$$ Seafood is king here, and special attention is given to the bouillabaisse and grouper dishes. Other standouts are the homemade chowders. For dessert, try the chocolate mousse and Key lime pie. An excellent wine list is available. ♦ Seafood ♦ M-Th 11:30AM-2:30PM, 4:30-10PM; F 11:30AM-2:30PM, 4:30-10:30PM; Sa 4:30-10:30PM; Su 4-10PM. 100 N. Indian Rocks Rd (In Plaza Shopping Center at W. Bay Dr) Bellair Bluffs. 585.6399

89 Belleview Mido Resort Hotel $$$ Perched on a bluff overlooking Clearwater Harbor, the Belleview Biltmore opened as a grand, seasonal hotel in 1897. Built by railroad tycoon **Henry Plant,** it is said to be the world's largest continuously occupied wooden structure. Truth is, the wooden shutters have been converted to aluminum siding to reduce costs and maintenance. Even its name was changed after a Japanese company bought it in 1990. Renovations by former and current owners have effected much-needed modernization, but a good deal of the spirit of other eras has been lost in the process. Still, guests will find themselves surrounded by Tiffany glass, chandeliers, gables, and peaked roofs. Facilities include two 18-hole golf courses (and access to a third), croquet, tennis courts, a swimming pool, and a European health spa. Guests may rent bicycles and use the complimentary shuttle service to the Cabana Club on the Gulf, which has 500 feet of beach. ♦ 25 Belleview Blvd (S. Fort Harrison Ave) 442.6171, 800/237.8947 (FL only), 800/282.8072 (US)

89 Shops at Sand Key Fine restaurants and several specialty shops are found in this Clearwater Harbor shopping center. ♦ 1241 Gulf Blvd, Sand Key

Within the Shops at Sand Key:

The Columbia ★$$$ This is the newest branch of Tampa's famous restaurant (see page 134). The decor is typically Spanish with tiles and dark woods, and the view is of Clearwater Harbor. ♦ Spanish ♦ M-Th, Su 11AM-10PM; F-Sa 11AM-11PM. 596.2828

Cha Cha Coconuts ★$$ Sandwiches, seafood, and finger foods—many with Caribbean seasonings—prevail in this casual tropical bar, a good vantage point for watching sailboats and sunsets. ♦ American ♦ M-Th 11AM-midnight; F-Sa 11AM-1AM; Su noon-11PM. 596.6040

90 Radisson Suite Beach Resort $$$ This new $40 million resort at Sand Key on Clearwater Harbor covers 7.5 acres. There are 220 one-bedroom suites with two televisions, wet bar, coffeemaker, microwave, and private balcony. Facilities include a free-form pool with a waterfall, a sun deck, a child care center, a fitness center, and dining facilities. Adjacent are the **Shops at Sand Key** with a branch of **The Columbia.** ♦ 1201 Gulf Blvd (Clearwater Pass) Sand Key. 596.1110, 800/333.3333

91 Sheraton Sand Key Beach Resort $$$ The hotel sits on 10 acres of secluded beach with a heated pool, a children's pool, a Jacuzzi, a volleyball court, and a wide selection of watersports. Other facilities include a coffee shop, a restaurant, a snack bar, a game room, a bar, and an entertainment lounge. For years, the hotel has been a favorite with international visitors. One of its rooms also gained notoriety because of the **Jim Bakker-Jessica Hahn** scandal. ♦ 390 rooms. 1160 Gulf Blvd (Gulf of Mexico) Sand Key. 595.1611, 800/325.3535

92 Sea Stone Suites Resort $$ There are 88 one-bedroom suites with kitchens in this six-story hotel that opened in 1988, and 65 rooms in the older Gulfview wing. The suites have kitchenettes and a living room. There is a pool, private dock, guest laundry, sun deck, and whirlpool. Rates include breakfast and a cocktail hour. The waterfront property is on the bay side of the island. ♦ 445 Hamden Dr (S. Gulfview Blvd-5th St) Clearwater Beach. 441.1222, 800/444.1919

93 Seafood & Sunsets at Julie's ★$$ A relaxed Key West-style atmosphere where casual or beach dress is the order of the day. Fish and chips, clam strips, grouper sandwiches, burgers, conch fritters, and a wide range of seafood are served. This is a great place to watch the beach activities or catch the sunset. ♦ Seafood ♦ M-Th 11AM-10 PM; F-Su 11AM-10:30 PM. 351 S. Gulfview Blvd (Mandalay Ave-Devon Dr) Clearwater Beach. 441.2548

94 Best Western Sea Wake Resort $$ Another beachfront property operated by the Seaton family, which owns the Gulf Sands and the Sea Stone. There is a heated pool, a restaurant where certain dishes are prepared tableside, and cabana rentals. Meals also are served on the tree-draped patio that overlooks the beach, a nice break from the heat. ♦ 110 rooms. 691 S. Gulfview Blvd (Big Pier 60-Bayway Blvd) Clearwater Beach. 443.7652, 800/444.1919

95 Gulf Sands Beach Resort $$ More than half of the rooms are efficiencies at this family-operated beachfront property known

for its friendly service. Facilities include a seafood restaurant, a poolside snack bar, a heated pool, a game room, volleyball, and shuffleboard. ♦ 655 S. Gulfview Blvd (Big Pier 60-Bayway Blvd) Clearwater Beach. 442.7171, 800/444.1919

96 **The Admiral Tour Boat** Sight-seeing luncheon and dinner-dance cruises are offered on this 300-passenger, triple-decked vessel that cruises the Intracoastal Waterway along Clearwater Beach, turns around in the Gulf of Mexico, and returns to dock at the Clearwater Beach Marina. A narrative history of the area accompanies the afternoon cruise. Schedules vary according to season. ♦ Admission. Memorial Causeway at Gulfview Blvd, Clearwater Beach. 462.2628, 800/444.4814

97 **Holiday Inn Clearwater Beach Surfside** $$$ Scarcely your standard roadside hostelry, the 427-room hotel and its pool sit right on prime beachfront with ample beach and water-sports rentals, volleyball, and a sun deck. The hotel is within walking distance of shops and restaurants at the beach's north end. A good value. ♦ 400 Mandalay Ave (Memorial Causeway) Clearwater Beach. 461.3222, 800/HOLIDAY

98 **Swim & Play** Extensive selection of beach and resort wear for women, including hard-to-find sizes. ♦ M-Sa 9AM-9PM; Su 10AM-5PM. 407 Mandalay (Papaya-Memorial Causeway) Clearwater Beach. 461.4499

99 **Clearwater Beach Hotel** $$$ This is the oldest hotel on the beach; part of it dates from the turn of the century, though the property was redone in 1988. Some of the rooms have small kitchens. There is an old and a new section for lodging. Other features are a heated pool, a library, and a sun deck. Locals stay here, including some area hoteliers. ♦ 160 rooms. 500 Mandalay Ave (Memorial Causeway-Bay Esplanade) Clearwater Beach. 441.2425, 800/292.2295

Within Clearwater Beach Hotel:

Clearwater Beach Hotel Dining Room ★★★$$$ Simply grand dining in a turn-of-the-century beach setting. Contemporary and nouvelle cuisine recipes elevate duck, salads, and vegetables dishes to new heights. ♦ American ♦ M-Th 7:30-10AM, 11:30AM-2:30PM, 5-10PM; F-Sa 7:30-10AM, 11:30AM-2:30PM, 5-10:30PM; Su 7:30-10:30AM, 11:30AM-2:30PM, 5-10PM. 441.2425

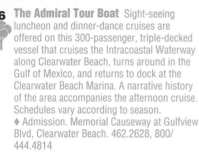

100 **Palm Pavilion Inn** $$ The 29-unit hotel, originally built in the 1940s, recently has been upgraded but retains its pink-and-blue

Art Deco exterior. The rooms, including two efficiencies, contain custom-built furniture to match the scale of the rooms. Other facilities are a guest laundry and a pool. Adjacent to the property is the **Palm Pavilion,** a classic

beach pavilion that opened in 1926 and has a snack bar that serves beer and wine. ♦ 18 Bay Esplanade (Mandalay Ave) Clearwater Beach. 446.6777

101 **Bob Heilman's Beachcomber** ★★$$$ There's no view of the water, but this restaurant has been a mainstay for more than 40 years. The menu offers a wide array of fresh seafood, including frog legs and Maine lobster. The steaks and prime rib also are tops. Fried chicken from an old family recipe is one of the most popular menu items; it's served with mashed potatoes and muffins. ♦ American ♦ M-Sa 11:30AM-10:30PM; Su noon-10PM. 447 Mandalay Ave (Bay Esplanade) Clearwater Beach. 442.4144

102 **Clearwater Marine Science Center** Live and model displays of area marine life are on exhibit at this research and rehabilitation center. One of the more popular exhibits is a tank containing baby sea turtles. There also are stingrays, small sharks, and dolphins. Children will like the "touching tank" with its small hermit crabs and other creatures. ♦ Admission. M-F 9AM-5PM; Sa 9AM-4PM; Su 11AM-4PM. 249 Windward Passage (Island Way) Clearwater Beach. 447.0980

103 **The Flagship** ★★★$$ A crowded fish house east of the main beach on the waterfront near the **Clearwater Marine Science Center.** Selections include salmon, crab, mahimahi, grouper, and snapper. Dishes may be cooked to order—fried, broiled, charbroiled, or blackened. This is one of the most favored fish houses in Pinellas County. ♦ Seafood ♦ M-Th, Su 11:30AM-10PM; F, Sa 11:30AM-10:30PM. 20 Island Way (Memorial Causeway) Clearwater Beach. Reservations recommended. 443.6210

Refer to map on page 128 for numbers 104-111

104 **Bella Trattoria** ★$$ This is the place to design your own one-person pizza with a variety of toppings. ♦ Italian ♦ M-Th 11:30AM-10PM; F 11:30AM-11PM; Sa 5-11PM; Su 5-10PM. 13505 Icot Blvd (Ulmerton Rd) 535.6224

105 **Heritage Park & Museum** A schoolhouse, a train depot, and houses ranging from a log cabin to a Victorian mansion have been restored and collected on 21 wooded acres in Largo. The historical museum depicts the county's pioneer lifestyle, and tours are led by guides attired in period dress. Spinning, weaving, and other crafts exhibits are held regularly. In the park, there are about 20 structures, including a turn-of-the-century bandstand, that have been moved from other parts of the county. The garden for the blind, where fragrant plants surround a gazebo, is an unusual feature. The annual Country Jubilee is held on the fourth Saturday in October. ♦ Tu-Sa 10AM-4PM; Su 1-4PM. 11909 125th St North (Walsingham Rd) Largo. 462.3474

106 Sturgeon Memorial Rose Garden

In 1985 this garden was approved by All-America Rose Selections as a public display garden, one of less than a hundred in the country. The only other accredited rose gardens in Florida are at **Walt Disney World, Cypress Gardens,** and Orlando's **Leu Gardens.** There are more than 850 bushes representing over 100 varieties. The garden is inside **Serenity Gardens Memorial Park,** a cemetery. The best months to visit are October and November. ◆ Daily sunrise to sunset. 13401 Indian Rocks Rd (Walsingham Rd) Largo. 595.2914

107 15th-27th Aves Street parking access to Gulf beaches, Indian Rocks Beach.

108 Keegan's Seafood Grille ★$ This modest restaurant presents seafood ranging from grilled fish to ceviche at modest prices. (The portions can be modest, too.) ◆ Seafood ◆ M-Th 11:30AM-10:30PM; F, Sa 11:30AM-11:30PM; Su 1-10:30PM. 1519 Gulf Blvd (15th-16th Aves) Indian Rocks Beach. 596.2477

109 1st and 8th Aves Street parking access to the beaches, Indian Rocks Beach.

110 Crabby Bill's ★★★$ While the atmosphere may be bare bones, there's nothing lacking in the seafood that is available at rock-bottom prices. Favorite dishes here are steamed shrimp, crab cakes, oysters, clams on the half-shell, oyster stew, catfish, and frogs legs. **Matt Loder** says his family decided to name the restaurant after his father, **Bill,** because he's "crabby all the time," and, of course, because they serve crab. The complex has three buildings that take up most of a block. Expect to wait. ◆ Seafood ◆ M-Th 11AM-10PM; F-Sa 11AM-11PM; Su 1-11PM. 401 Gulf Blvd (4th-5th Aves) Indian Rocks Beach. 595.4825

111 Hamlin's Landing This rambling, Victorian shopping-and-dining complex on the Intracoastal Waterway contains three restaurants and a half dozen shops. ◆ M-Th 10AM-8PM; F-Sa 10AM-10PM; Su 10AM-8PM for shops. Restaurant hours vary. 401 Second St East (Gulf Blvd-SR 688) Indian Rocks Beach. 595.9484

At Hamlin's Landing:

Starlite Princess The three-deck, 106-foot, Victorian-style paddle wheeler, built in 1986, offers a variety of cruises for sight-seeing, lunch, or dinner. Except for the summer months, the Starlite Princess leaves once a week for an eight-hour journey to **Harbour Island** at Tampa. The trip includes breakfast and a sit-down lunch. For an additional fee, the cruise line arranges transportation back to Hamlin's Landing. In the evening there is a three-hour dinner-dance cruise from Harbour Island. Entertainment includes Mississippi riverboat tunes and contemporary music. ◆ Two-hour luncheon cruises T, Th, F, Sa noon-2PM; three-hour luncheon dance cruise W noon-3PM; three-hour dinner dance cruise T, W, F-Su 7:30-10:30PM; three-hour dinner dance cruise from Harbour Island Th 7:30-10:30PM; eight-hour Tampa cruise Th 9AM-5PM. Closed June-Sept. Reservations required. 401 Second St East (Gulf Blvd-SR 688) Indian Rocks Beach. 595.1212, 800/722.6645

Gulf Boulevard

112 The Hungry Fisherman ★★$ It's not fancy, with its weathered wood facade, but this restaurant offers more than 40 seafood varieties at low prices. Selections include Danish lobster tails, Alaskan salmon, scallops, and snapper. ◆ Seafood ◆ Daily 11:30AM-10PM. 19915 Gulf Blvd (200th-199th Aves) Indian Shores. 595.4218

113 Scandia ★★$$ Paned windows, timbered walls, and Scandinavian items dress up this small chalet that doubles as a gift shop and restaurant. Norwegian smoked salmon, Swedish marinated herring, and Danish roast pork loin are hard to beat. Chef and owner **Poul Madsen** has been providing a cook's tour of his native Denmark and other Scandinavian countries since 1978. ◆ Scandinavian ◆ Daily 11:30AM-9PM. Closed Sept. 19829 Gulf Blvd (198th-199th Aves) Indian Shores. Reservations recommended. 595.5525

114 Holiday Villas II $$ These fully furnished condos with kitchens are right on the beach. Maid service, a laundry, and a pool, but weekly rentals only. ◆ 73 units. 19610 Gulf Blvd (196th Ave-Bay Pl) Indian Shores. 596.4852

115 Pepín on the Beach ★★★$$ Great pork chops, succulent aged beef, flaky pompano baked in salt, and authentic *caldo gallego,* a white bean soup with smoked pork, are excellent choices. This version of St. Pete's

popular eatery, Pepín, opened in 1985. ◆ Spanish ◆ Daily 5-11PM. 19519 Gulf Blvd (195th-196th Aves) Indian Shores. Reservations recommended. 596.9100; Also at: 4125 4th St North, St. Petersburg. 821.3773

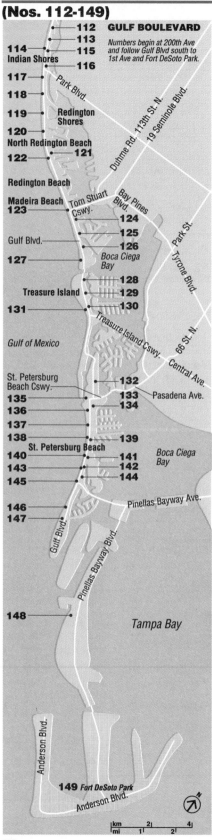

GULF BOULEVARD

Numbers begin at 200th Ave and follow Gulf Blvd south to 1st Ave and Fort DeSoto Park.

116 Le Pompano ★★$$$ Pompano prepared any number of ways is the specialty here: Try filets sautéed with small shrimp, mushrooms, and orange sections, baked *en croûte* with a julienne of seafood, or the more traditional *en papillote*. Other good bets are sole amandine, salmon steak with a sorrel beurre blanc, duckling à l'orange, chicken and veal *cordon bleu*, and rack of lamb. ♦ French ♦ Daily 4-10PM. 19325 Gulf Blvd (193rd-194th Aves) Indian Shores. Reservations required. 596.0333

117 Holiday Villas III $$ There are 75 condos and seven efficiencies located on the beach. Maid service, pool, game room, laundry, and private dock. Weekly rentals only. ♦ 18610 Gulf Blvd (186th Ave-Park Blvd) Indian Shores. 595.2335

118 Suncoast Seabird Sanctuary This refuge

for sick and injured birds is known worldwide for its preservation and rehabilitation of wild and endangered birds. Visitors can observe brown pelicans, cormorants, white herons, birds of prey, songbirds, and other species. ♦ Daily during daylight hours. 18328 Gulf Blvd (183rd-184th Aves) Indian Shores. 391.6211

119 Lobster Pot ★★★$$$ Lobster, prepared in

usual and unusual ways, is the house specialty. Standouts are the lobster stuffed with shrimp and scallops and the lobster bisque. Red snapper, grouper, fish chowders, and escargot are also excellent. The only drawbacks: it's small and noisy. Dressy. ♦ Seafood ♦ M-Th 4:30-10PM; F, Sa 4:30-11PM; Su 4-10PM. 17814 Gulf Blvd (Atoll-178th Aves) Redington Beach. Reservations recommended. 391.8592

120 Redington Long Pier Both fishermen and sightseers enjoy this pier, which stretches 1,021 feet into the Gulf of Mexico. Restrooms, a snack bar, and equipment rentals are available. This is also the best place to park for the Redington beaches, where parking is at a premium. ♦ Admission. Daily 24 hours. 17490 Gulf Blvd (175th Ave) Redington Beach. 391.9398

121 Wine Cellar ★★★$$$ You can start with Swiss cheese soup, Hungarian goulash soup, or soused shrimp in the rough—shrimp soaked in olive oil, garlic, and dry vermouth, with the tail portion left on for patrons to peel. Entrées include Wiener schnitzel, beef Wellington, and fresh Idaho rainbow trout. ♦ Continental ♦ Tu-Sa 4:30-11PM; Su 4-10PM. 17307 Gulf Blvd (173rd Ave) North Redington Beach. Reservations recommended. 393.3491

122 North Redington Beach Hilton $$$ Each room has a balcony with a view of either the Gulf or Boca Ciega Bay. This is one of the area's newest hotels, and the slickly decorated rooms have service bars, large bathrooms, and separate dressing rooms. It has its own 125 feet of beach with pool and deck. Parking is free. ◆ 17120 Gulf Blvd (171st Ave) North Redington Beach. 391.4000, 800/HILTONS, 800/447.SAND

123 Holiday Inn Madeira Beach $$$ All rooms have balconies or patios with a full or partial view of the hotel's 600 feet of beach. A restaurant and lounge overlook the Gulf. Other features are a heated pool, lighted tennis court, and beachside rentals, such as cabanas and water-sports equipment. ◆ 148 rooms. 15208 Gulf Blvd (Tom Stuart Causeway-153rd Ave) Madeira Beach. 392.2275, 800/HOLIDAY

124 Leverock's on the Bay ★$$ Fresh seafood is served at affordable prices, but there can be a long wait. No reservations. ◆ Seafood ◆ Daily 11AM-10PM. 565 150th Ave (E. Madeira Ave-Boca Ciega Bay) Madeira Beach. 393.0459

125 Omi's Bavarian Inn ★★$$ The Bavarian ambience is a bit overdone with taped oompah-pah music, but the food is authentic. Choose from schnitzel, sauerkraut, potato dumplings, red cabbage, and homemade soups. Wine and beer choices include many European imports. ◆ German ◆ M-Sa 4:30-9:30PM; Su noon-9:30PM. 14701 Gulf Blvd (147th-148th Aves) Madeira Beach. Reservations recommended. 393.9654

126 Grecian Isles ★$$ This small beachside bistro offers homemade bread, sausage, and innovative sauces for squid and lamb. ◆ Greek ◆ Daily 11AM-10PM. 14363 Gulf Blvd (143rd-144th Aves) Madeira Beach. 397.9352

127 141st-148th Aves Public access and metered parking for beaches at Madeira Beach County Park, Madeira Beach.

128 John's Pass Village & Boardwalk There are more than 60 shops and several outstanding seafood restaurants in this converted fishing village of tin-roofed buildings that overlooks "fish famous" John's Pass, home to a large commercial and charter fishing fleet. The 1,000-foot boardwalk provides a scenic view. Some shops carry the predictable tourist merchandise, but the majority are antique, arts and crafts, and handicrafts shops selling woodwork, glassware, and jewelry. **The Bronze Lady,** a longtime art gallery here, is the world's largest single dealer of works by comedian and artist **Red Skelton**. If you can find a spot, park here for the beach. ◆ Daily 9AM-6PM or later. 12901 Gulf Blvd (128th-129th Aves) Madeira Beach. 391.7373

129 Paradise Pier ★★★$$ This is a local landmark that has been around for years but is known only by word of mouth. It's casual, and its simple preparation of seafood continues to draw crowds, especially on the weekends. Located under the boardwalk at John's Pass. ◆ Seafood ◆ W-Su 5-9PM. 196 128th Ave East (Gulf Blvd) Madeira Beach. 393.1824

129 Captain Hubbard's Marina Try your hand at fishing here, either from the docks or catwalks, or from a party boat. Fishing sage Captain Hubbard claims that, on nine days out of 10, more fish are landed on boats here than on any other vessels along the Florida coast. Half-day, full-day, or overnight trips may be booked, but reservations are suggested. Schedules vary. ◆ 150 128th Ave (Gulf Blvd) Madeira Beach. 393.1947, 392.0167

At Captain Hubbard's Marina:

Friendly Fisherman ★$$ Amberjack, mullet, stone crabs, and other seafood have been brought in daily by the fleet of **Captain Wilson Hubbard,** the "friendly fisherman," for more than 50 years. Dine indoors or out on the boardwalk. ◆ Seafood ◆ M-Th, F-Sa 7AM-11PM; Su 7AM-10PM. 391.6025

129 Europa Sun Five- or six-hour cruises into the Gulf of Mexico with lunch or dinner are offered on this 275-passenger luxury ship. Casino gambling is allowed once the ship passes the state territorial limit 9.1 miles offshore. ◆ Schedules vary. 129th Ave at Gulf Blvd, Madeira Beach. 800/688.PLAY

130 The Kingfish ★$$ This fish house has bargain-priced seafood, but the best selections come from the raw bar. ◆ Seafood ◆ Daily 11:30AM-10PM. 12789 Kingfish Dr (Gulf Blvd) Treasure Island. 360.0881

131 77th-127th Aves Public access to the beaches with parking meters at 77th, 90th, 100th, 112th, 120th, and 126th Aves, Treasure Island.

132 El Gordo's ★$$ Since 1954, this family-owned restaurant has been the spot for homemade flan, *chilies rellenos,* and tamales. ◆ Mexican ◆ M-Sa 11AM-10PM; Su 8AM-10PM. 7815 Blind Pass Rd (79th-78th Aves) St. Petersburg Beach. 360.5947

133 Leverock's ★$$ The setting is simple but both the waterfront view and the service are delightful. Good bets are raw oysters and clams, peel-your-own shrimp, and any

number of grouper dishes. ◆ Seafood ◆ Daily 11:30AM-10PM. 10 Corey Ave (Boca Ciega Bay) St. Petersburg Beach. 367.4588. Also at: 4801 37th St South (49th-48th Aves South) 864.3883; 565 150th Ave (E. Madeira Ave-Boca Ciega Bay) Madeira Beach. 393.0459

134 Doe-Al Southern Cooking ★★★$ This local institution has been serving home-style Southern food for more than 20 years. Fried chicken and catfish, chitterlings, and barbecue are served family-style with generous portions of collards and black-eyed peas. ◆ Southern ◆ M-Sa 11:30AM-3:30PM, 4:30-9PM; Su 12:30-8PM. 85 Corey Circle (St. Petersburg Beach Causeway-Blind Pass Dr) St. Petersburg Beach. 360.7976

135 Woody's Waterfront ★$ Burgers, fried shellfish, and grouper are the favorites at this popular beach bar. ◆ American ◆ M-Sa 11AM-2AM; Su noon-2AM. 7308 Sunset Way (73rd-Corey Aves) St. Petersburg Beach. 360.9165

136 68th St Public access to Upham Beach and metered parking, St. Petersburg Beach.

137 Sandpiper Beach Resort $$ Toasters, coffeemakers, small refrigerators, and wet bars come with each room. Suites have a separate living room and full kitchen. Other facilities include a beachfront pool, an enclosed heated pool, air-conditioned racquet-sport courts, supervised children's activities, water-sports rentals, a game room, and an exercise room. ◆ 159 rooms. 6000 Gulf Blvd (60th Ave) St. Petersburg Beach. 360.1551, 800/237.0707

Tradewinds

138 TradeWinds $$$ Guests can ride motorized gondolas to their rooms on the meandering waterways that cut through the 13 acres of beach property of this sprawling hotel. The rooms, each with private balconies, are outfitted with coffeemakers, toasters, and wet bars; each suite has a separate living room and a fully equipped kitchen. Recreational facilities include four pools, a sauna, Jacuzzis, a fitness center, racquet sports, water-sports rentals, and supervised activities for children. ◆ 5500 Gulf Blvd (55th Ave) St. Petersburg Beach. 367.6461, 800/237.0707

Within TradeWinds:

The Palm Court ★★$$$ Grouper, lamb, roast duckling, and salmon prevail. French overtones blend remarkably well with fresh Florida ingredients. Lighter lunches are served. ◆ American ◆ M-Sa 11:30AM-2PM, 5:30-10PM; Su 10AM-2PM, 5:30-9:30PM. 5500 Gulf Blvd (55th Ave) Reservations required. 367.6461.

139 Silas Dent's ★$$ The weathered facade and decor are fashioned around a local folk hero, **Silas Dent,** the hermit of Cabbage Key. The white-bearded Dent made his living by fishing up and down the coast of West Florida. He was known locally as "Santa," because he gave out toys to the children every Christmas. According to local legend, he would occasionally leave his little island and row over to St. Petersburg Beach. Seafood choices range from alligator to amberjack, squid, sea bass, and coconut shrimp. Beef and chicken are also served. ◆ Seafood ◆ M-Th, Su 5-10PM; F, Sa 5-11PM. 5501 Gulf Blvd (56th and 55th Aves) St. Petersburg Beach. Reservations recommended. 360.6961

139 Bayside Market This center on the strip offers beachwear, T-shirts, and other tropical clothing. **The Shipwreck and Treasure Museum,** a 10,000-square-foot repository of recovered items, with a theater showing films on how they were found, is scheduled to open by 1992. ◆ Daily 10AM-9PM. 5501 Gulf Blvd (56th-55th Aves) St. Petersburg Beach. 367.2784

140 Sirata Sands Restaurant ★★$$ Longtime area restaurateur **Bill Nagy** is known for his creative concoctions. Try roasted duck with currant peppercorn sauce, the spinach salad, and the pâté plate, or a poultry mousse blended with brandy and cream and garnished with quail eggs, slices of cucumber, and cherry tomatoes. The restaurant is part of the Sirata Sands Best Western, which was built around the old El Sirata Hotel. Constructed in the 1930s, this facility sported an Art Deco theme—and it has been beautifully restored in peach and turquoise hues. ◆ American ◆ Daily 5-10PM. 5390 Gulf Blvd (54th-52nd Aves) St. Petersburg Beach. 367.2771

141 Swim & Play The store has a huge inventory of swimwear and beachwear, with such brands as Roxanne and Gottex, as well as hard-to-find sizes. ◆ M-Sa 9AM-9PM; Su 10AM-5PM. 4785 Gulf Blvd (48th-47th Aves) St. Petersburg Beach. 367.1713

142 Dolphin Village A two-story Art Deco shopping center with a glass-enclosed elevator features 50 outlets, including restaurants, a grocery store, and shops that feature shells, beach rentals, imports, and swimwear. ◆ Daily 9AM-6PM or later. 4615 Gulf Blvd (46th Ave) St. Petersburg Beach. 367.3138

Within Dolphin Village:

Kinjo ★★$$ Great sushi, an extensive menu of tempura, shrimp, and chicken prepared at a *teppanyaki* grill. ◆ Japanese ◆ M-Th, Su 5-10PM; F-Sa 5-10:30PM. 367.6762

143 46th St Access to Belle Vista Beach and metered parking, St. Petersburg Beach.

144 Brunello Trattoria ★★$$ Hearty soups, spicy salads, risotto, pastas, and grilled fish are tops, followed by *tiramisu* for dessert. ◆ Italian ◆ Tu-Su 5:30-10PM. 3861 Gulf Blvd (35th-50th Aves) St. Petersburg Beach. 367.1851

Restaurants/Nightlife: Red   **Hotels:** Blue
Shops/ ❦Outdoors: Green   **Sights/Culture:** Black

145 The Don CeSar, a Registry Resort $$$ The bubble-gum-pink stucco structure with its towers and high arched windows is a traffic-stopper. The imposing hotel was opened in 1928 as a seasonal winter hotel by an Irishman, **Thomas J. Rowe,** one of the great architects of the 1925 land boom in St. Petersburg. Rowe built the Don CeSar in gratitude for the money he made in the city and named it after his favorite grand opera character. The hotel flourished for the first two seasons and survived until 1941 when it closed. The Don, used as an army hospital in 1942, was slated for the wrecker's ball in 1969 and again in 1975 until preservationists intervened. Several renovations followed. The most recent was a $14 million overhaul by the Registry Hotel Corp. that dramatically replaced the old Spanish-style interior with luxurious and aristocratic English carpet, Italian crystal chandeliers, French furniture, and French and Italian marble—after which some have claimed to have seen Rowe's ghost at the hotel. The 277 rooms, including two grandiose penthouses, have marble baths and ocean views. The pool and tennis courts are right on the beach. Other features include a health club, a children's program, and various water-sports rentals. ♦ 3400 Gulf Blvd (54th Ave South) St. Petersburg Beach. 360.1881, 800/247.9810

Within the Don CeSar, a Registry Resort:

King Charles Restaurant ★★$$$$ Although the rack of lamb, smoked salmon, and duck are excellent, the elegant surroundings and obsequious service tend toward pretention. The elaborate Sunday brunch is a better choice than dinner, but no bargain. ♦ French ♦ Tu-Sa 5-10PM; Su 10:30AM-2:30AM. 3400 Gulf Blvd (54th Ave South) Reservations recommended. Jackets required for dinner. 360.1881

146 Keystone Motel & Apartments $ The 18 units include eight apartments and four efficiencies. There is a pool and laundry, and the location, right in the heart of Pass-a-Grille, is across from the beach. ♦ 801 Gulf Way (9th-8th Aves) 360.1313

146 Hurricane Seafood Restaurant ★★★$$ The recent addition of an upstairs deck at this Gulfside cafe has not diminished its quality. Without doubt the area's best and freshest grouper sandwiches are served here. Equally excellent are the grouper amondine and crab cakes. The jazz concerts W-Su 9PM-1AM are a local tradition. ♦ Seafood ♦ Daily 8AM-2AM. 807 Gulf Way (9th-8th Aves) Pass-a-Grille. 360.9558

146 Albion Cruises Shuttle service on a 32-passenger vessel is offered to **Shell Island,** an unspoiled, mile-long island south of St. Petersburg that offers excellent shelling. Schedules vary daily; a sunset cruise is sometimes included. ♦ 801 Pass-a-Grille Way (8th Ave) Pass-a-Grille. 360.2263

147 Evander Preston Contemporary Jewelry Celebrities **Carl Reiner, Peter Max,** and **Jimmy Buffet** have found their way to this creative oasis for one-of-a-kind jewelry in Pass-a-Grille Beach. Visitors are treated to a glass of white sangria as they peruse the chic inventory, which includes pieces priced from $100 to $25,000. ♦ Tu-Sa 10AM-5:30PM. 106 8th Ave (Pass-a-Grille-Gulf Ways) 367.7894

147 8th Ave Access to public beach and parking at Pass-a-Grille.

148 Michael's Conch Cafe ★★$$ Florida food is prepared with flair, from the house green salad with citrus to conch ceviche or chowder. An outstanding entrée is the grilled fish with black bean sauce. ♦ American ♦ M-Th, Su 5-10PM; F-Sa 5-11PM. 1110 Pinellas Bayway (Suite 206) Tierra Verde. 866.9158

148 Good Times Continental Restaurant ★★★$$ Tucked away near **Fort DeSoto Park,** this spot is owned by Czechs and frequented by a loyal local clientele, but word of the good dining continues to travel. In addition to potato pancakes, roast duckling, bratwurst, and hazelnut torte, the small restaurant offers almost 100 soups. ♦ Balkan ♦ Tu-Sa 5-10PM. 1130 Pinellas Bayway (Westshore-Anderson Blvds) 867.0774

149 Fort DeSoto Park The park consists of 900 unspoiled acres on five islands. Two bridges connect the park to the mainland. There are three miles of beach and two fishing piers, as well as picnic and camping areas, a concession stand, and restrooms. Although there are no boat rentals, there is a boat ramp and sea wall tie-up areas for those who bring boats. A fort, built during the Spanish-American War on **Mullet Key** and now listed on the National Register of Historic Places, offers panoramic views. ♦ 235 campsites. Pinellas Bayway at Anderson Blvd. 866.2662

St. Petersburg

St. Petersburg (also known as St. Pete) was named for the Russian hometown of Piott A. Dementieff. Dementieff, who changed his name to Peter Demens, was instrumental in 1887 in building the Orange Belt Railroad down the peninsula to the tip, which is now Gulfport. The

rail pier he envisioned is now a dining, entertainment, and shopping complex known as The Pier. A major citrus freeze in 1893 forced Demens to sell the rail line to Henry Plant. St. Pete, a town of about a quarter-million residents, is hopping in spring with its Festival of States, a three-week party coinciding with major league baseball's spring training. The festival features high school bands from around the country and includes a fishing tournament, parades, and a regatta.

(Nos. 155-178)

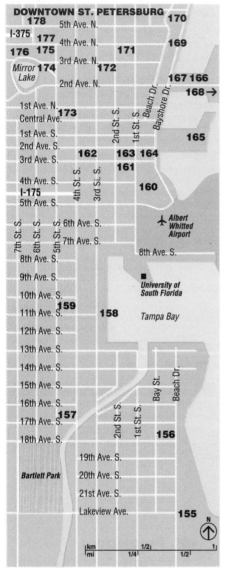

DOWNTOWN ST. PETERSBURG

Refer to map on page 128 for numbers 104-111

150 Sunshine Skyway Bridge This is Florida's first suspension bridge, modeled after the

Refer to map on page 128 for numbers 104-111

Tampa Bay Area

Bretonne Bridge over the Seine River in France and built over Tampa Bay to connect Pinellas and Manatee counties. An older bridge alongside it is being dismantled, and will be converted into the state's longest fishing pier—more than four miles lined with 83 individual artificial fishing reefs made from old cars, boats, concrete, and steel girders. The middle of the bridge's southbound span was knocked out by a freighter in 1980, killing 35 people. The state subsequently built a $250 million replacement bridge. The new bridge's yellow cables, resembling inverted fans, are illuminated at night. ♦ I-275 and US 19

151 Jack's Skyway Restaurant ★★$ Situated in a boat oasis, this is the top choice in town for breakfast in terms of price and quality. It's best known for its SOS—gravy and biscuits served with potatoes. Protests and petitions managed to save it when the highway was widened. Everything is well prepared, but there's usually a wait in tourist season. ♦ American ♦ Daily 5AM-3PM. 6701 34th St South (Pinellas Pt Dr) 866.3217

152 Leverock's Maximo Moorings ★$$ The service is friendly and the portions of seafood are ample at this waterside restaurant, which is cozily surrounded by private fishing docks. ♦ Seafood ♦ Daily 11:30AM-10PM. 4801 37th St South (49th-48th Aves South) 864.3883

153 Boyd Hill Nature Park Six trails meander through 216 acres of various Florida ecosystems: oak hammock, red maple swamp, cattail/willow marsh, pine flatwood, scrub, and lake. Wildlife (nesting bald eagles, gopher tortoises, flying and gray squirrels, possums, raccoons, snakes, frogs, and alligators) abounds in this park, and photo opportunities pop up on every trail. Other facilities are a playground, a picnic area, four aquariums, and an observation beehive at the nature center building. ♦ Admission. M, W-Th, Sa-Su 9AM-5PM; Tu, F 9AM-8PM. 1101 Country Club Way South (9th St South) 893.7326

154 Munch's ★★$ This community restaurant has creamy handmade milk shakes, burgers, grouper salad, and home-style cooking. Local memorabilia dominate the otherwise non-descript decor. You can still order a 99-cent breakfast special with unlimited coffee here. ♦ American ♦ M-Sa 7AM-8:30PM; Su 7AM-2PM. 3920 6th St South (40th-38th Aves South) 896.5972

The Chattaway

155 The Chattaway ★★$ This outdoor burger stand is a tradition among locals. Choose from burgers, a British breakfast, or Southern cooking. The onion rings are juicy but not greasy. There's a small sit-down section inside; picnic tables and a bar are outside. ♦ American ♦ 358 22nd Ave South (4th-3rd Aves South) 823.1594

156 Bayboro Bed and Breakfast $$ Located on the bay, in a quiet residential nook south of Bayboro Harbor. There are three rooms and a suite with a sitting area and kitchen in this many-gabled house that was built between 1903 and 1907. Each room is different, although they are all furnished with antiques, linens and lace, and private baths. Rates include a Continental breakfast served in the dining room or on the wraparound porch. ♦ 1719 Beach Dr SE (18th-17th Aves South) 823.4955

157 Bastas Ristorante ★★★$$$ Fine pasta and veal are served in elegant surroundings. The pasta is homemade, and all dishes are cooked to order. Steak and lamb are nicely prepared, too. ♦ Italian ♦ M-F 11:30AM-2:30PM, 5-11PM; Sa 5-11PM. 1625 4th St South (17th-16th Aves South) Reservations recommended. 894.7880

158 Salvador Dali Museum The bold, sometimes controversial work of **Salvador Dali** (1904-1989), the world-famous Spanish surrealist, seems out of place in sedate St. Pete. The world's largest collection, which encompasses 93 oils, 200 watercolors and drawings, and 1,000 other pieces ranging from graphics and sculptures to objets d'art, is valued at more than $125 million. The museum opened in 1982 after a nationwide search was conducted by Dali collectors **Eleanor** and **A. Reynolds Morse.** When you enter the gallery, go clockwise around the museum to appreciate Dali's work chronologically. Start with his early works (1914), move through his transitional period, and end up with his masterful surrealistic works. Among his most interesting pieces is *The Three Ages.* Look carefully for the faces of Infancy, Adolescence, and Old Age, which Dali painted using double images. Against the back wall are his floor-to-ceiling masterworks, painted between 1948 and 1970, including *The Discovery of America by Christopher Columbus* (1958), *Nature Morte Vivante* (1956), *Ecumenical Council* (1960), *Velázquez Painting the Infanta Margarita with the Lights and Shadows of His Own Glory* (1958), and *Hallucinogenic Toreador* (1970). If possible, take the highly entertaining docents' tours. Reproductions of the artist's work, posters, T-shirts, and books are sold in the museum store. ♦ Admission. Tu-Sa 10AM-5PM, Su noon-5PM. 1000 3rd St South (10th Ave South) 823.3767

159 Great Explorations This hands-on museum is more for children than adults, but it is educational and entertaining for both. Exhibits include a long, dark touch tunnel and laser pinball games, as well as sensory experiences and challenging puzzles. There's also a deli and gift shop. ♦ M-Sa 10AM-5PM; Su noon-5PM. 1120 4th St South (12th-11th Aves South) 821.8885

Hello, Dali

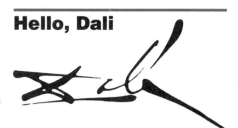

You might say it was the power of the press that helped bring the Dali Museum to St. Petersburg. When *The Wall Street Journal* reported that Cleveland industrialists **A. Reynolds** and **Eleanor Morse** were searching for a permanent home for their extensive collection of **Salvador Dali's** works, the paper's headline read: "U.S. Art World Dillydallies Over Dalis."

The article caught the attention of St. Petersburg attorney **James W. Martin,** who spearheaded a group that mobilized city and state support to bring the collection to St. Petersburg. An old downtown waterfront warehouse was renovated in 1982, and now the two-story center houses a museum, community room for workshops, kitchen, hurricane-proof vault, library, conference room, and office space (see "Salvador Dali Museum" at left).

The real story behind the Dali Museum in St. Petersburg began in 1941, however, when A. Reynolds Morse and his fiancée Eleanor Reese first viewed a traveling exhibit in Cleveland of Dali's early work. Excited about what they saw, the couple arranged a meeting with the painter in New York in December 1942. The meeting was the start of a lifelong friendship between the Morses and Salvador and Gala Dali.

The Morses purchased their first Dali oil painting, *Daddy Longlegs of the Evening...Hope!,* on their wedding anniversary in 1943. It was the start of a lifetime of collecting, which resulted in the world's largest private collection of Dali's art.

160 Bayfront Center Celebrity entertainment, special exhibits, ice shows, and plays are staged in this revamped facility on the downtown waterfront. ♦ The arena seats 8,400; the Mahaffey Theater seats 2,000. 400 1st St South (5th-4th Aves South) 892.5798

161 St. Petersburg Hilton and Towers $$$ The 15-story hotel has been the victim of mismanagement in the past. Yet it is strikingly done up in marble, crystal, and tile, and is within walking distance of the bayfront attractions and entertainment facilities. Rooms have views of the bay or city. Guests staying on the concierge level enjoy extras—bathrobes, shoe-shine machines, and a

miniature TV/radio in each bathroom. Other facilities include a restaurant, deli, lobby bar, lounge, outdoor heated pool, patio deck, Jacuzzi, and sauna. ♦ 333 rooms. 333 1st St South (4th-3rd Aves South) 894.5000, 800/HILTONS

February's Festival

Since 1904 Tampa has celebrated Gasparilla, a month-long festival of floats, parades, art shows, and concerts, named after legendary pirate **Jose Gaspar,** who plied the Caribbean and took refuge along Florida's west coast. You'll see his name everywhere along Florida's Gulf Coast, from street signs to the name of an island.

The celebration begins on the first of February when 500 "pirates" armed with sabers and cap guns sail an authentic-looking pirate ship into Tampa Bay to capture the city and lead a parade of floats and bands into Ybor City. Along the way they throw trinkets to the crowds. Concerts and dances lead up to an evening of fireworks.

More parades, as well as art shows, races, and balls, are held throughout the month, including two of the most popular events: the annual Gasparilla Distance Classic, a 9.3-mile run that regularly attracts about 14,000 runners, and the Gasparilla Sidewalk Art Festival, which brings in more than 100,000 art enthusiasts. For more information on the festival, call 800/44.TAMPA.

Sports Go Big Time

For years, big-time sports in Central Florida consisted of motor sports at Daytona International Speedway. Now there is a National Football League (NFL) team in Tampa, a National Basketball Association (NBA) team in Orlando, a National Hockey League (NHL) team in Tampa, and both Orlando and Tampa play host to New Year's Day college football bowl games.

Only major league baseball is absent in Central Florida, and both St. Petersburg and Orlando were among the finalists when the National League awarded expansion teams to Denver and Miami in 1991. However, residents and tourists get a taste of major league baseball in the spring when the **Grapefruit League** plays its spring training schedule. Florida cities, recently realizing the monetary benefits of having a team in town, have been vying for franchises to relocate teams by promising bigger and better facilities. Teams have begun playing one city against another, and each year franchises change location.

The hottest ticket in town is the **Orlando Magic** of the NBA. Virtually every game has been sold out in the first two seasons at the 15,077-seat Orlando Arena.

Tampa Bay Area

For football fans there are usually seats available for the **Tampa Bay Buccaneers.** Other football options include the powerful **University of Florida Gators** in Gainesville, and the New Year's Day bowl games—the **Florida Citrus Bowl** in Orlando and the **Hall of Fame Bowl** in Tampa.

Among the top motor-sport races each year is the world-famous **Daytona 500,** which is held every February on the 2.5-mile, high-banked Daytona International Speedway.

The Professional Golfers Association (PGA) has three stops in Central Florida. In March, a tournament is held at Arnold Palmer's Bay Hill Club in Orlando, and another tournament takes place at Ponte Vedra Beach, just north of St. Augustine. The golfers return in October to play the Disney courses.

There also is plenty of pari-mutuel wagering for those who like to gamble legally on spectator sports. The dogs run in Daytona Beach, Melbourne, Orlando, Tampa, and near St. Augustine. Jai alai, a sport brought to America by Basques, is played on three-walled courts called frontons. You can catch the fast-paced action in Daytona Beach, Ocala, Orlando, and Tampa. The only horse racing in Central Florida is at Tampa Downs.

The Tampa Bay Area offers two major complexes devoted to sports and concert viewing. Tampa Stadium, a common site for the NFL's Super Bowl, is also home to the Tampa Bay Buccaneers professional football team. The Florida Suncoast Dome is the site of a variety of indoor professional sports and big-name concerts.

Tampa Stadium

Florida Suncoast Dome

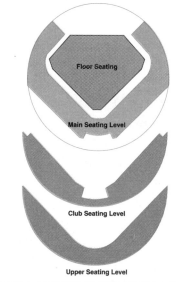

162 American Stage Co St. Petersburg's resident professional theater presents drama, comedy, and experimental plays in what was once a tobacco factory. This is the best local production company on the Pinellas side of the bay. ♦ 211 3rd St South (3rd-2nd Aves South) 822.8814

162 Florida Craftsmen Gallery The work of more than 100 Florida craftsmen is represented here. Many of the items are expensive, but moderately priced items can be found with a little browsing. Most are one of a kind. Works of art are composed from ceramics, wood, glass, fiber, metal, and paper. ♦ Tu-Sa 10AM-4PM. 235 3rd St South (3rd Ave South) 821.7391

163 The Presidential Inn $$$ The 30-room hotel, opposite **Al Lang Stadium,** is on the fifth floor of the **City Center** office building. The Inn caters to very upscale business travelers—the Florida governor and top entertainers who play at Baystreet Center have stayed here. Guests have access to an exclusive private club, **The Presidents Club,** that is also located in the City Center office building. All rooms have a view of the bay or the city and are elegantly decorated with signed and numbered contemporary prints in an oriental style, a theme prevalent throughout the inn. Each oversized bathroom comes equipped with a phone extension, a Jacuzzi, and a terry-cloth robe. Free covered parking is offered. The rates include a Continental breakfast. ♦ 100 2nd Ave South (1st St South) 823.7552

164 Al Lang Stadium This is the spring training home of the St. Louis Cardinals from mid-February to April. ♦ 230 1st St South (3rd-2nd Aves South) 893.7490

165 Demens Landing A 611-slip municipal marina and nine-acre waterfront park. There are permanent slips, along with an additional transit dock facility, available for rent. Boat supplies, fuel, and rental powerboats and sailboats are available. The park includes picnic facilities and a children's playground. ♦ 2nd Ave South at Bayshore Dr. 893.7329, 800/782.8350

166 St. Petersburg Historical Museum Thousands of pioneer artifacts and exhibits, including collections of china, glassware, coins, dolls, shells, pictures of early community landmarks, and old newspaper clippings. Notable are the green benches from the downtown's heyday as a retirement community, and baseball memorabilia associated with teams that have held spring training here. ♦ Admission. M-Sa 10AM-5PM; Su 1-5PM. 335 2nd Ave NE (Bayshore Dr) 894.1052

The Tampa Bay Hotel, which opened in 1891 at a cost of $3 million, was the first building in Tampa to be operated by electrical power. Six years after owner Henry Plant died in 1899, the city of Tampa bought the hotel and 150 acres for $125,000. The University of Tampa took over the building in 1933 after signing a 99-year lease with the city that calls for an annual payment of one dollar.

167 Museum of Fine Arts It's worth a visit just to see the collection of French Impressionist paintings that include Renoirs and Cézannes. There is a gallery of Steuben glass, and period rooms, antiques and historical furnishings. The museum has an important collection featuring American photographers including Ansel Adams, Margaret Bourke-White, and Phillip Hallsman. ♦ Donations accepted. Tu-Sa 10AM-5PM; Su 1-5PM. 255 Beach Dr NE (3rd-2nd Aves) 896.2667

168 The Pier This city landmark, an inverted pyramid structure, reopened in 1988 after a $9.7 million renovation. The five-level structure overlooks Tampa Bay and provides sweeping views of the water and the city skyline. A free trolley runs between the entrance and nearby parking lots. Among the restaurants here are **Cha Cha Coconuts,** a branch of Tampa's **Columbia Restaurant,** and a food court. The merchandise in the **Pier Shops** ranges from art and jewelry to souvenirs and crafts. Other features include an observation deck, boat and water-sports rentals, public boat docks, and two catwalks for fisherman. On the second level aquarium, giant tubes bubble with native and tropical fish, sharks, and invertebrates. ♦ Donations accepted for aquarium. M-Sa 10AM-9PM, Su 11AM-7PM for most shops. M, W-Sa 10AM-8PM, Su noon-6PM for aquarium. 800 2nd Ave NE (Bayshore Dr) 821.6164

At The Pier:

Cha Cha Coconuts ★$$ The taste of the tropics comes to The Pier at this restaurant, which also has a location at the shops of Harbour Island (see page 135). The drinks are great, and the daiquiris are made from fresh fruit. The menu includes hot black-bean chili and shrimp fritters. ♦ American/Caribbean ♦ M 11AM-midnight; Tu-Sa 11AM-1PM; Su noon-10PM. 822.6655

The Columbia ★$$$ Another branch of Tampa's Columbia (see page 135), this time at The Pier. ♦ Spanish ♦ M-Th 11AM-10PM; F, Sa 11AM-11PM; Su noon-10PM. 822.8000

Babe Ruth signed his first baseball contract in the lobby of the Tampa Bay Hotel.

Restaurants/Nightlife: Red **Hotels:** Blue
Shops/ 🌳Outdoors: Green **Sights/Culture:** Black

169 Straub Park 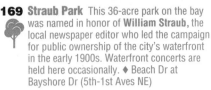 This 36-acre park on the bay was named in honor of **William Straub,** the local newspaper editor who led the campaign for public ownership of the city's waterfront in the early 1900s. Waterfront concerts are held here occasionally. ♦ Beach Dr at Bayshore Dr (5th-1st Aves NE)

170 Stouffer Vinoy Resort Aymer Vinoy **Laughner,** a Pennsylvania oilman, developed this Mediterranean Revival-style building as a luxury resort in 1925. It was host to the likes of **F. Scott Fitzgerald, Babe Ruth,** and **Calvin Coolidge.** For years, the Vinoy Park Hotel sat along the bay in disrepair and subject to vandalism. Recently opened in 1992, after a $92 million restoration, the new pink hotel includes a tennis complex, a tropically landscaped pool, a health club, and several restaurants. The main building, once sporting 375 rooms, has 258 large rooms, plus a 102-room tower. Listed on the National Register of Historic Places. ♦ 501 Beach Dr NE (6th-5th Aves North) 894.1000

171 Veillard House The rusticated block structure was built in 1901 by **Ralph Veillard,** a local merchant and political activist, who ingeniously combined bungalow and Queen Anne styles. It is one of the earliest surviving bungalow-style structures in St. Petersburg. Listed on the National Register of Historic Places. ♦ 262 4th Ave North (2nd-1st Sts North)

172 The Heritage Grill ★★$$ American cuisine is given new life in this old home with an updated, snazzy decor. This building is adjacent to the Martha Washington Hotel, built in the early 1920s. Such novelties as duck pizza and fruit and herb salsa are on the menu; soups and ice cream are made fresh and change daily. ♦ American ♦ M-F 11:30AM-2:30PM; 5-11PM; Sa 5-11PM. 256 2nd St North (3rd-2nd Aves North) 823.6382

172 The Heritage $$ The inn, formerly the Martha Washington Hotel from the 1920s, reopened in December 1986 after an extensive restoration. It is located in a quiet residential area within a few blocks of the heart of downtown. A wide veranda with a series of etched-glass French doors leads to the lobby, and the 71 guest rooms and suites still retain pieces of the original furniture. Other facilities are a heated pool, Jacuzzi, and lobby bar. A Continental breakfast is included in the rates. ♦ 234 3rd Ave North (3rd-2nd Sts North) 822.4814, 800/282.7829

173 Snell Arcade The Mediterranean Revival-style shopping arcade and office building was built in 1926 by land developer **Perry Snell.** The interior arcade serves as a passage to the

post office and was restored in 1982. Listed on the National Register of Historic Places. ♦ 405 Central Ave (5th-4th Sts)

173 US Post Office Once notable as the country's only open-air post office, but part of it is now enclosed. It was built in 1917 in the Mediterranean Revival style and designed locally by **George Stewart.** Listed on the National Register of Historic Places. ♦ 76 4th St North (1st Ave North-Central Ave)

174 Carnegie Library The city's first library building was built with a Carnegie Foundation grant in 1915. The Beaux Arts style in the old section was designed by **Henry Whitfield** of New York. Listed on the National Register of Historic Places. ♦ 300 5th St North (3rd Ave North)

175 St. Petersburg Lawn Bowling Club One of the country's oldest lawn bowling courts, built in 1926. Tournaments are held here each winter. Listed on the National Register of Historic Places. ♦ 536 4th Ave North (6th-5th Sts North) 822.3098

176 St. Petersburg Shuffleboard Club The world's largest such club dates from 1924 and houses the **National Shuffleboard Hall of Fame.** The sport was invented in Florida around 1912, and the courts are open to the public. In the Mirror Lake Park club building. ♦ Nominal admission. 7th St North at 3rd Ave North. 822.2083

177 Coliseum Ballroom This Mediterranean Revival-style building houses one of the country's oldest continuously operating Big Band-era dance halls. Since it was built in 1924, thousands have danced on the 13,000-square-foot maple ballroom floor, one of the country's largest. This downtown landmark was featured in the break-dancing sequence of the movie *Cocoon.* ♦ Admission. Dances M 1-3:30PM; W 1-3:30PM, 8-11PM; Sa 8PM-midnight. 535 4th Ave North (5th-4th Sts North) 892.5202

178 Boone House This house in the Classical Revival style was built in 1910 by pioneer land developer **Benjamin Boone.** The restored version serves as private offices. Listed on the National Register of Historic Places. There are no tours. ♦ 601 5th Ave North (7th-6th Sts North)

179 Central (St. Petersburg) High School This high school, designed by **William B. Ittner** in the Mediterranean Revival-style, was built in 1925 during the Florida land boom at a cost of $1 million. Listed on the National Register of Historic Places. ♦ 2501 5th Ave North (26-25th Sts North)

180 Stetson University College of Law The Mediterranean Revival-style structure was built as the Rolyat Hotel (Taylor spelled backwards), and was the climactic achievement of **I.M. "Handsome Jack" Taylor,** one of the chief architects of the frenzied St. Petersburg real estate boom of 1925. **Paul Reed,** a young Miami architect, based his concept for the hotel on a medieval walled Spanish village. It opened in 1925 in a blaze of glory; guests included golfer **Walter Hagen,** baseball's **Babe Ruth,** and prima donna **Freida Hempel.** The building also was used as a military academy before becoming Stetson University Law School. ♦ 1401 61st St South (15th-14th Aves South)

181 Ted Peters' Famous Smoked Fish
★★★$ This sidewalk cafe is a landmark and serves the best smoked fish in Florida. Try the smoked mullet or Spanish mackerel, served with hot German potato salad, thick slices of onion and tomato, and whole-wheat bread. ♦ Seafood ♦ M, W-Su 1:30AM-7:30PM. 1350 S. Pasadena Ave (Gulfport Blvd-14th Ave South) 381.7931

182 Horse & Jockey ★★$$ The Tampa Bay area's largest British pub offers fish and chips, meat pies, and other traditional pub fare. There are 11 British beers on tap. High tea is observed on weekdays, and dinner usually includes roast beef and Yorkshire pudding. ♦ British ♦ With 24-hour notice, high tea may be scheduled M-F 3-5PM. M-Th 11:30AM-10:30PM; F 11:30AM-11PM; Sa 8AM-11PM; Su 8AM-10PM. 1155 S. Pasadena Ave (Grevilla-Hibiscus Aves South) 345.4995

183 Sunken Gardens Once a sinkhole, this seven-acre garden has been converted into a tourist attraction with orchids, palms, and other exotica. Rare birds also are on display. The only entrance forces visitors to trek—the long way—through one of the largest and tackiest collections of souvenirs in Florida, including a tasteless Biblical wax exhibit. ♦ Admission. Daily 9AM-5PM. 1825 4th St. North (19th-18th Aves North) 896.3186

184 Wilson's Book Store New and rare comic collectibles at one of the Southeast's largest dealers of paperback and comic selections for 20 years. ♦ M-Th 9:30AM-6PM; 9:30AM-7PM; Sa 9:30AM-4:30PM. 2394 9th St North (24th-23rd Aves North) 896.3700

185 El Cap ★★$ A local hangout for residents and for major league baseball teams during spring training. Great grilled cheese sandwiches and chili, but this definitely is the place to find one of the area's best hamburgers—thick and juicy. There is baseball memorabilia throughout. ♦ American ♦ M-Th 11AM-11PM; F-Sa 9AM-midnight. 3500 4th St North (35th Ave North) 525.9122

186 Pepín ★★★$$ This local institution is resounding proof that all the good Spanish restaurants are not in Tampa. The shrimp *suprema*, chicken with yellow rice, pompano *à la sal*, and steak *milanesa* are always good. Memorable salads and hearty brown bread. ♦ Spanish ♦ M-F 11AM-11PM; Sa 11AM-11PM; Su 5-10PM. 4125 4th St. North (42nd-41st Aves North) 821.3773

In 1914 the warm, sunny retirement mecca of St. Petersburg made its way into the history books when entrepreneur Tony Jannus instituted the first regularly scheduled commercial air service in the world. The 11-mile flight from St. Petersburg to Tampa lasted about 20 minutes, including take off, landing, and taxi time, but it was a marked improvement over the two-hour drive around Tampa Bay to the peninsula.

187 Seabar ★★$$ Select fish by the pound at the fish market display and have it cooked to order. Prices fluctuate according to availability. Service is efficient. ♦ Seafood ♦ Daily 11AM-9PM. 4912 4th St North (50th-49th Aves North) 527.8728

188 Sawgrass Lake Park A mile of elevated boardwalk winds through a swamp filled with maple trees, and an observation tower provides a panoramic view of **Sawgrass Lake** in this 360-acre park. Booklets point out highlights for self-guided tours of nature trails. ♦ Daily 7AM-sunset. 7400 25th St North (74th Ave North) 527.3814

189 Derby Lane This Pinellas greyhound-racing track is open from January through June with 12 races daily. The track was founded in 1925 and claims to be the world's oldest in continual operation. Facilities include a lounge and restaurants. ♦ Nominal admission. M, W, Sa noon, 7:30PM; Tu, Th-F 7:30PM. 10490 Gandy Blvd (San Martin Blvd)

The Human Fish

Fishing, always a popular American pastime, peaked in the mid-1920s, when automobiles made distant lakes and streams accessible and new production techniques made quality fishing tackle affordable to the masses. This was especially true in Florida, which deservedly enjoyed a worldwide reputation for trophy-sized fish.

The "contemplative sport" soon gave birth to a peculiar brand of competition: anglers began to match their casting skills at tournaments throughout the country. The new boomtown of Orlando, a popular destination for northern anglers, resolved to hold a casting tournament of its own. In October 1925 members of the Orlando chapter of the **Izaak Walton League** gathered in the basement of the city hall building to plan their event. Prizes were determined, regional and national championships planned, and the date set for the following February, on the downtown shore of Lake Eola, during the city's annual Sub-Tropical Fair.

But **Walter Willman,** a transplant from Ohio, wanted more—a publicity stunt that would attract nationwide attention. He suggested a "human fish" event: He wanted to attach a fishing line to the bathing trunks of a strong swimmer to see how long it would take a well-known professional angler to land him. The league recruited **Fleetwood Peeples,** a young swimming instructor from nearby Rollins College, to serve as the human fish. The stunt was a huge success. Newspapers across the country snapped up the "Human Fish" story and newsreels replayed it in the nation's movie theaters.

For the record, it took US bait-casting champion **W.G. Fraser** of Huntington, West Virginia, a mere 10 minutes to reel in an exhausted Peeples, to the applause of hundreds of spectators.

Index

Index

Index

N

O

S

Restaurants

Only restaurants with star ratings are listed below. All restaurants are listed alphabetically in the main (preceeding) index. Always call in advance to ensure a restaurant has not closed, changed its hours, or booked its tables for a private party.

★★★

Ted Peters' Famous Smoked Fish $ 155
Tio Pepe's $$ 141
Victoria & Albert's $$$$ 71
Wine Cellar $$$ 146

★★

American Vineyards $$$ 53
Angel's Diner & Bakery $$ 16
Ariel's at the Beach Club $$$ 65
Aunt Catfish's $$ 98
Beauclaire $$ 121
Bernard's Surf $$$ 80
Bill Irle's $$ 141
Bill's Lighthouse $$ 137
Black Tulip $$$ 85
B-Line Diner $$ 28
Bob Heilman's Beachcomber $$$ 144
Bonfamille's Cafe $$$ 57
Brunello Trattoria $$ 148
Cafe de France $$$ 21
Cap'n Jack's Oyster Bar $$ 54
Capriccio $$$ 28
Captain Abbleby's Inn $$ 122
Chart House $$$ 102
Chattaway $ 150
Chefs de France $$$ 61
Columbia $$$ 135
Coral Reef Restaurant $$ 59
Cracker's Oyster Bar $$$ 12
Darbar $$$ 29
Donatello $$$$ 134
Don Quijote Restaurant $$$ 134
El Cap $ 155
Empress Room $$$$ 54
Eugen's $$$ 143
Fireworks Factory $$ 55
Fisherman's Deck $$$ 54
Forbidden City (Orlando) $$ 14
Hard Rock Cafe $$ 37
Heritage Grill $$ 154
Hollywood Brown Derby $$$ 67
Hops Grill & Brewery $$ 141
Horse & Jockey $$ 155
Hungry Fisherman $ 145
Jack's Skyway Restaurant $ 150
Kimonos $$ 65
King Charles Restaurant $$$$ 149
Kinjo $$ 148
Kringla Bakeri og Kafe $ 63
La Coquina $$$ 52
La Normandie $$$ 14
Le Pompano $$$ 146
Lombard's Landing $$ 36
Maison & Jardin $$$ 16
Mango Tree $$$ 81
Michael's Conch Cafe $$ 149
Ming Court $$$ 29
Munch's $ 150
Nannie Lee's Strawberry Mansion &
    Mister BeauJean's Restaurant $$ 78
Narcoosee's $$$ 71

Omi's Bavarian Inn $$ 147
Ottavio's Place $$$ 142
Outback Restaurant $$$ 54
Palio $$$ 65
Palm Court $$$ 148
Passage to India $$ 33
Paul's Seafood $ 137
Pebbles $ 9
Pebbles Walt Disney World 52
Pier House Restaurant $$$ 83
Portobello Yacht Club $$$ 55
Pure & Simple $ 64
Ran-Getsu $$$ 31
Restaurant Akershus $$$ 63
RG's Downtown $$$ 135
Sabals $$ 139
St. Regis Restaurant $$$ 101
Salt Water Cowboys $$ 109
Scandia $$ 145
Seabar $$ 155
Sea Grill $$ 139
Sirata Sands Restaurant $$ 148
Steerman's Quarters $$$ 54
Sum Chows $$$ 65
Teppanyaki Dining Rooms $$$ 61
Tex-Mex Cantina $$ 52
Yachtsman's Steakhouse $$$ 64

★

Alma's Italian Restaurant $$ 82
Aloha! Polynesian Luau $$ 27
Arthur's $$ 124
Backlot Express $$ 70
Beacham's Blue Note $$$ 12
Beaches & Cream $ 65
Bella Trattoria $$ 144
Benihana $$$ 53
Bergamo's Italian Restaurant $$ 31
Border Cantina $$ 21
Cactus Club $$ 136
Cafe Dora $ 122
Cafe Margaux $$ 85
Cantina de San Angel $ 63
Cape Sierra $$$ 86
Caruso's Palace $$ 29
Cha Cha Coconuts (Clearwater) $$ 143
Cha Cha Coconuts (St. Petersburg) $$ 153
Chef Mickey's Village Restaurant $$$ 54
Columbia (Clearwater) $$$ 143
Columbia (St. Petersburg) $$$ 153
Columbia Restaurant $$ 117
Dexter's $ 21
Dixie Crossroads $$ 93
Eduardo's $ 122
El Gordo's $$ 147

Enzo's on the Lake $$$ 16
Florida Cracker Cafe $ 117

Hotels

*Don CeSar
Registry Resort,
St. Petersburg*

Index

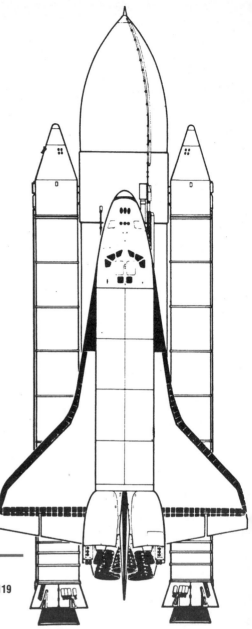

Features

Bests

ACCESS® Travel Diary

Page	Entry #	Notes

ACCESS® Travel Diary

Page	Entry #	Notes

ACCESS® Travel Diary

Page	Entry #	Notes

ACCESS® Travel Diary

Page	Entry #	Notes